Reconstructing Christian Theology

REBECCA S. CHOPP
MARK LEWIS TAYLOR
Editors

FORTRESS PRESS Minneapolis

RECONSTRUCTING CHRISTIAN THEOLOGY

Cover design: Orbit Interactive Communications

Library of Congress Cataloging-in-Publication Data

Reconstructing Christian theology / Rebecca S. Chopp, Mark Lewis Taylor, editors.
p. cm.
Includes bibliographical references and index.
ISBN 0-8006-2696-6 (alk. paper)
1. Theology—20th century. 2. Theology—21st century.
3. Christianity—United States—20th century. 4. Christianity—United States—21st century. I. Chopp, Rebecca S., 1952- . II. Taylor, Mark L. (Mark Lewis), 1951- .
BT30.U6R43 1994
230—dc20 94-2827
CIP

The paper used in this publication meets the minimum requirements of American National Standard for Information Sciences—Permanence of Paper for Printed Library Materials, ANSI Z329.48-1984. ∞™

Manufactured in the U.S.A. AF 1–2696

98 97 96 95 2 3 4 5 6 7 8 9 10

CONTENTS

PREFACE

Close collaboration has engendered this volume. In weekend meetings once or twice a year for the last four years, members of the Workgroup on Constructive Theology have attempted to articulate a strategy for introducing theology amid the intellectual and social turmoil that marks the end of Christianity's second millennium.

Although the Workgroup's members themselves exhibited real diversity in theological methods and even disciplines, they sought a pedagogy that would employ concern for today's cultural and social crises and that can inform a praxis of hope. This book is an invitation for students to delve into Christian theology's deep and rich traditions, truly engage in analysis and evaluation of those traditions and contemporary social challenges, and then to bring Christianity's chief doctrines, reconfigured or reconstructed, as hope-filled responses to these "crises of suffering."

Rooted in such challenges, the project is clearly contextual. Each chapter draws heavily from analysis of major cultural and social situations in the United States. Still, the editors and contributors are aware of the many limits of their efforts, especially the lack of sustained attention to some particular social groups and regions. We hope nonetheless that the reader will find the analysis and models developed here helpful for further addressing even more localized situations.

In conjunction with this volume, readers may also find helpful the other introductory volumes that the Workgroup has authored, *Christian Theology* and *Readings in Christian Theology,* both edited by Peter C. Hodgson and Robert H. King and published by Fortress Press.

In its many sessions discussing the shape and contents of this volume, the Workgroup benefited enormously from the reflections and observations of other members who are not chapter contributors in the volume itself. The editors wish to thank particularly Carl E. Braaten, Sheila Briggs, John B. Cobb, Jr., M. Shawn Copeland, Edward Farley, Mary Gerhart, Gordon D. Kaufman, David H. Kelsey, Robert H. King, and Marianne Sawicki. We all hope that this volume will help a new generation of students to learn and practice theology as a discipline instrumental in reconstructing our religious life and reenvisioning our world.

—Rebecca S. Chopp
Mark Lewis Taylor

CONTRIBUTORS

David B. Burrell, C.S.C., is Theodore M. Hesburgh Professor of Philosophy and Theology, University of Notre Dame. His recent work, notably *Knowing the Unknowable God* (1986) and *Freedom and Creation in Three Traditions* (1983), focuses on Islamic and Jewish influences on the formation of the classic Christian doctrine of God.

Rebecca S. Chopp is Professor of Theology and Dean of the Faculty at Candler School of Theology, Emory University, Atlanta, and author of *The Praxis of Suffering: An Interpretation of Liberation and Political Theologies* (1986) and *The Power to Speak: Feminism, Language, and God* (1989).

Dawn DeVries is Associate Professor of Church History at McCormick Theological Seminary, Chicago. She is translator and editor of *Servant of the Word: Selected Sermons of Friedrich Schleiermacher* (1987).

James H. Evans, Jr., is President of Colgate Rochester Divinity School/Bexley Hall/Crozer Theological Seminary in Rochester, New York. Among his previous publications are *Black Theology* (1987), *Spiritual Empowerment in Afro-American Literature* (1987), and *We Have Been Believers: An African-American Systematic Theology* (1992).

Peter Crafts Hodgson is Professor of Theology, Vanderbilt Divinity School. His recent publications include a new edition and translation of G. W. F. Hegel's *Lectures on the Philosophy of Religion* (3 vols., 1984–87), *Revisioning the Church* (1988), *God in History: Shapes of Freedom* (1989), and *Winds of the Spirit: A Constructive Christian Theology* (1994).

Catherine Keller is Associate Professor of Constructive Theology at Drew University Theological School, Madison, New Jersey, and author of *From a Broken Web: Separation, Sexism, and Self* (1986) and, forthcoming, *Apocalypse Now and Then: A Feminist Approach to the End of the World.*

Walter Lowe is Professor of Systematic Theology, Candler School of Theology, Emory University, Atlanta. He is author of *Mystery and the Unconscious* (1972), *Evil and the Unconscious* (1983), and most recently *Theology and Difference: The Wound of Reason* (1993).

Linda A. Mercadante is Professor of Theology at the Methodist Theological School in Ohio, in Delaware, Ohio. She is author of *Gender, Doctrine, and God: The Shakers and Contemporary Theology* (1990) and is presently researching the theological implications of addiction and recovery, for a book tentatively entitled *Victims and Sinners in an Age of Addiction.*

Sallie McFague is Carpenter Professor of Theology, Vanderbilt Divinity School. Formerly dean there, her recent writings include *Models of God: Theology for an Ecological, Nuclear Age* (1987) and *The Body of God: An Ecological Theology* (1993).

John T. Pawlikowski, O.S.M., is Professor of Social Ethics at Catholic Theological Union, Chicago. Editor of *New Theology Review,* he is also author of many volumes, including *Jesus and the Theology of Israel* (1989), and co-editor of *The Ecological Challenge: Ethical, Liturgical, and Spiritual Responses* (1994).

Elisabeth Schüssler Fiorenza is Krister Stendahl Professor of Scripture and Interpretation at Harvard Divinity School. A past president of the Society of Biblical Literature, she is author of *In Memory of Her* (1984), *Revelation: Vision of a Just World* (1991), *But She Said* (1992), and editor of *Searching the Scriptures: A Feminist Introduction* (1993). She is founding co-editor of the *Journal of Feminist Studies in Religion* and co-editor of feminist theology, *Concilium.*

Francis Schüssler Fiorenza is Charles Chauncy Stillman Professor of Roman Catholic Theological Studies at Harvard Divinity School, author of *Foundational Theology: Jesus and the Church* (1984), and co-editor of *Systematic Theology: Roman Catholic Perspectives* (2 vols., 1991).

Marjorie Hewitt Suchocki is Vice-President for Academic Affairs, Dean, and Ingraham Professor of Theology in the School of Theology at Claremont. Her works include *The End of Evil: Process Eschatology in Historical Context* (1988), *God, Christ, Church: A Practical Guide to Process Theology* (2d ed., 1989), and *The Fall to Violence: Original Sin in Relational Theology* (1994).

Kathryn Tanner is Associate Professor of Religious Studies at Yale University and author of *God and Creation in Christian Theology: Tyranny or Empowerment?* (1988) and *The Politics of God: Christian Theologies and Social Justice* (1992).

Mark Lewis Taylor is Associate Professor of Theology and Culture, Princeton Theological Seminary. He is editor of *Paul Tillich: Theologian at the Boundaries* (1987) and author of *Remembering Esperanza: A Cultural-Political Theology for North American Praxis* (1990).

Susan Brooks Thistlethwaite is Professor of Theology at Chicago Theological Seminary. She is author of *Sex, Race, and God: Christian Feminism in Black and White* (1989), co-editor of *Lift Every Voice: Constructing Christian Theologies from the Underside* (1990), and co-editor of *Beyond Theological Tourism: Mentoring as a Grassroots Approach to Theological Education* (1994).

Sharon D. Welch is Associate Professor of Religious Studies and Women's Studies at the University of Missouri—Columbia. She is author of *Communities of Resistance and Solidarity* (1985) and *A Feminist Ethic of Risk* (1990).

REBECCA S. CHOPP AND MARK LEWIS TAYLOR

INTRODUCTION: CRISIS, HOPE, AND CONTEMPORARY THEOLOGY

Contemporary students of theology face a world in crisis. Relations between peoples in the Northern and Southern Hemispheres are disastrously structured. While only 18 percent of the world's population lives in the region that combines North America, Northern Europe, and Japan, that region pulls in 82 percent of the world's income and has a per capita income twenty-six times greater than the entire rest of the world. The growing gap between rich and poor internationally has been sharply replicated within the United States. Women throughout the "Third World" and in North America bear a disproportionate share of the burden laid on the poor by combined market forces and nation-state politics. Further, within the United States, as elsewhere, women bear in their bodies and lives the marks of sexist practice: every eighteen seconds, still, a woman is battered. Consider also the ways people of color and Native Americans have been and still are assaulted by pervasive practices of white supremacism, and the rise of hate-crimes against diverse groups like gay and lesbian members of our society—all this and more easily sustains the sense of crisis.

The team of theologians represented here, having worked collectively over the past several years as the Workgroup on

Constructive Theology, is committed to careful analyses of these and other crises. If by nothing else, analysis is prompted by the fact that oppressing crises are not simple top-down phenomena. To be sure, there *are* oppressing agents who can be identified and dominator groups and elites to be named; but as Antonio Gramsci and Michel Foucault insist, oppression reaches crisis proportions because of forces that pervade the totality of political interaction, social patterning, and everyday personal struggle and living.

Suffering is structured as oppression through legal and economic systems, but suffering is also constructed as dehumanization through cultural images and even common linguistic metaphors. Structures of suffering are created through psychocultural systems of repression and psychic destruction that define certain experiences and feelings as normal. The crises of suffering are generated by large, autonomous systems that seem beyond the average person, by our daily face-to-face encounters with associates, friends, and strangers, and by our own inner feelings and forms of experiencing.

Although the essays in this book are rooted in such crises of suffering, the theologians represented here also see their analyses as a way toward authentic hope, a hope that embraces historical transformation. Hope springs from the voices of those belittled and oppressed who now speak; hope wells up in communities for whom new ways of living together are hallmarks of Christian praxis. Theologians craft expressions of hope in Christian symbols that envision personal and social transformation. This hope, in Cornel West's term, is a utopian realism: an anticipation of a new, transfigured reality based on a realistic analysis of the sufferings and desires of the present age.[1]

1. Cornel West, *The American Evasion of Philosophy: A Genealogy of Pragmatism* (Madison: Univ. of Wisconsin Press, 1989).

DISCURSIVE SHIFTS IN THEOLOGY TODAY

Theology in the United States has undergone major changes in the last twenty-five years. The changes concern who does theology; the problems that theology considers; the cultural, aesthetic, political, and philosophical contexts of theology; and even its genre and style. All these changes will not be discussed here. By way of introduction, however, we will discuss five of these changes as "discursive shifts" in contemporary theology. By "discursive shifts" we mean recent and pervasive changes in contemporary settings that have fundamentally altered theological discourse, that is, the ways in which theologians reflect, talk, and act. These shifts, being dimensions of wide-ranging new patterns and practices, pertain to the whole context within which theological work takes place as both theory and practice.

From Melting Pot to Collage

One of the dominant metaphors for the United States has been that of the society as a melting pot. In the myth of the melting pot, Americans supposedly shed their cultural particularities, their ethnic differences, their special languages and customs. The melting pot myth promised that if people left all such particularities behind, they could succeed, that is, they could become ideal Americans. This ideal American was imaged as a white Anglo-Saxon Protestant male who had a domestic wife and several children, who spoke without an accent, and who worked hard and was handsomely rewarded.

In recent years the myth of the melting pot and its heroic American figure has been revealed as false and dangerous. This constitutes a first discursive shift. The melting pot is false because most U.S. citizens—such as African Americans, Native Americans, Latinos, women of color, and white women—cannot finally live the myth. Try as they might to fit in, to melt down their differences for the common "pot," persons of color and women cannot match the image that serves as the goal of the melting pot: the image of the Euro-Anglo Protestant man. The myth is false also because it does not portray the day-to-day reality of the United States: a nation with many different groups marked by color, heritage, culture, region, sex and sexual orientation, and physical ability. There is no melting pot. Further, this belief far too often led to dangerous practices—legal, cultural, educational, religious—that assumed that if a person could not reflect the heroic ideal of the melting pot, then she or he was an inferior object to be both belittled and oppressed.

Today the myth of the melting pot is often replaced by the image of the mosaic or the collage of different faces and voices. The image of the collage highlights the real differences among Americans, reinforces that not everyone should or can fit the same mold, and celebrates the variety of traditions, perspectives, orientations, and communities as resources for flourishing together more richly.

Theology in the United States, therefore, has undergone a shift from using a melting pot model, in which theology as officially understood sought a dominant or common human experience, to a model that values the collage of different faces, voices, styles, questions, and constructs. Black theologies, Asian-American theologies, feminist theologies, womanist theologies, theologies from gay men and lesbian women, and theologies offered from the perspectives of the disabled are all presented on the scene today. Where once such differences were either ignored or belittled as "special interests," theology today is increasingly understood as having its vitality only insofar as its traditional resources embrace new voices and their differences. The fusion of voices in the theology of this book, then, is not so much a melting as an orchestrating of differences that are irreducible to one another, conflicting in their interests, but also mutually enriching.

Crises of Survival and Loss of Flourishing

These new voices in culture and theology are today not only speaking of their own particularity. They are also identifying crises relating to all of contemporary society and indeed to all the world. The emergence again in theology of the language of crisis constitutes another discursive shift.

Theologically speaking, this time of crisis requires Christians to name evil and sin in the midst of threats to the very survival of the earth, in the midst of unrelenting physical abuse of women and children, and in the midst of such practices as white supremacism, U.S. imperialism, and injustice toward gay and lesbian peoples. The theological task is to analyze the depravation of the conditions of life and the deprivation of human flourishing: the twin threats of utter destruction of creation and the constant loss of social and personal well-being. Such crises must be met with both denouncement and announcement—"denouncement" as lamentation, careful analysis, and opposition to all sinful structures and practices (personal, social, geopolitical), and "announcement" as envisioning grace as new ways of living through and beyond the crises.

What characterizes this discursive shift is the further awareness, on the part of Christian communities, that the denouncement of sin and announcement of grace are as much internal as external acts. That is, they entail refashioning Christian practices, including theological understandings, as much as speaking to societies other than the church. To put it differently, the problems of destruction, devastation, abuse, and imperialism have been reinforced and sustained, at least in part, by Christian practices and theological discourses. For instance, rates of physical abuse of women are exorbitant in the United States. One of the justifications given by abusers (and sometimes the abused) is that women are inferior in God's hierarchy and must be submissive to men. Religiously sanctioned notions of women's obedience and service are often obstacles to women's freedom from exploitation, as many workers in battered-women's shelters can today attest. Or to take another example, the destruction of the planet by massive environmental abuse has been, again in part, secured through religious ideologies of human domination of the earth. One of the contributing factors to the notion that humans can dominate the earth is a doctrine of creation in which humans are placed near or at the top of a hierarchy where all that is under them—other animals, rocks, minerals, the oceans, in sum, nature—is seen as "other" and less than humanity. The notion that humanity has the "responsibility" to exercise care over the earth from its higher position often results not so much in "stewardship" that guards the earth as in domination and exploitation.

The Ambiguities of Postmodern Culture

Cultural critics, from popular music deejays to philosophers, use the term "postmodern" to describe the present cultural scene, and the term has also entered theology. This discursive shift is generally associated with a new aesthetic sense focusing on diversity (collage itself is a popular "postmodern" term); a questioning of the abstract ideas of liberal humanism; and a foregrounding of values of ambiguity, fragmentation, and openness. In architecture, for instance, the term is associated with the razing of the Pruitt-Igoe housing development in St. Louis because it was judged to be an inhospitable environment. Pruitt-Igoe was portrayed as a machine for modern living. It exemplified a high modernism of architecture that functioned under the ideal of liberal humanism and its notions of what "autonomous man" needed. Postmodern architecture, by contrast, focuses on people in a small-scale way, combines in a collage-like fashion the pleasing aspects of former styles of architecture, and keeps itself open to the use of space in a variety of ways.[2]

2. For general treatments of postmodernity, see David Harvey, *The Condition of Postmodernity: An Enquiry into the Origins of Cultural Change* (Oxford and Cam-

The postmodern focus on ambiguity, fragmentariness, and openness has exerted an impact upon contemporary philosophy and theory. Modern philosophy operated with strict categories and within the limits of reason in order to discover the real foundations of truth. Modern theory thus strove for univocal clarity expressed in language that represented the essence of truth. Postmodern philosophy debunks the notion of foundational truth and suggests instead a process of truth-creating as an ongoing conversation. Theories of postmodernity, such as poststructuralism, invoke the multivalence of symbols, the openness of texts, and the construction and deconstruction of meaning in, as well as through, language.

Postmodernity stands not in opposition to limits so much as for blurring, questioning, and playing with them. In popular culture, MTV, with its brief video collages that neither correspond to nor oppose the music and lyrics being played at the same time, has the same effect of foregrounding ambiguity over clarity, and plurivocity over univocity. In political and economic systems, postmodernity names not so much the rise of new superpowers to oppose the old ones, but the dissolution of clear superpower categories and the new reality of shifting power relations among various political and economic networks, some of them nations-states, some multinational corporations, some ethnic and religious groups.

The values of postmodernism, such as openness and multiplicity, call upon theologians not only to speak in new ways to the culture but also to evaluate their theological understandings. "Modernity" was a day of great systems and large Protestant denominations in North America and parts of Europe, in relation to which the task of systematic theology was to elaborate a clear, logical, univocal system of thought that could answer all religious questions. Now theologians question that paradigm of expectations on cultural and religious grounds. Is theology an

bridge, Mass.: Basil Blackwell, 1989), and Ihab Hassan, *The Postmodern Turn: Essays on Postmodern Theory and Culture* (Columbus: Ohio State Univ. Press, 1987).

analytic logic that proves God, or is it about a poetics and a politics that name God's relation with the world? Does the coherence of theology depend upon deductive logic, or can the coherence of theology consist of the organic relatedness of hypothetical (abductive) logic that takes as its primary concern the imagining of new and healing ways of living? Is theology about sure foundations that never waiver and provide a closure against the winds of change (modernity), or is theology about envisioning new spaces for personal and social flourishing? Postmodernity, as a challenge to theology, consists of finding ways to address a culture with a penchant for the fragmentary, the open, the ambiguous, and the different. It invites refashioning the very task, genre, and style of theology so that it can help to point to new ways of living in postmodern culture.

A Postcolonial Sensibility

While the West now names its reality as "postmodern" and is critical of the theoretical and practical limits of modernity, much of the rest of the world resists the First World in both its modern and postmodern variants, seeing in each a form of economic, cultural, and political imperialism. Thus, as another discursive shift, we note the rise of a postcolonial sensibility.

During the rise of modernity an ongoing assumption of those persons in the First World was that their economic interests, belief structures, and political forms were superior to those in the rest of the world. Much of the rest of the world was seen as "primitive" and undeveloped. Modern Western empires set out to conquer the world, often justifying economic and political domination by a paternalistic understanding that treated newly discovered persons as inferiors or simply as children. In postmodernity, one danger is that those in the First World will simply turn their backs on global structures of oppression and become self-absorbed with the values of ambiguity, openness, and fragmentariness. Another danger is that if these postmodern values are not rendered through ethical criteria and structural analysis, they can be used to support multinational exploitation in the Third World. For example, the upscale multiethnic advertising of the Bennetton Corporation rarely reveals its dependence upon hidden outlays of big capital, enormous concentrations of international communications technology, and use of poor, non-unionized women who are often poorly compensated for their in-home labor.

Many of the new voices in theology from around the world join the postcolonial critique of both modernity and postmodernity.[3] From a postcolonial perspective, the problem of modernity lies not merely in its narrow limits and univocal reason but also in its use of such limits and reason to structure massive, worldwide oppression. Postcolonial theology examines how the superiority of the First World was constructed, including how Christianity supported such superiority through its beliefs and practices. Envisioning the transformation of worldwide relations is also a part of postcolonial theology, as theologians pursue how the global context might be restructured through forms of living together in community rather than perpetuating First World success through Third World exploitation.

From a postcolonial perspective, the problem with postmodernity is how to support its celebration of openness and fragmentation in a way that also responds to moral demands of the contemporary world. Working to free victims of colonial and neocolonial domination, such a postcolonial critique enriches postmodernism and prods it to move toward emancipation and not simply to dwell in self-indulgent play among cultures of privilege.

A Turn to the World's Religions

The last discursive shift we note is the turning of Christian theologians toward other religious traditions in a spirit of mutual critique and dialogue. Among these religious traditions, we

3. Gayatri Chakravorty Spivak, *The Postcolonial Critic: Interviews, Strategies, Dialogues* (London: Routledge, 1990).

include not only the other so-called great religions (Judaism, Buddhism, Hinduism, Islam, and others), but especially the long-threatened and particularly needed visions of indigenous peoples, those whom modernity often called primitive peoples.

This shift to dialogue with other religious traditions does not, of course, occur in isolation from the other shifts. The turn to other religious traditions is rooted in part, for example, in a postcolonialist critique of Christianity's often willing compliance with the devastating practices of Western civilization's empire building. Modernity and at times Western postmodernity have been reinforced by Christian ideologies that, in Enrique Dussel's terms, have said a "no-to-the-other"—a no to their religions and to their cultures.[4] The no was then embodied and implemented in exercises of extermination. They have included the Roman Catholic Church's complicity in conquistadors' violations in the Americas; Christians' deadly march against the Native peoples of North America; and certain Protestant groups' recent support for right-wing, Central American dictatorships that have pursued genocidal policies against indigenous peoples.

Resistance to both modernity's and postmodernity's imperialisms entails comprehensive critique of the political and the economic sovereignty of First World, Christian empires. This critique must also resist the cultural construct of non–First World peoples as "other," as "less than" and inferior. The "Orient," for instance, was a construct of modernity, dependent upon the West's strange fascination with the exotic nature of the Far East and its people's religions, customs, cuisine, sexual habits, and so on. Theologians today will often see in this "Orientalism," as Edward Said has termed it, the functioning of Christianity as a colonial ideology.[5] As such, Christianity has often deemed other religions of the world as inferior, as "pagan," or as "native," thereby refusing any kind of genuine dialogue with them.

4. Enrique Dussel, *A History of the Church in Latin America: Colonialism to Liberation, 1492–1979* (Grand Rapids: Eerdmans, 1981).

5. Edward W. Said, *Orientalism* (New York: Random House, 1979).

Christian theologians have pursued a number of approaches for dialogue with non-Christian religions. Some are interested in comparing particular beliefs from two or more religious systems. Others are interested less in comparison and more in developing Christian symbols and doctrines (for example, Christ and God) in ways they hope will prove meaningful for Christians' encounter with diverse religious groups. Still others may insist on establishing the dialogue between religions by reference to practical challenges, where pressing demands (for nation building or alleviating poverty or preventing war) call forth cooperative religious endeavors. Whatever the primary focus of these diverse approaches, a common tendency is to work well beyond the imperialist postures of the past and to respect the different religious traditions as authentic expressions of the sacred for diverse peoples. In the actual risking of one's own insights in dialogue, many of the old imperialist postures often reappear, but increasingly the dialogue is seen as the essential site for exposing and criticizing such postures. The spirit and tensions of Christian theologians who participate in this discursive shift are perhaps best displayed in a statement by theologian John B. Cobb Jr.: "The more deeply we trust Christ, the more openly receptive we will be to wisdom from any source, and the more responsibly critical we will be both of our own received habits of mind and of the limitations and distortions of others."[6] Many of the contributors to this volume display something like this spirit in their critique of Christianity's imperialisms and in their openness to other religions.

WHAT IS THEOLOGY?

The purpose of this book emerges more clearly when viewed in relation to these discursive shifts. The volume aims to address

6. John B. Cobb Jr., "The Religions," in *Christian Theology: An Introduction to Its Traditions and Tasks,* ed. Peter C. Hodgson and Robert H. King, 2d ed. (Minneapolis: Fortress, 1985), 373.

these kinds of current issues from the perspective of Christian doctrine and with the goal of shaping a revisioned Christian communal praxis. The authors of the various chapters and the editors of the volume all work, in a variety of settings, as Christian theologians. We work individually and collectively—as members of the Workgroup on Constructive Theology—to explore what theology is and can become in the contemporary situation.

Theology

Theology is, quite literally, language and knowledge about God. More important, perhaps, is a historical perspective that shows Christian theology to have two related senses: as "faith seeking understanding" and as the "scientific understanding" of God. For our purposes, "faith seeking understanding" signifies the rootedness of theological understanding in faith, viewing the latter as having to do with the whole concrete matrix of people's lives. Thus, this first sense signifies theological understanding's rootedness in practice and its function as guide to the ongoing practices of individuals and of Christian communities.

By using the term "scientific understanding," we are not raising issues of comparison between theology and natural or social sciences but rather emphasizing that theology has an interest in theoretical clarity. This clarity pertains not only to its beliefs but also to the way it analyzes its contexts and methods. In addition, this interest in theoretical clarity includes Christian thinkers' interests in presenting their claims as truth, according to contemporary views of truth.

Whether as faith seeking understanding or as scientific understanding, theology is always both historical and contextual. Although these latter terms are frequently invoked and used interchangeably, they are used here to specify some particular traits of Christian theology.

When we say that theology is *historical,* we mean that it changes through its various historical periods. The differences between Augustine's and Aquinas's theological writings are in part the result of their having lived in different historical periods that had different cultural issues to address, different philosophical systems to use, and different aesthetic images and visions to employ. Christian theology is a historical discipline, as Friedrich Schleiermacher argued, because it has to do with ongoing reflection on the historically dynamic life of Christians.[7]

But theology is historical not only because history changes but also because Christians understand that God acts continually and dynamically in history. Christianity therefore affirms, along with an ultimate revelation, the ongoing importance of God with us now, symbolized in the doctrine of the Spirit.

When we say that theology is *contextual,* we mean that even in a given historical period, theology is specific to a diversity of particular, local situations. In other words, theology is affected both diachronically (by differences due to passage through time) and synchronically (by differences occurring because of situational changes—social, political, cultural, gendered, and so on). For example, theological reflection from an inner-city, African-American community in Los Angeles, addressing tensions there, will be different from that emerging from a Latino or Korean community in the same city; and it will certainly be very different from that done by a suburban, Euro-Anglo community in Chicago as it attempts to address enormously high rates of depression, suicide, and drug use among its adolescents.

Awareness of contextuality leads to the understanding that all knowledge, theology included, reflects not only some general sense of meaning but also specific forms of interests. For instance, it was beneficial to the economic interests of white slave owners to have African-American slaves imaged as inferior, animal-like, and sinful. Given the structural as well as personal character of the crises that new voices are addressing, it is no surprise that what distinguishes the present era of theology is its

7. Friedrich Schleiermacher, *Brief Outline on the Study of Theology,* trans. Terrence N. Tice (Atlanta: John Knox, 1977).

attentiveness to the political character of theology. Theology is, of course, "political" in a very broad sense, including also dynamics of sexuality, gender, and culture. In general, though, a contextual approach works at the intersection of the analysis of power, interests, and meaning and is oriented toward the transformation of the present situation to greater social and personal flourishing.

What was said about the historicality of theology must be said also about its contextuality. Contextuality does not just name a way in which theology is changing and is affected by our different contexts and specific interests. The contextuality of theology also underscores a deep-seated theological belief that God acts in the world for transformation of specific contexts, inspiring and persuading toward liberation for human communities.

Symbols and Doctrines

Through its various living traditions, Christianity has shaped symbols and has developed explications of these symbols into doctrines. Theological notions such as God, creation, Christ, and church can be referred to as "symbols," as key areas or loci around which Christian communities construct their beliefs, spiritualities, practices, and relations to the world and other religions. In Christianity, these symbols are often found within the narratives of its Scriptures, and they accrue their meaning because of the way they occur in narrated stories. These symbols can be understood as "doctrines," especially when they are further developed conceptually and then related one to another to form a kind of basic grammar for Christian communities. In more traditional language, doctrines provide the content of what the church believes, teaches, and confesses.

Most of the authors in this volume preserve the important connection of symbol to doctrine without collapsing the two into each other. Doctrines are understood therefore as elaborated forms of symbolic knowledge; symbols and doctrines together constitute a type of practical wisdom in and for living Christian faith in the world. As a practical wisdom, theology enters into something like the fulfillment of the symbolic function. This is underscored if we recall that the Greek term *symballein* suggests "putting things together." Theology, through symbol and doctrine, therefore becomes the creation of spaces for Christian practice. This creation brings together analysis of social situations, biblical interpretations, fashioning of new meanings and practices, and forms of spirituality. The contributors to this volume are committed to just such a practical wisdom.

Praxis as Communal

This volume's focus on "*communal* praxis" is necessary because of the distorted systemic relations that mark the crises of our times. We use the term "communal" to refer to the structural, intersubjective character of Christian praxis. As communal, therefore, Christian praxis occurs in a variety of intersubjective domains: in local communities, in relation to a community that shares a historical tradition, and in broader communal networks that are social-symbolic or cultural-political.

It may also be important to clarify the notion of praxis. Here in the Introduction the term refers to integrations of theory *and* practice that intend an emancipative transformation. As such, "praxis" is a more complex term than "practices," focusing as it does on theory *and* practice in union toward an end.

The key point here, however, is that our focus on communal praxis directs theologians primarily toward intersubjective rather than individualistic considerations. Theology is done by and for particular communities rather than only by and for an abstract individual. Until recently, at least in white, Euro-Anglo theology, theology was assumed to be about "proving" whether or not individuals could justifiably believe in Christian doctrine. Modern, secular forms of knowledge widely assumed that "truth" was dependent upon empirical knowledge or the categories of thought and that since religion was neither empirically nor rationally verifiable by the human subject, religious belief was superstitious. Thus, Christian theologians had to argue that individual existence was more than merely empirical and that religious belief was not just superstitious but also reasonable. As Gustavo Gutiérrez has pointed out, this liberal theological agenda—or "progressive theology," as he calls it—was often aimed at the individual nonbeliever.[8] Even other theologies that criticized liberal theology's tendency to accommodate the Christian faith to a modern liberal agenda retained modernity's primacy of the individual. (An example is twentieth-century neoorthodoxy, which opposed anthropology as the starting point for theology and argued for a Christian faith in God as radically other to modern culture and reason.) To be sure, the individual was often discussed as a participant in the church community, but this was rarely accompanied by a full exploration of the complex intersubjective dynamics (cultural, historical, political, sexual) present in the church community.

At least four factors contributed to the shift away from the limited modern views of individuals and their crises of epistemology and faith to explorations of community and practical wisdom. First, the presence of voices such as those of African Americans, women, and Latin American scholars brought greater awareness to theology of the importance of community, and especially communal struggle, to the production of theological knowledge. Second, concern for the "practical" crisis of survival and flourishing worked to preempt concentration solely on problems of individual epistemology. Third, recognition grew within Christianity that it itself was a religion, one living in a global neighborhood with other religions, in one community with other communities. Fourth, there was a turn in the understanding of knowledge itself—it was increasingly seen as always intersubjective, as always formed through the mediation of communal traditions and through social-symbolic or cultural-

8. Gustavo Gutiérrez, *The Power of the Poor in History: Selected Writings*, trans. Robert R. Barr (Maryknoll, N.Y.: Orbis, 1983).

political processes as much as through empirical and analytic operations.

Since the first three factors were discussed in the first section of this Introduction, we can turn directly to the fourth. It recognizes that before we begin our empirical descriptions and analyses, the way we see the world, the feelings we have about it, and the actions we take in it are all shaped (not caused) through the forms of communal praxis from which we come and that we envision.

Awareness and study of these forms of communal praxis are sustained by several intellectual movements, and readers of this volume will see evidence of them throughout this book. First, the new voices of subjugated peoples have brought into theology the narratives of communal suffering. Second, studies in hermeneutics, or hermeneutical phenomenology, have reminded theologians that understanding in almost every field is mediated through concrete traditions that feature not only historical legacy but also a continual process of intersubjective conversation.

Third, contributors in this volume are often informed by what has been termed "critical theory," an intellectual project rooted in earlier approaches to the sociology of knowledge (like that of Karl Mannheim) that stressed that the "natural" ideas and assumptions of a period tend to cloak the interests of those in power. From this point of view theological knowledge is always laden with social and political interests. Fourth, many social sciences, such as cultural anthropology and political economy, have begun to study knowledge as itself a dynamic process of production that expresses cultural and political interests and social locations. Consequently, knowledge has to be understood as continually implicated in the dynamics of specific communal matrices. Fifth, some contributors here draw on traditions of process thought (Charles Hartshorne, Alfred North Whitehead), which assert not only that theories are related and mutually implicated with one another but also that theory and life are themselves always in relation. Theology, then, with its theories, symbols, and doctrines, is dynamically interacting always with the whole relational matrix, and communal praxis is stressed as part of this matrix.

Sixth, contributors here may be informed by various aspects of the neopragmatist revival in North America, a movement associated with figures like Charles Sanders Peirce, John Dewey, William James, and Richard Rorty. The focus here is less on philosophizing individuals or epistemology and more on keeping a conversation going among a community of interpreters, aiming at cultural criticism and transformation. Seventh, still other contributors may be informed by movements of poststructuralism, which may include thinkers as diverse as Jacques Derrida, Michel Foucault, and Julia Kristeva. Poststructuralism may be said to concentrate on the changing meaning of cultural signs and on how symbols and language construct human "reality." Perhaps one of the greatest contributions of poststructuralism is the special attention it gives to how power circulates through cultural structures.

From the perspective of each of these movements, students of theological knowledge are challenged to move beyond any individualist paradigms for theological study. More positively, they are equipped to study theology, indeed all knowledge, as shaped by and always related to intersubjective forces and structures. The authors in this book will address communal praxis in different ways, from different experiences, and from within varying intellectual traditions. But whether they employ insights from poststructuralism, neopragmatism, process thought, the social sciences, or critical theory, each is acknowledging the need for theology to respond to the intersubjective character of communal praxis.

DYNAMICS OF THEOLOGICAL INTERPRETATION

As diverse as our contributors' responses may be, the theologians offer an interpretation of their times and their traditions that exhibits three major dynamics of theological interpretation.

Although we have urged many contributors to this introductory volume to use these dynamics as section headings for structuring the sequence within their contribution, in most theologies these three dynamics are in a complex interaction, defying any easy sequence. The three dynamics can be briefly introduced here.

The first is *analysis* of the key features and immense structural problems of the current challenges to contemporary Christians and their communities. Such analysis includes careful attention to new voices and suffering voices of our time but also takes up a wide range of theories drawn from, say, literary criticism, anthropology, political economy, gender theory, and poststructuralism.

By analysis we also mean careful study of the religious and theological symbols and doctrines that often may be implicated in the very problems a theologian may wish to address. Theological doctrines, for instance, often may be patriarchally constructed and so underwrite traditions of gender injustice; or, notions of creation in Jewish and Christian doctrine may do as much to subvert as to support responsible relating to our fragile ecostructure.

The key point here is that this first dynamic entails careful study of the problems and of the theological traditions that provide resources for addressing such problems. It is necessary to focus not just on doctrine but also on the tradition's diverse relations to a complex world, the knowledge of which theologians cannot afford simply to leave to ad hoc engagements when Christian communities come under pressure. A theological response to racism, for example, must entail constant theorization of white supremacism in all its subtle forms, not simply addressing it when it appears in its blatant acts of domination or abuse. White supremacism in contemporary Los Angeles was and is present in the city's zoning laws and in ways of dividing and ruling minority peoples there, and not only in the vicious beating of Rodney King. From this perspective, the L.A. uprising in 1992 was not just people "rioting": it was people rebelling against a whole structure of ongoing destruction. Theologians rarely will attend to such a reality if they are not committed to a thorough analysis of the situation in its connections to doctrine.

Emerging from their analyses, the contributors to the volume exhibit a second dynamic, around which the volume is titled: *reconstruction*. This dynamic entails at least two major operations. The first is altering and reformulating theology's own resources of symbol and doctrine. In this sense of reconstruction, the changes in symbol and doctrine can take many forms. Even when a doctrine may be analyzed as a key contributor to structural crises, the reconstructive response may not simply be one of rejecting the doctrine. For example, for some writers today, the very word "God" may be so saturated with patriarchal meanings that only excising it seems an adequate response. For others, the reconstructive dynamic may entail a new appropriation of the term made possible by situating it in new contexts or seeing it in different ways. The point is that both are efforts in reconstructing Christian doctrine, and both remind us that there are a wide variety of reconstructive options. This book itself exhibits several of these.

A second operation that is included in our sense of reconstruction is the process of addressing our culture and society with new insights. This process moves forth from the symbols and doctrines of Christian traditions toward, and in conversation with, other theoreticians and activists. This sense of the reconstructive dynamic may entail not only new theoretical claims (for instance, theories about what a doctrine of creation suggests for Christian communities engaged in protection of the environment) but also insights offered in modes of address other than theory, experimenting with new genres and styles of communication. Alternative modes of address, perhaps employing the poetic or mixing words and images in novel ways, may be extremely important today for reconstructing an engagement of theologians with artists and activists, who are especially needed for social and ecclesial transformation.

"Reconstructing Christian theology" thus means both reworking theology's symbols and doctrines in various ways and also a continual re-engaging of the diverse communities that Christians address and with whom they must work today for an emancipative restoration of personal and social flourishing. This "re-engaging" operation in particular opens out into a third dynamic.

We term this third dynamic *envisioning emancipatory praxis*. It is not simply a "final step" in theological reflection. From its first moments, we propose, theological reflection grows from, and intends to flower in, new visions of emancipatory praxis. The dynamics of analysis and reconstruction presume and point toward such visions. We put it this way: in light of theology's ongoing analysis of structural challenges to personal and social flourishing, and facilitated by its ongoing reconstructive activity, there also emerges an emancipatory praxis. Emancipatory praxis embodies the reconstructions forged by theologians in community and the reconstructions they offer to an array of other communities they face in a pluralistic global life.

Envisioning emancipatory praxis means more than formulating a new awareness or set of beliefs for individuals. On the basis of what has already been said about the importance of communal praxis in contemporary theology, we can state that the new visions that practically embody our reconstructions must feature a communal or intersubjective character. All the contributors here included employ, at various points of their interpretations, proposals for setting in motion new communal modes of interaction. From this perspective, a reconstructed theological anthropology, for example, would not be complete until it issues in proposals for reforming our communal and political life together. Indeed, we might say that the social-symbolic or cultural-political nature of today's structural crises makes it incumbent upon theologians not to neglect this strategic dynamic of theological interpretation. Perhaps we are called as theologians to point toward emancipatory praxis as what

Schleiermacher in another context referred to as the "corporate grace" that is necessary to address today's all-pervasive "corporate evil." Amid today's structural evil and crisis—which drive many to despair because of the blatant and subtle realities of racial injustice, sexism, militarist spirals of violence, class exploitation, handicappism, and discrimination against gay and lesbian people—we may have a special challenge to point toward a grace abiding in history that promises nothing short of new *corporate* empowerment and flourishing. None of the contributors offers an easy hope; indeed, that would be nearly impossible if one grasps the full significance of the systematic character of our crises. Nevertheless, in their interpretations, the writers in this volume persist in hope and so weave their visions of emancipatory praxis around the other two dynamics of theological interpretation—analysis and reconstruction.

STRUCTURE OF THE BOOK

This book's very structure can be viewed as part of an emancipatory project in that it focuses theological questions at the intersection of questions of oppression, meaning, and power. It seeks to link interpretations of the meanings of theological loci (God, creation, sin, Christology, and so on) to distortions of power that afflict our times. In the titles of each chapter, therefore, readers will find a theological notion paired with a particular structural challenge or problem that is salient especially for the contemporary situation (white supremacy, religious pluralism, colonialism, and so on).

Yet chapter titles also include a third term, one that in each case names what is envisioned as a centerpiece of hope, a crucial feature of an emancipatory praxis. So, for instance, the pairing of the doctrine of creation with environmental crisis, in the chapter by Kathryn Tanner, is further complemented by the term "ecological justice," naming the aspect of hope relative to her set of problematics.

No claim is being made here that other scholars will necessarily have to develop links between doctrinal symbols and structural problems, as we have in this book. Theology can address the structural problem of ecological crisis, for instance, out of other doctrinal loci, as well as from its doctrines of creation. Catherine Keller, for example, illustrates this by approaching that same crisis in relation to eschatology. To prevent any supposition that there is necessity in the kinds of linkages we have forged, we often have included essays that move toward different structural issues from the same doctrine, as well as chapters that treat the same structural issue from the perspective of different doctrines. In this way we hope to introduce readers not only to theological interpretation as disciplined reflection but also to the variety of approaches possible when one explores the whole intricately related "web of meanings" that constitutes theological reflection.

The purpose of the linkages in each chapter—between doctrinal locus, structural issue, and emancipatory hope—is to invite readers to explore ways in which properly theological meanings can illumine contemporary cultural-political and social-symbolic issues.

We stress that this theological effort is only *part of* an emancipatory project. Indeed, several emancipatory projects need forging among different religious communities, political parties, community organizations, or international networks. But even in the area of Christian theology's engagement with today's crises, we are aware of the partial character of this book's contribution. We have aimed for considerable comprehensiveness in coverage of both doctrinal symbols and the structural challenges. It should be noted, however, that missing from the list of doctrinal loci are the notions of providence, the Trinity, pneumatology, and the sacraments. Equally significant are omissions of discussions of crises such as the pervasive injustice of heterosexism and the specific racial injustices faced by Latino and Asian-American communities in North America.

It is our hope, however, that although these and other omissions may be problematic and revealing of our limitations as a workgroup in constructive theology, the structure of the volume and the nature of the theological interpretations displayed will be instructive even for readers who need theologically to analyze and address issues not taken up here. What is of utmost importance to us is introducing a mode of theological interpretation that continually exhibits the mutually interplaying dynamics of analysis, reconstruction, and envisioned emancipatory praxis. In so doing, we hope to move ourselves and our readers into an emancipatory discourse that features not simply one more theological set of constructions but also a distinctive discourse for making some small difference in a time suspended between crises and hope.

MARJORIE HEWITT SUCHOCKI

1. GOD, SEXISM, AND TRANSFORMATION

Her problem was simple. From childhood she had worshiped in her small community, participated in the various ministries of laity, and felt drawn to pastoral leadership in the church. But her church was one that refused to ordain women for clearly stated reasons: Jesus was male, and as the incarnation of God, he represented the maleness of God the Father; further, he called only men to be his disciples. Therefore, because the ordained ministry is to be a representative office, only those who represent maleness can be ordained. She must seek another vocation.

Behind the apparent simplicity of this reasoning lie enormously complex issues involving the sociology of power and the relationship between the structure of any society and the ideas through which that society understands itself and fashions its ideal visions. Included within the latter, particularly for religious institutions, are the complexity and function of the doctrine of God. The purpose of this essay will be to explore the function of God within the church, both through the tradition and through the contemporary context of North American theology. This will necessarily involve the sociological context of the doctrine and thus should illumine the issues in our presenting case of the woman seeking ordination.

There is a close relation between the doctrine of God, the interpretation of evil, and the structure of society. The doctrine of

God is developed so as to ensure that there is an answer to the problem of evil as defined by the society. The problem of evil is social as well as individual, including natural as well as moral disruptions, and one of the functions of any society is the ordering of human life so as to minimize insofar as possible the disruptions humankind faces. The notion of God as a power sufficient to address the problem of evil is therefore at the same time a power sufficient to authenticate social structures that are consonant with the doctrine. And so our young woman who felt called to ordained ministry found herself facing not simply the prejudice of a particular church but also the result of this long process: she was a challenge to a doctrine of God and a corollary social system designed to address an interpretation of evil no longer pertinent to her world.

So long as a particular interpretation of evil remains vibrantly cogent to a community, the social structure and the correlative doctrine of God will hold. When the interpretation of evil changes, both the social structure and the doctrine of God will creak and groan and then either be adapted or snap and be cast aside. Sometimes the adaptation will be little more than finding new reasons to maintain the same doctrine and social structure, but such superficial changes are themselves brittle and shallow. Deeper changes require going to the roots of the complex system and being open to the new structures that such reorganization will present. The woman requesting ordination has moved into precisely this challenging juncture.

What were the dynamics of the doctrine of God she was challenging? How had the doctrine addressed effectively a dominant understanding of evil? How was this interpretation of evil reflected in the social structure of the church? What are the forces leading to a reinterpretation of the contemporary understanding of evil in North America? What are the doctrinal implications for how we understand God and the social implications for the structure of the church?

ANALYSIS OF A DOCTRINE: THEN AND NOW

For nearly fifteen hundred years the Christian interpretation of evil has focused upon the problems of lust, ignorance, and death, each of which was seen to follow from the misuse of the will by finite, mutable human beings. But in the contemporary North American context, the interpretation of evil is deeply influenced by perceptions of evil as oppression, whether related to race, gender, sexual orientation, handicapping conditions, class, or the environment. Such issues were not addressed in the tradition and therefore are not immediately encompassed redemptively in the doctrine of God. The extent to which the traditional doctrine can be adapted or expanded to include these issues is currently in question. One possibility is to reexamine the hierarchical dualisms of the traditional doctrine of God—dualisms such as transcendence/immanence, immutability/dynamism, unity/plurality. In each of these pairs, the first has been dominant, but the new interpretation of evil as oppression pushes toward a revaluation of this dominance. Before exploring this, it is important to see why the dominance lay as it did in the traditional notion of God.

Augustine, who wrote in the late fourth and early fifth centuries, typifies traditional thought, for he not only wove together many of the themes from the Christian centuries preceding him but also provided the pattern for Christian doctrine in the subsequent centuries. Thus the following exposition generally follows Augustinian lines. However, with various changes of emphasis and adaptation to different cultural contexts, it could apply to most pre-Enlightenment forms of Christian theology.

Like many persons in the classical age, Augustine was troubled by the changeable character of the human situation: to be human is to be subject to the instability of desires, to the death and decay attendant upon finitude, and to the ignorance of things eternal. These three factors illustrated the problem of evil, but of the three, the instability of desire, also called lust, was fundamental.

Lust indicated not only the sense in which reason could not control the emotional and sensual life but also the way in which all of one's being is awry through love directed to finite realities rather than toward God. Augustine held that we are born with a bent toward things that, like ourselves, are mortal and unstable and that can in no way give the soul the life it craves. But rather than turn our love to the immortal and immutable God in whom alone we can find the source and sustenance of our life, we persist in turning to finite things. This misdirected will yields a drifting of desire hither and yon from one finite reality to another in a ceaseless ocean of sin. It is the root of the problem of evil, for consequent upon this inability to focus one's love upon God come the attendant problems of death and ignorance.

Augustine understood death in three increasingly severe modes: the deprivation experienced through the death of those we love, the death of our own physical being, and the eternal death of the unredeemed soul. All three follow upon the human predicament of misplaced love. Yet within the human soul is the yearning for permanence and the everlasting overcoming of death. Such an overcoming is not possible for beings who orient themselves to finite loves. Because we are not rooted through love in the source of life (God), we live toward a physical death that is followed by a spiritual death in which soul and body eternally coexist in a state of war and pain. The overcoming of death can be achieved only through the immortality of God.

The final aspect in Augustine's triad of evil is the ignorance that follows from the instability of our misdirected will and our finitude. Basically, all human knowledge is subject to error when the objects of human knowing are themselves unstable and changing. Knowledge tends to fix things in categories—but those things that are "fixed" are in fact finite and therefore mutable; to "fix" them is to falsify their essential nature. That which we call knowledge is but a sophisticated form of ignorance. Only that which is permanent can be the basis for true knowledge. The dilemma is that the finite mind is inadequate in itself for the knowledge of immutable permanence, which is God, and apart from being rooted in the knowledge of God, there is no basis in the human mind for anything other than a superficial knowledge of even finite things.

These three problems—lust, death, and ignorance—are each rooted in the mutability of the human condition; the answer rests with the immutability of God. For example, the unchanging nature of God represents an absolutely fixed will that provides the corrective for the mutability of the human will turned from God. Salvation is God's turning of the human will back to the divine orientation for which it was intended. Thus corrected, the finite will is released to love finite things not in and for themselves, but in and through God. With regard to death, the immutability of God ensures the eternity of the divine life; God is absolute life. God's gracious turning of the human will toward God is at the same time a turning of the human person toward the source and sustenance of all life, God. This constitutes redemption, for the soul thus grounded in God need undergo no "second death" following physical death.

The issues of knowledge are also answered through the immutability of God and the gracious turning of the will toward God. When God reorients the will, then just as the person is in touch with the ground of life, the person is also connected with the source and norm of all knowledge. The permanence of God provides the standard by which all things are known truly. Thus one loves in and through God, and the lust of the misdirected will is corrected; one lives in and through God, and the fear and loss of death are overcome; one knows in and through God, and the problem of ignorance gives way to the knowledge of things in the light of eternity.

The essential immutability that provides the means to answer the problem of evil indicates that all of the qualities of God are static and fixed. God's power is omnipotent and total. God is omnipresent, for there could be no place where God is not if God is immutable. To be absent from a place once for an immutable being would be to be absent always: God must be omnipresent. In this scheme, God's knowledge is omniscient, which essentially means that God's knowledge is eternal, not subject to the vagaries of temporality and change. Thus for the omniscient God, there is no future and no past; all is known in an eternal present. Immutability implies omnipotence, omnipresence, and omniscience, each of which is eternally the same.

But in the description of the human plight given above, there is the hint of a drama, of divine action that changes the human situation. Since all humans are born inheriting a defective will, humans are incapable of reorienting their own wills toward God. To ask them to do so would be like asking a person with broken legs to walk: the means for walking are precisely the problem; first the legs must mend, and then the person can walk. Even so, a will turned from God is defective, incapable of doing anything other than continuing in its disastrous bent away from God. The will must first be healed: but it cannot heal itself. Only God is able to heal the human will by redirecting it toward God's own self. Once the will is thus reoriented, the issues of lust, death, and ignorance can be addressed as noted above. For Augustine, such action denoted the supreme graciousness of the immutable God, but to speak of grace and immutability injects an inner tension into the doctrine. The drama of the human story indicates a divine story of God taking initiative within human history. And so it is not sufficient to speak of the classical God as simply the immutable being containing all power, presence, and knowledge; the classical God must be dynamic as well. To account for this, the doctrine of the Trinity answered the tension between immutability and grace, suggesting a divine story that touched human history.

Early Christians witnessed to God's incarnation in history as God's way of answering the human problem. The immutable God acted in history through Jesus Christ in order to overcome the human predicament of evil. The immutability of God required that this act be eternally decreed so as to introduce no new thing into God. Rather, incarnation must simply be a finite manifestation of that which had always taken place in God and hence had always been known to God. The omnipresence of God made the incarnation consistent with divinity, for how could the omnipresent God be absent anywhere? Nonetheless, the presence of God in Christ was a different order of divine presence. Whereas omnipresence indicated the universality of the divine power, incarnation indicated a very particular manifestation of the divine character under the conditions of human history. In order to account for this manifestation, Augustine further developed the already established patristic trend of considering God triune.

If God were triune, then there would be a way of accounting for God's actions in history even while maintaining the immutability that guaranteed the divine perfections. In a sense, the doctrine of immutability guaranteed the qualities in God that contrasted with and answered the human problem of evil, and the doctrine of the Trinity guaranteed the ability to apply these qualities to human history.

Since incarnation was portrayed through birth and since God is immutable, then there must be that in God which is eternally giving birth or generating a life that is at once the same and other. Accordingly, the generation of the Son of God in time was considered a finite manifestation of an eternal generation whereby God is always Father of the Son within the divine self. Human birth is a matter of both likeness and unlikeness: from the substance of a woman and a man, a woman generates a child who is from the woman and man and like them and yet who is a separate self. Given the dominant patriarchy in the classical culture, the birthing God was seen as male rather than female, but the birthing imagery is apt. God as Father eternally generates that which is both of the Father and like the Father, but nonetheless irreducibly distinct from the Father. That which generates is the Father, but that which is generated is the Son.

The third aspect of the doctrine of the Trinity, which is God as the Spirit, accounted for the continuing presence of God in salvation history. The notion of the Spirit explained the actual application of redemption to individual souls or the experienced grace of God in the turning of the will to God: that is, conversion. It also named the power of God in the community of the church, and the sanctifying grace of God at work through sacramental life. And since this identification of the continuing redemptive power of God in human history stemmed from the immutable nature of God, then God as the Spirit must also be eternal. Just as the Spirit in history is the reconciling power of God that unites us with God and with one another, even so within the inner life of God the Spirit must be a uniting reality, ever expressing the love and therefore the union between the Father and the Son.

This triadic structure of God qualifies the divine immutability by introducing an essential dynamism within the nature of deity. Given the dynamism within the godhead, there is a consistency with the external expression of this dynamism in salvation history, which includes creation, redemption, and reconciliation. Creation is the external act that outwardly expresses the generativity within God whereby God is Father of the Son; incarnation is that external act that outwardly expresses the inward distinction of being generated; reconciliation is that outward act giving historical expression to the inward union within God. The technical terms for these are the "immanent Trinity," or the dynamics of God's inner being, and the "economic Trinity," or the external manifestation of God's character in creation.

Thus the notion of trinity became an answer to account for the dynamic action of an immutable God: since the immutable nature of God contained a triadic dynamism, it was consistent even with God's immutability that the dynamism be expressed externally as well as internally. In fact, the immutability of God might even be said to have required the external expression, for God must act in accordance with the divine character. The very unchangeability of God indicates that if God is internally dynamic,

God must also be externally dynamic. Otherwise, the external nondynamism would represent a change from the internal dynamism.

Through the dynamism introduced by trinity, the salvific qualities of the immutable power, presence, and knowledge of God could be communicated to human beings torn by the problems of lust, death, and ignorance. That is, the substance of the doctrine relative to evil rested with the immutability and transcendence of God; the application of the doctrine was guaranteed through the dynamism and immanence of God. The former were seen as essential to deity, the latter, as essential to grace. While in a formal sense neither ought to be valued over the other, in fact the immutability and transcendence of God took precedence in that these qualities provided the essence of the salvation that was conveyed through dynamism and immanence, or involvement with the human world. Also, insofar as the human world was itself devalued, those aspects of God most closely associated with the world were likewise valued less than the more exalted qualities of immutability and transcendence, with their attendant omnipotence, omnipresence, and omniscience.

I referred above to the social structures that relate to the doctrine of God. It is, of course, difficult or impossible to sort out neatly the causal relation between the structures and the doctrine, for the ancient interpretations of evil and of God took place within a highly patriarchal and elitist social structure. Women, slaves, and barbarians were assumed to be less valuable than civilized men, and these social suppositions gradually overcame the more egalitarian roots of Christianity. By the time of Augustine, women and slaves were certainly still included in the Christian vision, but their marginal and to varying degrees oppressed status was not at all understood to be a problem by the formulators of theology. To the contrary, if "all evil is the result of sin and its punishment," there was a real sense in which the misfortunes of women and slaves were in fact theologically justified. Their salvation was from lust, death, and ignorance, not from marginality and servitude. Hence the interpretation of evil itself reflected the patriarchal structure of the wider society. Far from countering the cultural patriarchy, the structure of the church replicated it. Its role within the culture was to guarantee that lust, death, and ignorance could be held at bay during this temporal life pending their ultimate resolution in the life to come. Since lust was the fundamental issue in this triad, it played the most important role in the developing hierarchy of the church.

The leadership of the church focused upon celibacy as a counter to lust, which of course was most exemplified in sexual desire. Fourth- and fifth-century exclusion of women from leadership was rationalized not on the principle that Jesus called male disciples but by associating women with a ritual impurity based precisely on their gender. Femaleness was taken to symbolize sexuality and lust, and hence women did not qualify for leadership in a church dealing with lust as sin. Further, their exclusion facilitated the celibacy of a male clergy. These rationalizations fit well with the patriarchal assumptions not only of the church but also of the Roman culture in which it was embedded at the time.

Centuries later and a continent removed, there are still persons within the diversity of a North American religious context who define evil through the classical definitions of lust, death, and ignorance brought about by a misdirected will. However, quite different suppositions lie behind such North American appropriations, for finitude and mutability are no longer so negatively valued. To the contrary, literary heroes such as David Thoreau and Walt Whitman well expressed the delight in nature that still typifies American sensitivity, and both the United States and Canada have placed a high value upon novelty. Immutability in the strong classical sense simply does not grip the American imagination, much less serve as a model for salvation.

If the basis of evil as lust, death, and ignorance no longer connects deeply with experience, what does? The quick answer has already been indicated at the beginning of this chapter: oppressions that deny the dignity and freedom of persons in community tend to be perceived by Americans as problematic at best and evil at worst. Oppression is the social name of evil, and broken relationships and selves are the personal dimensions of oppression. Freedom and egalitarianism have been rallying cries in the United States since the beginning of the nation, despite the fact that the founding fathers were as blind to the value of freedom for women, slaves, and indigenous Americans as were the ancient Romans to women, slaves, and those not possessed of Roman citizenship. But in the American context, the blindspots with regard to freedom were needled by the very values on nature and on novelty suggested above. In a context devaluing finitude and valuing immutability, ideal worlds and social structures both take on a deceptive aura of permanence; in a context valuing nature and novelty, the empirical world and its givenness to change provide a ground for bringing all manner of things into question. The nineteenth-century trauma of beginning to come to grips with slavery and beginning to raise the question of women moved into the twentieth century as a long and still continuing struggle to cope with the depths of racism and sexism. This struggle in its turn has opened up the myriad of ways by which our social structures lead to the systematic oppression of persons different from those in the dominant power base. With these discoveries, oppression has become the new name of evil. Can the notion of God constructed to address evil as lust, death, and ignorance be stretched to address oppression salvifically? This is the question of feminists—and it is the question symbolically represented by that woman standing before the hierarchy of her church and asking for ordination.

FEMINIST METHODOLOGICAL STRATEGIES

The feminist approach to redevelopment of doctrine maintains that all theology is rooted in experience and that the structure of experience is mediated through socially constructed language, which in turn is affected by one's embodiment as male or female. While the emphasis upon experience is certainly fundamental to feminist analysis, it is deeply rooted in American empiricism. From Jonathan Edwards through William James through the Chicago school of the early twentieth century, North Americans have a history of connecting religious faith not simply with theological definitions and expressions but also with particular analyses of experience that link human consciousness with the wider environment of nature and culture. Feminists deepen this empiricist trend by asking the further question of the relation of one's interpretation of experience not only to nature and society but also to one's embodiment—specifically, to one's male or female embodiment.

When the dimension of embodiment is brought into view, then the question of distortion must be raised concerning linguistic and social interpretations of experience that neglect this ever-present factor. The inevitable result of this distortion is a universalization of the masculine experience that enters into the formulations of theology and culture, along with the exclusion or rejection of the female as substandard. Since the universalization of the masculine has been the assumed norm of all Christian theology, particularly as it developed through the patriarchal tradition, then all theology must now be questioned by a more authentically recognized criterion of fully human experience—female as well as male.

Furthermore, women's problems are not individualistic but social and corporate in origin and nature. Social structures create individual ills. And social structures are linguistic—they are created, sustained, and mediated through language. Oppression, then, is not simply a physical reality but a psychic reality, for one's perceptions of self and world are formed linguistically, and the language is received from the social reality within which one is embedded. When this language makes the male gender systemically normative, then women as the other gender are precisely that: other, outsiders, marginalized. In addition, insofar as the language pervades the culture, all of the institutions within that culture will reflect and perpetuate the normative and therefore privileged status of the male as over against the female. This pervasiveness not only includes the religious institutions within the culture; indeed, insofar as religious institutions are the culturally appointed conservers of value, these institutions become prime guardians of the patriarchal status quo.

Thus all feminist theological constructions tend toward a strong interest in language and its use; they take the empirical ground of theology with great seriousness; they are deeply aware of the connections between doctrine and social structures. They bring a "hermeneutic of suspicion" to doctrine, their own as well as the patriarchy's, asking the question of whose interests are served or violated by the doctrine. And the criterion by which doctrine is measured is the degree to which that doctrine facilitates the mutual well-being of diverse peoples in community. There is a bias in favor of pluralism, theological as well as social. Given these suppositions and strategies, what is the result with regard to reconstruction of a doctrine of God hitherto very much favorable to male elitism?

RECONSTRUCTION OF THE DOCTRINE

Given the fact that patriarchal theology is intrinsically biased in favor of male dominance, many feminists have renounced the possibility of dealing in Christian theology at all, choosing rather to define themselves as post-Christian feminists. Insofar as such feminists name a power for the good that is not reducible to individual human experience, they often name this power Goddess. Goddess thealogies are grounded in the ancient past and often imply a collective unconscious realm through which goddesses can emerge within the psyche for the empowerment of individual women.

Among those feminists who relate to the tradition as well as to the norms drawn from women's experience, there is an increasing diversity: womanists, who critique the racism within feminism and the sexism within black theology and who develop reformulations of doctrine from the uniqueness of black women's experience; mujerista theologians, who give voice to Hispanic women's struggles for liberation; Asian feminists, who often integrate Asian and Christian traditions for feminist reconstruction; lesbian feminists, who name the heterosexual bias that is combined with patriarchy; ecofeminists, who highlight the environmental concerns that are a part of all feminist thought; and white, middle-class feminists. All are committed to transforming their patriarchal Christian traditions. Given this rich feminist diversity, no single doctrine of God emerges from feminist experience. However, there are common themes emergent within the feminist critique and reconstruction of the notion of divine being, and each theme in some way addresses the issue of evil as oppression.

Relationality over Immutability

The immutability of God required by the patriarchal devaluation of finitude and mutability is almost totally absent in feminist reconstruction. Finite mutability is recast as relationality and as such is valued as integral to all experience—even divine experience. Hence immutability as the essential quality of God is not simply irrelevant; it is anachronistic and dangerous. Anachronistically, it casts the category of God into philosophical criteria designed for an age with far different assumptions about the nature of reality. If reality is made up of unchanging bits of stuff that undergo accidental changes, then immutability in God is a way of guaranteeing the eternity of that unchanging "bit of stuff" that constitutes deity. But if reality is essentially relational, so that everything is constituted in and through relationality, then immutability applied to God contradicts not only the life of God but the existence of God. Thus it is anachronistic, in a relational age, to apply immutability to God. The danger of the quality is already apparent: immutability as a divine value sanctions immutable structures in society; these, in turn, become bastions of power for the perpetuation of privilege.

In the patriarchal tradition, the notion of trinity was invoked in order to indicate a dynamism *within* the immutable God, which in turn accounted for the external activity of God. Thus immutability and trinity were corollary concepts. The Christian feminist repudiation of immutability hesitates over a similar repudiation of trinity, since "trinity" can arguably be expressive of an internal relationality within God. Barbara Brown Zikmund argues in "The Trinity and Women's Experience"[1] that the relationality posited of the Trinity is akin to the feminist notion of community and may indeed be explored as a model of community. The trinitarian relationality depends upon an irreducible diversity of aspect and function within the one divine nature. Further, the unity of the divine nature depends upon the irreducible diversity and functions in an egalitarian way: no member of the Trinity is subordinate to another, and the designations of "first," "second," and "third" have nothing to do with priority, but only with distinction. All of this runs directly counter to the homogeneity of patriarchy's insistence on conformity, whether in theology or culture, race or gender. If the trinitarian formula could be divested of its masculine terminology, it could provide a mandate for Christian communities to seek and celebrate irreducible diversities in order to achieve unity.

But that, of course, is the issue: trinitarianism has been so interwoven with the male language of Father and Son that it is questionable whether it can be extricated from this language. The feminist use of "Creator," "Redeemer," and "Sustainer" substitutes the functions attributed to God relative to the world for the intratrinitarian patriarchal names. The problem with such a move is that the focus on the economic Trinity loses the value of the dynamic intratrinitarian language that depicts God as an egalitarian, irreducibly diverse unity. Since it is precisely this

1. Barbara Brown Zikmund, "The Trinity and Women's Experience," *Christian Century*, April 15, 1987, 354–56.

intratrinitarian model of God that so dramatically contradicts oppressions, the move to the use of the titles Creator, Redeemer, and Sustainer can be experienced as merely proposing stand-ins for the *real* designations of what Mary Daly calls "Father, Son & Co." Thus, far from serving as feminist reappropriations of God that can challenge patriarchal oppression, the use of the titles Creator, Redeemer, Sustainer may simply perpetuate the oppressively male aspects of the Christian notion of God. Whether feminists can reappropriate the communal notions of the trinitarian God without lapsing again into its patriarchal aspects is still an open question. Regardless of the outcome, the very discussion is witness to the feminist shift from immutability to relationality as a central category in the reconstruction of the doctrine of God.

Immanence over Transcendence

While the classic, patriarchal notion of God included the categories of immanence and transcendence, the emphasis was on transcendence, sometimes in extreme form, as in the early work of Karl Barth, where God is conceived as wholly other. Feminists also tend to keep both categories, but the emphasis is reversed—and at times immanence tends to overwhelm transcendence, as in Carter Heyward's *The Redemption of God,* where God appears to be solely the empowering relationality of egalitarian human community.[2]

Perhaps the most interesting tension between immanence and transcendence is manifested in Mary Daly's works. Daly, whose role in feminist theology was as a reformist in her first two works and thereafter as a radically post-Christian feminist, develops the notion of God as dynamic energy, ever unfolding, drawing creation toward itself. In *Beyond God the Father,* God is the Verb, a force that is transcendent but no longer in a way that suggests an "over and above" creation. Rather, God the Verb is in advance of creation, always transcending history by evoking new

2. Carter Heyward, *The Redemption of God: A Theology of Mutual Relation* (Lanham, Md.: Univ. Press of America, 1982).

history, feminist history. The Unfolding Verb is the empowerment of women and the call to the sisterhood of all humankind in new modes of community. In *Gyn/Ecology,* a work that came after *Beyond God the Father,* Daly moves almost totally to immanence: God the Verb of the earlier work is replaced by an Intransitive Verb that is incarnate in the female self and in words spun from that space. But in the following work, *Pure Lust,* we find Be-ing the Verb, which again is transcendent as well as immanent.[3] The word "Goddess" used in *Gyn/Ecology* is replaced by "Metabeing," used to designate "the Powers of Be-ing, the Active Verb in whose potency all biophilic reality participates."[4] Finally, in *Wickedary,* Be-ing the Verb is both immanent in a way consistent with the use in *Gyn/Ecology* ("The ultimate Guide of each Weaver/Journeyer is her Final Cause, her indwelling, unfolding Purpose") and transcendent, as in *Beyond God the Father* ("Goddess the Verb: Metaphor for Ultimate/Intimate Reality, the constantly Unfolding Verb of Verbs in which all be-ing participates; Metaphor of Metabeing").[5] For Daly and for all feminists, immanence is no lesser category than transcendence; the two are inseparably linked, with immanence usually being predominant.

Perhaps the best way of characterizing the feminist transformation of transcendence is to note that whereas in patriarchal theology transcendence seemed to have spatial connotations of remoteness, feminist usage of transcendence tends to connote the irreducibility of God to human experience. There is that which is more even than collective humanity, and that "more than" is a power for relation. A number of feminists utilize Charles Hartshorne's process metaphor of "the world as God's body"[6] as a way of indicating the closeness of God to the world and yet the

3. Mary Daly, *Beyond God the Father* (Boston: Beacon, 1973); idem, *Gyn/Ecology: The Metaethics of Radical Feminism* (Boston: Beacon, 1978); idem, *Pure Lust: Elemental Feminist Philosophy* (Boston: Beacon, 1984).

4. Daly, *Pure Lust,* 26.

5. Mary Daly and Jane Caputi, *Webster's First New Intergalactic Wickedary of the English Language* (Boston: Beacon, 1987), 55 and 76.

6. See, for example, Sallie McFague's works *The Body of God: An Ecological The-*

"more than" that is God in relation to the world. Transcendence is harnessed by immanence.

The relation between this shift in emphasis and oppressive structures in the world lies primarily in the implications of immanence. If God's transcendence does not contradict the presence of God with us, for us, among us, and even in us, then the reality we call God co-experiences with the world: this is what immanence means. But if God co-experiences with the world, then God is not separated from the suffering of the world. God is the co-victim of oppression. Oppressions against humanity—and nature—are also oppressions inflicted upon the immanent God who is with us. It is not enough to say that God must then be a resource enabling one to endure and triumph over oppression, for too often oppression claims its victims with a brutal finality. One must rather say that in the name of God and in the name of humanity, oppression must be judged as evil and give way to the transformation to justice.

Unmaleness

The patriarchy-endorsing maleness of God is resoundingly repudiated by feminists, but in different ways. For some feminists, particularly in early feminist works, God is portrayed by female as well as male imagery. Feminists such as Phyllis Trible, a biblical scholar, called attention to the way biblical texts use female as well as male images and symbols for God. Under feminist influence it is not uncommon for worship liturgies to include the phrase "God as Mother." However, since the use of gendered language for deity draws from and tends to perpetuate gendered stereotypes in society, many feminists feel that simply including female- as well as male-gendered language cannot resolve the problem; God must be degendered. Womanist theologian Delores Williams argues for shifting the dominance of God-language to Spirit-language, thus avoiding the use of

ology (Minneapolis: Fortress, 1993) and *Models of God: Theology for an Ecological, Nuclear Age* (Minneapolis: Fortress, 1987).

gender altogether.[7] Rosemary Radford Ruether coins the word "God/ess" to go beyond stereotypical maleness or femaleness, denoting instead a unifying power that is both the substratum of matter and creative spirit.[8] However, since women have traditionally been associated detrimentally with matter and men have been associated positively with creative spirit, even such a use of God/ess has its dangers of perpetuating the male/female stereotypes that endorse women's oppression.

Like Daly, Rebecca Chopp repudiates patriarchal maleness by using "Word" as the primal metaphor for God. This metaphor *replaces* God as "Father" since its fundamental connotation is the ultimate contradiction of that term. In Chopp's development, this is because the Word is a perfectly open sign, whereas "Father" is inherently restrictive. The open sign that is the Word lives through humans (and is thus immanent) and is communicated through textual words but ultimately transcends both humanity and texts. Thus the metaphor "Word" builds upon the infinite potentiality of words to encompass many things, so that every specific word used of God must imply its own limitations by its connection to yet other words. The criterion that governs any specificity to "Word" is its transformative power toward ever-more inclusive communities of well-being in the world. God as "Word" thus judges and transforms oppression.[9]

Liberation through Empowerment

In the classical doctrine, the patriarchal God redeemed "man" by turning the broken will back to God's own self. "Man" was essentially passive in this act because part of the corrective of salvation was to counter the aggressive pride of "man." Thus grace,

7. Delores Williams, "Womanist Theology," in *Weaving the Visions: New Patterns in Feminist Spirituality,* ed. Judith Plaskow and Carol P. Christ (New York: Harper and Row, 1989).

8. Rosemary Radford Ruether, *Sexism and God-Talk: Toward a Feminist Theology* (Boston: Beacon, 1983).

9. See Rebecca Chopp, *The Power to Speak: Feminism, Language, and God* (New York: Crossroad, 1989).

in this view, represents the divine initiative whereby God, apart from any human act whatsoever, heals the broken will.

Feminists, like other liberation theologians, find such passivity a part of the problem: when passive marginalization is imposed by patriarchy, a passive salvation is a contradiction in terms. Hence the word "liberation" replaces the words "salvation" and "redemption," for in "liberation" the activity of women and men replaces the passivity that had dominated the human role in the patriarchal scheme. This liberation is not the healing of a broken will but the empowerment to seize salvation, both personally and socially. Furthermore, this empowerment comes through the very act of seizing; liberation is experienced in the process of the struggle toward liberation.

Given the dominance of immanence in feminist theology, it is not surprising that the empowerment from God comes in and through relationship with one another in community. Whether that community is "women-church" (Ruether) or "the community of equals" (Elisabeth Schüssler Fiorenza) or "sisterhood as anti-church" (Daly), empowerment is not an individualistic but a social term, a "withness" that generates the ability to act toward transformation.[10]

The feminist reconstruction of soteriology in terms of a relational power toward liberation radically changes problems that typically perplexed Christian theologians through the ages. If salvation comes only by divine initiative acting through divine grace, with humans passively receiving this salvation, why is there so much evil in the world? Why isn't this God just a bit more generous with grace, thus alleviating some of the gross problems of human evil? The feminist shift to liberation as empowerment reframes the issue. God does not—indeed, God *cannot*—overcome oppressions "for" us. We are responsible for

10. These themes are developed, respectively, in Rosemary Radford Ruether, *Women-Church: Theology and Practice* (New York: Harper and Row, 1985); Elisabeth Schüssler Fiorenza, *In Memory of Her: A Feminist Theological Reconstruction of Christian Origins* (New York: Crossroad, 1984); and Mary Daly, *Beyond God the Father.*

the oppressions we create, and we are responsible for drawing upon divine power as available through the community to transform oppressions. The problem of human evil is not a question of God's withholding grace but rather is a matter of our withdrawal from an ever-present offer of divine grace that is mediated to us in and through communal relations. The answer to oppression is not divine intervention from above but divine and human cooperation through the positive power of relationality.

Nondualism

The patriarchal God presided over dualisms hierarchically valued in terms of superior/inferior. This included the primal split between male and female, which then implied further dualisms of spirit and body, mind and matter, civilization and nature. In each of the dualisms, the second named was subordinate to the first. The feminist construction of God does away with these dualisms, but in so doing, the notion of liberation must overcome not only the male/female dualism but all other oppressive dualisms as well.

Consequently, the empowerment for liberation is not simply grasped as the betterment of women. To transform the role of women in society is to transform society itself, to unmask its patriarchal substructure and replace it with egalitarian relations stressing mutuality rather than hierarchy. But the transformation of society requires at the same time the transformation of the human relation to the environment. No longer can the world around us be taken as a passive substance immune to its own exploitation. The nonhuman world, animate and inanimate, participates in the world of relation embraced by feminism and is included in the vision of relations of respect for all things.

These themes—relationality rather than immutability; immanence conditioning transcendence; liberation as empowerment rather than salvation passively received; degendering the notion of God; and nondualism—tend to characterize all feminist reconstructions of the notion of God. As has been suggested above, various feminist theologians take one or the other of these themes as primary and therefore as conditioning the way they develop the other themes, so that there is a rich variety among feminist reconstructions of God. Given the bent for diversity within the feminist community and the sense in which feminists assume the metaphorical rather than literal nature of all of their constructions, it belongs to the richness of feminism that it welcomes diversity rather than uniformity in doctrinal construction. To value irreducible diversity in community and to have a vision of the world as a community of diverse communities, each with its own integrity, each with its own forms of mutual well-being, is also to value diversity in theological expression. There is therefore no single feminist doctrine of God; there are rather unifying themes that mark doctrines of God as feminist.

GOD AND SEXISM: THE DOCTRINES APPLIED

Just as the patriarchal concept of God addressed the patriarchal interpretation of evil, even so feminist conceptions of God address the feminist interpretation of evil. Evil is experienced as the patriarchal oppression of women through women's social and personal marginalization, subordination, and devaluation relative to men, and by extension, evil is named as all oppression of peoples or environment. Since the patriarchal concept of God is implicated in oppression, that concept is part of the problem and therefore cannot adequately describe the liberating God.

By bringing the unifying themes of feminist construction together, we might indicate the following as a composite image of God. The liberating God described by feminists is internally and externally relational. Internally, God is already in some sense communal; externally, God relates to the world in and through community. God relates to the world by empowering it to reach toward a new future, one that more closely approximates the inclusive well-being of all the world, human and nonhuman. A relational God empowers relation—not as one great mega-community, however, for that notion harks back to the "Big Brother" world of enforced conformity that is the extreme development of patriarchy. Rather, the relational God empowers diverse communities of relation.

The liberating God is "eminently immanent," to be found in community as well as in our unfolding selves. The transcendence of this God comes to us as the vision and call into liberation and into more deeply inclusive communities of well-being. The liberating God is nondualistic and therefore neither male nor female; it is Spirit. The empowerment of this nondualism is its embrace and celebration of diversity in the unity of well-being. The omnipotence of patriarchy is transformed into the empowerment of feminism; the omniscience of patriarchy is transformed into the vision of feminism; and the omnipresence of patriarchy is transformed into the communal presence of God in feminism. These transformations of God are corollary to the transformation of women, and the transformation of women is the transformation of society and the world.

So, then, if such a construction of God were prevalent, we might rewrite our introductory story like this. A woman—or a person with handicapping conditions, or a person oriented to the same sex, or a person whose ethnicity differs from that of the dominant social class—has long been a part of a local community. Through the years, this person has been very active in lay ministry, serving with others in the community in a variety of local endeavors, all of which have been carefully developed to ensure a deeper well-being in the congregation's local setting. Eventually this person feels convinced that her life's work is in ordained ministry, and so she approaches others in her community to discuss this call. They encourage her to pursue it further, and the strength of their confirmation deepens her own strong sense of call. And so this person approaches those in her tradition who are responsible for guiding people into the best ways of answering such a call. This group hears this woman and hears also the confirmation from her local community. Noting the unfortunate uniformity that plagues ordained leadership because of too long a patriarchal interpretation of ministry, they rejoice in this new opportunity to add diversity to the leadership of the church. There will now be an increased richness of the community as it mirrors in its own way the irreducibly diverse and egalitarian unity that is God. So this woman will study, will eventually be ordained, and will then lead a congregation. She will share with them the seminary studies that enriched her, so that they too will be equipped and empowered for ministry with her. Their guiding vision will be threefold, encompassing a vision of God, of themselves, and of their surrounding community. They envision that the diverse unity that is the love in and of God spills over, empowering the congregation to rejoice in its diversity and to create modes of mutual well-being. Its love also spills over, so that it becomes a power toward transformation in society. Its energy is drawn from relatedness to each other in and through God, and to God in and through each other. Its work in society—of which it is a part—is not to force that society into conformity with itself but to work with it to explore ever deeper modes of well-being in their common community. Such a story, enacted again and again and again and again, would be a force answering oppression everywhere with well-being.

DAVID B. BURRELL, C.S.C.

2. GOD, RELIGIOUS PLURALISM, AND DIALOGIC ENCOUNTER

A major question that can be posed among persons of diverse religious faiths is: Do we worship the same God? There are philosophical puzzles as well as theological problems built into the question, as we shall see, but we cannot escape asking it. What might have posed little difficulty at all from a tribal perspective, where the question would usually not even arise, becomes a major issue for us, for what has tended to separate one tribe from another is precisely the difference in their gods. Yet once the unity of the universe is seen as implying the oneness of God (and vice versa), then another argument can begin: Whose god is this one God? Since the major traditions that form the focus of this exploration—Judaism, Christianity, and Islam—share that perspective, the question arises sharply in our comparative study. We should note, however, how this question provokes precisely because it conflates perspectives: as though the one God could belong to a single group. Yet we must acknowledge that the history of religions insistent on God's uniqueness seems equally intent on confusing these perspectives, and fatally so. When conceptual confusion instills and fuels animosities, then political authorities have but one alternative: sever "religion" from the civil order; relegate it to personal preference and conviction, and urge civic tolerance. This is a history and a dynamic that Americans readily recognize and are accustomed to applauding.

If a full-blown peace be impractical, we can at least hope for nonhostility.

The alternative has been all too clear since the seventeenth century: communal violence in defense of a group's identity, often reinforced by adherence to that group's God. We are inclined, then, to consider societies enlightened to the extent that they adopt a personalist view of religious faith. Yet the upshot of such a policy is to downgrade the Creator to one dimension of our lives and so in practice to subvert the sovereignty of the one God. The social strategy that exalts personal faith opens the doors to a practical polytheism: one god for the home, another for the workplace; one to be worshiped on the proper day of worship, another to be served during the rest of the week. In the wake of that initial bifurcation yet other divinities will assert their hegemony over further dimensions of our lives: physical fitness, erotic satisfaction, aesthetic enjoyment, intellectual improvement. Only time, opportunity, and energy will limit the list.

So the presumed consensus among philosophers and theologians regarding God's uniqueness is hardly limited to metaphysical concerns. In fact, it finds its psychological corollary in the human aspiration to wholeheartedness, a pull quite contrary to the inherent fragmentation of desire by many attractive objects. It is this attraction to unity of purpose that is addressed in Jesus' renditions of the "greatest and the first commandment: you must love the Lord your God with all your heart, with all your soul, and with all your mind" (Matt. 22:37, citing Deut. 6:5), as well as in rabbinic and Islamic teachings regarding the unity of God. While this insistence may have focused initially and polemically on there being one rather than many gods, the teaching itself soon took on a more substantive cast: God's being *one* intends to concentrate into one the diverse aspirations to which many gods had long answered. It is not difficult to see this dynamic operative across the three major religious traditions that affirm God to be one.

Jewish faith is expressed as a duty: for instance, a Jew is to recite Deut. 6:4 ("Hear, O Israel: the Lord our God is the one, the only Lord") twice daily. Whoever negates the truth stated in this text is said to deny the primary principle of the faith, so that " 'he who denies the root' (kōfēr bā-'Iqqār) is not therefore just one who denies God generally, but one who disavows God the Creator of the universe, the God who gave the Torah and the commandments."[1] So faith in one God entails trust in divine providence, in the One who creates and rules the universe. Meister Eckhart, a fourteenth-century Dominican, comments on John 14:8 ("Lord, show us the Father, and it is enough for us") by reminding us that "unity is attributed to the Father. But every desire and its fulfillment is to be united to God, and every union exists by reason of unity and it alone. . . . Therefore, when he says 'Show us the Father, and it is enough for us,' he asks us to be united to God and for this to be enough."[2] The first reason why Philip asks that the Father be shown to us is "that God, insofar as he is Lord and God, is the Principle of the creature, as the Father is Principle of the Son."[3] As the source of all, both begotten and created, the Father is preeminently one, and thus the One to whom all creatures aspire. Al-Ghazālī, a twelfth-century Muslim religious thinker, offers a summary statement of Islamic *tawḥīd* (faith in divine unity):

> For whoever says: "There is no God but God" alone, and "there is no sharer with Him," and "to Him belong sovereignty and praise, and He is the Able to do all things" (64:1)—to that one belongs the faith which is the root of trust in God. That is, the force of this assertion induces a property inherent in the heart which rules over it. Now faith in divine unity is the source and much could be said about it: it is a knowledge of revelation, yet certain knowledges of revelation depend upon practices undertaken in the midst of mystical states, and knowledge of religious practices would not be complete without them. So we are only concerned with [faith in divine unity] to the extent that it pertains to practice, for other-

1. Ephraim Urbach, *The Sages* (Jerusalem: Magnes, 1979), 27.
2. See *Meister Eckhart: Teacher and Preacher,* ed. Bernard McGinn (New York: Paulist, 1986), 182.
3. Ibid., 189.

wise, the teaching of divine unity is a vast sea which is not easy to negotiate.[4]

So each of these Abrahamic faiths insists that God's unity is not an attribute of divinity so much as a constitutive feature of the faith of those who believe in such a One and a formal feature of this God. (A formal feature does not describe an object but reminds us what sort of thing we are talking about.) So in this case insisting that the God whom Jews, Christians, and Muslims worship is one God does not correct a misapprehension regarding how many gods there are so much as it lets believers and nonbelievers know what it is to believe in such a One. So we are reminded, for example, that those for whom "their belly is their god" cannot be worshiping the God whom Jews, Christians, and Muslims have encountered.

Moreover, while we shall focus on these three Abrahamic traditions, since their shared faith in a free Creator makes our inquiry easier to follow, what will interest us throughout are the ways in which their *differences* enhance our understanding of the faith of each. Rather than seek for a common perspective, we will search for differences that help move us out of settled patterns of discourse into ways of understanding "the other" and a consequent fresh appreciation of our own traditions. The fact that all religions make totalizing claims is a constituting feature of such faiths; it is not up to us to relativize them from some purportedly superior perspective. But we can come to understand one relative to another and so appreciate the ways in which traditions need to be poised to respond to challenges that their world is too small. When this is carried out not in the abstract but among believers, that mutual appreciation becomes an avenue to friendship as well. This is the tantalizing fruit of interreligious dialogue when it is presented as a new way of understanding ourselves along with the other.

4. Al-Ghazālī, *Kitāb at-Tawhīd wa at-Tawakkul* (Book of faith in divine unity and trust in God), in *Iḥyā' 'Ulūm ad-Dīn* (Beirut: al-Fikr, 1989), 4.261 (*Biyān haqīqah at-tawhīd*).

ANALYSIS OF THE DOCTRINE

A Persistent Challenge

If the affirmation of God as one is so pregnant an assertion, the doctrine of God will set itself the task of capturing the resonances of so radical a faith. The challenge has been to articulate God's unitary existence in terms that relate this One to our world and yet do not pretend to speak of God as though speaking of another item "alongside" the universe. For then God would be one in the sense of "single," and we would be misinterpreting the faith-assertion as giving information about how many gods there really are. So the spontaneous move has been to follow the lead of the Scriptures—Bible or Qur'an—and see God as the origin of all-that-is. That framework allows one to move either of two ways: that the One is such that all-that-is comes forth from it by "overflow" or emanation or by way of intentional activity. In the medieval period this polarity dominated discussions between philosophers and people of faith. Philosophers found the derivation of premises from principles to offer an elegant model for the coming forth of all-that-is from the One.[5] Religious thinkers in all three traditions resisted a formulation that seemed to compromise divine freedom in originating the universe and could even be construed to say that God needed the world so emanated to be fully divine.

Yet we may also be invited to think of originating freedom more as spontaneity than as choice, and especially in the case of the One who is the sole source of all, for there would as yet be nothing to "choose between." So other religious thinkers in these traditions could also be enticed to explore the emanation model as a way of articulating the one God without postulating another item over against the universe that God creates.[6] For if

5. See my "Creation or Emanation: Two Paradigms of Reason," in *God and Creation: An Ecumenical Symposium,* ed. David Burrell and Bernard McGinn (Notre Dame, Ind.: Univ. of Notre Dame Press, 1990), 27–37.

6. For the Christian tradition, see Bernard McGinn, "Do Christian Platonists Really Believe in Creation?" in *God and Creation,* 197–219; for the Islamic tradition, we shall

the logical overtones of emanation lead to necessity, the anthropomorphic resonance of "making" leads one to think of a God poised over against the world, so that the totality of all-that-is would contain two items: God and the universe. We have already seen, however, that faith in God's unity does not assert that there is one God out there so much as it directs us to God as unitary source of all-that-is. Plotinus, the Neoplatonic philosopher, was compelled to say that this One was "beyond being," as a way of insisting on the unalloyed unity of the One, whereas Thomas Aquinas preferred to identify the divine essence with existing itself. That formula also met the needs of Moses Maimonides and of al-Ghazālī (who adapted it from the thought of Ibn Sīnā [Avicenna]), so that all three religious traditions that aver the free creation of the universe also adapted the metaphysical wisdom of the Greeks to assert the connection of Creator with creation.

Yet they employed that metaphysics in such a way as to assert the "distinction" as well. Indeed, reconciling these dual requirements of *connection* and of *distinction* fairly defines the "doctrine of God." We can see this quite clearly if we think that there must be *something* in terms of which God and the universe can both be understood, yet if there were such a *thing,* then there would be something other than the source of all that links that source with all-that-is. So whatever the connection is between God and the universe, it must come from God's creating activity. That reminder runs usefully counter to our native propensity to conceive God as parallel to or over against the universe;[7] however, once we have insisted on God's being the sufficient source for all-that-is, then we need to assert "the distinction" of God from what God causes-to-be, since one might easily conclude that the world was but another appearance of

consider Ibn al-'Arabī; for the Jewish tradition, see Seymour Feldman, "The Theory of Eternal Creation in Hasdai Crescas and Some of His Predecessors," *Viator* 2 (1980): 289–320, an article that presents with admirable clarity the complex logic of the debates.

7. Kathryn Tanner's salutary warnings against this intellectual tendency are worked out in *God and Creation in Christian Theology* (Oxford: Blackwell, 1988).

the divine—or other crudely monistic articulations.[8] "Connection" and "distinction" here function parallel to theologians' use of "immanence" and "transcendence": the One who creates all-that-is must by that very fact *transcend* the universe that it originates, yet since *all*-that-is comes from it, that same One must be present to all-that-is, and immediately so, hence *immanent* to creation.

When this unique relation was expressed by the image of *emanation,* the teaching of the three religious traditions on creation looked very much like a form of explanation, since the resolution of the multiplicity of beings in the universe into a unitary source showed the elegance of a deductive system. In this respect, the emanation scheme worked out by al-Fārābī and adopted by Ibn Sīnā differed but little from that of Plotinus. Yet the Islamic philosophers at least intended to offer a model for the Qur'an's insistence on the origination of all things from a Creator, while Plotinus was not responding to the demands of a revelation but to the inner impulse of reason. Plotinus sought to secure the transcendence of the One, moreover, by removing from it all attributes whatsoever—indeed, by placing it "beyond being." In al-Fārābī's hands, the simplicity of the One was secured by identifying essence (*dhāt*) with existing (*wujūd*) in it alone. On both of these schemes, however, it was inevitable that the relation of the One with all that emanates from it should be considered more natural than intentional. If creating the universe is a free act, it could only be seen as pure spontaneity, yet at such a remove from experience and ordinary grammar, "pure spontaneity" could be read either as a "necessary overflow" or as a free (or intentional) action. And when the language of emanation remains so ambiguous, what is in jeopardy is the "distinction" of the One from all that emanates from it.

In contrast, the image of *making* seemed quite anthropomorphic and was in fact tied to Plato's picture (in the *Timaeus*) of

8. Robert Sokolowski's *The God of Faith and Reason* (Notre Dame, Ind.: Univ. of Notre Dame Press, 1982) develops "the distinction" in clear and cogent detail.

the Demiurge who crafts things out of preexisting matter according to heavenly archetypes. So a Creator who is a maker does not need to be the sole source from which all-that-is comes; there can be something already there for such a one to fashion. Nonetheless, religious thinkers beholden either to the Hebrew Scriptures or to the Qur'an found it more workable to remove the anthropomorphic residue from the Creator/maker picture than to accept the implication of "necessary outflow" that easily accompanied emanation. (There has always been a minority voice on the other side, however, and one often associated with the more mystical strains of each tradition—see note 6.) Aquinas's strategy is illuminating here: by removing any hint of preexistent matter, he was able in one fell swoop to insist that creation is an action that does not involve change, since there is nothing that perdures through it, and that, hence, no process accompanies it. So the image of maker is radically transformed. All that is left is the intentional character, and that was the very reason for preferring *making* to *emanating*.

What is illustrative here is the way in which Scriptures and philosophical schemes interact to develop a virtual consensus in formulating a religious doctrine. No single statement of the Scriptures decides the issue, but a series of constraints offer cumulative criteria for preferring one formulation rather than another. Since no scheme can be expected to articulate matters adequately, however, alternative formulations remain possible, provided one can show that they too meet those same constraints. A further advantage of the image of making lies in its power to distance the doctrine of creation from expectations that it provide an explanation of origins. For asserting an intentional producer of all-that-is suffuses the universe with meaning without requiring that features of the world display their divine origin. If there is no natural (or necessary) connection between the source and what is originated, no specific traces need be found, and God is free to shape creation to meet divine concerns, as in giving the Torah or handing down the Qur'an. In fact, for both al-Ghazālī and Maimonides, it is this fact that makes them decide against the model of speculative knowing embodied in emanation and in favor of the model of practical reason that *making* suggests.[9] So we can see how a community's experience with revelation tends to shape its teaching about creation, thereby reminding us that the doctrine of creation envisages far more than origins: the very meaning and destiny of the universe are at stake.

Doctrines of God in Western Contexts

This interrelation of explanatory schemes with religious traditions, including practices of worship and of formation in community, was interrupted by the pretensions of an enlightened West to a manner of doing theology more akin in meaning to that of the Greeks: rational reflection on the universe. Religious *differences* became a scandal to educated persons, who were at once repelled by the religious wars and attracted by Descartes's dream of a universal reason that would ground beliefs about God and the universe not in faith but in the very deliverances of reason. This confidence in "natural theology" took a different form in England than on the Continent, but for the history of theology the parallels are more telling than the differences.[10] The search for grounds for faith in a universal reason led to the reinvention of philosophy and even of metaphysics as disciplines independent of insights gained from faith, since they were to provide it the warrant of intellectual respectability. And if reason can discover the whence and the whither of the universe, "sciences of the human" will not be far behind. The next step,

9. See al-Ghazālī's discussion in his *Tahāfūt al-Falāsifa,* best located in Averroës's refutation: *Tahāfūt al-Tahāfūt,* ed. and trans. Simon van den Bergh (Cambridge, Mass.: Gibb Memorial Trust, 1978), "Third Discussion," 87–155; and Maimonides, *Guide of the Perplexed,* trans. Schlomo Pines (Chicago: Univ. of Chicago Press, 1963), 3.21; see my "Why Not Pursue the Metaphor of Artisan and View God's Knowledge as Practical?" in *Neoplatonism and Jewish Thought,* ed. Lenn Goodman (Albany: State Univ. of New York Press, 1992), 207–15.

10. I am beholden to Michael Buckley's *At the Origins of Modern Atheism* (New Haven: Yale Univ. Press, 1987) for much of this optic, although one should consult John Milbank's review of Buckley in *Modern Theology* 8 (1992): 89–92.

then, was into social theories, each of which offered such normative deliverances on the scope of human existence that they became virtual substitutes for theological discourse. A telling history of sociological theory cast in this mold has been written by John Milbank, where the argument reminds us that any pretension to articulate the aims and goals of human existence must perforce present itself as a *theology;* the names Durkheim, Weber, Hegel, and Kant stand paramount in the drama Milbank stages.[11]

In the case of the cosmologies offered in the name of pure reason, as well as the anthropologies undergirding a new practical reason, however, faith was disbarred from an initiating or intellectually validating role, so it became incumbent on theologians to align their discourse with that of social theory in order to gain legitimacy. Enter the phenomenon known as liberal theology, with the resulting polarities within the churches between those intent on preserving orthodoxy and those desirous of adapting to the modern world. Part of what today's postmodern optic brings to such matters is the legitimacy of a faith-perspective, so that the insights gained from participation in a particular community of faith once more become relevant to human discourse about God, the universe, and the destiny of human beings. One of the signal advantages of this shift in the intellectual valence of the knowledge that comes to us by faith has been an opening to worlds vastly more extensive than the presumptively superior European one in which the "enlightened" discussions took place. This setting leads us beyond familiar theological analyses of the discussion about God in the West to an appropriate reconstruction of the doctrine.

11. John Milbank, *Theology and Social Theory: Beyond Secular Reason* (Oxford: Blackwell, 1990); for a set of critical appreciations, see *Modern Theology* (1992).

RECONSTRUCTION OF THE DOCTRINE

Christianity's Presumptive Hegemony

As Western Christianity made its peace with the Enlightenment, in one way or another, at an intellectual level, most of humanity continued to seek tangible symbols, and many of them alien to Christianity. Yet those who had made their peace with Enlightenment reason found themselves confronted with the threatening spectacle of other Gods—not just other "gods"—in the shape of YHWH and Allah. Threatening, since the God of reason owed its ethical superiority, at least ancestrally, to Christian revelation, so theologian and philosopher alike simply presumed Judaism to be *passé,* intellectually as well as theologically. (The "reformed" movement in Judaism was in large part motivated, in its search for an ethical core to Jewish teaching, by this pervasive judgment. If such a core were to be the substance of Judaism, then no unwelcome particularity would remain except in the residue of ritual.) Islam represented but the exotic fringe of the known world, once the "discoveries" had allowed Europe to bypass the Muslim heartland in search of the pleasures of life. A few hardy travelers composed haunting adventure tales, while "the Turk" became a feared yet fascinating figure. Yet none of this led to any desire to understand Islam, about which enlightened Europeans remained even less instructed than their medieval forebears, who had at least exploited Islamic scientific and philosophical culture.

Thus while the presumptive (even if now defunct) hegemony of Christianity in the West vitiated anything more than curiosity regarding the religious teaching of Jews or Muslims, the possible presence of other ways to God, and so in effect other Gods, offered a potential threat to religious believer and secular believer alike. Secular Westerners believed in the superiority of that ancestral Christian hegemony no less than their religious counterparts, and what proved threatening to each was both the fact that there might *be* another God (for secular thinkers respected the power of symbol even when they had evacuated the reality) and the "relativism" which that possibility entailed for them. Indeed relativism seems to be an even more powerful bugbear for secular than for religious thinkers since it threatens the intellectual counterpart of the presumptive Eurocentrism that shaped their shared convictions. Moreover, out beyond the respectable boundaries of monotheism, in the "Far East," lay Hindu and Buddhist worlds of belief and practices, which were regarded less as theological contenders than as cultural fascinations. So long as the Eurocentric presumptions of Enlightenment rationality were in league with Christian doctrinal superiority, the threat remained quite latent, since if one could still believe anything at all, one would certainly be a Christian believer. However, as the universality of Western reason became suspect, and some Christians began to wonder aloud about there possibly being other ways to God, perhaps even as part of God's own "dispensation," the specter of relativism would become more palpable.

The Specter of Relativism

Yet the specter of relativism gains in stature and threat as a function of Enlightenment presuppositions about reason and truth, for they presume a normative set of rational criteria available to all, over against which any claim to other sets of criteria is utterly unsettling. That is what we mean by relativism: that there are no longer any operative norms across human discourse; so power or even violence will have to arbitrate. However, like earlier debates over natural law, there may be other ways of thinking about those criteria that are not so laden with specific beliefs but that have to do with the fact that believers formed in quite diverse traditions can discourse with one another. Once the idol of pure reason has been shattered, and we can learn to accept diverse ways of arriving at conclusions, we will also find that we can employ the skills learned in our tradition to follow reasoning in another. Traditions, in other words, may indeed be *relative* to one another in ways that can prove mutually fruitful rather than isolating. Those traditions that prove to be so will be those that avail themselves of human reason in their development, and the patterns of stress and strain in their evolution will display their capacity for exploiting the resources of reason.[12] In short, relativism gives way before the fact that all inquiry takes place within a tradition, and the specter that it evoked turns out to be the shadow of our faith in pure reason, that is, in the possibility of human inquiry outside of any tradition.

So the discovery of reason that every inquiry employs presuppositions that cannot themselves be rationally justified opens the way to self-knowledge on the part of Enlightenment philosophy itself, which can then take its place among the traditions.[13] Once that has been accomplished, the specter of relativism dissolves in the face of developing the skills needed to negotiate among traditions, which can be accomplished because the traditions can be seen to be related one to another. Because we have become accustomed to associating faith with tradition, we must then renounce the normative Enlightenment view that represented faith as an addendum to the human condition. For if that view itself reflects *a* tradition whose account can be rendered in historical terms (like a reaction to the devastating religious wars in Europe), then it too will have a recognizable convictional basis, and faith will once more emerge as part of a shared human legacy. Then the intellectual task, on the part of reason operative in any tradition that survives the test of time, becomes one of learning how such traditions develop and how one might learn from the other. *Reason,* in other words, becomes a functional notion, displayed in practices that cut across traditional boundaries, rather than expressing a set of substantive beliefs that must be adhered to *in those very terms* before discourse can be undertaken. *Rationality* will then show itself in practices that can be followed

12. Alasdair MacIntyre, *Whose Justice? Which Rationality?* (Notre Dame, Ind.: Univ. of Notre Dame Press, 1988), chaps. 18–19.
13. Ibid., chap. 17.

and understood by persons operating in similar fashion from different grounding convictions.[14]

What those persons have in common is the need to talk about what they believe. Here emerges the analogy with debates about natural law: what is so shared and common as to be dubbed "natural" are not necessarily substantive norms regarding human actions so much as the demand that any normative "law" must express itself in a coherent discourse. That very activity, which displays the fruitfulness of human ingenuity, also contains operative parameters whose function can be tracked by astute participant-observers who recognize analogies across traditions of inquiry, as Socrates' assembling linguistic reminders for Thrasymachus made him abandon his projected discourse without Socrates' having to exert any force at all (*Republic* bk. 1). Those reminders have to do with the possibility of any discourse at all and so governed the tradition Thrasymachus was defending as well as the totally opposed one that Socrates had set out to elaborate. Book 1 of the *Republic* does not defend Socrates' own position so much as display the terms for any debate. One may, of course, go on to imbed those terms in a much larger framework, as Plato does in the subsequent books of the *Republic,* but the exchange with Thrasymachus can stand on its own as displaying the coherence of the very practice that makes the rest possible. We will need to elaborate that coherence into a "philosophy" because practice alone seldom offers a persuasive display of its own cogency. These reflections, however, should remind us that the elaboration is secondary, and there may even be many such, yet they will be able to be elucidated *relative* to one another. The fact and the possibility of dialogue begin to emerge as the shape that reason takes in our pluralistic age. We can gain perspective on that task by employing some salient ex-

14. Here the reference is usually to the work of Ludwig Wittgenstein, notably the *Philosophical Investigations* (New York: Macmillan, 1956), and the extensive elaboration of reason as a human practice, which that seminal work spawned.

amples from Christianity as it faced a pagan world as well as from the history of Islam.

God and the Universe: Parsing a Key Relation

The primary opposition in the classical scenario was that between God and "the gods." It is originally a Hebrew opposition, so it was presumed among Christians, yet forcefully reiterated by Muslims. The opposition turns on what Robert Sokolowski has dubbed "the distinction" of God from the world: the insistence that God has no need of the universe to complete what it is to be God; that there is no way of moving by logic alone from divinity to world, and so *a fortiori,* the world cannot be conceived as a part of God.[15] These stipulations are taken to be grammatical reminders mirroring the metaphysical status of God, by contrast with "the gods," who represent a higher (and usually the highest) portion of the universe. It is usual to describe the relation between this God and the universe as free: that is, the universe cannot be said to derive from divinity as conclusions can be regarded as drawing out the virtualities of a logical premise. This need not imply an absolute beginning; such a spontaneous origination could well be everlasting and so (loosely speaking) "co-eternal" with God. Yet originated the universe must be, on this account of divinity, and in such a way as not to imply that it "completes" or "fills out" the divine Creator. So it is that the correlative terms "Creator," "creature," and "creation" have assumed the full-blooded sense that they have, especially for Jews, Christians, and Muslims.

Logically speaking, then, the very notions of *God* and *universe* must be parsed in terms of one another. The God who is Creator will differ from the One that necessarily emanates the universe as part of what it means to be that One. And the universes will differ as well, as Ibn Sīnā reminded us when he did not hesitate to suffuse the world with the same quality of neces-

15. Sokolowski, *God of Faith and Reason,* chaps. 3–5.

sity that realizes it: the logic of the emanation scheme, modeled on logical derivation, pervades his system, while a free Creator can have several kinds of relation to the universe spontaneously originated. The affirmation of creation, then, by contrast to an emanation scheme, will be compatible with diverse theologies or manners of elucidating that "distinction" of God from God's world. Some of these may even veer close to a kind of "monism" that eviscerates the distinction itself, but that will be for the respective traditions to discern. By a curious inverse logic, Hindu thought allows for "theologies" creationist in tone even when Hindu Scriptures are not so insistent on "the distinction." Hinduism seems to celebrate such diversity, softening the opposition between God and "the gods" as well, while tolerating "theologies" from monist to creationist. So this tradition will contain within itself the very debates that Jews, Christians, or Muslims would invariably strike up with Hindus. Monitoring those debates would help test our contention that the notions of God and universe must be parsed in terms of each other and would probably prove more fruitful than trading polemics about "logics"—Western and Eastern. Once again, the intellectual promise comes from understanding that such traditions are indeed *relative* one to another and that those who discover that fact have not thereby assumed a higher plane from which to peruse them all neutrally, but are rather reaching out from their own tradition to appreciate analogies with another, and thereby recognizing blind spots in their own as well.

It is a simple epistemological corollary of God's "distinction" from the world that such a One is unknowable: that is, *not* one of the items in the world. A sane epistemology will normally presuppose that our range of knowing is coextensive with the kinds of beings we are in such a way as to deflate pretensions to knowledge about things quite beyond us. That range cannot be equated with "our experience," however, and not simply because the term "experience" is notoriously protean. It is rather that our knowledge must extend to things presupposed to our experiencing anything at all, which might be called the "structures" of our experience. In fact, our greatest joys in discovery can come in domains like mathematics, where the elegance of an otherwise indiscernible "structure" is communicated to us. Yet the test of our grasp will certainly be our ability to communicate that discovery to others, so the limits of knowledge will reflect the kind of beings we are, in the sense of what can be communicated among us. Medievals like Thomas Aquinas used the scaffolding of the emanation scheme to depict our place in the universe as linking spiritual with material realms, thereby designating the "proper object" of human beings to be "the quiddity of material things," where our intellectual (spiritual) capacity to ask "What is that?" focused us on the "quiddity," while our bodily constitution linked us directly with "that" by *pointing* to it. Though little of that scaffolding may remain with us, the double orientation perdures in epistemology, however naturalist it may purport to be.

Free Creation as the Axis of a Renewed Doctrine of God

So the origin-of-all will be accessible only through the relation linking it with all-that-is, since it is not itself a member of that set—however paradoxical that may sound. Again, the philosophical attractiveness of the emanation scheme flows from its modeling that relation on logical deduction, thereby connecting the One with all the rest in a fashion otherwise available to us. But that also made it suspect to religious believers whose revelations accentuated "the distinction," for the first principle from which a set of conclusions may be derived is not itself adequately distinct from that deductive chain. So a Creator from whom all-that-is freely originates cannot be cast as the One from which all-that-is emanates in logical array. It is no less *one,* of course, yet such a One will have to *be* in a manner specifically distinct from the manner in which all-that-is exists. As noted above, Plotinus, in an effort to escape these logical constraints, insisted that the One was "beyond being," while subsuming the polarity *necessary/free* under the transcendent expression "spontaneous," so that it remains a nice question (as we shall see) whether his One is adequately distinct from the universe it spontaneously emanates. His phrase "beyond being," however, certainly intends to secure the semantic and epistemological distinction just noted. So the relation linking the origin-of-all to all-that-is will not be accessible to us; in fact, it must expressly be one that transcends relations among items in the world.

If the relation that relates God to the universe cannot itself be characterized, neither of course can God—at least in any way that might amount to a description. In that sense, then, in which God cannot be described as an object in our epistemological "world," God must be said to be unknowable. Yet that need not mean that we can know nothing at all about *the source-of-all,* for we do know that God answers to that formula. (It is, in fact, the "verbal definition" with which Aquinas begins his treatment of God in the *Summa Theologiae.*) This fact has led thinkers in Jewish, Christian, and Muslim traditions to insist that we may then attribute to God what we assess to be *perfections* in the world—with the proviso, however, that such attributions to divinity cannot be understood to be in God in the same *manner* in which they are in us, since this One must *be* in a unique fashion that sets it off from all-that-is. In fact, we may rightly attribute what we deem to be perfections to God only if we understand that their manner of being in divinity is quite unlike their manner of being among us. For that assures that we are attributing the perfection itself, as it were, bereft of the particular manner in which we encounter it. Astute readers will recognize immediately that we are hardly privy to the "perfection itself," so there is an unknowing in the very act by which we may be said to know anything about God! So be it; yet we can offer some clues: what can only be said *concretely* in our sphere ("Socrates is just") will be said of God both in that way ("God is just") and *abstractly* as well ("God is justice"). In fact, to be accurate in predicating such things of divinity, one must understand that they will only be said in one way if they can also be said in the other way as well. That semantic rule reminds us that God does not merely happen to be just but is just as the source of justice is just. It stands to reason that we cannot fully know what that would be like, as our very use of "just" demands that the norm outstrip our current conception, for we need to be able to ask whether justice as we conceive it is indeed just.

Yet such attributions can and must be said truly to be in God, if we are to consistently affirm that the Creator is the source of all being and of all worth. These attributions, however, will be in God not as something "added to" God but as part of what it means to be God. Their manner of being in God must cohere with God's own manner of being, which we saw had to be utterly different from that of all-else-that-is, lest God belong to what God creates. We have noted that Plotinus's way of expressing that difference was to insist that the One is "beyond being"; Aquinas's preferred way was to note that in God alone what-God-is is identical with God's existing—a formula already employed by Maimonides and al-Ghazālī as well, and hence apposite for all three traditions. Here again we have a formula that could never be mistaken for a description of anything in our world but that can and must be said to be true of the God who is the origin-of-all. It is formulas like these that allow us to assert *of* God that God is unknowable: that is, we can know enough by what they state to insist that such a One cannot be located within the world of objects familiar to us, nor indeed as an object *in* any imaginable world. Yet we can make such statements only because of the link we have taken as our starting point, that God is the source-of-all, without thereby pretending to be able to characterize that link in terms familiar to us. All of this apparent contortion becomes germane to our topic—God and religious pluralism—precisely because there are limits to pluralism, and they are set by the demands shared by these religious traditions regarding the meaning of the term "God." God, here understood, is contrasted with "the gods," and if we wish to establish linkage with Hindu tradition, we are speaking of that One from which all-that-is emanates. If such a One, for Hindus, is not so radically opposed to "the gods" as it is for Jews, Christians, and Muslims, we will nonetheless be permitted to establish the analogies we can with that subset of Hindu assertions about divinity that reflects commonalities with our discourse. With Buddhists, however, who cannot subscribe to this metaphysics at all, the challenge is more radical, which pushes Christian theologians into a much starker form of the unknowability of God, one closer to Karl Barth's famous *totaliter aliter.*[16]

Interestingly enough, however, it is not "alien" religious traditions that threaten to undermine the distinction of God from the world so much as those Christian theologies that seek to reduce the distance between God and creatures, as they find the metaphysical corollaries we have seen associated with the source-of-all to present a quite inaccessible divinity. This presentation has tried to meet their concerns by highlighting a feature of Christian theology that has until recently been left all too implicit: creation. If creation is the spontaneous action of the One from whom all comes, then it is the primary "grace" or gift. Yet Christian theology has been content to treat it as a mere *given,* so adopting an effectively pagan stance toward the universe. (That stance, epitomized by Aristotle, treats the universe as the given context in which all else takes place and so one that need not itself require any explanation.) A concatenation of three reasons offers a plausible historical account of this situation, beginning with the liturgical replacement of the Sabbath by the day of the Lord, which in effect invited the community of believers to let redemption eclipse creation. A rabbinic understanding of the Sabbath, rooted in the Genesis account, had it that God created the world in a well-ordered fashion but left it to human beings to perfect. The point of the Sabbath rest, however, was our penchant to presume that we had made it as well, so long as we were

16. See David Tracy, *Dialogue with the Other: The Inter-Religious Dialogue* (Grand Rapids: Eerdmans, 1990), chap. 4.

busy perfecting it. So we were forbidden to take part in those sorts of activities that contribute to culture on the Sabbath, thus inviting us to recognize how the world went on without us and so offering us the opening to return praise to its Creator.

Much later, in the thirteenth century, Philip the Chancellor introduced a distinction that proved to be crucial to the assimilation of Aristotle: that of *natural/supernatural.* One of the corollaries of this distinction would identify "grace" with the "supernatural life" given in baptism, thus leaving people to surmise that whatever was *natural* must not be a gift but a *given.* This distinction became a bifurcation in the nineteenth century, when philosophers wrought a cleavage between *nature* and *history,* placing all redemption into history and leaving nature for science to explain. So it was, in fact, Christianity that impoverished its own self-understanding by a peculiar theological development. If recovering its roots in creation has become an ecological imperative, one of the side-effects of this movement has been to highlight Christian parallels with Judaism and with Islam regarding the free creation of the universe, as well as to recover classical modes of expressing "the distinction" of God from the world. Once we grasp the implications of the doctrine of free creation, we will not be tempted to conceive God over against the world, so that we will then be constrained to make such a one "more accessible"; rather, understanding God as the freely originating source of all-that-is, we will find in that gracious "transcendence" all the "immanence" we might need.[17] What must by its very nature *not* be an item in the world will nonetheless be known by its traces in a world originating from it. What remains crucial to such a scenario, however, is that the initiative rest with the free Creator, without whose self-revelation

17. Tanner (*God and Creation*) traces the disastrous effects for Christian theology of neglecting the free relation of God to the world in creation. Her insistence that God not be construed "parallel to" or "by way of simple contrast to" the world may well be illuminated by certain Hindu discussions of "nonduality." I am indebted to Bradley Malkovsky for this suggestion, which he attributes to the work of the Belgian theologian Richard deSmet, who has long participated in dialogue in Hindustan.

we could never have suspected ourselves to be so graced. Creation, by contrast with various theories of emanation, is itself a matter of revelation.

Testing the Limits: Plotinus and Ibn al-'Arabī

We have so far been showing how a doctrine of God must attend to the distinction of God from the world, a position reflected most clearly in those religious traditions that avow free creation. We have also seen how that avowal of creation secures the distinction in a way that does not threaten to alienate God from creatures, as more simple-minded parallel constructions of God and world invariably tend to do. Yet the act of creation remains inaccessible to us, so diverse philosophical attempts to articulate it will inevitably emerge. Contrasting these with the stark assertions associated with "the distinction" may help us cast some light on the way in which one's understanding of God reflects one's understanding of the world and of the Creator's relation to it. As we shall see, much will turn on the contrast of *necessary* with *free,* which long characterized a debate between philosophers and religious thinkers. Asserting creation to be a free act of divinity seemed to allow divinity an arbitrary sovereignty over all things, so philosophers tended to adopt a relation they could understand: the necessity of logical derivation. Moreover, when explicating the manner in which God is free to create, religious thinkers often imported into divinity notions of *choosing* that seem quite anthropomorphic. So while the notion of creation as the primary gift of a gracious God is a precious legacy, especially of Jews, Christians, and Muslims, finding an idiom appropriate to explicate that relation remains a formidable intellectual task.

Two classical thinkers offer interesting test cases. One is usually classified as a pagan; the other as a heterodox Muslim. Plotinus (205–270) lived in two environments inhabited by Jews and Christians—Alexandria and later Rome—but was never impressed with their "philosophy." Yet his way of casting the relation of the One to all-that-is has largely come down to us in its particular assimilation by Augustine (354–430) and Thomas Aquinas (1225–1274). Here we shall consider how his expression of that relation might well have proved amenable to such a recasting, yet in itself offered a formidable alternative to faith in a Creator. Ibn al-'Arabī (1165–1240) was an Andalusian Sufi master who completed his immense corpus of writings in Damascus. His expressly mystical teaching, when separated from the context of spiritual discipline, has been read as a form of "existential monism" that focuses so intently on the sustaining presence of God to the world as to elide "the distinction."[18] Other readers are less critical,[19] however, and the contrast with "orthodox Islam"[20] appears less stark in more recent studies of this "greatest master."[21] While Ibn al-'Arabī considered himself at the very heart of Islam, whatever his contemporary and posthumous critics might aver, Plotinus presented himself as a pagan, perhaps even as offering an alternative to Christianity. In any case, while Augustine found in his philosophy a serendipitous stepping-stone to faith, his friends who styled themselves "Platonists" presented their own lives as a viable alternative to Christianity. Yet in presenting Plotinus's thought to our era one writer will note how "in some respects his position was similar to Philo's."[22] So each of these figures will provide fruitful contrasts with the received forms of those traditions with which we shall place them in conversation.

From the perspective sketched here of free creation, Plotinus has long been seen as the prime proponent of "necessary emanation" and as the one who provided the intellectual base for

18. Louis Massignon, *The Passion of al-Hallaj,* trans. Herbert Mason (Princeton, N.J.: Princeton Univ. Press, 1982), 3:58.

19. Annemarie Schimmel, *The Mystical Dimensions of Islam* (Chapel Hill: Univ. of North Carolina Press, 1975), 263–74.

20. Fazlur Rahman, *Islam,* 2d ed. (Chicago: Univ. of Chicago Press, 1979), 146.

21. William C. Chittick, *The Sufi Path of Knowledge: Ibn al-Arabi's Metaphysics of Imagination* (Albany: State Univ. of New York Press, 1989).

22. James Jordan, *Western Philosophy from Antiquity to the Middle Ages* (New York: Macmillan, 1987), 254.

the Islamic emanation scheme elaborated by al-Fārābī and introduced into Western thought by Ibn Sīnā, often via Moses Maimonides's influential *Guide of the Perplexed*.[23] More recent studies, however, place him in the context of Platonic theologies of the time and show how he moved beyond them to a fresh synthesis of philosophy and theology, one ripe "for its subsequent absorption into the Abrahamic theological world . . . , providing it with a rich philosophical vocabulary and an account of divine primordiality."[24] As we have already noted, Plotinus was intent on articulating "the distinction": "[T]he One must be such that it depends on nothing distinct from itself and that everything distinct from itself is absolutely dependent upon the One." It is this primary constraint that dictates a simple ontological constitution for the One, and "the One must be said to be beyond 'being' in order to be represented as simple and ultimate." Moreover, since "what is most simple is also the productive source of all lower levels of reality,"[25] according to middle- and Neoplatonic axioms, the One will be productive of all-that-is. But how so: freely or necessarily?

That question is not so simple as it looks, for if our tendency to associate *necessity* with *need* seems to make that alternative unworthy of the One, so our propensity to link *freedom* with *choosing* makes that activity similarly beneath the dignity of the One, whose "will is in perfect conformity to its eternal activity."[26] So while the One may have no choice about the matter, it is hardly constrained to create by something like a need, so in that sense we would be tempted to call its action "free." A corollary to Plotinus's insistence that the One is beyond being, however, may well be to place its action beyond our polarities of

23. David B. Burrell, *Knowing the Unknowable God: Ibn Sina, Maimonides, Aquinas* (Notre Dame, Ind.: Univ. of Notre Dame Press, 1986).

24. John Peter Kenney, *Mystical Monotheism: A Study in Ancient Platonic Theology* (Providence: Brown Univ. Press, 1991), 156.

25. See ibid., 101, 102, 103.

26. L. P. Gerson, *God and Greek Philosophy: Studies in the Early History of Natural Theology* (London: Routledge, 1990), 219.

necessity or freedom. Yet what we know of all that comes from it makes us "confident that the *energeia* [activity] of the One does indeed result in production."[27] While the extent to which this production is "personal" and so can be said to be a "gift" remains quite implicit for Plotinus, one may argue that "the personal is in a way already constitutive of the One as an inferred cause of being."[28] Yet such a reading of Plotinus, which sees him as completing an explanation for the cosmos promised but never executed by Aristotle,[29] also suggests why Augustine will find this pagan scheme yearning for fulfillment in a more resolutely personal idiom: while "these books of the Platonists served to remind me to return to my own true self [and] prompted [me] to look for truth as something incorporeal, [nevertheless] their pages have not the mien of the true love of God" (*Confessions* 7.10, 20, 21). That judgment summarizes a chapter wherein Augustine cites Paul's paean to "your grace [by which] he is enabled to walk upon the path that leads him closer to you, so that he may see you and hold you" (ibid., 7.21): an idiom in which one could hardly speak of or to Plotinus's One. All this suggests that the *freedom* that Jews, Christians, and Muslims attribute to divine creation is not preoccupied with *choice* so much as with a particular divine initiative, reminding us once again that "free creation" is a matter of revelation rather than a philosophical inference and that each tradition's understanding of it will be modeled on the pattern of revelation proper to it. Here is where our insistence on the fact that inquiries reflect a tradition of faith allows us to learn from each without attempting to colonize others in the name of a "unique" Christianity.

Ibn al-'Arabī's thought, when summarized, seems to display those features of theosophy that attempt to *say* what cannot be said: "[F]rom the perspective of Unity and multiplicity, the Divine Presence appears as a circle whose center is the Essence and

27. Ibid., 216.
28. Ibid., 217.
29. Ibid., 140

whose full deployment is the acts in their multiple degrees and kind."[30] Each of these acts is itself a manifestation of the activity of the One, according to the various perfections articulated in the "beautiful names of God." So the dialectic between reality and its manifestation, imaged as the interplay of light and darkness, attests to the evanescent character of created being—a kind of intermediate reality "that separates a known from an unknown," a *barzakh*.[31] Light is the dominant image: the One is hidden from view in inaccessible light while whatever we can apprehend will be some admixture of light and darkness. The "distinction" between the One and all that depends on it for its existence, then, will be expressed as the difference between light that is pure and inaccessible and various adulterations of it. "Emanation" becomes a handy expression for the relation of the center to its successive peripheries, and the journey of all creatures during their lifetime reflects their inbuilt desire to return to the source from which they derive. This return is inscribed in every creature, but human beings are given the task of realizing their natures by free actions aimed at developing those character traits (*akhlāq*) that will manifest specific names of God.

What such summaries invariably miss is the movement whereby this return to the source is also the realization of the virtualities implicit in existence bestowed, so that the difference between "unity of being" (*wahdat al-wujūd*) and "unity of witnessing" (*wahdat al-shuhūd*) is minimized in practice. In other words, one may be, at root, a manifestation of the divine and so *think* of oneself in terms that express a "unity of being," yet that very unity remains to be realized in such a person, whose path of realization will involve all of the actions and trials that shape those "friends of God" whose lives give witness to divine unity as their vibrant source. What seems to matter most is the manner in which Ibn al-'Arabī is read: whether as a metaphysician or as a master and guide. While his idiom is resolutely metaphysical,

30. Chittick, *Sufi Path,* 25a.
31. Ibid., 118.

readers who are also potential novices (*murīd*) will understand that they must supply the activities that the master's writings presume to be taking place. Indeed, such a reading is the only one congruent with the metaphysics itself, for the *manifestations* of the One are not presented as passive "appearances" so much as loci of the divine activity's emergence into existence. And "existence" here "defines our 'location' for all practical purposes: its most obvious characteristic is its ambiguous situation, half-way between Being and non-existence, light and darkness, He and not-He."[32] The last characterization of the One and all-that-is as He (*huwa*) and not-He (*lā-huwa*) does express starkly "the distinction," while "half-way between" seems to elide it.

Such is ever the expression of Ibn al-'Arabī, which seems as well suited to express the sense of participation in the divine light that guides novices on their path as it is ill suited to secure the integrity of their strivings. Yet one who is expending considerable energy on the ascent is unlikely to read one's master in a "monistic" manner, so the difference in readers seems crucial to the task of interpretation here. A Western reader could be assisted by the ways in which Carl Jung is characteristically misread, perhaps most of all by those who call themselves Jungians. Jung himself is party to the misreading because he has such a penchant for flights of metaphysical expression, yet he also warns us that his writing is forged in the analytic encounter and ought to be heard always in reference to such a practice. In short, the key terms in his analyses find their focus in the interaction of analyst and client, and one unfamiliar with that "work" (which he explicitly likens to the "work" of alchemy) will be quite oblivious to the interior effort that any accurate use of such expressions involves.[33] So the theology and the metaphysics of Ibn al-'Arabī will be doomed to misunderstanding on the part of Western readers whose own religious studies have not characteristically required so interior a

32. Ibid., 7b.

33. David B. Burrell, *Exercises in Religious Understanding* (Notre Dame, Ind.: Univ. of Notre Dame Press, 1975), chap. 5.

response from their inquirers. Like Jung, however, he seems to be party to obtaining for himself the label of "existential monism," for he cannot resist placing his directions in an idiom that will be read as a series of statements. Or put another way, his statements will not ordinarily be read as also embodying directions for seekers along the way precisely because of their declaratory mode of expression. Perhaps this explains why those engaged on the path salute him as "the greatest master" while other readers excoriate him as a danger to Islam. Again, it all turns on "the distinction" and how a tradition effectively secures it. The example of Ibn al-'Arabī shows how religious writers can be read in different ways within a tradition and by its onlookers and how one might discriminate between two very different readings.

Our attempt to understand each of these writers underscores the way in which we are always hard-pressed, as creatures, to formulate that relation with the Creator that we avow to be constitutive of our very selves. We need some sort of philosophical scheme to articulate it, but no scheme will be up to the task. For we are attempting to speak of the One from whom all-that-is derives, and no metaphysical scheme can pretend to encompass more that all-that-is! So our reading of various attempts will have to be tempered by our prior realization that such a task will have to stretch human conceptualities beyond their proper limits. As I have suggested, it will be our respective faith communities that will give us the tolerance necessary to see that endeavor through and to respect the stretching that will have to take place.

PRAXIS

I have tried to show how diverse religious traditions will exhibit in quite different fashion a fundamental feature of divinity, namely its "distinction" from the universe that is said to derive from it. This is clearest, of course, in those religious traditions that avow free creation of the world but will also manifest itself in others that do not. Indeed, theological variants that seem to elide the crucial difference of creature from Creator will emerge within those traditions that avow a free creation, but these may often be read as presupposing that "distinction" if we attend to the "depth grammar" of the statements made. This brief treatment also offers a way for theology today to exploit the diverse traditions that are becoming more relevant to its inquiries and capitalize on the fact that they can be read "relative to" one another. Yet this cannot be done in the abstract, as the American experience with Jewish-Christian dialogue has already taught us. We need to step outside our presumptive certainties—those of our own faith as well as those of a Western intellectual superiority that would minimize the truth claims of any religious tradition in the name of a radical pluralism. We must allow others the freedom to speak in their own voice, even when that voice threatens to eclipse our own. *All* religions will make totalizing claims; thence comes the sustaining passion of the convictions displayed. What the Enlightenment reacted against as fanaticism we can also recognize as sustaining human faiths. Genuine dialogue is a risky endeavor, for it requires that all participants forgo their own presumed superiority, yet the fruits appear abundantly worth the risks involved. Besides dissolving the abstract specter of relativism, a sustained practice of dialogue will invariably issue in an enhanced understanding of the reaches of our own faith—often reaches hitherto unexplored and even unsuspected. Moreover, what emerges through such practice in the faith of Christians is a fresh appreciation of the trinitarian dimensions of their faith, dimensions often less explicit in Christian self-understanding than in the classic professions of faith. What manifests itself in the confidence with which Christians can invite and undertake dialogue is indeed the presence of the Holy Spirit, a presence that animates the community of believers and that seems intimated in other religious faiths as well.

This reference to the Holy Spirit is far more than honorific, however, for the practice of dialogue is unnerving as well as enhancing. Indeed, it can expand the horizons of our faith only in the measure that it threatens the formulations with which we have become accustomed. This is especially true for North Americans, who can so easily presume themselves and their faith to offer the paradigm of what it is to be human. Where our predecessors had characteristically to contend with the challenge of atheism, we confront the lure of other faiths. This fact presents theology with what Karl Rahner has dubbed a *crisis,* for we lack categories appropriate to contending with conflicting claims that all articulate divinity in a way that calls for a wholehearted faith-commitment.[34] Yet this impasse, which might cripple a philosopher, need not debilitate a person of inquiring faith, for one can presume that the illumination worked in allowing the formulations of our faith to be stretched in encounter with the faith of others will also unveil gaps in our self-understanding and in our understanding of divinity, gaps that will let "the Other" reveal itself that much better than our categories have permitted thus far.[35] Such a confidence is the very stuff of faith in the revealing Spirit and hence sounds the most distinctive note of Christian faith. Its outworking in dialogue among partners in diverse religious traditions can effect that signal trace of the Holy Spirit among us: friendship. Those who have experienced the fruit of interfaith dialogue have done so in a context in which discussion fueled by mutual respect becomes an exchange carried out in enhanced esteem of the faith-traditions manifested in the life and practice of one's partners. And all that can take place because in the process people have become friends walking together in an inquiry that is as existential as it is intellectual and in which mutual needs and insights can be found strengthening one another.

34. Karl Rahner, "Towards a Fundamental Interpretation of Vatican II," *Theological Studies* 40 (1979): 716–27.

35. For an illuminating set of essays outlining this way of proceeding among religious traditions, see Gavin D'Costa, *Christian Uniqueness Reconsidered* (Maryknoll, N.Y.: Orbis, 1990).

ELISABETH SCHÜSSLER FIORENZA

3. THE BIBLE, THE GLOBAL CONTEXT, AND THE DISCIPLESHIP OF EQUALS

Every time we turn on our television sets we meet our neighbors in the global "village." National and international "town" meetings discuss issues of the day. Satellite dishes, telecommunications, fax machines, and mass tourism have made us business partners in the global village. The broadcast of national and international ecological disasters; the threat of nuclear accidents and biological-chemical warfare; the displacement of whole populations because of war, hunger, and political or religious persecutions—all these have increased our awareness of global interdependence.

In recent years radical democratic movements around the globe have fought for the freedom and power of the people and are now faced with ruthless economic exploitation and nationalist strife. These are signs that an intense struggle has begun over the nature of the global "village." This "village" will be fashioned either into a global, democratic confederation governed by concern for the economic-political well-being of all its citizens or into a tightly controlled, patriarchal dictatorship that concentrates all economic and cultural resources in the hands of a few and relegates the majority to a permanently impoverished and dehumanized underclass. In this struggle, telecommunications and the media can serve to keep the dream of freedom alive before the eyes of the disenfranchised, or they can be used to encourage a nationalist "bunker mentality" and the scapegoating of the disadvantaged by the so-called middle class. This scapegoating has been intensified by the fact that their economic and educational potential has been steadily eroded during the 1980s. Economists,[1] for instance, point out that only 15 to 20 percent of North Americans—the wealthiest and most highly skilled—have benefited from the global economy, whereas two-thirds of all North-American citizens are more and more relegated to the status of the working poor, unemployed, and welfare recipients. This economic and educational erosion of the middle classes engenders an economic-political situation in which the dividing line between the so-called First and Third Worlds is increasingly drawn *across* the world and runs between the haves and have-nots living in the same city, county, or country. In other words, my neighbor who works for an international computer firm has more in common with her counterparts in Europe, Latin America, or Japan than with the woman on welfare who lives three blocks away.

DOMINANT FORMS OF BIBLICAL INTERPRETATION

How, then, must the Bible be read in such a global context? How should it be studied, used, and proclaimed? Neoconservative fundamentalist groups quote the Bible constantly and read it in the context of an explosion of fundamentalist movements around the globe.[2] These fundamentalist movements—whether the electronic churches of the United States, technologically sophisticated Islamic fundamentalism, the ultraright movement of Rabbi Kahane, biblicist and revivalist movements in Latin America, emergent Hindu fundamentalism in India, or fundamentalist Shintoism in Japan—all exhibit common traits: they employ

1. See, for instance, Robert B. Reich, *The Work of Nations* (New York: Vintage, 1992).

2. See John Stratton Hawley, ed., *Fundamentalism and Gender* (New York: Oxford Univ. Press, 1993); and Reich, *Work of Nations.*

modern media technology in very sophisticated ways and generally advocate nationalism or religious exclusivism. Yet while they embrace modern technological science as well as modern industrialism and nationalism, they reject many of the political and ethical values of modern democracy: basic individual rights; pluralism; freedom of speech; equal rights for women; the right to housing, health care, and work; equal compensation for equal work; social market measures; a democratic ethos; sharing of power and political responsibility.

I recently gave a lecture in which I argued for a critical feminist interpretation of the Bible—that is, for a sociopolitical reading of the text. A young woman, university-educated, middle-class, and a member of a conservative fundamentalist student group, was chosen as one of my respondents. She berated me not only for promoting feminism, which according to her entices women to hate men and to destroy the Christian family, but also for understanding biblical interpretation in sociopolitical terms. Jesus came to save souls and not bodies, she insisted. She argued that personal acceptance of and a spiritual relationship with Christ—not a striving for justice and liberation—are the defining Christian hallmarks. Such fundamentalist notions did not challenge her to question her privilege or to engage in political struggles for justice and well-being. Instead such a reading allayed the psychological insecurity of a young woman desiring the assurance of love and placated the unacknowledged economic insecurity of a female student who might easily end up in a low-paying, dead-end job.

Biblicist fundamentalism not only reads the Bible with the theological lenses of individualized and privatized bourgeois religion but also asserts militantly that its approach is the only legitimate one. It thereby neglects that different Christian communities and churches use the Bible differently and that throughout the centuries different models of biblical interpretation have been and still are developed by Christians. Although such spiritualized biblicism berates mainline churches for succumbing to modernity and secularization, it has adopted its own particular modern understanding of religion and the Bible.

The dominant understanding of religion and the Bible that has developed in modernity is privatized and individualistic. It holds a similar view of religion and women—they belong to the private sphere and are affairs of the heart. This understanding of religion approaches the interpretation of the Bible with four basic assumptions that inform Christian bourgeois readings in the global village.[3] (1) *Interiorization:* this involves the insistence that the biblical message addresses the individual. It concerns our hearts and souls and serves to facilitate our personal relationship with God. (2) *Otherworldliness:* this is the claim that the biblical message belongs to a totally different world and does not affect societal or political structures. Christians who suffer in this world as Christ has suffered will receive their just reward in heaven. The *basileia*—the reign of God—is "not of this world." (3) *Individualist ethics:* this involves the assumption that the biblical message proclaims universal moral values and attitudes that appeal to the conscience of the individual. The message promises redemption from personal sin, salvation of the soul, and eternal life. Any human accomplishment involves pride, which prevents us from accepting Jesus as our sole savior and Lord. (4) *Ahistorical verbalism:* this is the view that the Bible is the verbally inspired and inerrant word of God in which Christians must believe. This emphasis implies that the Bible and its interpretation transcend ideology and particularity. It obscures the interests at work in biblical texts and interpretations and reduces faith to intellectual assent rather than to a way of life. It promotes belief in the Bible rather than in God and screens out the notion that God's loving intention and liberating praxis for the world have been paradigmatically realized through the ministry of Jesus.

3. For these characterizations of bourgeois biblical readings, see Johannes Thiele, "Bibelauslegung im gesellschaftlich-politischen Kontext," in *Handbuch der Bibelarbeit,* ed. W. Langer (Munich: Kösel, 1987), 106–14.

In line with this modern, privatized, biblicist understanding of the Bible, biblical scholarship claims to be scientific, objective, and disinterested. Nevertheless, biblical scholarship also tends to focus on the word and to claim that it produces a nonideological reading of the Bible. Its sociopolitical location is not fundamentalist religion but the university with its positivist understandings of language and reality. Biblical scholars no longer read the Bible as a code by which to decipher moral directives for individual spiritual edification. Rather, they either understand the Bible in a positivist way as a historical source whose information pertains to antiquity, or they read it as religious literature whose meaning can never be fixed in a definite reading. Both "scientific" strategies of interpretation share in the social location of the Enlightenment university. These scholars participate in an interpretive community that is dedicated to rational, scientific, and value-detached inquiry and proud of being apolitical and agnostic.

This scientific ethos of biblical reading insists that readers must silence their own interests and abstract themselves from their own sociopolitical situation in order to respect the "alien" character of the Bible and the historical chasm between us and the biblical text. What makes scientific biblical interpretation possible is ostensibly radical detachment—emotional, intellectual, and political. Disinterested and dispassionate scholarship enables biblical critics to enter the minds and worlds of biblical texts, to step out of our own time, and to study history or literature on its own terms, unencumbered by contemporary experience, values, and interests. Apolitical detachment, objective positivism, and scientific value-neutrality are the rhetorical postures that determine the interpretive strategies of modern biblical interpretation understood as a science. This rhetoric of disinterestedness and presupposition-free exegesis silences reflection on the political interests and functions of biblical texts and interpretations. Its claim to public scientific status suppresses the rhetorical character of biblical texts and readings and obscures the power relations by which biblical interpretation is constituted.[4]

According to this modern understanding of biblical interpretation, a "division of labor" is called for. Scientific exegesis has the task of elaborating what the text of the Bible *meant,* whereas ecclesial theology and private "spirituality" must articulate what the text *means* today. The task of the exegete consists in delineating as objectively as possible what the text meant in its original historical or literary contexts. The rights of the text must be respected, it is maintained, and the chasm between the world of the text and that of the present-day interpreter must be maintained. Biblical interpretation is here construed in patriarchal terms insofar as the reader has to submit herself to an unequivocal meaning of a text claiming the authority of God for its content. Moreover, this scientific model of interpretation shares in the pathology of modernity, which, according to Jürgen Habermas, consists in splitting off expert cultures from everyday cultural practices and life.[5] By understanding the "first" meaning of the biblical text as a deposit of the definitive meaning of the author, historical-scientific interpretation runs the risk of shutting up the meaning of the text in the past and turning it into an artifact of antiquity that is accessible only to the expert in biblical history or philology.

Theologians, ministers, and the faithful in turn are interested in the religious, spiritualized meaning of biblical texts for today.[6] Through "application," they seek to liberate the text from

4. For discussion of the scientific ethos of biblical scholarship and hermeneutics, see my book *Bread Not Stone: The Challenge of Feminist Biblical Interpretation* (Boston: Beacon, 1984), 117–50; see also Archie L. Nations, "Historical Criticism and the Current Methodological Crisis," *Scottish Journal of Theology* 36 (1983): 59–71; and W. S. Vorster, "The Historical Paradigm: Its Possibilities and Limitations," *Neotestamentica* 18 (1984): 104–23.

5. Jürgen Habermas, *The Theory of Communicative Action* (Boston: Beacon, 1987).

6. See my article "Theological Education/Biblical Studies," in *The Education of the Practical Theologian*, ed. D. S. Browning, D. Polk, and I. S. Evison (Atlanta: Scholars Press, 1989), 1–20; idem, "Commitment and Critical Inquiry," *Harvard Theological Review* 82 (1989): 1–11. See also Rebecca S. Chopp, *The Power to Speak: Feminism, Language, and God* (New York: Crossroad, 1989).

its historical captivity in order to rescue the message of the Bible for Christians today. One form of this rescue and liberation of the text is accomplished by updating and actualizing aspects of it: by translating and rendering its mythic images into contemporary frameworks of meaning, by selecting those passages that still speak to us and illumine our own questions, by reducing its multiple voices to theological or ethical principles and themes, and especially by psychologizing its main characters and worlds of vision. Another form of theological application of biblical texts is achieved by correlating the text's "pastoral" situation with present-day religious problems. Whereas theological liberals frustrated by the mythological content or outdated injunctions of the Bible look for approaches that enable them to squeeze the living water of revelation and theological truth out of the hard stone of ancient biblical facts, biblical fundamentalists insist on the inerrant literal sense of the text as a given fact.

Insofar as scientific exegesis, like biblicist interpretation, seeks to distill the universal truth or univocal word of God from the Bible's multivalent and often contradictory meanings, it denies its particular perspective and rhetorical aims.[7] By spiritualizing, psychologizing, and privatizing Scripture it religiously legitimates and makes palatable injustice and domination. In order to become accountable to and to promote the well-being of all inhabitants of the global village, biblical interpretation must engage in the formation of a critical historical, cultural, and religious consciousness. It can do so by paying attention both to the kind of sociosymbolic worlds and moral universes biblical

7. For discussion of the rhetorical paradigm shift in general and in biblical studies in particular, see Brian Vickers, ed., *Rhetoric Revalued* (Binghamton: State Univ. of New York Press, 1982); Brian Vickers, *In Defence of Rhetoric* (Oxford: Clarendon, 1988); William A. Beardslee, "Theology and Rhetoric in the University," in *Theology and the University,* ed. David R. Griffin and Joseph C. Hough (Albany: State Univ. of New York Press, 1991), 185–200; Wilhelm Wüllner, "Hermeneutics and Rhetorics: From 'Truth and Method' to 'Truth and Power,' " *Scriptura S* 3 (1989): 1–54; Burton L. Mack, *Rhetoric and the New Testament* (Minneapolis: Fortress, 1990); for my contributions to this development, see "Rhetorical Situation and Historical Reconstruction in 1 Corinthians," *New Testament Studies* 33 (1987): 386–403; and *Revelation: Vision of a Just World* (Minneapolis: Fortress, 1991).

writings construct and to the way biblical texts and visions function in contemporary struggles for a radical democratic world order that can promote civil and human rights, equitable political power, socioeconomic equality, and the right of all citizens to adequate education, health care, employment, housing, and security.[8]

A CRITICAL FEMINIST BIBLICAL INTERPRETATION FOR LIBERATION

Feminist liberation theologies of all colors do not borrow their lenses of interpretation from the modern individualistic understanding of religion and the Bible. Rather they shift attention to the politics of biblical interpretation and its sociopolitical contexts. They claim the hermeneutical privilege of the oppressed and marginalized for reading the Bible in the community of faith. Interpretation is carried out from the social position of the poor and marginalized. The purpose of such biblical interpretation is not primarily to seek information about the past but to interpret daily life in the global village with the help of the biblical God of justice and salvation and to inspire Christians to transformation with the biblical vision of a world freed from the structural sin of patriarchal domination. Such a reading from the social position of the oppressed is ecumenical and liberating. It seeks to enable and to defend life that is threatened or destroyed by hunger, destitution, sexual violence, torture, and dehumanization. Such a biblical reading aims to give dignity and value to the life of exploited women in whose struggles and survival the presence and image of God can be experienced in our midst. Therefore, it does not restrict salvation to the soul but seeks to promote the well-

8. See my SBL presidential address "The Ethics of Biblical Interpretation: Decentering Biblical Scholarship," *Journal of Biblical Literature* 107, no. 1 (1988): 3–17; Fred W. Burnett, "Postmodern Biblical Exegesis: The Eve of Historical Criticism," *Semeia* 51 (1990): 51–80; Gary Phillips, "Exegesis as a Critical Praxis: Reclaiming History and Text from a Postmodern Perspective," *Semeia* 51 (1990): 7–50; and Robert M. Fowler, "Postmodern Biblical Criticism," *Foundations and Facets Forum* 5 (1989): 3–30.

being and radical equality of all; it aims to inspire Christians to engage in the struggle for transforming patriarchal structures of domination.[9]

In contrast to fundamentalist and liberal theology, feminist liberation theologies of all colors see the greatest problem for faith today not as the threat of secularization but rather as the jeopardization of human life by dehumanization, exploitation, and extinction. They shift the question from How can we believe in God? to the following questions: What kind of God do Christians proclaim? Does Christian faith make a difference in the struggle for the well-being of all in the global village? How is the Bible used in this struggle for liberation and transformation? Which texts legitimate the status quo and which promote God's intention for the well-being of all? In short, liberation theologies insist that salvation is not possible outside the world or without the world. God's vision of a renewed creation entails not just a new heaven but also a new and qualitatively different Earth.

Feminist theologies proclaim that such a world must be freed of domination and dehumanization inflicted by patriarchy.[10]

9. See the various contributions in Katie G. Cannon and Elisabeth Schüssler Fiorenza, eds., *Interpretation for Liberation,* Semeia (Atlanta: Scholars Press, 1989); see my "The Politics of Otherness: Biblical Interpretation as a Critical Praxis for Liberation," in *The Future of Liberation Theology: Essays in Honor of Gustavo Gutiérrez,* ed. Marc Ellis and Otto Maduro (Maryknoll, N.Y.: Orbis, 1989), 311–25; see also the essays in Susan B. Thistlethwaite and Mary Potter Engel, eds., *Lift Every Voice: Constructing Christian Theologies from the Underside* (San Francisco: Harper and Row, 1990).

10. For a review of the category of patriarchy, see V. Beechey, "On Patriarchy," *Feminist Review* 3 (1979): 66–82; Gerda Lerner, *The Creation of Patriarchy* (New York: Oxford Univ. Press, 1986), 231–41; Christine Schaumberger, "Patriarchat als feministischer Begriff," in *Wörterbuch der feministischen Theologie* (Gütersloh: Mohn, 1991), 321–23. For a discussion of patriarchy in antiquity, see Monique Saliou, "The Process of Women's Subordination in Primitive and Archaic Greece," in *Women's Work, Men's Property: The Origins of Gender and Class,* ed. Stephanie Coontz and Helen Henderson (London: Verso, 1986), 169–206; W. K. Lacey, "Patria Potestas," in *The Family in Ancient Rome: New Perspectives,* ed. Beryl Rawson (Ithaca, N.Y.: Cornell Univ. Press, 1986), 121–44. For the development of the "political philosophy of otherness" as legitimizing patriarchal societal structures of domination in antiquity, see Susan Moller Okin, *Women in Western Political Thought* (Princeton, N.J.: Princeton Univ. Press, 1979), 15–98; Elizabeth V. Spelman, *Inessential Woman: Problems of Exclusion in Feminist Thought* (Boston: Beacon, 1988), 19–56; and especially Page DuBois, *Centaurs and Amazons: Women and the Pre-history of the Great Chain of Being* (Ann Arbor: Univ. of Michigan Press, 1982).

The terms "feminist" and "patriarchy" evoke in many audiences not only a complex array of emotions, negative reactions, and prejudices but also a host of different understandings and meanings. Therefore, it is necessary here to explicate the way in which I employ the terms in my own work. The diverse theoretical articulations of feminism generally agree in their critique of masculine supremacy and hold that gender roles are socially constructed rather than innate or ordained by God. The root-experience of feminism is that cultural "common sense," dominant perspectives, scientific theories, and historical knowledge are androcentric—that is, male-biased—and are therefore not objective accounts of reality but ideological mystifications of patriarchal domination.

Feminism as I understand it, however, is not just concerned with gender inequities and marginalization. Rather, feminism is a movement of those women and men who seek to transform patriarchal structures of subordination. Patriarchy perpetrates not only dehumanizing sexism and gender stereotypes but also other forms of women's oppression, such as racism, poverty, religious exclusion, and colonialism. The field of feminist studies, therefore, has the goal of fundamentally altering the nature of our knowledge of the world by exposing its deformations and limitations in and through androcentrism, racism, classism, and cultural imperialism; it thus has the further goal of reconstructing more comprehensive and adequate accounts of knowledge.[11]

11. The literature is, of course, immense. See, for instance, Sandra Harding and Merill B. Hintikka, *Discovering Reality: Feminist Perspectives on Epistemology, Metaphysics, Methodology, and Philosophy* (Dordrecht: Reidel, 1983); Susan Harding, "The Method Question," *Hypatia* 3 (1987): 30; idem, *The Science Question in Feminism* (Ithaca, N.Y.: Cornell Univ. Press, 1986); N. Hartsock, "Rethinking Modernism: Minority vs. Majority Theories," *Cultural Critique* 7 (1987): 205–6; Rosemary Henessy, "Women's Lives/Feminist Knowledge: Feminist Standpoint as Ideology Critique," *Hypatia* 8 (1993): 14–34; Louise M. Antony and Charlotte Witt, eds., *A Mind of One's Own: Feminist Essays on Reason and Objectivity* (Boulder, Colo.: Westview, 1993); Ruth A. Wallace, ed., *Feminism and Social Theory* (Newbury Park, Calif.: Sage, 1989); Carolyn J. Allen, "Feminist Criticism and Postmodernism," in *Tracing Literary Theory*, ed. Joseph Natoli (Urbana: Univ. of Illinois Press, 1987), 278–305; Karen Dugger, "Social Location and Gender-Role Attitudes: A Comparison of Black and White Women," *Gender and Society* 2 (1988): 425–48; Carole Ann Taylor, "Positioning Subjects and Objects: Agency, Narration, and Rationality," *Hypatia* 8 (1993): 55–80.

While women always have read and interpreted the Scriptures, feminist hermeneutics—the theoretical exploration of the exegetical and theological presuppositions of biblical interpretation in the interest of women—is of very recent vintage. Only in the context of the women's movement in the last century, and especially in the past twenty years or so, have feminists in the churches begun to explore the implications and possibilities of a biblical interpretation that takes the institutional ecclesial silencing of women into account. Books and articles on biblical women's studies not only have enlisted a wide readership in the churches and synagogues but are also very slowly making inroads into the academy.

As a movement and strategy for change, Christian feminism engages in the struggle to transform the patriarchal church into the *ekklesia* understood as a discipleship of equals.[12] Therefore, it seeks to expose and to redress women's subordination, exploitation, and oppression in society and church. Feminists in biblical religions seek to break the structures of silencing and exclusion that have prohibited women's ecclesial self-determination and leadership and have prevented them from asking their own theological questions and from articulating theology in light of their own experiences of struggle. Feminist theologians and biblical interpreters therefore first of all engage a critical strategy that theoretically can explore the ways in which the structures and ideological systems of patriarchy have shaped and still shape biblical self-identity, memory, theology, and communal practice. Since feminist critical theological reflection is motivated by the hunger and thirst for justice, it also seeks to reclaim positively those biblical visions, memories, and unrealized possibilities that can sustain resistance to oppressive structures and inspire energy and hope for their transformation.

Reclaiming the authority of women for shaping and determining biblical religions, feminist theology asks new questions in

12. For a fuller development of such an understanding, see my book *Discipleship of Equals: A Feminist Ekklesialogy of Liberation* (New York: Crossroad, 1993).

order to reconceptualize the act of biblical interpretation as a moment in the global praxis for liberation. Relying on a critical theory of language and the insights of liberation movements, I have sought to develop a critical feminist biblical interpretation for liberation and transformation as a distinct approach in biblical women's studies. Such a model attempts to articulate biblical interpretation both as a complex process of reading and reconstruction and as a cultural-theological praxis of resistance and transformation. To that end it utilizes not only historical, literary, and ideological-critical methods that focus on the rhetoric of the biblical text in its historical contexts. It also employs storytelling, role playing, bibliodrama, pictorial arts, dance, and ritual for creating a "different" historical imagination. In short, this approach does not subscribe to a single reading strategy and method but employs a variety of theoretical insights and methods for articulating its own practices of reading the Bible. It seeks to recast biblical interpretation not in positivist but in rhetorical terms. It does not deny but recognizes that biblical texts are rhetorical texts, produced in and by particular historical debates and struggles.

Such a critical process of feminist biblical interpretation for liberation presupposes feminist conscientization and systemic analysis. Its interpretive process has four key moments.[13] It begins with a *hermeneutics of suspicion* that scrutinizes the presuppositions and interests of biblical interpreters and commentators as well as the androcentric strategies of the biblical text itself. Androcentric biblical language, texts, literary classics, and visual art; androcentric works of science, anthropology, sociology, and theology—these do not fully describe and comprehend reality. Rather they are ideological constructs that produce the invisibility and marginality of women. Therefore, a critical feminist interpretation insists on a hermeneutics of suspicion that can unmask the ideological functions of androcentric biblical

13. For a practical elaboration of such an understanding, see my book *But She Said: Feminist Practices of Interpretation* (Boston: Beacon, 1992), esp. 51–78.

texts and commentary. It does not do so because it assumes a patriarchal conspiracy of the biblical writers and their contemporary interpreters but because women do not, in fact, know whether we are addressed or not by grammatically masculine generic texts.

A *hermeneutics of historical remembrance and reconstruction* not only works to increase the distance between ourselves and the time of the text but also works for an increase in historical imagination. It displaces the androcentric dynamic of the text in its literary contexts by reconstructing the text in a sociopolitical model that can make the subordinated and marginalized "others" visible. It seeks to recover women's biblical history and the memory of their victimization, struggle, and accomplishments as women's heritage.

A *hermeneutics of proclamation or of ethical and theological evaluation* assesses the oppressive or liberatory tendencies inscribed in biblical texts as well as their function in contemporary struggles. It insists for theological reasons that Christians must cease to preach patriarchal texts as the word of God, since by doing so they proclaim God as legitimating patriarchal oppression.

Finally, *a hermeneutics of creative imagination and ritualization* retells biblical stories, reshapes biblical vision, and celebrates our biblical foresisters in a feminist key.

Such a critical process of interpretation for liberation is not restricted to Christian biblical texts but can be applied successfully to Scriptures of other religions. It can also be employed in a wide variety of contexts. It has been used in graduate education, in parish discussions, in college classes, and in work with illiterate Andean women. This model of feminist biblical interpretation conceives of church as well as of theology as a site of struggle and conscientization. It challenges other modes of biblical reading to become more comprehensive and sophisticated by highlighting the shortcomings of their sociopolitical location and function in relation to the global feminist struggle for a more just and inclusive church and world.

Since such a critical process of biblical interpretation seeks not just to understand biblical texts but to change patriarchal biblical religions in the interest of the well-being of all, it requires a theological reconception of the Bible as a formative root-model rather than as a normative, timeless, abstract, mythic archetype of Christian faith and community. To read the Bible not as an unchanging archetype but as a structuring prototype is to understand it as an open-ended paradigm that sets experience in motion and makes transformation possible.

To be sure, the experiences that the biblical root-model has generated are not always liberating. They often are oppressive because of unfaithful or false interpretations and bad readings. Biblical texts and writings can also foster relations of oppression because they were formulated in their original contexts in order to maintain patriarchal sociopolitical structures and religious identities. Therefore, a critical interpretation for liberation must clearly identify and mark biblical texts and traditions that promote patriarchal structures and religious visions that legitimate injustice and oppression.

Christian identity that is grounded in the Bible as its formative prototype must in ever-new readings be deconstructed and reconstructed in terms of a global praxis for the liberation not only of women but also of all those dehumanized by patriarchal societies and religions. As a root-metaphor, the Bible informs but does not provide the theological perspective for a critical feminist reading of particular biblical texts in the interest of liberation. Rather, I have argued, evaluative criteria or theological lenses must be developed in contemporary struggles for justice and liberation. A positioning of biblical readings not in terms of modern, privatized understandings of religion but within the *ekklesia* as the democratic assembly of free citizens, who gather to deliberate their own affairs, engenders a different notion of biblical authority and truth.

Examining ancient Greek legal, philosophical, and literary texts on torture, the feminist philosopher Page DuBois argues that classical Greek philosophy developed the concept of truth as something hidden, something to be excavated or extracted by the torture of slaves.

> This logic demands a closed circle, an other, an outside, and creates such an other. And in the case of the Greek city, the democracy itself used torture to establish this boundary, to mark the line between slave and free, and to locate truth outside.[14]

Western philosophy understands truth as something that is not known; as something buried, secreted in the earth, in the body, in the woman, in the slave, in the totally "other"; as something that must be extricated through torture or sexual violence. In a similar fashion, biblical revelation has been understood in traditional theology as an uncovering of a hidden mystery that is located in the unknown and in the beyond. It is directly known to only a select few, and it can be extracted only through arduous labor. The "canon within the canon" approach, for instance, seeks to uncover, to distill, or to extract a universal truth or authoritative norm from the multilayered meanings of biblical texts and the often contradictory writings collected in the Bible.

According to Page DuBois, this patriarchal understanding of truth is articulated in reaction to the "logic of democracy" as the "notion of equal power among members of a community. . . . Such a notion of democracy required the radical distribution of wealth, the elimination of social and political hierarchies. For some ancient thinkers, even slavery itself was eventually called into question."[15]

14. Page DuBois, *Torture and Truth* (New York: Routledge, 1991), 125.

15. Ibid. On Roman slavery, see K. R. Bradley, *Slaves and Masters in the Roman Empire: A Study of Social Control* (New York: Oxford Univ. Press, 1986); Dale B. Martin (*Slavery as Salvation: The Metaphor of Slavery in Pauline Christianity* [New Haven: Yale Univ. Press, 1990], 1–49) paints a positive picture of slavery, probably in order to justify Paul's use of this metaphor. Orlando Patterson (*Freedom in the Making of Western Culture,* vol. 1 of *Freedom* [New York: HarperCollins, 1991]) claims to have written the first such emancipatory history of freedom. His historical reconstruction of the struggles for freedom in antiquity recognizes women's crucial participation and contribution to these struggles.

The contextualization of biblical interpretation in the paradigm of democracy produces a notion of truth different from that held by Western philosophy. It does not understand truth as a metaphysical given hidden in the text but seeks to achieve the interactive deliberation of a multiple, polyvalent assembly of voices. Truth is a process not of discovering what is hidden or lost but rather of public deliberation and "creation in democratic dialogue." The truth of democracy is produced in struggle and debate as an alternative discourse to torture. In this paradigm, truth is best understood as an "absent presence," a moment in an interpretive political process, a progressive extension of rights and equality to all residents of an expanding community. Such a notion of truth comes close to the biblical notion of "doing the truth."

In Christianity the theological discourses of the *ekklesia* as the discipleship of equals have been submerged and marginalized in patriarchal theological articulations. Nevertheless there are still traces of the praxis of the discipleship of equals inscribed in biblical and theological-ecclesial practices that allow for a reconceptualization of Christian identity in terms of radical democracy. Within this democratic paradigm, scriptural truth is not something hidden and to be found but something to be constituted in and through communicative practices of biblical and theological interpretation under the guidance of the Holy Spirit. Active engagement with Scripture (not submission to it) and the practice of its truth are appropriate for reading the Bible in the global village. To quote John's Gospel: "If you continue in my word, you are truly my disciples, and you will know the truth, and the truth will liberate you."

A critical feminist theological hermeneutics of liberation, therefore, must attempt to reconstruct the traditional spiritual practice of discerning the spirits as a deliberative rhetorical practice. As theological subjects, Christian feminists must claim their spiritual authority to assess both the oppressive as well as the liberating imagination of particular biblical texts. They must do so because of the patriarchal functions of authoritative scriptural claims that demand obedience and acceptance. By deconstructing the all-encompassing patriarchal rhetorics and politics of subordination, critical feminist discourses are able to generate new possibilities for the communicative construction of biblical identities and emancipatory practices. The theological criteria that allow us to test how much biblical texts and symbols perpetrate patriarchy may be informed by biblical experiences but cannot be abstracted from them.

Instead, the "canonical standard" for discerning biblical texts and imagination must be articulated in a systemic analysis of structures of domination and confronted with contemporary struggles to end kyriarchal oppression.[16] It is from these struggles that we gain the perspective with which we can confront the religious vision of the Bible and discriminate among its diverse theological tendencies. Whereas the traditional scriptural principle rests on the identity of the divine and androcentric word, the understanding of the biblical canon as a formative root-model generates a plurality of readings and experiences.

To that end we have to revision Christian church and faith as a radical egalitarian movement for the liberation and welfare of all without exception. Participants in emancipatory movements, including the women's liberation movement, do not struggle for equal rights as citizens in church and society in order to become elitists and oppressors. Rather they struggle in order to achieve the rights, benefits, and privileges of equal citizenship that are legitimately theirs but that are denied to them by the patriarchal-kyriarchal regimes of Western societies and religions. Such movements cannot afford to substitute truth claims for

16. In order to distinguish a multiplex analysis of patriarchy from the dualistic understanding that is prevalent in feminist discourses, I have introduced the term *kyriarchy:* that is, the rule of the lord/master/father (*Herrschaft*). Scholars tend to use the term "hierarchical" when they characterize such a pyramidal system of domination/subordination. However, the term *kyriarchal* is more appropriate and accurate because "hierarchical" refers to a sacred pyramidal system such as is found in the later "malestream" church. For a more fully developed argument and documentation, see my book *But She Said,* 102–32.

their claims to human dignity, equal rights, emancipation, equality, self-determination, and well-being for everyone. Rather, they must interrogate biblical texts, Christian traditions, and institutional practices for religious visions that foster equality, justice, and the logic of the *ekklesia* rather than that of patriarchal domination. Only when they question the patriarchal theological discourses of exclusion inscribed in Christian Scriptures and traditions are they able to uncover the radical democratic religious roots of Christian church and faith.[17]

Utilizing a feminist approach and analysis, I have sought in *In Memory of Her*[18] to reconstruct early Christian beginnings in terms of such a democratic and inclusive model as the practice of the discipleship of equals. Such a reconstruction must, however, not be understood as a transcript of the egalitarian beginnings of the Christian movements. Rather it is a *reconstruction* of those early Christian roots that have engendered radical egalitarian Christian visions and movements throughout the centuries. The project of the *ekklesia* as the discipleship of equals is already and not yet. It is the eschatological project of the *basileia,* the intended world of God, that must be realized in and through struggles against the evil powers of patriarchy.

Jesus and his first followers, women and men, already stood in a long line of Israel's prophets and witnesses. They sought the renewal and well-being of Israel as the people of God. Jesus and his movement followed the Jewish vision of the *basileia,* of God's society and world that are free of domination and do not exclude anyone. This "envisioned" world is already present in the inclusive table-community, in the healing and liberating practices, as well as in the domination-free kinship-community of the Jesus

17. For the fuller development of such an emancipatory reconstructive argument, see my article "A Discipleship of Equals: Ekklesial Democracy and Patriarchy in Biblical Perspective," in *A Democratic Catholic Church,* ed. Eugene C. Bianch and Rosemary Radford Ruether (New York: Crossroad, 1992).

18. Elisabeth Schüssler Fiorenza, *In Memory of Her: A Feminist Theological Reconstruction of Christian Origins* (New York: Crossroad, 1984).

movement, which found many followers among the poor, the despised, the ill and dispossessed, the outcast, and women.[19]

Such elements of that "radical democracy" can also be detected in the early Christian missionary movements that practiced "the equality of the Spirit." A segment of those movements abolished all religious and social status-distinctions and privileges between Jews and Greeks, women and men, slave and free, and understood itself to be called to freedom. Its equality in the Spirit was expressed in alternating leadership and partnership, in equal access for everyone—Greeks, Jews, barbarians, slaves, the free, the rich, and poor women and men. Therefore, its proper name is *ekklesia,*[20] the full decision-making assembly of free citizens who are alien residents in their societies and constitute a different third "race."

The so-called household-code texts[21] or injunctions to patriarchal submission can be understood only when they are seen as rhetorical statements seeking to adapt the egalitarian and therefore subversive Christian movement to its Greco-Roman patriarchal society and culture. They are not "church orders" or historical reports but rhetorical injunctions. They would not have been necessary if from their inception the Christian community and faith had existed as patriarchal formations. Rather the patriarchal rhetorics of the early Christian writings allows

19. For the discussion of the social reconstructions of the Jesus movement, see M. Ebertz, *Das Charisma des Gekreuzigten: Zur Soziologie der Jesusbewegung* (Tübingen: Mohr, 1987); and especially Richard A. Horsley, *Sociology of the Jesus Movement* (New York: Crossroad, 1989).

20. The common classical meaning of *ekklesia* is found in Acts 19:21-41 where the town clerk of Ephesus, probably the chief civil officer in the city, urges silversmiths and other people not to solve the issue at hand in the near-riotous *ekklesia* now in session but to bring the matter before the lawful *ekklesia* where such matters were decided (19:39-41). For discussion of the formation of the *ekklesia,* see Wayne A. Meeks, *The First Urban Christians: The Social World of the Apostle Paul* (New Haven: Yale Univ. Press, 1983), 74–110; and H. J. Klauck, *Hausgemeinde und Hauskirche im frühen Christentum* (Stuttgart: Katholisches Bibelwerk, 1981).

21. See my book *Bread Not Stone,* 65–92, and especially Clarice J. Martin, "The *Haustafeln* (Household Codes) in African American Biblical Interpretation: 'Free Slaves' and 'Subordinate Women,' " in *Stony the Road We Trod: African American Biblical Interpretation,* ed. Cain Hope Felder (Minneapolis: Fortress, 1991), 206–31; D. Balch, "Household Codes," in *Greco-Roman Literature and the New Testament,* ed. D. Aune (Atlanta: Scholars Press, 1988), 25–50.

us to glimpse the "dangerous memory" of a movement and community of radical equality in the power of the Spirit.

A liberative theological integration of notions of liberty and democracy with the radical egalitarian vision of the "discipleship of equals" can engender biblical interpretations and discourses of possibility and vision for a different church and society in the global village. The task of liberation theologies of all colors is to read the Bible in order to envision a Spirit-center for a radical democratic citizenry of global dimensions. Affirming cultural and religious particularity and pluralism, such a "rainbow" theology of liberation can claim as its common ground the commitment to the struggles of all persons for dignity, freedom, and well-being. Biblical religions can do so, however, only if they overcome their exclusive patriarchal formations and articulate a vision of faith and hope in a liberating God who is "justified by all Her children" (Luke 7:35 Q) struggling against kyriarchal oppression and dehumanization.

KATHRYN TANNER

4. CREATION, ENVIRONMENTAL CRISIS, AND ECOLOGICAL JUSTICE

Contemporary Christians are citizens of a planet gravely troubled by the reckless and rapacious enterprises of its human inhabitants. Human industries, spurred by the technological innovations of the last several centuries, have turned the earth into a commodity for human purposes. The earth's geological features and animal and plant life are routinely sacrificed before the altars of corporate profit and a moneyed public's ever-expanding hunger for consumable goods. Modes of production and patterns of consumption in the industrialized nations proceed as if the earth were an infinitely malleable object of human mastery readily bent for any human use, or as if the harm done by human enterprises to the earth and its life-forms were of no real importance or concern.

Scientific developments and common human experience show the inadequacy of these irresponsible and anthropocentric attitudes that Western modes of production and consumption institutionalize. The ecological outlook of modern biology informs us that the natural world is not a supremely plastic material for the imprint of human purposes. To the contrary, the natural world is comprised of fragile networks of interrelationships among organisms and environment. The capacity of human beings to disrupt these networks is dramatically evident—for example, in the drastic loss of species diversity in many areas of the United

States. Human neighborhoods were once visited—even in my lifetime—by more than sparrows, pigeons, squirrels, and the seagulls that feast on our garbage.

The cold war specter of nuclear war and the fear of nuclear power plant accidents after Chernobyl and Three Mile Island have destroyed all smug confidence about the beneficial effects of human efforts to harness the forces of nature. The enormous complexity of the ecological balance among environmental conditions and planetary life counters, moreover, human presumption that the powers and resources of the earth are ours to master. The unexpected chains of cause and effect from (for example) aerosol hairspray and Styrofoam cups, on the one hand, to destruction of the earth's life-giving ozone layer, on the other, make one doubt human abilities to anticipate and so control the outcomes of human influence on the environment. Even seemingly minor human-initiated changes can have, we now know, undreamed-of repercussions. The undeniably harmful effects on human health of automobile exhaust, industrial waste, and airborne toxic chemicals should persuade even the most human-centered planners against implementing technological advances in our productive powers without thought for the environmental consequences.

Ecological sciences make clear, indeed, that human needs cannot be served without attention to the well-regulated functioning of wider biosystems. Human life is a part of larger life patterns and is therefore dependent upon them. Knowing that, one cannot suppose human beings somehow stride blithely above the world with blueprints in hand for their own advancement. They are themselves susceptible to every bit of environmental havoc they wreak for their own ends. Ecological science in this way turns human action away from simple self-interested concerns. Human beings are dependent for their well-being on wider ecosystems, and what maintains the delicate balance of these ecosystems is not necessarily what serves a human profit motive.

The crisis proportions of the environmental situation and the delusional nature of the human attitudes that have brought us to this point call every Christian, as they do every thoughtful North American, to work to change the business-as-usual of production and consumption in our industrialized, technologically sophisticated continent. Recognizing the power over life on this planet that we wield, we must make it our business both to remedy past harms and to limit the destructive impacts of present human action. In accepting such responsibilities, we must act with caution, considering all relevant factors in a broad ecological context and assessing carefully the possible environmental consequences of human initiatives. Rather than approach the minerals, plants, and animals of the earth with an exploitative eye, we must set the pursuit of human goods within a broader, nonanthropocentric context of environmental well-being and therefore bind that pursuit by concern for the good of the nonhuman.

Christians must join forces, moreover, with all other persons of social conscience to work for environmental causes in a socially responsible way. The poor, here or abroad, should not be the ones to feel the brunt of calls for restraints on the environmentally hazardous production of goods and services. Poor neighborhoods or poor nations should also not be, as they increasingly are today, the dumping ground for "dirty" industries or their toxic wastes.[1] The opportunity to live in a healthy environment, to breathe clean air and drink clean water, must not be thought of as the privileges of the well-to-do or the powerful.

The environmental crisis calls Christians in particular to confront their own religious tradition's complicity in the present crisis and in the attitudes toward the natural world that con-

1. Low-wage earners, immigrants, and people of color are usually employed in the most health-hazardous jobs in the United States and usually live in the most polluted communities. See, for example, Eric Mann, *LA's Lethal Air* (Los Angeles: A Labor/Community Strategy Publication, 1991), chap. 4; Commission for Racial Justice, *Toxic Wastes and Race in the United States* (New York: United Church of Christ, 1987).

Regarding corporate plans to export pollution to the Third World, see the text of a purloined memorandum by World Bank chief economist Lawrence Summers in the February 1992 issue of *The Economist,* and discussion of it by Michael Albert, "Market Maladies," *Z Magazine* 5, no. 3 (March 1992).

tribute to it. Social scientists tell us that the religious beliefs people hold often have a marked influence on their overall outlook toward the world.[2] Christianity has been, and arguably remains, the dominant religious influence in the United States and many other industrialized nations with very poor environmental records. From these facts alone, one can presume the likelihood of some Christian complicity in the present environmental crisis. The extent and nature of Christian responsibility may remain a matter for argument.[3] But whatever the character and degree of the fault—whether Christianity has been a minor or major player in the ignominious relations of human beings with the natural world so far, whether Christian beliefs have directly inspired these rapacious and exploitative relations, rendered them indirect aid, or simply allowed them to proceed unimpeded—Christians are summoned to repent of their fault. They are required, that is, according to the original Greek sense of the term "repentance," to turn around and rethink their Christian commitments in light of their possible environmental consequences. This is the special task that environmental crisis calls Christians to perform as they work for change.

Of central importance in this task of rethinking Christian commitments are Christian beliefs about creation, beliefs about God's relation to the world as its Creator. Christian beliefs about the relations that human beings have with the natural world are of obvious relevance when considering Christian attitudes with possible environmental repercussions. But these beliefs are determined in large part by Christian beliefs about the relations that God maintains with the various inhabitants of the world that God creates. The terms for understanding the relations between humans and the natural world are set by the understanding of

2. See Max Weber, *The Sociology of Religion* (Boston: Beacon, 1963), for an account like this of religion's influence.

3. See Lynn White, "The Historical Roots of Our Ecologic Crisis," in *Ecology and Religion in History,* ed. David Spring and Eileen Spring (New York: Harper Torchbooks, 1974), and the controversy it has generated over the years.

God's relations with both humans and nature as the beings God creates.

Although based upon many of the same biblical texts and early creedal statements, Christian beliefs about creation have taken many different forms. In the next section, I isolate three distinct bodies of these beliefs that have had the greatest historical influence upon Christian attitudes toward the natural world. My intent in separating Christian thinking about creation into several distinct strands is to clarify the strengths and weaknesses of Christian beliefs about creation for coping with environmental concerns. I suggest that, for different reasons, none of these strands is adequate to meet the present demands of environmental crisis.

I argue in a subsequent section, however, that certain other, rarely tapped aspects of a Christian theology of creation do indeed meet such demands. The need for a nonanthropocentric and socially responsible environmental activism at the present time prompts my emphasis and development of these beliefs. The beliefs I specify are long-standing features of a preexisting religious tradition, however; they are not newly minted in order to meet such a contemporary need. They therefore have the capacity, as we see in the final section of this essay, to make their own distinctive contribution toward moving human beings beyond attitudes and actions in which mastery, exploitation, and domination of the earth and its inhabitants, be they human or nonhuman, are the order of the day. Actions and attitudes that are informed by these beliefs about creation should help us move, I argue, beyond environmental crisis toward what I call ecological justice.

ANALYSIS OF THE DOCTRINE: THREE STRANDS OF A CHRISTIAN THEOLOGY OF CREATION

Christian theologies of creation can be separated into three distinct strands. None of the three strands adequately addresses, however, the present-day challenges of environmental crisis.

Imitation of God's Rule

The first strand of a Christian theology of creation to be assessed with reference to environmental concerns can be termed an "imitation of God's rule" strand. Human relations with the nonhuman are modeled on God's relation to the world. In other words, human beings are to behave toward animate and inanimate nature in the way God behaves toward the whole created order. Human beings can claim such a stance toward nature because they alone among creatures are like God. As Gen. 1:26-30 implies, human beings are created in God's image, and therefore they are to exercise a God-like dominion over the earth and all its inhabitants.[4]

The consequences of such an account of creation for environmental concerns obviously depend a great deal on how God's relations with the world are understood. Christians have commonly affirmed God's free sovereignty with respect to the world God creates. This affirmation can easily combine with the connotations of "dominion" to suggest that human beings rightfully rule over the natural world like despots. Human beings imitate God in doing whatever they like with the earth and its life-forms. Modeling their relations with the natural world on a God who directs the world according to purposes of God's own choosing, human beings are led simply to use the natural world for their own ends without regard for any damage they might cause to it.

As an alternative to a model of despotic rule, Christians can stress the care that God expresses for the world as its Creator. They can therefore stress God's rule as one that bestows blessings.[5] This idea of God clearly suggests that human relations with the world should be less exploitative and anthropocentric

4. Indeed, in more recent times the image of God in human beings is sometimes equated with the exercise of dominion. See James Barr, "Man and Nature: The Ecological Controversy and the Old Testament," in *Ecology and Religion in History,* 60.

5. See Claus Westermann, *Creation* (London: SPCK, 1971), 51–53, for this interpretation of biblical language concerning God's dominion. See also John Passmore, *Man's Responsibility for Nature* (London: Duckworth, 1974), 9.

in their orientation. But whatever the account of God's intentions toward the world, traditional Christian suggestions of God's infrustrable and unconditional power are likely to give human beings an illusory sense of their own powers of mastery vis-à-vis the natural world. Even if the God they model themselves on is a beneficent God, human beings are not educated thereby to be mindful of their own limits. The world may be infinitely malleable in God's hands, but it is not perfectly plastic in ours, as this strand of Christian thinking about creation easily leads one to presume. God may be able to bring everything back to the good, but human beings are wise to forgo this model of God's working when thinking of their own. Christians would better remember the limited capacities of their own foresight and the commonly unintended consequences of their own best intentions.

The justification that this "imitation of God's rule" strand of Christian thinking about creation gives for modeling human relations with nature on God's relations with the world remains highly problematic, moreover, for environmental concerns. Far from highlighting human life's place within an ecological whole, talk of human beings as the image of God can have the effect of raising them out of the world altogether. Human beings seem to have some sort of ontological standing that puts them on the divine side of the divide between God and the world. Human beings exhibit certain qualities or capacitics—usually identified as rational or spiritual ones—that no other creatures on Earth exhibit, and these qualities or capacities establish an exceptional relation between human beings and God. Exceptional qualities and an exceptional relation with God become the excuse, in turn, for self-congratulatory claims of human superiority. In that way a path is cleared for uninhibited human domination of the earth. Nonhuman beings have little or no value compared to humans, and therefore human needs and interests may willfully override all others. When oriented around the exceptional relation that human beings have with God, Christian notions such as sin, grace, sanctification, and salvation establish no commonality of focus within which the goods of the human and the nonhuman might be considered together. Redemption, communion with God, and other concepts tend to be understood in anthropocentric and exclusive ways: the good of creatures other than human beings either is subordinated to an end of human fulfillment or drops out of religious purview altogether.[6]

A Great Chain of Being

In a second strand of Christian thinking about creation, which I term a "great chain of being" strand, human relations with nature are not modeled on God's relations with the world but are set firmly within the ordered world that God establishes. According to this second strand of Christian belief, human beings are not *above* the world but *of* it. They are parts of an immense whole arranged to suit God's purposes, links in a great chain of beings held together by the way the qualities and activities that are natural to such beings have been coordinated by God to achieve a divine end. This is a classically medieval idea, which may be developed in either a Neoplatonic or Aristotelian fashion (in the writings, for example, of Dionysius the Areopagite and Thomas Aquinas, respectively). Similar ideas in more modern dress still hold attractions for theologians concerned about the environment.

This "great chain of being" strand of Christian thinking about creation seems to support a more holistic outlook than the first strand and therefore might be thought to favor something like an ecological sensibility. In its classic form, one is directed to consider the lower links of the chain as beings created to promote the functions of those higher up. And one is directed to consider the way beings higher up the chain affect lower ones by achieving the ultimate purposes for which those lower beings were created.

What generates a holistic attitude here—the idea that purposes have been written into the nature of things by the God

6. See Paul Santmire, *The Travail of Nature* (Philadelphia: Fortress, 1985).

who creates them—conflicts, however, with the conclusions of most forms of modern science. The blind run of atoms in an eighteenth-century mechanistic view of the world is not a teleologically ordered world, a world ordered according to natural ends. After Darwin, scientists do not appeal to purposes to explain animal demographics. No one any longer believes, for example, that polar bears have thick fur so that they can live in the Arctic and provide hide for Eskimos' coats. Ecological science, while obviously more amenable to the idea of functional interplay within the natural world than a mechanistic theory, still discredits the idea of a teleological ranking of beings. From an ecological point of view, it makes as much sense to say animal and plant life exist for the sake of the humans who eat them, as it does to say human beings exist for the sake of the viruses that kill them.[7] From Teilhard de Chardin on, modern theologians who try to update the teleological perspective of a great chain of beings are therefore in danger of distorting the conclusions of science to meet theological demands.

"Great chain of being" views are generally, moreover, quite anthropocentric. The purposes that the order of the world serves center on human beings. The rest of the beings in the world exist with the God-given qualities and capacities they have in order ultimately to further ends that benefit human existence. Nonhuman beings might exist in order to direct human beings to God, or harry them into repentance for their sins, or, more crudely, simply to feed and clothe them and so make their lives more comfortable for the pursuit of greater spiritual ends. Once understood in an anthropocentric way, this strand of thinking about creation tends to be irremediably anthropocentric, since the centrality of human concerns will be thought of as part of the very nature of things.

This strand of Christian thinking about creation does set some limits on the pursuit of human ends. It has the potential, there-

7. See Passmore, *Man's Responsibility,* 14. Also, Murray Bookchin, *The Ecology of Freedom* (Palo Alto, Calif.: Cheshire, 1982), 26.

fore, to check wild flights of human arrogance in the use and appropriation of the natural world. Human beings are not alone in the pursuit of ends; their purposeful activities take place within a wider world that is teleologically ordered throughout its heights and depths. When pursuing their own ends, human beings must respect this wider order; they must respect the distinctive roles and functions of other beings in the grander scheme of things. Within this grander scheme, the nonhuman may sometimes, moreover, be serving purposes with no obvious relation to human ends. As the Book of Job makes clear, God will bring "rain on a land where no one lives, on the desert, which is empty of human life, to satisfy the waste and desolate land, and to make the ground put forth grass" (Job 38:26-27). Finally, the opening for a simple exploitation of nature that we saw the first strand of Christian thinking about creation produce is closed off here. Although human beings may be "on top" in a great chain of being, they are not so in virtue of any absolute distinction between the human and the nonhuman. Humans are distinguished from nonhumans, instead, along a slow hierarchical grade of being and value. None of the qualifications I have just been mentioning necessarily disturbs, however, the essentially anthropocentric character of the "chain of being" position.

This second strand of Christian thinking about creation also remains problematic for a situation in which human beings need to take responsibility for the ecological destructiveness of their acts. Especially in its classic form (which maintains the special creation of each individual species and the fixity of the total number of species), this strand stresses the idea that nonhuman existence is *already* ordered in a felicitous way to serve human ends. Human beings are not enjoined to take any special measures themselves to ensure that order. Human action that alters the natural, matter-of-course run of things endangers God's own designs for the world. While such a perspective on human action might favor a hands-off, preservationist mentality and so discourage destructive human interventions into stable ecosystems, it suggests, contrary to much ecological science, that human activity is somehow excluded from the natural interrelations of beings in the world to begin with and that stasis is the "normal" state of environmental order. In a world already damaged by irresponsible human action, these ideas promote a false optimism about the benefits of simple human passivity. They discourage any renewed sense of active human responsibility for environmental well-being.

A teleological creation theology like this can be modified, however, in order to incorporate the idea of human beings working to bring about the kind of harmonious interplay among creatures that God intends. The nonhuman world may have been created to further human ends but that does not mean that human beings do not need to act, for example, as cultivators of the earth or raisers of livestock, in order to bring out the potentials of an essentially hospitable environment. Such action may be especially necessary after the fall, which disordered the proper relations among things as they were originally created by God. Benedictine monasteries seemed among the first to operate according to such principles.[8]

Considered from the standpoint of a world in dire environmental straits, a teleological perspective that is modified in this way seems admirably activist; it encourages a sense of human responsibility for the well-regulated functioning of the natural world. But such a perspective is surely overly sanguine in its assumption that human interventions are necessarily beneficial. Our experience with the enormous destructive powers of human technology makes us less confident that human initiatives mark the site of nature's own improvement.

Stewardship

When the "imitation of God's rule" strand of Christian thinking about creation is modified so that human beings model their

8. See Clarence Glacken, *Traces on the Rhodian Shore* (Berkeley: Univ. of California Press, 1976).

action on a beneficent God, and the "great chain of being" strand of Christian thinking about creation is modified to make clear the need for human action, these strands are on their way to a third. Here the human dominion over the earth that Genesis texts discuss is understood as a kind of stewardship. Unlike the first strand of Christian thinking about creation, human relations with the natural world are understood with reference not to God's own way of relating to the world but to the God-ordained place of human beings within the world God establishes. Human beings are special not in virtue of qualities that raise them out of the created order but in virtue of the special place they fill within it. Unlike, however, the second strand of a Christian creation theology, human beings hold this special place in an administrative rather than ontological capacity.[9] In other words, human beings are viewed as the primary workers of God's will for the world rather than the prime beneficiaries of a world constructed by God with certain ends in mind. As the primary administrators of God's will, human beings are charged with special responsibilities by God, delegated crucial functions in the fulfillment of God's plans, deputized as God's agents. These responsibilities bring along with them certain legal rights or entitlements of use with respect to nonhuman beings. Human beings are licensed as God's agents to direct the nonhuman toward ends conformable to God's will; human beings are commissioned by God to look after or manage the world God has created.

Since human beings are the primary administrators of God's will rather than the highest beings within the world, the anthropocentric presumption of this third strand of Christian thinking about creation is weaker than that of the "great chain of being" strand. It is not proper to say that nonhuman beings exist and exhibit a particular arrangement simply for the sake of human beings. In another way, however, this "stewardship" strand of Christian thinking about creation frees human action for a more

9. Santmire draws a contrast like this in *The Travail of Nature,* 42.

anthropocentric focus. An emphasis on the administrative primacy of human beings frees human action from respecting the integrity of nonhuman operations found in a "great chain of being" strand. The more human beings are viewed as privileged agents of God's will, the more nonhuman existence tends to be considered formless putty in human hands, to be shaped at will.

The "stewardship" strand of creation theology does, however, set standards for responsible human action vis-à-vis the nonhuman. There are clear limits to what human beings are entitled to do. Human rights vis-à-vis the nonhuman are circumscribed by obligations. First of all, to God: human beings as God's agents are bound by God's purposes. Those purposes, moreover, are not equatable with human ends as easily as they are in the "great chain of being" strand of creation theology where the privileged value of human beings in God's sight can be assumed from their high placement on an ontological ladder. The divine purposes, for all we know, may include the whole of the created order, human and nonhuman alike. God's plans may include the good of animals and plants, as well as the good of human beings. Human beings, as the agents of God's will, should work in that case not only for their own good but also for the well-being of the entire world. Furthermore, as agents with only a delegated authority, human beings have rights of use, but they do not finally *own* what they work on. Human beings have no *absolute* rights over the nonhuman since the nonhuman remains God's own. The earth and all that is in it are the Lord's (Psalm 24). The natural world is not human property but is leased, so to speak, from God. Human beings are therefore not given a license for the plunder or wanton destruction of the nonhuman; they are to make a planned and constructive use of it. The relations between human lenders and borrowers are appropriate for the relations between human beings and God. One should keep safe what one has on loan; while one cannot be called to account for misusing or damaging one's own property, it is wrong to mistreat or destroy that over which one has only been given rights of use.

The "stewardship" strand's emphasis on responsible human governance of the nonhuman world is to be applauded. This emphasis does not prevent, however, the nonhuman from being employed primarily for human purposes. Indeed, the primacy of human ends tends to be an unargued-for presumption of this third strand of Christian thinking about creation. The charge to exercise responsibility typically qualifies, therefore, only the *manner* of a human-centered use. For example, human cruelty or pleasure involved in the suffering of animals intended for slaughter may be condemned, while the slaughter itself remains outside the bounds of moral concern.

This third strand can encourage human responsibility for the well-being of *both* the human and the nonhuman and can therefore prove helpful in a world threatened with destruction from careless human self-interest. Unfortunately, however, respect for nonhuman well-being does not necessarily challenge a view of nonhuman life as primarily oriented for human use. As God's deputies, "the righteous know the needs of their animals" (Prov. 12:10), but these animals are otherwise still theirs to use for their own purposes.

The idea of legal rights in the "stewardship" scheme gives human beings, moreover, too grand a sense of their own prerogatives and authority over the course of world affairs. The world is subject here to the self-conscious planning of human beings in a way that disguises their dependence on forces, living and nonliving, outside their control. Human beings are easily led to think of themselves as sovereign observers and directors of a world that is theirs to manage as they see fit. Recent history, which hammers home the unforeseen harmful consequences of even the best-intentioned human action, makes such confidence in human stewardship seem laughably (and tragically) naive.

Finally, although human beings in this third strand of Christian thinking merely manage someone *else's* property, the earth and its inhabitants still appear to have a status similar to commodities. The earth and its inhabitants are objects of ownership and lease, of deals and exchanges between God and human beings over which they have no say. Too great an agreement exists here with the instrumentalist and use-oriented attitudes toward the natural world that have brought us to our present environmental crisis.

The idea of human stewardship of the earth can be modified to avoid some of these implications. The elevated claims made for human planners can be lessened by viewing human beings as just one class of contributors in a genuinely cooperative venture for the well-being of the whole. The impression that nonhuman beings are commodities subject to exchange and utility calculations can be lessened by making clear that human beings are to use their special capacities for reflection and planning in order to act as facilitators, rather than self-interested manipulators, of nonhuman processes.[10] The essential anthropocentrism of the "stewardship" strand of Christian thinking about creation remains problematic, however, in a world that suffers so obviously from human hubris.

RECONSTRUCTING A CHRISTIAN THEOLOGY OF CREATION

What we learn from this assessment of historically dominant strands of Christian thinking about creation is mostly negative. The three strands we have looked at can be modified to meet the demands of modern science and worries about the well-being of the earth. Even when so modified, however, these strands remain problematic for a world in environmental crisis. The general source of their failure is nevertheless instructive.

These strands, at their best, introduce broader, more holistic concerns within fundamentally anthropocentric frameworks; they mitigate anthropocentric starting points by making refer-

10. See, for example, the work of John Cobb, *Is It Too Late? A Theology of Ecology* (Beverly Hills, Calif.: Bruce Books, 1972).

ence to holistic concerns that widen the scope of moral purview and set human beings within the world as fully natural beings in essential relations with others. In all three of the strands human beings are given a privileged position from the start—as the bearers of God's image in the first, as the beings on the highest rungs of an earthly ladder of beings in the second, and as the special agents of God's purposes in the third. The existence, order, and destiny of the world God establishes revolve, therefore, in one way or another, around human beings—always as the prime beneficiaries, and sometimes as the prime executors, of what is to happen there. Recognition of the value and needs of the nonhuman and recognition of the wider order in which human being and action subsist may check this initial anthropocentrism, but as mere caveats or qualifications of a human-centered focus, they never finally undermine it.

The pressing concerns of the environmental crisis arguably demand more from Christian theology. Why not reverse the priorities of the theological strands we have looked at and thereby undermine their anthropocentrism more radically? Why not make more holistic elements of a Christian theology of creation the starting points for theological reflection and subordinate any discussion of special human prerogatives or obligations to them? In forming an ecologically sensitive theology of creation, why not put what human beings share with the earth and its inhabitants into first place, rather than their differences? In that way one could make a single horizon of moral concern including all the earth and its life-forms the basis for any subsequent talk of special human privileges or powers.

Such a strategy would also help a Christian-based ecological activism to be socially responsible. Theologies that privilege humans on account of their differences from nonhumans have been implicated historically in nonegalitarian proposals for human relations. Discourses about the proper treatment of people and of nonhuman beings (particularly animals) are often mixed up together in the history of Western thought, especially prior to the eighteenth century.[11] Parallels are drawn between relations among different classes of persons and relations between humans and nonhumans. The idea that differences between humans and nonhumans justify a lesser standard of treatment for the latter is paralleled by the idea that differences between white and black men, men and women, nobles and peasant, and so on, justify unequal distributions of power and privilege in human society.

Thus, the "imitation of God's rule" strand of a Christian theology of creation has been associated with proposals for very extreme differences in power among human beings. The relation between God and the world in which God rules with absolute authority is not only to be reproduced in human relations with the natural world. It is also to be reproduced in the king's relations with his subjects, in men's relations with women, in fathers' relations with their children or servants, and so on.[12]

The "great chain of being" strand of a Christian theology of creation is part of a whole theory of "correspondences" between the human and the nonhuman realms; according to this theory, hierarchical relations between human beings are established by nature just as they are throughout the entire chain of being. Social roles are thought to be rigid and immutable because "natural," and assignment to these roles is fixed by intrinsic characteristics or capacities that supposedly suit one for just those functions in society one happens to perform.

The "stewardship" strand of a Christian theology of creation has supported, and in turn been supported by, paternalistic relations between human beings of unequal social standing, for example, relations with servants or laborers in one's employ. In

11. See Keith Thomas, *Man and the Natural World* (New York: Pantheon, 1983), esp. chap. 1. The qualities of animals were often attributed to certain orders of people—workers, peasants, women, foreigners, subjugated persons, nonwhites, the insane—to justify their substandard position in human society. In the early modern period, all sorts of human beings began to be pulled onto the human side of the divide between animals and people while a sharp difference between the two was left standing and was in fact insisted upon. Poor treatment of certain classes of people was wrong, it was argued, because it involved treating them like animals. Justice for human beings in this case trades off an ideology of human domination over animals.

12. The *locus classicus* of this position is Robert Filmer's *Patriarcha* (ca. 1640).

the seventeenth century, treatment of beasts and laborers could be considered in the same breath under a model of stewardship: good managers of God's estate should let both animals and people in their employ have some rest (on Sundays) and not treat them injuriously.[13] As late as the early nineteenth century, English parliamentary discussion proposed that if one were in doubt about the propriety of striking a beast, the criterion was the same as that determining when it was proper to strike an apprentice—sometimes but not often, presumably, and only for their own good.[14]

The injustice of paternalism, hierarchy, and autocratic rule gives us another reason, then, to undermine Christian anthropocentrism and stress holistic elements of Christian theology that put human and nonhuman together within a single leveled plane of moral concern. There might be many ways of doing this. Let me explore one such possibility now.

Instead of being used as a simple justification for human prerogative, Christian ideas about God as Creator can place human and nonhuman within the same plane of consideration. God is the Creator of all—of rivers and mountains, of grasses and goats, of human beings. The earth and all its inhabitants can be considered together as God's creatures and, qua creatures, as the objects of God's continuing concern. God as the Creator of all bestows blessings on all and tenderly watches over even the most insignificant and peculiar of them (from a human point of view)—the tiniest birds of the air (Matt. 6:26), the weirdest beasts of the deep (Job 41).

Differences among creatures, differences in particular between human beings and other inhabitants of the earth, are part of God's gifts (like everything else). They exist and no doubt have some significance in God's plans for the world. But they are

13. Thomas, *Man and the Natural World,* 156.

14. Ibid, 190. This sort of parallelism could obviously work in favor of animal rights when standards for the treatment of apprentices, servants, paid laborers, and so on, rose (with no help from the idea of stewardship!).

relativized under a status before God that all beings share: the standing of *creaturehood,* which remains beneath all the different forms of being and activity that the inhabitants of the earth exhibit.

This shared standing of creaturehood need not be a mere backdrop for an anthropocentric reading of God's plans and purposes. It can establish the overriding context for discussion of God's relations with human beings. Human ends become in this way simply an integral part of salvific and providential intentions of God that encompass the whole created world. God providentially speaks and summons the earth itself from the rising of the sun to its setting (Ps. 50:1). God covenants after the Flood not just with human beings but with every living creature (Gen. 9:10-17). God wishes to save both "humans and animals," according to Ps. 36:6. Christ, who was with God in the making of heaven and earth, comes to bring about not just a redeemed human community but a renewed cosmos (Col. 1:15-20).[15]

The earth and its inhabitants are not deemed valuable by God just insofar as they are objects of God's concern. They have, as creatures, a value in themselves. God looks out on the world God creates and *sees* that it is good; God *recognizes* its inherent value (Genesis 1). The world God produces, the world God establishes in its own created existence, must be itself good, since God, according to Christian belief, is a good God and the source of goodness. This inherent value of the earth and its inhabitants calls out for respect not just from God but also from human beings. The human purview of concern should therefore be as extensive as God's own as Creator of heaven and earth.

The inherent value of creatures, which human beings must recognize, puts all the beings of the earth on a par for human consideration. If the beings of the earth are valuable as God's creatures, all of them share in this value equally. None of the beings of this earth is any more or less the creature of God,

15. For a very interesting cosmos-centered rereading of God's relations with human beings, see Santmire, *The Travail of Nature,* chap. 10.

and therefore none of these beings is more or less valuable than another in that respect.

Treatment appropriate for beings so valuable must be extended, consequently, to all beings of the earth in the same degree. The same care and concern that are owed human beings as God's creatures are owed also to nonhuman ones. Here, then, is a vision of cosmic justice in which all beings are due equal consideration at some basic level of moral concern.

What such consideration amounts to depends upon what it is about creatures that has inherent value. Creaturehood gives all beings inherent value, but *what about them* is valuable for that reason? One can answer this question by considering the sort of blessings a good God bestows as Creator. These blessings include, at a minimum, the existence of the beings of this earth, in the distinctive forms that set them off one from another, and those beings' engagement in the various activities whose pursuit seems to fulfill them. All God's creatures are therefore due treatment that respects both the value of their continued existence as the beings they are and the value of those activities and achievements proper to them.[16]

Creatures' own entitlements, according to this strand of Christian thinking about creation, force an activist stance appropriate for a time of environmental crisis. Human beings must repent of their ill-treatment of nonhumans in the past; they must see such ill-treatment as a form of injustice demanding present remedy. Consequences of human enterprises must be carefully assessed for their impacts on nonhuman as well as human beings. The universal range of appropriate consideration—humans and nonhumans, plants and animals, air, sea, and land—makes highly nuanced forms of decision making necessary in which attention to ecological networks of dependencies will be of paramount importance.

16. For a more technically sophisticated version of this argument see Kathryn Tanner, *The Politics of God* (Minneapolis: Fortress, 1992), chap. 5.

Here, indeed, on the question of active human responsibility for the well-being of the earth, a difference between human and nonhuman may come to the fore. Humans are perhaps alone on the earth in their capacities for analysis and foresight. Or, if that is too much, they are probably alone in their abilities to imagine a universal community of moral concern when exercising these capacities for analysis and foresight. Among the beings of this earth, human beings therefore have a special responsibility to foster a world in which all receive their due as God's creatures.

Differences between human and nonhuman may also be important factors for consideration in the real circumstances of human decision making where a proper respect cannot be shown all the beings due it. In such circumstances, the different qualities and capacities of creatures may supply grounds for judgments of differential value over and above the value ascribed equally to all beings as God's creatures. One might be able to argue, for example, that a human being, in virtue of its distinctive qualities and capacities, has some greater value of this sort than an insect and, therefore, that where circumstances prohibit all from enjoying what they are due as God's creatures, decisions favoring human life are in order. The value and entitlements shared by all beings as creatures of God remain, however, the overarching context for such judgments. All beings continue to *have* this shared value and these shared entitlements, even in circumstances where, because of, say, scarce resources or finite human capacities, all beings cannot be shown the same respect for that value and cannot equally enjoy what they are due. This continuing context for decision making rules out any simple subordination of nonhuman interests to our own, where "subordination" implies a lesser degree of *entitlement* on the part of nonhuman beings as creatures of God. Nonhuman beings remain a focus for moral concern; an ideal of equal *enjoyment* of entitlements remains the ultimate goal for human action. Complacency in situations where nonhuman interests are subordinate to human ones is therefore inexcusable. Human beings always have the obligation to explore ways in which human action might alter circumstances of competition and bring the earth closer to a vision of a truly universal, world-inclusive, equal justice.

IMPLICATIONS FOR PRACTICE

Putting human and nonhuman beings together in this way within a single community of moral concern helps resolve certain issues for human decision making. For example, if research into human diseases supposed such a context of decision making, a concern for both human beings and animals would prompt researchers to culture disease-producing organisms without the use of animal hosts. Were this not possible, researchers would choose to culture these organisms in living animals that are not made sick thereby. Monkeys, for instance, would be a suitable experimental host for HIV because they do not come down with AIDS. Researchers, moreover, would be obliged to do everything possible to foster the well-being of the animals involved. Monkeys helping in AIDS research, for example, would be due extremely fine care—for example, adequate space and time for social interactions, as much control over their activities as possible, even periodic entertainment from the staff to alleviate their stress and boredom.

The complications of such a wide-ranging focus in human decision making will often, however, increase its difficulty. First, more factors than usual will have to be taken into account when considering environmental issues. Questions of human justice, for example, will have to be included from the start. Thus, North American worries about the destruction of Brazilian rain forests cannot be acted upon without considering the plight of the Brazilian underclasses who have been encouraged to farm there as one of their only hopes for economic advancement. Calls for the preservation of rain forests should therefore lead immediately into questions of national and global economies and their possible restructuring toward more equitable distributions of income and opportunities.[17] Second, the decisions reached will often remain agonizing. Where the well-being of both the human and nonhuman cannot be achieved at once, the bad consciences of human beings cannot be finally assuaged by claims of a difference in value between humans and nonhumans or by claims of human incapacity to alter circumstances of scarcity or competition. Decisions under such conditions never lose an edge of tragedy. Or, better said, a deep sense of unease and regret over them unfolds beneath the hope for a new heaven and earth of cosmic justice to come and prompts ever-renewed efforts to bring that world of justice closer.

Christians, finally, are brought to a new understanding of the environmental movement. Environmental concerns have historically been disassociated from concerns about justice issues. A preoccupation with the preservation of wilderness areas or the protection of wild animals has often provided a pleasing distraction from the inhumanities of economic injustice suffered by others; it can easily become an excuse for neglecting these injustices. Environmental activism can make one seem a responsible citizen of the planet even as it allows one to ignore the plight of one's fellow human beings. This is a time-worn maneuver: in the late eighteenth and early nineteenth centuries in England, worries about cruelty to animals could suggest the benevolent sensibilities of an industrialized age even as the age failed to extend the same benevolence to its workers.[18] Singing the praises of animal life and untamed wilderness is easy when one will not starve if such land remains fallow or suffer economic hardship if those animal habitats are preserved. Ecological sensibilities have often, indeed, provided a measure for class distinction. Being a nature lover in the early history of an industrialized society like the United States marked one as a member of a class distant from the hand-to-hand struggle to eke a humanly consumable prod-

17. The concluding statement of the recent United Nations Conference on Environment and Development (April 4, 1992) shows the beginnings of such an analysis.

18. See Thomas, *Man and the Natural World*, chap. 6.

uct from nature. It meant one was not a farmer or cattleman, for example. At any time, it makes clear one's membership in an economically secure class, with the leisure time for nature appreciation and the disposable income to get in a position to see it. The rarity of the conditions for such appreciation has been a great part of its appeal.[19] In eighteenth- and nineteenth-century England, nostalgic praise of country life by economically comfortable city dwellers masked the fact that human beings labored there, exploited by an enclosure system, to serve urban needs.[20] In this century, environmentally minded calls for restraint on industrial production in poverty-stricken areas of the world help protect the outrageous consumption levels of the upper classes in industrialized nations; similarly outrageous consumption levels cannot be had by all.

Christians who think through a belief in God as the Creator of the world in the ways I suggest should repudiate any such alternative between concerns for environmental well-being, on the one hand, and sensitivity to issues of human justice, on the other. They should join efforts in their communities to build coalitions across environmental groups and organizations working for minority and workers' rights.[21] People must be empowered to force corporate, industrial America away from a narrow concern for profit and toward more responsible action for the well-being of the environment, their workers, and the communities of which they are a part. Christians, from their own distinctive starting point in beliefs about God and the world, can encourage a broad social movement that combines worries about the environment and a just society within a single focus of moral concern. They can help sustain a movement of ecological justice, in other

19. See Roderick Nash, *Wilderness and the American Mind* (New Haven: Yale Univ. Press, 1967).

20. See Raymond Williams, *The Country and the City* (New York: Oxford Univ. Press, 1973).

21. A sterling example of such an effort at coalition building is the Los Angeles–based WATCHDOG group. For a description of their activities, see Mann, *LA's Lethal Air,* chaps. 6 and 7.

words. However they come to understand such engagement from a Christian point of view, complex times of environmental crisis and social irresponsibility demand nothing less from them than action for such an end.

DAWN DeVRIES

5. CREATION, HANDICAPPISM, AND THE COMMUNITY OF DIFFERING ABILITIES

PRESENTING THE PROBLEM AND THE DOCTRINE

Naming the Problem

The problem of handicappism—discrimination against persons on the basis of physical or mental disability—is neither new nor peculiarly North American. Handicappism has existed wherever the "able-bodied" have wielded the power to make laws and organize the structures of social reality. What is new in North America is the refusal of people with disabilities to accept their marginalization with quiescence. Relatively recent congressional legislation, including the Rehabilitation Act of 1973 and the Americans with Disabilities Act of 1990, represents the culmination of years of political organizing and activism on the part of persons with disabilities.

In Christian communities consciousness about handicappism has slowly been raised through the insistence of members with disabilities, and their families and friends, that they ought to be able to participate fully in the life of the church. In 1975, the Fifth Assembly of the World Council of Churches in Nairobi resolved: "The Church cannot exemplify 'the full humanity revealed in Christ,' bear witness to the interdependence of humankind, or achieve unity in diversity if it continues to acquiesce in the social isolation of disabled persons and to deny them full participation in its life. The unity of the family of God is handicapped where these brothers and sisters are treated as objects of condescending charity. It is broken where they are left out."[1] More recently, many of the mainline churches have issued policy statements on the church's ministry to persons with disabilities and on the need for more inclusive forms of worship, architecture, and activities.[2]

Yet, although persons with disabilities have become more visible in society, and although people in and outside the Christian community are beginning to recognize handicappism as a form of discrimination just as unacceptable as racism and sexism, the problem persists: persons with disabilities do not enjoy the same rights and privileges as their "able-bodied" neighbors.

Presenting the Doctrine

The doctrine of creation has been used for many purposes in the history of Christian thought. It has been invoked to repudiate metaphysical dualism, to affirm the inherent worth of the natural order, to assert the absolute sovereignty of God or otherwise to characterize the God of Christian faith, to establish the quality of relation between God and God's creation, to explain the origin of the world, and to give an etiology of human existence. In the modern world, and perhaps more prominently among Protestant than Roman Catholic theologians, the doctrine of creation has often been reduced to the last two of these options: cosmogony and etiology.

This narrow focus of the doctrine of creation on the question of origins should not be surprising, if for no other reason than that the biblical *locus classicus* for the doctrine falls in a

1. Geiko Müller-Fahrenholz, ed., *Partners in Life: The Handicapped and the Church*, Faith and Order Paper No. 89 (Geneva: World Council of Churches, 1979), 177.

2. See, for example, *That All May Enter: Responding to People with Disability Concerns* (Louisville: Offices of the General Assembly of the Presbyterian Church [U.S.A], 1989).

book with the title "Genesis." But at least two developments in modern theology further help to explain the contemporary preoccupation with the question of origins. First, the progress of biblical criticism in the eighteenth and nineteenth centuries raised the question: To what extent may biblical narratives be relied upon to present accurate and true accounts of historical events? The creation narratives of Genesis 1–3 have been subjected to this line of questioning in a variety of ways in the last two hundred years. Some theologians assume that the narratives do intend to give an account of the facts of creation, and thus they ask simply whether the account may be considered to be literally factual. Other theologians argue that the narratives should be taken as belonging to the genre of myth rather than chronicle. Yet even these theologians may question whether the mythical picture of creation given in Genesis is coherent with a particular scientific account of the origins of the universe and of biological life-forms. In short, the questions raised by critical approaches to the text of Scripture have encouraged theologians to focus on the question of origins when speaking about the doctrine of creation.

Second, with the rise of evolutionary biology in the nineteenth century, many Christian theologians were faced with a full frontal attack on the truth of Christianity itself. The doctrine of creation became the place for playing out the battle, even though other doctrines were equally threatened (as was, for example, theological anthropology). The questions posed by the new science were broader than those raised by historical criticism. Now theologians asked not only whether the Genesis narratives were reliable historical sources but also whether Christian beliefs about the kind of world we live in were truthful.

These two developments in modern theology have defined the agenda for the doctrine of creation for a very long time. Creationism, the doctrine that the Genesis narratives are reliable accounts of the origins of the world, is the subject of much theological writing—both for and against. And the dialogue between theology and the natural sciences has generated a huge literature.[3] I will argue, however, that this identification of the doctrine of creation with the question of origins is something of a modern aberration—a tendency that is neither faithful to Scripture and tradition nor helpful in describing the experience of believing Christians. Moreover, as we shall see below, this approach to the doctrine of creation presents particularly difficult problems for people with disabilities.

The patterns of thought and structures of belief that support handicappism are deeply ingrained in North American culture. Sadly, some experts in the field of disability and rehabilitation studies point to religious beliefs and theologies as prime ideological foundations for the suppression and marginalization of persons with disabilities.[4] In particular, the Christian doctrine of creation is often used to assert the notion of an originally "perfect" and "normal" world, beside which all impairment and disease are seen as evil deviations—the result of sin.

Must the doctrine of creation be so conceived? And are there other ways in which this fundamental Christian doctrine supports the marginalization of persons with disabilities? Or does the Christian tradition contain within itself a liberating view of the meaning of divine creation for human life in the world—a view that values the inherent worth of the environment and of all persons? These are the questions that we must attempt to address in this chapter. In the following section we will analyze the structures of belief that are used to justify discrimination against persons with disabilities. Next (in the section entitled "Analyz-

3. For an overview of the literature on creationism, see Roger E. Timm, "Scientific Creationism and Biblical Theology," in *Cosmos as Creation,* ed. Ted Peters (Nashville: Abingdon, 1989), 247–64. For a historical account of the dialogue between theology and the natural sciences, see John Hedley Brooke, *Science and Religion: Some Historical Perspectives* (Cambridge: Cambridge Univ. Press, 1991), and David C. Lindberg and Ronald L. Numbers, eds., *God and Nature: Historical Essays on the Encounter between Christianity and Science* (Berkeley: Univ. of California Press, 1986). Peters's volume *Cosmos as Creation* presents a good summary of the range of theological perspectives on the doctrine of creation and modern science.

4. See, for example, Myron G. Eisenberg, et al., eds., *Disabled People as Second-Class Citizens* (New York: Springer, 1982), 5–6, 10, 35.

ing the Doctrine") we will examine the ways in which Christian beliefs about creation have either supported or challenged the structures of discriminatory thinking. Finally, in the concluding section, we will attempt to reconstruct the doctrine in such a way as to address the problem of handicappism in North America on the eve of the twenty-first century.

ANALYZING THE PROBLEM AND THE DOCTRINE

Analyzing the Problem

One need not look long before discovering evidence of rampant handicappism in our culture. A startling article in the *Chicago Tribune* recounted the tale of what happened on the Northwestern University campus after one of the busy cafeterias hired a handicapped woman to check student identification cards at the entrance. The manager at first received quiet complaints: "You know we're all for hiring the handicapped, but she's very slow." But it was not long before the complaints were taken to the student newspaper in astonishing letters to the editor. One blamed the food service for hiring a "token" handicapped employee who was clearly unqualified and inefficient. Another letter suggested that "perhaps some people would like to train parakeets to perform . . . [the employee's job] as well."[5]

What are the structures of belief that allow for this kind of discriminatory discourse? Perhaps one of the most powerful is the tyranny of the "normal." We are a culture almost obsessed with assessing ourselves against standard measures, not only of physical growth and mental capacity but also of developmental stages and skills. Such measurement can serve useful purposes in diagnosing illness and in appropriately challenging people to learn and grow. But often assessment is used to force individuals

5. *Chicago Tribune,* Thursday, February 21, 1991, sec. 2, p. 1. Of course, no one will deny that the initial problem is that people are in a hurry and have a limited period of time in which to have lunch. But the emotive language used and the excessive anger expressed betray handicappism.

into categories that identify what is "normal" and to ostracize those who do not fit. It is precisely persons with disabilities who often suffer from this practice; they are identified, usually from birth, as abnormal people who will always need special help to overcome their "handicaps."[6]

The tyranny of the normal also appears in the fear of difference and intolerance of eccentricity. Not only people with disabilities but also people of color, women, and many other groups are seen as "the other"—something that is alien and dangerous. Even the eccentricities that might be seen as harmless expressions of individuality are rarely accepted in the broad mainstream of North American culture. To be accepted is to conform.[7]

Closely related to the solitary focus on normality is the myth of an original uniformity that preceded diversity. This myth has been powerfully reinforced by images from the Bible that have been significant in shaping North American consciousness. The myth of original uniformity is often invoked to explain why there is social or political turmoil in our culture. Consider, for example, recent debate about whether English should be the legally

6. One of the most difficult problems in writing on this subject is that of finding an appropriate and acceptable language for persons with disabilities. The word "handicap" is taken from the practice used in racing of equalizing the chances of winning by giving artificial advantages or imposing disadvantages on certain contestants. Therefore, a "handicap" is taken to be a disadvantage that makes achievement unusually difficult. "Disability" implies inability to do something because of physical or mental impairment or limitation. But to call *persons* "handicapped" or "disabled" is to reduce them to the particular disability they possess. "Handicapped," in any case, is a word laden with hidden assumptions. A particular disability, say blindness, does not necessarily make *any* achievement unusually difficult. Only in a society designed by and for those who can see will blindness be perceived automatically as a handicap. The currently favored expression "differently abled" well expresses that persons should not be reduced to their disabilities, but it also tends to discount the reality of the specific challenges faced by persons with disabilities. Disabilities to see, to hear, to walk, and so on, do exist, and they need to be acknowledged. But a person who cannot see is not a "disabled person," because he or she will have many other abilities that are potent and effective. It seems best, therefore, to speak of persons with disabilities rather than of "the disabled"; and it certainly is worth noting that the very word "handicapped" used to describe a person is an example of handicappism, in that it presupposes the superior value of a world defined by able-bodied persons. For a fuller discussion of this matter see Stewart D. Govig, *Strong at the Broken Places: Persons with Disabilities and the Church* (Louisville: Westminster/John Knox, 1989), 1–4, 120–21.

7. Paul Tillich's description of American culture as "democratic conformism" remains accurate on this point (*The Courage to Be* [New Haven: Yale Univ. Press, 1952], 103–12).

binding language of the United States or whether bilingualism is preferable. The proponents of an English-only policy often assert that it is the fault of recent immigrants that the question even arises. In the "good old days" everyone spoke English as a matter of course. This argument, whatever the merits of the position it is intended to support, simply fails to acknowledge the multilingualism of the North American continent from the very beginning of its European colonization; it owes more to the myth of original uniformity than to historical reality.

This myth functions in other subtle ways as well. For example, it paints the picture of the "typical" American—a construct used not only in informal speech and journalism but also in academic and scientific writing and research. This "typical" American has certain characteristics and behaviors, and deviation from these is taken as representative of "otherness." Perhaps the most striking recent example of this use of the myth of uniformity is the disclosure that the majority of research on cardiovascular disease has been performed on middle-aged white men. Even though this sample represents a relatively small segment of the society, the results of the research have been considered uniformly applicable. And the myth not only provides the most perfect subject of study (that is, the "original" or most basic North American person) but also sets the agenda for the questions or problems that will be investigated (that is, those of this "original" person—the middle-aged white male). Federal dollars are poured disproportionately into medical research on the health problems of this "typical" American, while the challenges of substantial portions of our population are ignored (for example, research on the prevention and treatment of breast cancer). These inequalities in medical research, of course, land us squarely in the midst of issues of classism, racism, and sexism. These, no less than handicappism, are often buttressed by the myth of original uniformity.

A third structure of belief that supports handicappism in North America is what might be called a "subjective idealism" in the moral realm. What I mean by this is the common assumption that what cannot be seen is not real and thus cannot be a problem (*esse est percipi*!). In passing the Americans with Disabilities Act of 1990, Congress estimated that forty-three million Americans had one disability or more. This is no small minority. In fact, estimates suggest that between 8 and 10 percent of the world population have disabilities.[8] Unfortunately for the citizens of this continent who have disabilities, however, the lack of accessible public space has rendered them invisible to many of their neighbors; and this invisibility has, in turn, functioned precisely to convince those neighbors that they do not exist, rather than to persuade them that people with disabilities are the victims of society's neglect.

A final structure of belief that supports handicappism is stigmatization. This can occur in relatively benign, as well as more aggressive, modes. The "kind" face of stigmatization is seen in patronizing attitudes and in excessive pity. The *person* is not seen—only the disability counts. And the disability is taken to be *very* disabling. The more malevolent form of stigmatization is seen in the blaming of persons with disabilities for their own and society's ills and in the avoidance of these persons as if their disabilities were contagious.[9]

Analyzing the Doctrine

For better or for worse, the doctrine of creation has customarily been developed from an exegesis of Genesis 1–2 and its sequel in chapter 3 (for in practice creation is almost never considered apart from the fall). Whether the narratives are taken to be literally true or whether they are regarded as myths, theologians throughout the history of Christian thought have used this story to derive certain principles about God and God's relationship to the world. What are some of these principles?

Perhaps most important is that God created the world *ex nihilo*. Ironically, much recent biblical scholarship maintains

8. Müller-Fahrenholz, ed., *Partners in Life*, 6–7.
9. Eisenberg et al., eds., *Disabled People*, 3–12.

that this concept cannot be derived from the biblical account of creation, where God is, rather, one who brings order from chaos.[10] Nevertheless, Christian theologians have insisted that God's creative activity is not like human creativity since God calls something into being from nothing. Thus, while everything that exists is ultimately dependent upon God, God is transcendently free of all God's creatures. And God does not share the status of "Creator" with another: God, the one God, is the source of all that is.[11]

Second, the Genesis narratives suggest that God's way of relating to the world is personal or at least person-like. God is represented as deliberating about what to create and in what order to create. Sharing the human characteristic of aesthetic sense, God takes delight in the created order and pronounces it "good." God is also presented as one who "walks" and "converses" with the human inhabitants of the Garden of Eden. All of these qualities are personal or person-like. Many theologians argue, therefore, that, despite the alleged difference between human and divine creativity, God must be "personal" in some sense. This is true even of theologians who candidly acknowledge the mythical, anthropomorphic quality of the Genesis narratives.

Third, it has been inferred from the story of creation in Genesis 1–2 that the creation is a completed act of God.[12] Of course few present-day theologians would say that the creation occurred in six twenty-four-hour days, as many premodern theologians

10. See Jon D. Levenson, *Creation and the Persistence of Evil: The Jewish Drama of Divine Omnipotence* (San Francisco: Harper and Row, 1988). Cf. Rosemary Radford Ruether, *Sexism and God-Talk: Toward a Feminist Theology* (Boston: Beacon, 1983), 72–92.

11. A powerful twentieth-century argument for the doctrine of *creatio ex nihilo* may be found in Langdon Gilkey, *Maker of Heaven and Earth: The Christian Doctrine of Creation in the Light of Modern Knowledge* (Garden City, N.Y.: Doubleday, 1959). But this doctrine is not without its critics in contemporary theology. See, for example, Michael Welker, "Was ist 'Schöpfung'? Genesis 1 und 2 neu gelesen," *Evangelische Theologie* 51 (1991): 208–24.

12. On this point, as well, contemporary biblical scholarship would demur; see Levenson, *Creation and the Persistence of Evil.* In addition, the generalization must be tempered by the recognition that the ancient notion of a *creatio continua* has also been significant in the history of Christian thought.

believed. But Christian theology has traditionally distinguished (and still does) between two divine activities in relation to the world: creation and providence. Creation is the act that got things going, so to speak, and providence is the activity that keeps the machinery running—the maintenance operation.[13] The work of creation, understood in this bifurcated scheme, is a completed work, while the doctrine of providence becomes, for many theologians, the way to ensure a continuing relationship between God and the world. For few Christian theologians could tolerate the idea of a God who sets the created order in motion and then withdraws to allow it to run according to its own inner principles.

Fourth, the story of the temptation and fall of the first humans, in Genesis 3, is often used to establish a causal link between sin and evil. Before the fall, it is argued, there was no evil. The created order was free from the flaws, both natural and social, that we term "evil." Harmony and bliss reigned supreme in the primordial paradise. But the sin of Adam and Eve changed all that: evil was introduced, not incidentally, but directly and intentionally by God as a punishment for sin. And in what does this evil consist? Death, first and foremost, followed closely by exhaustion in work and pain in childbirth. Theologians whose reading of the text is literal believe that there was a time when these seemingly natural realities were not a part of human existence. But even theologians who read the text as mythical argue that these evils are not a part of the structure of being but rather a distortion of it.[14] All human beings since the first human pair, then, are born too late, to a world grown weary with the results of sin. We can only mourn the loss of our original perfection.

13. A notable exception to this way of organizing the system of doctrine is Friedrich Schleiermacher, who argued that the doctrine of providence (or preservation) is the fundamental doctrine describing God's relation to the world and that the doctrine of creation is simply absorbed by it (*The Christian Faith,* trans. of the 2d German edition, ed. H. R. Mackintosh and J. S. Stewart [1928; reprint, Philadelphia: Fortress, 1976], §§33–39).

14. See, for example, Paul Tillich, *Systematic Theology* (Chicago: Univ. of Chicago Press, 1957), 2:29–59.

This brings us to a final inference drawn from the Genesis creation narratives: that is, that the world is profoundly in need of re-creation. The divine pronouncement of goodness was not permitted to stand without challenge: sin, and consequently evil, disrupted the brief period of innocence that the world and its first inhabitants enjoyed. But this distortion of goodness is also not the last word. Christian theologians have used the doctrine of creation, then, as a presupposition of the doctrine of redemption. Creation sets up the conditions for the possibility of the new creation, secured by the reconciling work of Jesus Christ. The doctrine of creation presents the relationship between God and the created order that is presupposed by the doctrine of reconciliation.

Now we must ask what these five very common theological principles drawn from the Genesis narratives have to say to persons with disabilities. The idea of creation *ex nihilo* is, I believe, a helpful one in that it places all creatures in the same relationship to God: namely, that of absolute dependence. In this sense, the Christian doctrine of creation is nonhierarchical. Whatever "orders" of creation there may be, no individual part of the creation can claim ontological superiority. Only God exists *a se*. To this extent, the "able-bodied" cannot claim an elevated status in creation; nor can humans over animals, or animate over inanimate matter. Ultimately, all stand, qua creatures, in the same creaturely relation to God, and all partake of the rights and benefits that belong to creaturehood.

The concepts of divine personality and of creation as a finished act are perhaps best considered together. While there are good reasons for maintaining that God is in some respects person-like (for example, to avoid a mechanistic understanding of ultimate causes), there are also dangers that present problems, especially for persons with disabilities. As noted above, the doctrines involving God's relation to the world are traditionally separated into the rubrics "creation" and "providence." And just as the God of creation is seen as person-like, so also the God is who providentially sustains the world. This means, among other things, that God consciously deliberates about what to do and when to do it. Thus, natural phenomena, such as floods or droughts, famines, blizzards, plagues, and birth defects, may all be said to be the results of ad hoc divine deliberation. God "decides" to do this or that, now or later, here or there. For the person with a disability, this inevitably raises the question of theodicy: Why did a good and omnipotent God choose to do this thing rather than another? And why did God do it to me?[15]

The problem is further complicated by the view of creation as a finished act. The original creation was good, but sin introduced evil into the system. Now the fact that evil is permitted to persist in the created order is, according to this view of divine causality, surely also the result of divine deliberation. The "original perfection" of the created order is lost, and we can only look back wistfully to what might have been. Although we have no experiential knowledge of a world without disability, the view of creation as finished act invites the view that disability is not a part of the essence of God's creation but rather a perversion of it. Disability, therefore, is either willed or allowed by God, not as a part of the original good plan of creation but rather as the punishment for sinful deeds: disabilities are necessarily evils.

This leads us, of course, to the fourth principle derived from the Genesis narratives: the connection between sin and evil. This is perhaps the most dangerous territory for persons with disabilities, for their disabilities, as we have just seen, are commonly regarded as evils introduced by the fall. Before considering the connection of sin and evil, however, let us look first at the understanding of evil presented in Genesis 3. Pain, exhaustion, and death are seen as the primary evils. But are these things always evils? Must we, that is, assign them no positive, natural function but see them only as divine penalties? Does not pain help a per-

15. For more on problems with the notion of divine personality, see J. M. E. McTaggart, *Some Dogmas of Religion* (London: Edward Arnold, 1906), 186–220, which remains one of the best discussions of this subject.

son to attend to his or her injuries, rather than to ignore them? And does not exhaustion force otherwise driven people to rest? And what of death? Could it not be the height of human presumption to assume that we are not like other living things, for which death is a part of life? Granted there are forms of pain and exhaustion that seem purposeless, and death seems at some times more cruel than at others. But the restrictive definition of evil derived from Genesis 3 is at lcast open to question.

Now the issue of whether disabilities can be defined as evils in themselves is similarly open to debate. While I do not discount the suffering experienced by persons with disabilities, I do wish to question why we automatically define disability as evil. Human beings are an amalgam of thousands of abilities, and each of us has different abilities in different degrees. Often the limitation of abilities in one area contributes to the excellence of abilities in another. Is this perhaps a part of the infinite variety of human life intended and proclaimed good by the deity?[16] If one considers human beings in this way, it is difficult to imagine what would be the definition of a "perfectly normal" human person.

If, nevertheless, we allow that some disabilities are in some sense evils, what of the connection traditionally made with sin? Clearly, much of the stigmatization suffered by persons with disabilities stems from the notion that disability is the punishment for sin. Jesus encounters this problem in the disciples' question regarding the man born blind (John 9:2): Who sinned, this man or his parents? The present-day version of this story is played out in the maternity ward of many a modern hospital: What did the mother do, or what did she ingest, during her pregnancy to make the baby this way? Sometimes, of course, the question is entirely

16. Many persons with disabilities will testify that they have acquired new and important skills precisely because of their disabilities. For an interesting instance of this kind, see Viktor E. Frankl, *Man's Search for Meaning: An Introduction to Logotherapy,* 3d ed. (New York: Simon and Schuster, 1984), 147–48. In fact, some persons with disabilities argue that the special skills they acquire as a result of their identities outweigh any supposed "disadvantage" they may be assumed to be burdened with. See, for example, the interesting discussion of the Deaf Culture Movement in Edward Dolnick, "Deafness as Culture," *Atlantic Monthly* 272 (September 1993): 37–53.

appropriate, but just as often it expresses what Jesus saw as a false habit of mind (cf. also Luke 13:4). Even the way in which many people avoid persons with disabilities betrays their deep-seated horror at something gone terribly wrong. Seeing a person with a disability calls to mind both one's own vulnerability and one's own culpability. The traditional conception of the connection between sin and evil is particularly problematic for the way in which others see persons with disabilities.

Finally, the notion that the world is in need of re-creation may, at least, be more helpful on the question of handicappism, provided that re-creation is not understood as *merely* the restoration of an original ideal. Re-creation can be seen to stand in tension with the notion of creation as finished act insofar as it suggests that God is not yet finished with the universe and its inhabitants. New developments, fresh insights, unexpected possibilities await the world. Does this mean that we can expect a world free from pain, exhaustion, and death? Perhaps. Does this mean that eventually there will be a world free of disability? Perhaps. We cannot see the telos because we are a part of the web of nature; but we can suspend our judgments about what is "normal" and "original" to this world in the expectation that God's creative work is making everything new. It seems to me that the "new creation" could be understood not in terms of restoration of the "old" order but as the fashioning of a new order in which pain, exhaustion, and death are inducements to a new understanding of community.

RECONSTRUCTING THE DOCTRINE AND ADDRESSING THE PROBLEM

Reconstructing the Doctrine

What must the doctrine of creation look like in order to avoid contributing to the problem of handicappism in North America? Within the limits of the present chapter we can only provide a brief outline of what the reconstruction might look like. In short, creation must not be taken to be about origins so much as about relationships.[17] Rather than giving an account of how the world came to be or how human beings came to be the kind of beings that they are, the doctrine of creation intends to define the order for which we are called to work while it is day (John 9:4). This just order (1) sees all humans as related to God as their source of being without reducing human diversity to some supposed original uniformity; (2) accepts a connection between sin and evil only as it applies to the entire web of the natural and social orders and refuses to atomize it as an exact and invariable rule in the life of the individual; (3) insists that right relationship with God is integrally connected to right relation to the entire web of created being; and (4) understands creation/providence, or God's work with the world, to be an ongoing process rather than a finished act.

Each of these points, I believe, not only helps to address the issue of handicappism but also retains or recovers the best of the Christian tradition. The first point captures the radical meaning of the doctrine of *creatio ex nihilo:* that in relation to God we are all alike God's creatures, even though we are all very different in relation to each other. The faithful response to this doctrine is an attitude of humility, in which we recognize that we are bound together with all other creatures in our utter dependence on God.

The second point acknowledges that there is often a connection between sin and evil but sees it on a structural, rather than a personal and individual, level. This approach does not exacerbate the theodicy question for the individual; it condemns the practice of stigmatizing or scapegoating those who suffer from evil.

The third point retains the idea that creation provides the vi-

17. See Janet Martin Soskice, "Creation and Relation," *Theology* 94 (1991): 31–39; cf. B. A. Gerrish, "Nature and the Theater of Redemption: Schleiermacher on Christian Dogmatics and the Creation Story," in *Continuing the Reformation: Essays on Modern Religious Thought* (Chicago: Univ. of Chicago Press, 1993), 196–216.

sion of a just order to be achieved by reconciliation. This just order includes not only humanity's relationship with God but also humans' relations with their fellows and with nature, as well as nature's own inner relations. Reconciliation, then, cannot by definition be otherworldly. It is precisely this world and this humanity that God is reconciling to Godself. And humans can participate in God's reconciling work insofar as they work to realize the vision of a just order in their own lives.

The fourth point recovers the biblical view of creation as process. God's work with the created order is ongoing, and perfection stands ahead of us as the telos of creation. The old dogmatic division of creation and providence, therefore, seems no longer helpful.

Addressing the Problem

When the doctrine of creation is constructed in the way I have outlined above, it can address the structures of belief that lead to handicappism. It undercuts the tyranny of the normal by questioning the very existence of a "normal" human being. Similarly, it deflates the myth of original uniformity. Creation is in process; if one wishes to project a concept of "original perfection," then one must see it in the future and not in the distant past. "Subjective idealism" in the moral realm is ruled out by the normative relations that the doctrine of creation establishes. Inattention to any of God's creatures is tantamount to inattention to the Creator: the neglect of neighbor or of the environment is rebellion against God.[18] Finally, the stigmatization of persons with disabilities cannot be supported by a doctrine of creation that refuses to atomize the sin/evil connection. The pressing moral issue is not to locate the blame for sin but to participate in God's act of taming

18. John Calvin says this well: "Therefore... let all readers know that they have with true faith apprehended what it is for God to be Creator of heaven and earth, if they first of all follow the universal rule, not to pass over in ungrateful thoughtlessness or forgetfulness those conspicuous powers which God shows forth in his creatures, and then learn so to apply it to themselves that their very hearts are touched" (*Institutes of the Christian Religion,* trans. Ford Lewis Battles, ed. John T. McNeill [Philadelphia: Westminster, 1977], 1.14.21 [p. 181]).

chaos, destroying evil, and reconciling the world to Godself. The new order that comes into existence through reconciliation is a community of interdependent persons, *all* of whom are differently abled: "For just as the body is one and has many members, and all the members of the body, though many, are one body, so it is with Christ. . . . God has so adjusted the body . . . that there may be no discord in the body, but that the members may have the same care for one another. If one member suffers, all suffer together; if one member is honored, all rejoice together" (1 Cor. 12:12, 24b-26).

SALLIE McFAGUE

6. HUMAN BEINGS, EMBODIMENT, AND OUR HOME THE EARTH

Traditional Christian theology, including North American theology, has not taken the body seriously: Christianity has focused on saving souls, not on ministering to bodies. And yet Christianity is the religion of the incarnation, the religion of embodiment, as proclaimed in its central doctrines of Christology (the Word made flesh), the Eucharist (the body and blood of Christ), and the church (the body of Christ). The refusal of Christianity to take seriously its own proclaimed incarnationalism—and even worse, its historical disparagement of bodies, especially the bodies of women, as well as the natural world—has contributed to our present ecological crisis.[1] Christian hierarchical dualism of spirit over flesh, male over female, and human beings over the natural world has been a factor in the Western utilitarian and imperialistic attitude toward the earth.[2] This attitude says: it is here for our use and subject to our control. To be sure, Christianity is not alone responsible for the deterioration and destruction of our planet, and there are traditions within Christianity that sup-

1. See the work of Margaret Miles, especially *Practicing Christianity: Critical Perspectives for an Embodied Spirituality* (New York: Crossroad, 1988), and *Carnal Knowing: Female Nakedness and Religious Meaning in the Christian West* (Boston: Beacon, 1989).

2. Lynn White in his famous essay entitled "The Historical Roots of Our Ecological Crisis" puts this case strongly, though others have qualified it (White's essay can be found in *Ecology and Life: Accepting Our Environmental Responsibility*, ed. Wesley Granberg-Michaelson [Waco, Tex.: Word, 1988]).

port the well-being of creation, but Christianity has not preached a gospel of embodiment, has not proposed an earthly anthropology, and has not taught us to think of our planet as our home.

It should do so—not only because our dying planet needs every helpful voice but also because as the religion of the incarnation, which proclaims that the *whole creation* is the theater of God's saving activity, its most basic goal ought to be the well-being of bodies of all sorts. It should insist on the cosmological context for doing theology, which is one of the classic contexts along with two others, the psychological and the political.[3] The cosmological context is the oldest and broadest one and is being revived in present-day ecological theology. In the last few hundred years, however, this context has been narrowed to the psychological, which focuses on the redemption of individual human beings. In the past few decades various liberation theologies have insisted on the broader political context in order to address the needs and well-being of oppressed groups of people. We need now to widen the circle still further to include all oppressed creatures as well as the deteriorating ecosystems that support all life-forms, including human ones. The gospel of Jesus is proclaimed to the oppressed, to the poor: in our time nature is oppressed, nature is the new poor.

Thus, justice and ecology issues join hands in a theology of embodiment. The focus is on bodies and their basic needs: food and water, shelter, companionship. An earthly theology, epitomized in the model of the world as God's body, claims that *bodies matter,* and whatever else salvation means, it starts with the needs of bodies, all the wonderful, various, strange, and beautiful bodies on our planet.[4] In this theology the needs of human bodies are central but not unique or absolute, for the entire creation,

3. For an analysis of these three contexts, see George S. Hendry, ed., *Theology of Nature* (Philadelphia: Westminster, 1980), chap. 1.

4. For a fuller treatment of this model see chap. 3 of my book *Models of God: Theology for an Ecological, Nuclear Age* (Minneapolis: Fortress, 1987), as well as *The Body of God: An Ecological Theology* (Minneapolis: Fortress, 1993).

the whole world, is in God's hand. All bodies live and move and have their being in the body of God—a model that radicalizes Christian incarnationalism. God is Emmanuel not only in Jesus of Nazareth but also in the flesh of our planet.

ANALYSIS: THE COMMON CREATION STORY AND OUR PLACE IN THE SCHEME OF THINGS

Turning toward Nature

What does a Christian embodiment theology say about the place of human beings? How does it change how we think about ourselves, other creatures, and the earth? A brief meditation on space will help us to answer this question. An embodiment theology is a theology of space and place. It is a theology that begins with the body, each and every body, which is the most basic, primary notion of space: each life-form is a body that occupies and needs space. A theology of embodiment takes space seriously, for the first thing bodies need is space to obtain the necessities to continue in existence—food, water, air. Space is not an empty notion from an ecological perspective ("empty space"), but a central one, for it means the basic world that each and every creature inhabits. Finding one's niche, one's space that will provide the necessities for life, is the primary struggle of all life-forms, including human ones.

Space is an earthy, physical, lowly category unlike time, which is a peculiarly human, often mental, and sometimes grand notion.[5] In Christian thought, space has often been connected with "pagan" fertility religions that are earthy and celebrate the rebirth of life in the spring after its wintry death. The eternal return of the earth's physical cycle is contrasted with the historical movement toward the eschatological fulfillment of creation in the kingdom of God, a fulfillment beyond earthly joys. In space

5. One of the few contemporary theologians to deal with space is Jürgen Moltmann. See chap. 6 of his *God in Creation: A New Theology of Creation and the Spirit of God* (San Francisco: Harper and Row, 1985).

versus time, the old dichotomy of nature versus history is played out. The dichotomy is certainly not absolute, for history takes place in nature, and nature itself has a history, as the common creation story clearly demonstrates; however, for the past several hundred years at least, the focus and preference of Western thought have been on history to the detriment of nature. The importance of time and history in relation to evolutionary development, both biological and cultural, can scarcely be overstated: we *are,* everything *is,* only as it has become and is becoming through the complex machinations of temporal development. However, since this essay deals with bodies and their most basic needs, it will focus on a neglected necessity for bodies: space. For us, now, space should become the primary category with which we think about ourselves and other life-forms. Let us look at a few reasons why this ought to be the case.

First, space is a leveling, democratic notion that places us on a par with all other life-forms. This is certainly not our only status, for as is becoming increasingly evident and as this essay will underscore, we are the self-conscious, responsible form of life on our planet and therefore have an awesome vocation to work for its well-being. But we need to begin our anthropology (who we are in the scheme of things) with the basics. The category of space reminds us not only that each and every life-form needs space for its own physical needs but also that we all exist together in one space, our finite planet. We are all enclosed together in the womb-like space of our spherical planet, a tiny part of God's body, but to us the indispensable space from which we all derive nourishment. Each and every different life-form needs its own particular space and habitat in which to grow and flourish. This includes, of course, human beings, who need not only food, water, and shelter but also loving families, education, medicine, meaningful work, and (some would say) music, art, and poetry. Spaces are specific and different for the billions of species on our planet; hence, the notion of space helps us to acknowledge both the basic need of all life-forms for space to satisfy their physical needs as well as the specific environments needed by each life-form, given their real differences. And yet all these differences and special needs must be satisfied within one overarching space, the body of our planet. We are united to one another through complex networks of interrelationship and interdependence, so that when one species overreaches its habitat, encroaching on that of others, sucking the available resources out of others' space, diminishment and death must occur at some point. This process (natural selection) has been going on since the beginning of the earth and has resulted in the rich, diverse planet we presently inhabit. The issue now, however, is whether one species, our own, has encroached so heavily on the space, the habitats, of other species that serious imbalance has occurred. As the dominant species for the last few thousand years, we have forgotten the primary reality of planetary space: it is limited, and therefore attention to the primacy of space for other life-forms entails a leveling move toward egalitarianism. We need to remember that at a basic level all life-forms are the same: all need a space for the basics of life.

The second reason we need to turn from a historical (temporal) to a natural (spatial) perspective is because space highlights the relationship between ecological and justice issues. The crisis facing our planet is, in a sense, a temporal one: How much time do we have left for preserving life in community? But the reason time matters is that we are misusing space. Theoretically, we have plenty of time, at least the five billion years of our sun's life, but we may have only a few hundred because of what we have done and continue to do to our plants, trees, water, and atmosphere. We are ruining the space, and when this occurs, justice issues emerge centrally and painfully. When good space—arable land with clean water and air, comfortable temperatures, and shade trees—becomes scarce, turf wars are inevitable. Wars have usually, and not just accidentally, been fought over land, for land is the bottom line. Without good land, none of the other goods of human existence is possible. Geography, often considered a trivial subject compared to more splendid history (the feats of the forefathers), may well be *the* subject of the twenty-first century. Where is the best land and who controls it? How much good space is left, and who is caring for it? Justice for those on the underside, whether these be human beings or other vulnerable species, has everything to do with space. In a theology of embodiment, space is the central category, for if justice is to be done to the many different kinds of bodies that comprise the planet, they must each have the space, the habitat, they need.

The third reason that we ought to focus on nature rather than history, on space rather than time, is that we need to realize that the earth is our home, that we belong here, that this is not only our space but our *place.* Christians have often not been allowed to feel at home on the earth, convinced after centuries of emphasis on otherworldliness that they belong somewhere else—in heaven or another world. That sojourner sensibility has faded with the rise of secularism, but it has not been replaced with a hearty embrace of the earth as our only and beloved home. Rather, many still feel, if not like aliens or tourists, at least like lords of the manor who inhabit the place but do not necessarily consider it their only, let alone beloved, home. Christian theologies as well as works of spirituality have not encouraged meditation on the beauty, preciousness, and vulnerability of the earth and its many creatures. The profound ascetic strain within the tradition that has feared too close association with human bodies has extended this to other animals and the body of the earth. But what if we were not only allowed but encouraged to love the earth? What if we saw the earth as part of the body of God, not as separate from God (who dwells elsewhere), but as the visible reality of the invisible God? What if we also saw this body as overlain by the body of the cosmic Christ, so that wherever we looked we would see bodies that are incorporated into the liberating, healing, inclusive love of God? Would we not then feel obliged to love the earth and all its many bodies? Would that not be the first duty of those who not only belong to the earth but know we belong to it? We *do* belong to the earth: it is not only our space but our place, our beloved home.

Our meditation on space and place has suggested that we keep our eyes on the earth as we begin our theological anthropology. An embodiment anthropology must start with who we are as earthly, physical creatures who have evolved over billions of years as pictured by postmodern science. This is a modest, humble beginning but one with enormous consequences for how we view both our status and our responsibilities. Reflections on our place in the scheme of things will provide clues to where we belong, our proper place, and hence what improper behavior might be. Thus we will look first at the place (space) of human beings, not primarily from a Christian or even a religious perspective, but from the broad parameters of the common creation story. Our reflections on our proper place and behavior, in light of contemporary science, will show that we have been *decentered* as the point and goal of creation. The paradigmatic Christian story will suggest that we have been *recentered* as God's partners in helping creation to grow and prosper in our tiny part of God's body. A new place and a new vocation have been given to us: these are informed both by contemporary science and by Christian faith, for they are grounded in the mundane and the physical but are shaped by a new calling that evolutionary science could never have envisioned—the calling to solidarity with all other creatures on earth, especially the vulnerable and needy ones.

Toward a Postmodern Theological Anthropology

The first step in a theological anthropology for our time is not to follow the clues from the Christic paradigm or even from the model of the universe as God's body, but to step backward and to ask, Who are we in the scheme of things as pictured by postmodern science? Who are we simply as creatures of planet Earth, quite apart from our religious traditions? That is not a question Christians have usually asked, believing that theological anthropology had little relationship with so-called secular views of human nature. Failing to ask that question, however, has often meant that Christian reflection on human existence has been "docetic": human beings come off as a little lower than the angels—not fully human. We have not been seen as mundane, as being of this earth, of the earth, earthy. Our place and duties have been defined primarily in relationship to God (First Great Commandment) and secondarily in relationship to other human beings (Second Great Commandment), but seldom in relationship to the earth, its creatures, and its care. A first, sobering step, therefore, is to look at ourselves from the perspective of the earth, rather than from that of the sky. The contemporary scientific picture of reality will by no means tell us all we need to know about ourselves, but it will give us a base in reality (as understood in our time), so that what we say about ourselves from the perspective of belonging to the body of God will be grounded, literally rooted, in the earth.

As we begin this task, let us briefly describe the central features of the postmodern scientific view of reality. At its heart is the common creation story.[6] In broad strokes, the story emerging from the various sciences claims that some fifteen billion years ago the universe began with a big bang that was infinitely hot and infinitely concentrated. This explosion eventually created

6. Over the past decade or so, a large number of books have appeared that were written for the educated layperson and that give various aspects of this story. Here are a few of them: Robert K. Adair, *The Great Design: Particles, Fields, and Creation* (New York: Oxford Univ. Press, 1987); John D. Barrow and Joseph Silk, *The Left Hand of Creation: The Origin and Evolution of the Expanding Universe* (New York: Basic Books, 1983); Marcia Bartusiak, *Thursday's Universe: A Report from the Frontier on the Origin, Nature and Destiny of the Universe* (Redmond, Wash.: Tempus, 1986); Paul Davies, *The Cosmic Blueprint: New Discoveries in Nature's Creative Ability to Order the Universe* (New York: Simon and Schuster, 1988); Freeman Dyson, *Infinite in All Directions* (New York: Simon and Schuster, 1988); George B. Field and Eric J. Chaisson, *The Invisible Universe: Probing the Frontiers of Astrophysics* (Boston: Birkhauser, 1985); Stephen Jay Gould, *Wonderful Life: The Burgess Shale and the Nature of History* (New York: Norton, 1989); other relevant writings include: Stephen Hawking, *A Brief History of Time: From the Big Bang to Black Holes* (New York: Bantam, 1980); Alan Lightman, *Ancient Light: Our Changing View of the Universe* (Cambridge, Mass.: Harvard Univ. Press, 1991); James Trefil, *The Moment of Creation: Big Bang Physics from before the First Millisecond to the Present Universe* (New York: Basic, 1983).

some hundred billion galaxies of which our galaxy, the Milky Way, is one, itself containing billions of stars including our sun and its planets. From this beginning came all that followed, so that everything is related, woven into a seamless network, with life gradually emerging after billions of years on our planet (and probably on others as well) and evolving into the marvelously complex and beautiful earth that is our home. All things living and all things not living are the products of the same primal explosion and evolutionary history and hence have been interrelated in an internal way right from the beginning. We are distant cousins to the stars and near relations to the oceans, plants, and all other living creatures on our planet.

We need to highlight several features of this story as we consider how it might help reformulate a postmodern theological anthropology, that is, who we are in the scheme of things. The world here is, first of all, the universe, beside which the traditional range of divine concern mainly with human subjects dwindles, to say the least. In this view, God would relate to the entire fifteen-billion-year history of the universe and all its entities and inhabitants, living and nonliving. On the clock of the universe, human existence appears a *few seconds* before midnight. This suggests, surely, that the whole show could scarcely have been put on for our benefit; our natural anthropocentrism is sobered, to put it mildly. Nevertheless, since it took fifteen billion years to evolve creatures as complex as human beings, the question arises as to our peculiar role in this story, especially in relation to our planet.

A second feature of the new picture is its story character: it is a historical narrative with a beginning, middle, and presumed end, unlike the Newtonian universe, which is static and deterministic. It is not a realm belonging to a king or an artifact made by an artist, but a changing, living, evolving event (with billions of smaller events making up its history). In our new cosmic story, time is irreversible, genuine novelty results through the interplay of chance and law, and the future is open. This is an unfinished universe, a dynamic universe, still in process. Other cosmologies, including mythic ones such as Genesis and even earlier scientific ones, have not been historical, for in them creation was finished. At the very least, this suggests that in our current picture God would be understood as a continuing Creator, but of equal importance, we human beings might be seen as partners in creation, as the self-conscious, reflexive part of the creation that could participate in furthering the process.

A third characteristic of the common creation story is the radical interrelatedness and interdependence of all aspects of it, a feature of utmost importance in the development of an ecological sensibility. It is one story, a common story, so that everything that is traces its ancestral roots within it, and the closer in time and space entities are, the closer they are related. The organic character of the universe in no sense, however, supports a leveling or simplifying direction, that is, a lack of individuation. Precisely the opposite is the case. Whether one turns to the macrocosm or the microcosm, what one sees is an incredibly complex, highly individuated variety of things, both living and nonliving. No two things, whether they be exploding stars or the veins on two maple leaves, are the same: individuality is not just a human phenomenon—it is a cosmic one. At the same time, however, the exploding stars and the veins on the leaves are related through their common origin and history. The implications of this feature of the universe for theological anthropology are immense. The common character of the story undercuts notions of human existence as separate from the natural, physical world; or of human individuality as the only form of individuality; or of human individuals existing apart from radical interdependence and interrelatedness with others of our own species, with other species, and with the ecosystem. Were this feature of the scientific picture to become a permanent and deep aspect of our sensibility, it would be the beginning of an evolutionary, ecological, theological anthropology that could have immense significance in transforming how we think about ourselves as well as our relations and responsibilities toward other human beings, other species, and our home, planet Earth.

A fourth feature is the multileveled character of the universe, from the flow of energy in subatomic reality to the incredibly complex set of levels that comprise a human being. One critical aspect of this complexification is increasing subjectivity or the ability to experience and feel. Whatever one might or might not want to say about subjectivity in atoms or rocks, it surely increases as one progresses to animals and its present culmination in human self-consciousness. This means that there is no absolute distinction between the living and the nonliving, for life is a type of organization, not an entity or substance. Thus, as Ian Barbour puts it, "[T]he chemical elements in your hand and in your brain were forged in the furnaces of the stars."[7] What is significant, however, for a theological anthropology is not only the continuity from the simplest events in the universe to the most complex but also their inverse dependency, which undercuts any sense of absolute superiority. That is, the so-called higher levels depend on the lower ones rather than vice versa. This is obviously the case with human beings and plants; the plants can do very nicely without us, in fact would do better, but we would quickly perish without them. But it is also the case with aspects of our earth that we have until recently taken for granted, such as clean air and water. This very important point needs to be underscored: *the higher and more complex the level, the more vulnerable it is and the more dependent upon the levels that support it.* For theological anthropology, this is a very sobering thought, especially for a tradition that has been accused of advising human beings to subdue and have dominion over all other created beings. It has profound implications for reconceiving the place of human beings in the scheme of things.

Finally, the common creation story is a public one, available to all who wish to learn about it. The full implications of other

7. Ian Barbour, "Creation and Cosmology," in *Cosmos as Creation: Theology and Science in Consonance,* ed. Ted Peters (Nashville: Abingdon, 1989), 147.

creation stories, the cosmogonies of the various world religions, tend to be limited to the adherents of those specific religions. Our present one is not so limited, for any person on the planet has potential access to it and simply as a human being is included in it. This common story is available to be remythologized in different ways by any and every religious tradition and hence is a place of meeting for the religions, whose conflicts in the past and present have often been the cause of immense suffering and bloodshed as belief is pitted against belief. Moreover, the common story itself can be enriched by various ancient organic creation stories. What this common story suggests is that our primary loyalty should be not to nation or religion, but to the earth and its Creator (albeit that Creator would be understood in different ways). We are members of the universe and citizens of planet Earth. Again, were that reality to sink into human consciousness all over the world, not only war among human beings but ecological destruction would have little support in reality. This is not to say that they would disappear, but those who continued in such practices would be living a lie, that is, living in a way out of keeping with reality as currently understood.

RECONSTRUCTION: SIN—THE REFUSAL TO ACCEPT OUR PLACE IN THE SCHEME OF THINGS

Who are we, then, according to the common creation story? According to the major characteristics of that story, human beings are radically other than what either the Christian tradition, especially since the Reformation, claims we are or what secular, modern culture allows. These two views differ in critical ways: the religious picture focuses on the importance of those human beings who accept Jesus Christ as savior, whereas the secular picture elevates individualism, consumerism, and technology. In both cases, the focus is on human beings, especially in terms of individual well-being. In light of the common creation story, however, this is a narrow vision indeed. Yet it is so profoundly a part of the post-Enlightenment consciousness that we, for the most part, accept it as natural, that is, as the proper order of things.

Decentering and Recentering Human Life

But, according to postmodern science, the religious/secular/modern picture of human reality is a lie, a very large and dangerous lie. According to the common creation story, we are not the center of things by any stretch of the imagination, although in a curious reversal, we are increasingly very important. That is, even as the sense of our insignificance deepens when we see our place in an unimaginably old and immense universe, nonetheless, at least on our tiny planet at this time, because of the wedding of science and technology, we are in a critically important position. We have the knowledge and power to destroy ourselves as well as many other species, *and* we have the knowledge and the power to help the process of the ongoing creation continue. This means, in a way unprecedented in the past, we are profoundly responsible.

The several characteristics of the common creation story we have highlighted suggest, then, a decentering and a recentering of human beings. From this story we learn that we are radically interrelated with and dependent on everything else in the universe and especially on our planet. We exist as individuals in a vast community of individuals within the ecosystem, each of which is related in intricate ways to all others in the community of life. We exist with all other human beings from other nations and religions within a common creation story that each of us can know about and identify with. The creation of which we are a part is an ongoing, dynamic story that we alone (we believe) understand and hence have the potential to help continue and thrive or let deteriorate through our destructive, greedy ways. Our position in this story is radically different than it is, for instance, in the king/realm story, one of the major models in Western religion. We are decentered as the only subjects of the king and recentered as those responsible for both knowing the common creation story and helping it to flourish. In this story we feel profoundly connected with all other forms of life, not in a romantic but in a realistic way. We *are* so connected, and hence we had better live as if we were. We feel deeply related, especially, to all other human beings, our closest relatives, and realize that together we need to learn to live responsibly and appropriately in our common home.

In light of this story it is obvious that the model of the human being seeking its own individual salvation, whether through spiritual or material means, is not only anachronistic to the postmodern sense of reality but dangerous. We need to think holistically and not just in terms of the well-being of human beings. We need to move beyond democracy to biocracy, seeing ourselves as one species among millions of other species on a planet that is our common home.[8] This is not the only context in which we need to view ourselves, but it is an important, neglected perspective. Our loyalty needs to move beyond family, nation, and even our own species to identify, in the broadest possible horizon, with all life: we *are* citizens of planet Earth.

We began our theological anthropology with the place of human beings as seen in the common creation story rather than as a reflection of divine reality, understood either from revelation or from fundamental theology. It is important to underscore that this is a modest thesis that is not directly concerned with the liberation and salvation of the outcast and the oppressed—in other words, with the heart of Christian faith, as I understand it. The focus has been on our empirical, cosmic setting as earthlings. This setting has been for the most part neglected in recent theology and needs to be recalled and reinterpreted. Christian theologians will want to say more and other things about who we are, but we need to begin with our planetary citizenship.

8. See Thomas Berry, *The Dream of the Earth* (San Francisco: Sierra Club Books, 1988), 161.

It is a modest thesis, but given the great differences between the understanding of our proper place in post-Reformation Christianity and the common creation story, theological reflection conducted in terms of the new story would have revolutionary results. Once the scales have fallen from our eyes, once we have seen and believed that reality is put together in such a fashion that we are profoundly united to and interdependent with all other beings, everything is changed. One sees the world differently, not anthropocentrically, not in a utilitarian way, not in terms of dualistic hierarchies, not in parochial terms. One has a sense of belonging to the earth, of having a place in it, and loving it more than one ever thought possible.

Theological anthropologies emerging out of this understanding of human being can and will vary greatly, given the tradition, social context, and kinds of oppression experienced by different communities and individuals. The context with which we are dealing is the broadest one possible—the human being as species. It is, nevertheless, but *one* context, not the only one. But were it to become a feature of theology for the planetary agenda, it would contribute some of the following notes: a focus on gratitude for the gift of life rather than a longing for eternal life; an end to dualistic hierarchies, including human beings over nature; an appreciation for the individuality of all things rather than the glorification of human individualism; a sense of radical interrelatedness and interdependence with all that exists; the acceptance of responsibility for other forms of life and the ecosystem, as guardians and partners of the planet; the acknowledgment that salvation is physical as well as spiritual and, hence, that sharing the basics of existence is a necessity; and finally the recognition that sin is the refusal to stay in our proper place—sin is, as it always has been understood in the Jewish and Christian traditions, living a lie.

A Deeper Understanding of Sin

The sense of place—proper and improper—is one of the most important insights that theological reconstruction can gain from the common creation story.[9] We need, then, to delve more deeply into the issue of sin. The common creation story helps us with this issue because it gives us a functional cosmology, a working cosmology. It gives us a way of understanding where we fit. It tells us that we belong and where we belong: it is both a welcoming word celebrating our grandeur as the most developed, complex creatures on our planet to date and a cautionary word reminding us that we belong in *a* place, not all places, on the earth. In the words of James Gustafson, human beings are thus reminded of "their awesome possibilities and their inexorable limitations."[10] The Genesis myth no longer functions for most people as a working cosmology, a framework providing a sense of both space and place, grandeur and groundedness, possibilities and limitations, for the conduct of daily living. The Genesis myth, rich and profound as it still can be shown to be, does not strike most people as a working model or construct within which the ordinary events and details of their lives can be understood. Moreover, the creation story that does function, at least implicitly, in Western culture is one heavy with otherworldly overtones, seeing human beings as resident aliens on the earth. In contrast, the common creation story orients human beings within this world, this planet, and therefore has credibility for many as soon as they first hear it. "So this is where I, we, fit, not as a little lower than the angels but as an inspirited body among other living bodies, one with some distinctive and mar-

9. The notions of "where we fit" and "proper place" in the scheme of things are *not* meant to support, in any fashion, cultural stereotypes of subservience and quietism, as when certain ethnic groups or children are told to "know their place" or "keep their place." Rather, the concept of limited space and a proper place for human beings vis-à-vis other species (as well as other members of our own species) carries the connotation of not taking more than one's share: the implication is of justice for all, not the subservience of some.

10. James Gustafson, *Theology and Ethics,* vol. 1, *Ethics from a Theocentric Perspective* (Chicago: Univ. of Chicago Press, 1983), 96–97.

velous characteristics and some genuine limitations. I am of the earth, a product of its ancient and awesome history, and I really and truly belong here. But I am only one among millions, now billions, of other human beings, who have a place, a space, on the earth. I am also a member of one species among millions, perhaps billions, of other species that need places on the earth. We are all, human beings and other species, inhabitants of the same space, planet Earth, and interdependent in intricate and inexorable ways. I feel a sense of comfort, of settledness, of belonging as I consider my place in this cosmology but also a sense of responsibility, for I know that I am a citizen of the planet. I have an expanded horizon as I reflect on my place in the common creation story: I belong not only to my immediate family or country or even my species, but also to the earth and all its lifeforms. I *do* belong to this whole. I know this now. The question is, Can I, will I, *live* as if I did? Will I accept my proper place in the scheme of things? Will *we*, the human beings of the planet, do so?"

This little meditation suggests that the common creation story, in giving us a functional cosmology, also gives us a grounded or earthly understanding of sin. One of the advantages of starting our reflections on human existence with our possibilities and limitations as seen in light of the common creation story is that it keeps them from being either overstated or spiritualized. In this story we are not a little lower than the angels, nor the only creatures made in the image of God: our particular form of grandeur is in relation to the earth and derived from it—we are the self-conscious, responsible creatures. Likewise, in the common creation story we are not sinners because we rebel against God or are unable to be sufficiently spiritual: our particular failing (closely related to our peculiar form of grandeur) is our unwillingness to stay in our place, to accept our proper limits so that other individuals in our own species, other individuals of other species, as well as other species in general can also have needed space. From the perspective of the common creation story, we gain a sober, realistic, mundane picture of ourselves: our grandeur is our role as responsible partners helping our planet prosper, and our sin is just plain old selfishness—wanting to have everything for ourselves.

What is the relation of this ecological view of sin to the classical Christian view? It both deepens and grounds it. The classical view can be summarized with the phrase "living a lie," living out of proper relations with God, self, and other beings. Sin, in the Hebrew and Christian traditions, is a relational notion, having to do with the perversion of fitting, appropriate attitudes and actions in relation to other beings and the source of all being. Sin is, therefore, thinking, feeling, and acting in ways contrary to reality, contrary to the proper, right relations among the beings and entities that constitute reality.

An autobiographical note might clarify the point. When I was first introduced to Christian theology as a college student, I recall being deeply impressed with its view of sin—it struck a chord of authenticity in me—while I remained unmoved by the various traditional interpretations of redemption. The classical understanding of sin focuses on wanting to be the center of things, and I already knew and knew deeply that longing. Augustine calls it "concupiscence," literally sexual desire, but more broadly it is wanting to have it all, whatever the all is—that is, sin is limitless greed. As a privileged member of the world's elite, I was an easy target for this view of sin. While as a female in the American 1950s I perhaps lacked an overbearing sense of my self-worth—or sin as pride—by class and race I fitted the pattern of the voracious Western appetite for more than my share: I was an "ecological" sinner. The Augustinian view, in focusing on the bloated self, the self that wants it all, the self that refuses to share, highlights the ecological dimension of sin. From this perspective, selfishness is the one-word definition of sin—at least for us First World types.[11]

11. To say that sin is selfishness does not entail claiming that righteousness is selfless-

The common creation story deepens and grounds this view of sin because it forces us, as a first step, to apply it to our relations with other members of our own species, other species, and the natural world that is our common home. It advises us to ask: What does selfishness mean in relation to other human beings? What does the refusal to share mean in relation to other animals? What does our unwillingness to stay in our proper place, our space, mean in relation to nature?

Us versus Us: Living a Lie in Relation to Other Human Beings

The evidence of disproportionate space and place of some human beings in contrast to others—the rich and poor within nations and between nations—is everywhere and growing.[12] If the most basic meaning of justice is fairness, then from an ecological point of view, justice means sharing the limited resources of our common space. From the perspective of the one home we all share, injustice is living a lie, living contrary to reality, pretending that all the space or the best space belongs to some so that they can live in lavish comfort and affluence, while others are denied even the barest necessities of physical existence. The disproportion here, epitomized in the billionaires versus the homeless, the standard of living of the First World versus that in the Third World, the swollen stomachs of starving people versus obesity in others, forces us to think concretely and physically about sin.

ness. Traditional understandings of sin as pride fail, as Valerie Saiving pointed out in her classic essay over thirty years ago, to acknowledge women's problem of a lack of self in our society ("The Human Situation: A Feminine View," in *Womanspirit Rising: A Feminist Reader,* ed. Carol P. Christ and Judith Plaskow [San Francisco: Harper and Row, 1979], 25–42).

12. "The global balance-sheet is sobering. Since the 1972 United Nations Conference on the Human Environment the gap in living standards between the world's rich and poor has steadily grown. Industrialized countries and some parts of the developing world have prospered, but a billion people live in absolute poverty. Per capita income in the world's 41 poorest countries is well below $300, a sharp contrast to the $14,500 average of developed market-economy countries. Some 70 per cent of the world's income is produced and consumed by 15 per cent of the population" (Foreword, *Notes to Speakers,* Earth Summit '92: The United Nations Conference on Environment and Development [New York: United Nations Department of Public Information, 1991]).

The common creation story deepens the classical view of right relations in regard to members of our own species: it suggests that loving the neighbor must be grounded in mundane issues of space, turf, habitat, land. Every human being needs an environment capable of supporting its sustenance and growth. While this might at first glance appear to be a minimalist view, reducing human beings to the physical level, it is precisely the minimum that those individuals and nations bloated with self, living the life of insatiable greed, refuse to recognize. It is far easier as well as less costly to one's own lifestyle to offer spiritual rather than material goods to the poor. The ecological view of sin refuses to raise its eyes above the minimalist view, insisting that justice among human beings means first of all adequate space for basic needs. It also means, for some, staying in their own proper, limited place.

The issue on which to focus when we consider justice versus ecological issues is not our species versus other species (the rights of humans versus the rights of other animals), but *some members* of our species versus other members. While it is certainly the case that the human population is too large and encroaches on the habitats of other species, lumping human beings all together as *the* ecological problem masks the profound justice issues within our own population. Those to whom this essay is addressed—we relatively well-off Westerners—need to admit that the first lie we live is in relation to others of our own kind. *The* ecological sin is the refusal of the haves to share space and land with the have-nots. It has been shown that human populations stabilize when the standard of living improves; hence, the problem is not only our gross numbers but also the disproportionate way in which space is controlled by some humans to the disadvantage of others. Over the long haul, stabilizing the human population at a sustainable level is primarily a justice issue between human beings. Thus, justice issues *within* the human species have a direct effect on environmental issues between our species and other species. Simply put, we need to do some housecleaning as a first step. Until we rectify gross injustices among human beings, in other words, begin our ecological work at home, we will have little chance of success abroad, that is, in relation to other species and the planet as a whole.

Us versus Them: Living a Lie in Relation to Other Animals

The ecological view of sin deepens when we realize that other animals, beside human ones, must have space, that they too have a place. While the model of the universe as God's body tells us that we are united with the physical bodies of all other animals, the common creation story gives detail and depth to this statement. While there are tens of billions of known kinds of organic molecules, only about fifty are used for the essential activities of life. Molecules are essentially identical in all plants and animals. "An oak tree and I are made of the same stuff. If you go back far enough, we have a common ancestor."[13] If some degree of intimacy is true of us and oak trees, it is astonishingly true of us and other animals. We not only *are* animals but also are genetically very similar to all other animals and only a fraction of difference away from those animals, the higher mammals, closest to us. And yet one would scarcely suspect this from the way animals are conventionally regarded as well as used in our culture. While most people now have or pretend to have a raised consciousness in regard to the needs of all human beings for the basic necessities of life, the same cannot be said for attitudes about other animals. This is not the place for a review of human use and misuse of animals as manifest in pleasure hunting, excessive meat eating, the fur trade, circuses and traditional zoos, vivisection, testing of cosmetics on animals, and so on.[14] But even listing a few of our more callous practices in regard to animals illustrates

13. Carl Sagan, *Cosmos* (New York: Random House, 1980), 34.

14. See Tom Regan, ed., *Animal Sacrifices: Religious Perspectives on the Uses of Animals in Science* (Philadelphia: Temple Univ. Press, 1986); Tom Regan, *The Case for Animal Rights* (Berkeley: Univ. of California Press, 1983); Carol J. Adams, *The Sexual Politics of Meat: A Feminist-Vegetarian Critical Theory* (New York: Continuum, 1991).

our degree of insensitivity to their needs, wishes, and feelings. In fact, it is by suppressing any thought that they might have needs, wishes, or feelings, in other words, that they are *anything like us* (or we like them—the more valid evolutionary comparison), that we can continue such practices with good or at least numbed consciences.

What does it mean to live a lie in relation to other animals? What is ecological sin in regard to them? The common creation story helps us answer this question most specifically by providing a realistic picture of who we are in relation to other animals, both our profound intimacy with them and our important differences from them. We recall that one of the special features of this story is the way both unity and diversity are understood: the interrelationship and interdependence of all living things *and* distinctive individuality and differences among living forms. The common creation story helps us to move into a new paradigm for responding to our fellow animals, one in which we appreciate the network of our interdependence with them as well as their real differences from us. In the conventional model, the model that views them as resources or means of recreation, as something to serve us or amuse us, we can appreciate neither their profound closeness nor our genuine differences: they are simply "other." The new paradigm, however, presses us into a much more complex, highly nuanced relationship with other animals, one that refuses either a sentimental fusion or an absolute separation. In this paradigm, we are neither "a species among species" nor "the crown of creation." Who, then, are we?

We are like other animals in complex ways; we are also different from them—and they from one another—in complex ways.[15] We have simplified our relationship with other animals by focusing on one human characteristic, a kind of rationality divorced

15. One highly interesting, provocative analysis of our relationship with other animals—and one to which I am indebted—is in the various writings of Mary Midgley. See *Animals and Why They Matter* (Athens: Univ. of Georgia Press, 1983); *Beast and Man: The Roots of Human Nature* (Ithaca, N.Y.: Cornell Univ. Press, 1978); *Evolution as a Religion: Strange Hopes and Stranger Fears* (London: Methuen, 1985).

from feeling, which has allowed us to put ourselves on top with other animals as inferior to us and radically different from us. The operating model here is the ladder, with rationality at the top and ourselves as its sole possessor. Everything that does not possess rationality is alien, including our own feelings and bodies as well as other animals, plant life, and the earth. But what if the evolutionary model were the bush rather than the ladder, a model much closer to what the common creation story tells us? A bush does not have a main trunk, a dominant direction of growth, or a top. There is no privileged place on a bush; rather, what a bush suggests is *diversity* (while at the same time interconnectedness and interdependence since all its parts are related and all are fed by a common root system). The bush model helps us to appreciate different kinds of excellence, each of which is an end in itself. In this model other animals are not defined by their *lack* of rationality. "Is there nothing to a giraffe except being a person *manqué*?"[16] Or the same point, asked positively: Would a dolphin think that we could swim, a dog be impressed with our sense of smell, or a migrating bird with our sense of direction?[17] We are profoundly and complexly united with other animals as well as profoundly and complexly different from them and they from each other.

Our most important difference is not perhaps our grand rationality but a more humbling trait, one that we share with young children and that the poets and artists among us retain into adulthood: our ability to wonder. We are the creatures who *know* that we know. Many creatures know many things; intelligence is not limited to human beings. But the ability to step back, to reflect on *that* we know and *what* we know—in other words, self-consciousness—may well be our peculiar speciality. As Annie Dillard notes, "[T]he point is that not only does time fly and . . . we die, but that in these reckless conditions we live at all, and are vouchsafed, for the duration of certain inexplicable

16. Midgley, *Animals and Why They Matter,* 358.
17. Ibid., 225ff.

moments, to know it."[18] To live at all and to know it: these are the roots of wonder. It is a wonder to be alive, but it is a deeper wonder to know it. Knowing that we know places special possibilities as well as special responsibilities on us. Self-consciousness is the basis of free will, imagination, choice, or whatever one calls that dimension of human beings making us capable of changing ourselves and our world. In relation to other animals, our ability to wonder, to step back and reflect on what we know, places us in a singular position: our place in the scheme of things may well be to exercise this ability. We are the ones, the only ones we believe, who know the story of life and the only ones who know that we know: the only ones capable of being filled with wonder, surprise, curiosity, and fascination by it. A first step, then, toward a healthy ecological sensibility may well be a return, via a second naïveté, to the wonder we had as children at the world, but a naïveté now informed by knowledge of and a sense of responsibility for our planet and its many life-forms.[19] We know that we know: we have a choice to act on behalf of the wonderful life that we are and that surrounds us.

Living a lie in relation to other animals, then, is pretending through numbed consciences that they are so totally unlike us that they do not need space, places, to eat and rest and raise their young, to run and fly and swim and do all the other wonderful things that each different one does so well. Living a lie in relation to them also means refusing to accept our special difference from them: our ability to know the common creation story that unites us all and that we alone can become partners in helping to continue.

18. Annie Dillard, *Pilgrim at Tinker Creek: A Mystical Excursion into the Natural World* (New York: Bantam, 1974), 81.

19. The phrase "second naïveté" is Paul Ricoeur's and refers to the possibility of returning to the most basic roots of our being by a conscious, informed route when intuitive acceptance found in our own youth and the youth of the human community is no longer possible for us.

Us versus It: Living a Lie in Relation to Nature

John Muir, the eminent American naturalist, wrote at the end of his life: "I only went out for a walk and finally concluded to stay until sundown, for going out, I discovered, was actually going in."[20] This is a summary statement of a lifelong conversion to the earth, the realization that one *belongs* to the earth. It is not natural for most of us to believe, let alone feel, that we belong to nature, to realize that by going out one is actually going in. Susan Griffin, poet and ecofeminist, eloquently expresses our complex in-and-out relationship with nature: "We know ourselves to be made from this earth. We know this earth is made from our bodies. For we see ourselves. And we are nature. We are nature seeing nature. We are nature with a concept of nature. Nature weeping. Nature speaking of nature to nature."[21] We are the self-conscious ones who can think about, weep for, and speak of nature, but we are also one in flesh and blood with nature. It is this dual awareness of both our responsibility for nature and our profound and complex unity with it that is the heart of the appropriate, indeed necessary, sensibility that we need to develop.

The proper balance of this dual awareness in relation to nature, specifically the earth, the land, may be even more difficult than in relation to other people and other animals, for we have a clearer notion of the ways we are both united to and distinct from them than we do with such things as oceans, plants, and land. For most Westerners the tendency is to objectify nature so totally that human beings are essentially distinct from it. One way to overcome this is to enlarge our sense of self—that is, what we include in our definition of who we are.[22] A narrow

20. As quoted by Bill Devall and George Sessions, *Deep Ecology: Living as if Nature Mattered* (Salt Lake City: Peregrine Smith, 1987), 205.

21. Susan Griffin, *Made from This Earth: An Anthology of Writings* (New York: Harper and Row, 1982), 343.

22. See analysis of this concept by Warwick Fox, *Toward a Transpersonal Ecology: Developing New Foundations for Environmentalism* (Boston: Shambhala, 1990), chap. 8.

self-definition includes only one's nearest and dearest: family and friends or, at most, one's tribe or nation. A broader self-definition takes in not only all people but also some of the higher or more interesting animals (at least the poster ones, such as baby seals, panda bears, and snowy egrets). But a cosmological or ecological self-definition acknowledges that we are part and parcel of everything on the planet, or, as Alan Watts puts it, "the world is your body."[23]

Only as we are able both to think and to feel this enlarged definition of self will we be able to begin to respond appropriately and responsibly to the crises facing our planet. We need to be radicalized into a new way of looking at the earth in which we are decentered as masters, as crown, as goal, and begin to feel empathy in an internal way for the sufferings of other species and even for the earth itself. As Aldo Leopold comments, "For one species to mourn the death of another is a new thing under the sun."[24] It is indeed new and requires an expanded self-identification, a sense that I care about another species in a way analogous to the way I care about those near and dear to me. I do not merely regret the loss, but I feel and weep for it. Can we also expand this sense of self to include ecosystems and even the planet? When we read of the pollution of the oceans or the destruction of rain forests, do we feel grief for the earth itself, for that beautiful blue-green living marvel of a planet spinning alone in space?

We are *a part* of the whole, and we need to internalize that insight as a first step toward living truthfully, rightly, on our planet. But we need more than a sense of oneness with the earth to live appropriately on it. An environmental ethic in regard to nature—the land, ecosystems, the planet—must be based on knowledge of and appreciation for the intrinsic and particular differences

23. As quoted in the introduction to J. Baird Callicott and Robert Ames, eds., *Nature in Asian Traditions of Thought: Essays in Environmental Philosophy* (Albany: State Univ. of New York Press, 1989), 62.

24. Aldo Leopold, *A Sand County Almanac and Sketches Here and There* (New York: Oxford Univ. Press, 1949), 110.

of various species, biotic regions, oceanic ecosystems, and so on. We need to learn about these differences and make them central in our interaction with the environment. A sense of oneness with the planet and all its life-forms is a necessary first step, but an *informed* sensibility is the prerequisite second step. Leopold is on the right track when he tells us that we need a "land ethic," an ethic toward the land that no longer sees it as mere property, entailing privileges but no responsibilities. A land ethic that aims "to preserve the integrity, stability, and beauty of the biotic community" is an example of living appropriately on the land, refusing to live the lie that we are the conquerors, the possessors, the masters of the earth.[25] A land ethic deals with the issue of space—the primary issue for an environmental anthropology—in its broadest and deepest context. *The* space, the ultimate space, as it were, that we *all* share is the land, oceans, and atmosphere that comprise the planet. The complex question facing us is how to share this space with justice and care for our own species, other species, and the ecosystems that support us all. How can we live appropriately and justly with others that inhabit this space, realizing that we have a place but not all places, that we need space but cannot have the whole space?

Our reflection on sin in three contexts—as living a lie in relation to other human beings, other animals, and nature—has highlighted space as a central category for an ecological anthropology. In each case, we have insisted that attention to *difference,* while at the same time acknowledging and *feeling* our profound unity with these others, is central.

PRAXIS: A NEW PLACE FOR HUMANITY

A new way of being in the world begins to emerge from our reflections on our place in the scheme of things as pictured by the common creation story. We have been decentered as the point

25. Ibid., 224–25.

and goal of evolutionary history; hence, ecological sin means living as if we were the center, denying space and place to other human beings, other species, and the ecosystems of the planet. But that same history suggests, in the words of biologist Stephen Jay Gould, a recentering for us as "the stewards of life's continuity on earth."[26] We have arrived at these conclusions by looking at ourselves from the pedestrian, mundane, earth-up perspective, by seeing ourselves as part of the profound, intricate kind of unity that characterizes the contemporary organic model of reality as well as seeing the special sort of difference that distinguishes us from other beings on the planet. The new place for humanity is not only, however, a product of who we are in the common creation story; for Christians this also involves being members of God's body qualified by the liberating, healing, and inclusive love of Christ. This identification presses us beyond stewardship of life on earth to solidarity with all earth's creatures, especially the vulnerable. The Christic shape for humanity is built upon our evolutionary distinction but is also a radical intensification of it.

To be stewards of life's continuity on earth and partners with God in solidarity with the oppressed is an awesome vocation, a far higher status than being a little lower than the angels or subjects of a divine king or even the goal of evolutionary history. We now realize that our knowledge of the common creation story and where we fit into it means that we are responsible for taking evolution to its next step, one in which we will consciously bond with other human beings and other life-forms in ways that will create a sustainable, wholesome existence for the rich variety of beings on our planet. To be stewards of life on our planet and, even more, to side with the oppressed life-forms on earth is a sublime, formidable, and baffling vocation for mere human beings. It is not one we probably would have chosen, but it has been thrust upon us as the self-conscious ones and as Christians.

26. Stephen Jay Gould, *The Flamingo's Smile: Reflections in Natural History* (New York: Norton, 1985), 431.

We need to recall, however, that we are not the creators or redeemers of creation, only the stewards and partners of the Creator and savior. Christians believe that our efforts on behalf of the planet are not ours alone and that the source and power of life in the universe is working in and through us for the well-being of all creation, including our tiny bit of it. A reading from a lover of the planet, novelist Alice Walker, has given me courage as I think about our new vocation, and I share it in closing:

> Helped are those who love the Earth, their mother, and who willingly suffer that she may not die; in their grief over her pain they will weep rivers of blood, and in their joy in her lively response to love, they will converse with trees....
>
> Helped are those who find the courage to do at least one small thing each day to help the existence of another—plant, animal, river, human being. They shall be joined by a multitude of the timid.
>
> Helped are those who lose their fear of death; theirs is the power to envision the future in a blade of grass.
>
> Helped are those who love and actively support the diversity of life; they shall be secure in their differentness.
>
> Helped are those who *know*.[27]

We *do* know and we ask for help.

27. Alice Walker, "The Gospel according to Shug," in *The Temple of My Familiar* (New York: Simon and Schuster, 1989), 288–89.

SHARON D. WELCH

7. HUMAN BEINGS, WHITE SUPREMACY, AND RACIAL JUSTICE

White supremacy: harsh words, conjuring images of an ugly reality. The term "white supremacy" is most often used to refer to neo-Nazis or the Ku Klux Klan (KKK), hate groups who attack people who are racial and ethnic minorities. White supremacy is expressed in the alarming rise in acts of vandalism and personal attacks against racial and ethnic minorities in the United States and Europe. These extreme, blatant acts of hatred and violence deserve condemnation and require a careful scrutiny of the social and political climate that allows them to emerge.

The extreme acts of hatred perpetrated by neo-Nazis and members of the KKK do not exist in a vacuum. These violent acts are not the only manifestations of the assumption that white people are more deserving of cultural and political power than racial minorities. White supremacy lies behind a wide spectrum of actions, from uninformed indifference to the concerns of people of color, to willful, intentional acts of bigotry and racial discrimination.

In this essay I will be addressing white supremacy in its broadest forms. I will not examine blatant outbursts of racial violence but will address the more subtle, but no less damaging, manifestations of white supremacy in people who would not consider themselves racist, much less consciously and directly espouse doctrines of racial superiority.

All forms of white supremacy—the complex interaction of racism, bigotry, and prejudice—are worthy of attention by theologians. In choosing to focus on only one dimension of this complex of behaviors, and in focusing on one strata within even the phenomenon of white supremacy, I am making a methodological move that is central to theologies of liberation. Liberation theologians (feminist, black, Latin American, Asian) argue that reflection on the meaning of faith is most profound when based in particular contexts, the actual struggles of people of faith. Liberation theology is engaged theology and, as such, reflects complex and concrete theological, political, and cultural struggles. In one essay, it is impossible to do justice to the many dimensions of work for racial justice. I will, therefore, throughout this essay be making a series of moves from the general to the particular and concrete.

DIMENSIONS OF WHITE SUPREMACY

I have first chosen to examine the experiences of whites rather than the experiences of any of the groups who are the targets of racial exploitation. I am Euro-American and, as such, responsible for understanding the ways in which whites perpetuate racial injustice. I am also responsible for challenging patterns of racial oppression, personally and politically. In this work I am informed by the lives and work of those who are the targets of racial oppression. The effects of racism on people of color are deep and profoundly tragic. The drama of resistance to racism is equally deep and profoundly awe-inspiring. People of color are far more than victims of racism. The struggle for human dignity in the face of racial oppression is a complex story of politics, culture, and religion, all shaping a people's ability to survive and transform conditions of oppression. African-American, Asian-American, Hispanic, and Native American writers and theologians have explored the legacy of this century's long work for racial justice.[1] I have learned much from this work about the depth and hold of racism; I have learned much about the strength of the human spirit, our ability to resist and defy systems of oppression.

Here, I wish to explore the "spiritual malaise" of white supremacy, a malaise inextricably bound up with oppression, yet not at all identical to the phenomenon of being oppressed. Starhawk, in a critique of the men's movement, makes a helpful distinction between spiritual malaise and oppression:

> Oppression is what the slaves suffer; malaise is what happens to the slaveowners whose personalities are warped and whose essential humanity is necessarily undermined by their position. Malaise and oppression are both painful but they are not comparable. The necessary first step in the cure for what ails the slaveowner is to free the slaves.[2]

How can we understand the spiritual malaise of racism? What stands in the way of whites reaching for our full humanity by "freeing the slaves," by ending the systemic oppression of people of color? In order to understand how and why racism is maintained by whites, it is helpful to note the distinctions between prejudice, bigotry, racism, and white supremacy. These four terms are interrelated yet can be used to describe different aspects of the phenomenon of racial oppression.

Prejudice is most often used to refer to the act of erroneously generalizing about an individual or a group of people, assuming that one has significant information about a person's character, habits, and intelligence simply by seeing that person as a member

1. Ann Perry, *Harriet Tubman: Conductor on the Underground Railroad* (New York: Simon and Schuster, 1955); Cornel West, *Prophetic Fragments* (Grand Rapids: Eerdmans, 1988); Cornel West, *Prophesy Deliverance!* (Philadelphia: Westminster, 1982); Lewis Baldwin, *There Is a Balm in Gilead: The Cultural Roots of Martin Luther King, Jr.* (Minneapolis: Fortress, 1991); Katie G. Cannon, *Black Womanist Ethics* (Atlanta: Scholars Press, 1988); William R. Jones, *Is God a White Racist? A Preamble to Black Theology* (Garden City, N.Y.: Anchor, 1973); bell hooks, *Yearning: Race, Gender and Cultural Politics* (Boston: South End, 1990); Martin Luther King Jr., *Stride toward Freedom: The Montgomery Story* (New York: Harper and Row, 1958).

2. Starhawk, in *Women Respond to the Men's Movement: A Feminist Collection*, ed. Kay Leigh Hagan (San Francisco: HarperCollins, 1992), 29.

of a particular group. Prejudice refers to the attitudes of individuals. Prejudices are often negative, but even when seemingly positive ("Black women are strong"), they are grounded in a negative and dangerous reality: the oversimplification of a people's complex experience and the tendency to base perceptions on a narrow, often erroneous understanding of a people's history. The opposite of prejudice is informed and open-ended knowledge of other groups of people. Someone who is not prejudiced knows that many African-American women have exhibited great strength but also knows the costs of that strength and the difficulty of living up to a romanticized, idealized image.[3] Someone who is not prejudiced knows that the history of any group and the life of any individual within that group are too complex and multifaceted to support broad generalizations. As a result, our encounters with members of other groups are characterized by openness to learning more about a particular person or people.

Bigotry is an extreme form of prejudice. It may be expressed as a deep-seated hatred of people from different social groups. A person who is bigoted thinks that other groups are dangerous to society, inferior in ability and intelligence, and lacking in moral virtue. Bigotry may also be condescending rather than hateful, the paternalistic assumption that members of another group are less able and in need of our guidance and control ("We need to bring them up to our level of achievement"; or "They need us to take care of them"—the white man's burden).

Bigotry and prejudice both refer to the attitudes held by individuals about people in different groups. *Racism* refers to a structure of economic, political, social, and cultural discrimination and oppression. Prejudice plus collective, structural power equals racism.[4] Racism is carried by systems, by institutions,

3. Patricia Hill Collins, *Black Feminist Thought: Knowledge, Consciousness and the Politics of Empowerment* (New York: Routledge, 1991).

4. I first became aware of the distinctions between prejudice and racism and sexism through the teaching of Dorothy Haecker, director of women studies at the University of Missouri from 1982 to 1988. The facilitators of the Equity Institute also make the distinction. They explain the equation "Prejudice + Power = 'Ism' " as follows: "Oppres-

and by structures; it exceeds individual attitudes and intentions. American society is rife with racist structures: blacks are less likely to receive small-business loans, home mortgages, or even disability benefits. Even when educational qualifications are matched, blacks are less likely to be promoted to well-paying jobs with decision-making responsibilities; schools that are predominantly black are drastically underfunded; and blacks are more likely than whites to be beaten and even killed by police officers—the Rodney King case was no aberration.[5] Angela Davis describes one indicator of racism, the unemployment rates of black college graduates:

> Unemployment is three times higher among Black male college graduates than among white male college graduates. It is indeed scandalous that young Black college graduates today have an unemployment rate almost as high as that of white high-school dropouts. About one out of every four Black college graduates is unable to find a job.[6]

There are two key distinctions that follow from this definition of racism. First, once prejudice is entrenched in systems and institutions, people's actions may be part of maintaining that structure without their conscious or direct assent. Second, people who are the targets of racial discrimination may be prejudiced, but in the United States as it is now structured, they cannot be racist. In the United States, an individual who is African-American may be prejudiced but cannot be racist. African Americans lack the political, economic, and cultural power

sion [is] the systematic subjugation of a social group by a group with access to social power, or prejudice and power. Prejudice [is] a set of negative beliefs, generalized about a whole group of people. Social power [is] access and availability to resources needed to get what you want and influence others" ("Training of Trainers Intensive Program" (training manual, from a program in the San Francisco Bay Area, January 13–17, 1992, conducted by Equity Institute, p. 7).

5. "Between 1976 and 1987, the most recent period studied, some 1,800 black persons and about 3,000 whites were killed by law enforcement officers. So given their proportion of the population, black Americans have a three times greater chance than whites of dying form a policeman's bullet" (Andrew Hacker, *Two Nations: Black and White, Separate, Hostile and Unequal* [New York: Scribner's, 1992], 189).

6. Angela Davis, *Women, Culture, and Politics* (New York: Vintage, 1990), 181.

to systematically exclude whites from access to legislative, economic, or judicial power. While individuals and small groups of African Americans may have a degree of power in relation to some individuals who are white (an African-American supervisor and white employees, for instance), as a whole, white people still have control of the major institutions of our society.

White supremacy is the attitude or cultural ideology that lies behind racist structures and systems. I am working here with the definition of white supremacy developed by George Frederickson in his comparative study of the United States and South Africa:

> Few if any societies that are "multi-racial" in the sense that they include substantial diversities of physical type among their populations have been free from racial prejudice and discrimination. But white supremacy implies more than this. It suggests systematic and self-conscious efforts to make race or color a qualification for membership in the civil community.[7]

When white supremacy is fully developed, one finds the racist policies of "color bars, racial segregation, and restriction of meaningful citizenship rights."[8] Frederickson states that white supremacy in the United States and in South Africa has created "a kind of *Herrenvolk* society in which people of color, however numerous or acculturated they may be, are treated as permanent aliens or outsiders."[9]

A vivid example of white supremacy was the 1991 *Time* issue on the "browning of America."[10] Behind these concerns about the growing numbers of people of color is the assumption that African, Asian, and Hispanic Americans are somehow less American than Euro-Americans, many of whose ancestors came to North America far later than the ancestors of many African Americans and Hispanics.

7. George M. Frederickson, *White Supremacy: A Comparative Study in American and South African History* (New York: Oxford Univ. Press, 1981), xi.
8. Ibid.
9. Ibid., xi–xii.
10. "Whose America?" *Time,* July 8, 1991.

Racist structures reinforce and are sustained by the cultural matrix of white supremacy. Joel Kovel, in his 1970 study of racism, draws distinctions between several dimensions of white supremacy.[11] By examining two of his distinctions, we can gain a clearer, if not exhaustive, understanding of the depth of white supremacy and the power it exerts in American society.

In his work, Kovel uses the term "racism" for what others now call white supremacy. In my summary of his work, I will use the terminology being developed here, and in the direct quotations I will append the terms that are consistent with the differentiation between racism as systemic institutional practices and white supremacy as the ideology and attitudes that accompany those practices.

Kovel distinguishes between two types of white supremacy—dominative and aversive. He gives as an example of dominative white supremacy the leader of the Southern Populists, Tom Watson. Early in his political career, Watson supported the union of poor whites and poor blacks in a common struggle against economic exploitation. At the turn of the century, his views changed dramatically.

> Watson underwent a radical change in sentiment when the realignment of national forces at the turn of the century brought Jim Crow segregation to the South. He, who had been the black man's friend, could later say that the Negro simply had "no comprehension of virtue, honesty, truth, gratitude and principle." The

11. Joel Kovel, *White Racism: A Psychohistory* (New York: Pantheon, 1970), 30. In his study of white racism, Kovel argues for the existence of a further level of racial oppression, metaracism. He defines it as follows: "Racism, which began with the random oppression of another person, and moved from directly dominative, systematic control of his being, into abstracted averted use of his degradation, now passes beyond consciousness, holding only to its inner connections with the symbolic matrix. Metaracism is a distinct and very peculiar modern phenomenon. Racial degradation continues on a different plane, and through a different agency: those who participate in it are not racists—that is, they are not racially prejudiced—but metaracists, because they acquiesce in the larger cultural order which continues the work of racism" (pp. 211–12). In future work I will argue that metaracism is only temporary, a function of the isolation of whites from contact with significant numbers of racial minorities. When there is exposure to a number of minorities sufficient to challenge the power of naming and ordering reality (what Rosabeth Moss Kanter and others call the "tipping point"), whites often revert to "dominative" or "aversive" behaviors.

> South had to "lynch him occasionally, and flog him, now and then, to keep him from blaspheming the Almighty, by his conduct, on account of his smell and his color."[12]

Watson's irrational hatred of people with darker skin and his justification of barbaric acts of cruelty are not an aberration. Far too many whites were and are dominative white supremacists, ready to oppress black people directly, eager to resort to violence when threatened by people who are black.[13]

If whites escape the cultural formation of dominative white supremacy, we face the equally insidious complex of attitudes, beliefs, and mores of aversive white supremacy. According to Kovel, the aversive white supremacist oppresses black people "indirectly, through avoidance." When threatened by demands for justice by African Americans, the aversive white supremacist "turns away and walls himself [or herself] off."[14] Kovel gives as an example of aversive white supremacy the actions of Woodrow Wilson:

> Perhaps the most telling example of the other, remote, variant of reformer *cum* racist was Woodrow Wilson. The most morally pure of American leaders, certainly a far-seeing advocate of principled reform, Wilson stated in 1912 that he wished to see "justice done to the colored people in every matter; and not mere grudging justice, but justice executed with liberality and cordial good feeling." Yet Wilson was in the American mainstream that equated white virtue with power. . . . [A]t home, despite fine ideals, Wilson put the *coup de grace* to the misfortunes of black Americans by issuing an executive order which racially segregated the eating and toilet facilities of federal civil service workers. His final blow was to give Southern federal officials the right to discharge or downgrade without due process any black employee on any ground they saw fit. Needless to add, it was an opportunity well seized. And when a group of black leaders protested to the President, he, offended, sent them summarily from his office.[15]

12. Ibid., 31–32.
13. Ibid., 32.
14. Ibid., 30–31.
15. Ibid.

Three aspects of Kovel's definitions are especially important for theological analysis. Kovel writes that

> under the terms of racism [white supremacy], the white self was either swollen, as in dominative racism [white supremacy], or pure, as in its aversive form, while the black person was less than a person, less than a self: either a concrete body-thing, or as time went on, a no-thing.[16]

White selves: either arrogantly larger than life or pure, seemingly unsullied by complicity with structures of oppression; black selves: objectified, reduced, ignored in their full human complexity, dignity, and richness. Such are the terms of white supremacy.

RECONSTRUCTION

Human Equality: Affirmations from Liberation Theology

The central tenets of white supremacy, the confidence in the intrinsic superiority and right to cultural and political power of whites, stand in glaring contradiction to Christian affirmations of the fundamental worth and the intrinsic equality of all human beings in the eyes of God. As Joseph Hough writes, Christianity is "a faith that affirms the universal worth of human beings before an all-loving God."[17] From the strains of familiar Sunday school songs through theological statements to impassioned pleas for justice, Christians have long affirmed that all humans are equal in the sight of God. In Sunday school, countless children are taught to sing,

16. Ibid., 215.

17. Joseph C. Hough Jr., *Black Power and White Protestants: A Christian Response to the New Negro Pluralism* (New York: Oxford Univ. Press, 1968), 134. Hough emphasizes the need for power relations between blacks and whites to be changed in order for there to be racial justice; Christian ideals alone are insufficient: "I am not so pessimistic as to say that neither Christianity nor democratic ideals have had any part in the changing character of race relations in the United States.... Yet, the loyalty of Christians and other Americans to their ideals is not alone a sufficient basis for hope that change can really take place." Hough goes on to emphasize the need for a "better balance of power": "Hence, if there is to be any constructive attack made upon the caste barrier to justice in this country, it is necessary that a more equitable balance of power be achieved. That this is precisely what the new Negro strategy is attempting to do is already clear" (p. 135).

Jesus loves the little children...
red, brown, yellow, black and white,
they are precious in his sight.[18]

This clear affirmation of human equality has long led people to challenge the political and cultural expressions of white supremacy. Anna Julia Cooper, an African-American educator, was one of many late nineteenth- and early twentieth-century activists and writers who found in Christianity a basis for social critique and a vision of human equality.[19] Karen Baker Fletcher provides a succinct account of Cooper's convictions:

> Women, men, and persons across color lines of white, red, and black are created sacred, in the image of God. Cooper had a keen sense of the rights and dignity of the individual, and challenged white women to recognize individual human rights across racial lines.[20]

In the late twentieth century, feminist, black, and Latin American theologians base their critiques of unjust political structures on theological affirmations of human equality. Nathan Wright, for example, describes the theological mandate that propelled theologians and laity to affirm black power:

> Black power is a positive, creative concept.... [It] speaks to human dignity. It is a clear and uncompromising assertion of the worth of that human handiwork of God which had been systematically desecrated in the nation's culturally conditioned life.[21]

The National Committee of Black Churchmen, writing in 1969, described the challenge that a theological anthropology of human equality posed for blacks and for whites:

> [Black theology] is the affirmation of black humanity that emancipates black people from white racism, thus providing authentic

18. Anonymous, "Jesus Loves the Little Children," in *The Broadman Hymnal* (Nashville: Broadman, 1940).

19. See Karen Baker Fletcher, "A 'Singing Something': The Literature of Anna Julia Cooper as a Resource for a Theological Anthropology of Voice" (Ph.D. diss., Harvard Univ., August 1990).

20. Ibid., 226.

21. Nathan Wright, as cited by James Cone, *For My People: Black Theology and the Black Church* (Maryknoll, N.Y.: Orbis, 1984), 37.

> freedom for both white and black people. It affirms the humanity of white people in that it says no to the encroachment of white oppression.[22]

The theological challenge is clear: Christian faith has, at times, led to an affirmation of the humanity of all, emancipating those who have been denied the recognition of that humanity and challenging whites by freeing us from white supremacy, returning us to the limits of being human in relationship to other humans.

Liberation theologians—black, feminist, womanist, Asian, Asian-American, and Latin American—claim that the power of Christian faith is expressed in freedom from internalized oppression. In the past twenty years, these theologians have described the power of faith in moving people to resist forces of dehumanization. The practical and theoretical emphasis on emancipation, on living out the theological mandate of human equality, is clearly expressed in James Cone's affirmation of the work of Gustavo Gutiérrez. Cone agrees with Gutiérrez that the fundamental theological problem is not "the unbeliever as created by the European Enlightenment" but "the nonperson as created by European colonization and exploitation of the Third World."[23]

While theological affirmations of human dignity and equality have been effective in some degree in "emancipating black people from white racism," they have not been as effective in "say[ing] no to the encroachment of white oppression."[24] That is, many African Americans have taken the declaration of human equality in the eyes of God as a profound truth that sustains hope, propels activism, and creates havens of dignity and justice. While white racism has not been eradicated, African-American cultural and political life resounds with fierce affirmations of human worth and dignity.[25]

22. National Committee of Black Churchmen, "Black Theology" (June 13, 1969), cited by Cone, *For My People,* 53.

23. Cone, *For My People,* 70.

24. Ibid., 53.

25. See the following works: Cannon, *Black Womanist Ethics;* James Cone, *God of the Oppressed* (New York: Seabury, 1975); Garth Baker-Fletcher, *Somebodyness: Martin Luther King, Jr., and the Theory of Dignity* (Minneapolis: Fortress, 1993).

Has internalized racism been utterly vanquished? No. The struggle for self-affirmation and community empowerment is demanding and ongoing. Yet there are theological resources clearly at work in these struggles. James Cone describes, for example, the theology of hope embodied in African-American spirituals. This musical tradition emerged from political and religious struggle and has played a pivotal role in African-American spirituality and politics from the days of slavery, through the Civil Rights movement, and into present work for racial justice.[26]

Given the centrality of the spirituals, Cone raises a pointed question to white theologians: Why have they not seen this tradition and learned from it? Why has this tradition been ignored even in the theologies of hope?

> The songs of hope, the "Negro spirituals," seemed to be the logical places to turn for any North American theological reflection on hope. Why were they ignored by white North American theologians who claimed to be interested in applying the ideas of hope and promise to life in the United States? Their silence baffles me, because the spirituals played such a dominant role in the civil rights movement. Furthermore, many of these same theologians were present at the march on Washington and had marched with King in Selma, singing the same songs as everyone else, because of the empowerment and the courage they bestowed upon the marchers. Why, then, did they ignore them when they sat down at their seminary or university desks to reflect on hope? Were white theologians too blinded by their own racism to hear the truth of the gospel that was erupting from the struggles of the poor?[27]

What is "the truth of the gospel" that "erupts from the struggles of the poor"? And, more specifically, What are the truths that white theologians have failed to hear? When I listen to these spirituals, I find truths that are systematically excluded from serious theological work, truths that are, not coincidentally, central to work for racial justice.

26. See Theophus Smith's thorough discussion of the fusion of spirituality, art, and politics: Theophus H. Smith, "The Spirituality of Afro-American Traditions," in *Christian Spirituality: Post-Reformation and Modern,* ed. Louis Dupre and Don E. Saliers, in collaboration with John Meyendorff (New York: Crossroad, 1989).

27. Cone, *For My People,* 69.

There are no widely accepted theological justifications for white supremacy. The few who attempt to find such justifications, such as members of the KKK, are sharply criticized by other Christians. And yet the political and cultural life of the United States is rife with the assumptions of white supremacy. Even whites who are outraged by racism often find ourselves in complicity with systems of racism or find ourselves isolated, paralyzed, or confused in our work against structures of racial injustice.

For whites motivated by a theological anthropology of human dignity and equality, there still remain fundamental collective structures of action, of imagination, of interpersonal relationships that thwart our work for racial justice. These structures are more practical than conceptual, more spiritual than theological, a matter more of collective mores than individual intent. What is lacking is a thorough understanding of the practices that enable us to live out the theological mandate of human dignity and equality. And it is these practices, habits of prayer, worship, friendship, and politics, that are embodied in African-American spirituals.

The problem of white supremacy is a conceptual matter only insofar as theology has not expanded the range of its analysis to a thorough exploration of the dynamics involved in the practice of faith. Once theology fully takes up this challenge, which is the focus of theologies of liberation, resources for systematic thinking emerge, but most importantly, resources for acting are brought to the fore.

Human Equality: Western Theology's Ambiguous Affirmation

Liberation theologians stress the interaction between praxis and faith—the many ways in which faith propels us into action, the many ways in which action leads us to new understandings of our faith. The relation is not without its ambiguities. There are some cases in which theological symbols and concepts contribute to particular forms of oppression. There is, for example, a mutually reinforcing connection between exclusively or primarily masculine symbols for deity and patriarchal cultures.[28] In the case of white supremacy, however, the Christian tradition is forthright and unambiguous in its condemnation. Given a theological anthropology that posits the fundamental equality of human beings, there is no plausible religious justification for white supremacy.

The spiritual malaise of white supremacy is not primarily caused by faulty concepts or inadequate symbols. The Christian tradition and even the Enlightenment philosophical tradition contain resources for denouncing any forms of white supremacy. How do we account for the disparity then between ideals and practice? This disparity plagues Enlightenment philosophy as much as it does the Christian tradition. Enlightenment assertions of the fundamental equality of all human beings have coexisted with the oppression of women and people of color.[29] While there may be ways in which our notions of human equality could be refined, I find the primary error to be one of practice.

Patricia Williams writes of the alchemical fire that gives life to aspirations for justice and equal rights. Williams is a professor of law and is in dialogue with scholars critical of rights discourse. She argues that equal rights have not been fairly extended to women and people of color and cites such outrageous denials of equal rights as the Tuskegee syphilis experiment. From 1932 until 1972, doctors with the U.S. Public Health Service withheld treatment for syphilis from black men. Approximately six hundred men died.[30]

What went wrong in the Tuskegee experiment? Williams

28. For a detailed discussion of this point, see the following works: Mary Daly, *Beyond God the Father: Toward a Philosophy of Women's Liberation* (Boston: Beacon, 1973); Rosemary Radford Ruether, *Sexism and God-Talk: Toward a Feminist Theology* (Boston: Beacon, 1983); Sallie McFague, *Models of God: Theology for an Ecological, Nuclear Age* (Philadelphia: Fortress, 1987).

29. See Cornel West's discussion of the Enlightenment and racism in *Prophesy Deliverance!*

30. Patricia J. Williams, *The Alchemy of Race and Rights* (Cambridge, Mass.: Harvard Univ. Press, 1991), 161.

claims that the failure here is not one of theory but one of practice: "This country's worst historical moments have not been attributable to rights *assertion* but to a failure of rights commitment."[31]

What can sustain rights commitment? Williams writes of the centuries-long process of giving practical form to cherished ideals:

> To say that blacks never fully believed in rights is true. Yet it is also true that blacks believed in them so much and so hard that we gave them life where there was none before.... This was the resurrection of life from ashes four hundred years old. The making of something out of nothing took immense alchemical fire—the fusion of a whole nation and the kindling of several generations.... But if it took this long to breathe life into a form whose shape had already been forged by society, and which is therefore idealistically if not ideologically accessible, imagine how long the struggle would be without even that sense of definition, without the power of that familiar vision.[32]

What is the alchemical fire that can transform the "familiar visions" of human equality into impassioned work for social justice? What is the alchemy that can free whites from the soul-destroying distortions of supremacy? Do we need a reformulation of our theological doctrines of human agency, worth, and accountability? No. What we need is greater attention to practice, to the habits of living, and to the practices of faith that can give us the courage and vision to live out the mandates of faith. Patricia Williams and James Cone alike challenge whites to look at the practical resources that have enabled African Americans to take the vision of human equality and forge from it passionate work for social justice.

Patricia Williams offers an intoxicating, inspiring vision of a society committed to the extension of rights, not only to all people but to all of nature:

31. Ibid., 158.
32. Ibid., 163.

> In discarding rights altogether, one discards a symbol too deeply enmeshed in the psyche of the oppressed to lose without trauma and much resistance. Instead, society must *give* them away. Unlock them from reification by giving them to slaves. Give them to trees. Give them to cows. Give them to history. Give them to rivers and rocks. Give to all of society's objects and untouchables the rights of privacy, integrity, and self-assertion; give them distance and respect. Flood them with the animating spirit that rights mythology fires in this country's most oppressed psyches, and wash away the shrouds of inanimate-object status, so that we may say not that we own gold but that a luminous golden spirit owns us.[33]

To be owned by a "luminous golden spirit": Is this not the energy and power expressed in spirituals, in the passionate fusion of faith and work for political transformation?

PRAXIS

James Cone writes of the "empowerment and courage" that the spirituals bestowed upon those who worked for civil rights. It is precisely these qualities that are needed to sustain white attempts to overcome white supremacy. I will focus on three examples of the struggle of whites against white supremacy—college students at Berkeley, the contemporary women's movement, and whites working against racism in their workplaces—and will demonstrate the failure not of ideals but of practice in these, as in many other, movements for social change.

Troy Duster, a professor of sociology at the University of California at Berkeley, interviewed Berkeley students about what it takes to "make diversity a constructive experience."[34] The following scenario describes the conceptual and practical barriers to racial justice:

> What our hundreds of interviews showed is that there is a sharp difference between the ways black and white students feel about racial politics. . . . White students tend to arrive with an almost

33. Ibid., 164–65.

34. Troy Duster, "They're Taking Over! and Other Myths about Race on Campus," *Mother Jones*, September/October 1991, 30–33, 63–64.

> naive good will, as if they are saying, "I think I'll just go and have some diversity," while the music from *Peter and the Wolf* plays in the background. They expect to experience the "other" without conflict, without tension, without anything resembling bitterness or hostility. Meanwhile, many blacks arrive after being told in high school that Berkeley is a tough place, an alien environment, and that in order to survive, they should stick with other black people.
>
> Imagine then what happens in the first few weeks of the first semester. White students looking for diversity run into black students already sure that race is political.... They might say something offensive without knowing it and get called "racist," a word they use to mean prejudging a person because he or she is black. *Why do you call me racist? Hey, I'm willing to talk to you like an ordinary person.*
>
> But when black students use the term, they tend to aim it at a person they see participating in a larger institution that works against black people.[35]

Dunster points to a conceptual problem: white students think that racism is primarily a matter of individual prejudice and thus remain ignorant of racism as a system of discrimination and oppression. Behind the power of the conceptual "error" is a collective structure: the expectation of white students that racial justice can be achieved readily, easily, "without conflict, without tension, without anything resembling bitterness or hostility." Once conflict arises, many whites are shocked, unable to understand the depth of anger felt by many black students, unable to find the resources to work through these conflicts. What is missing are practices that can sustain whites through the bitter struggles needed to move beyond white supremacy.

Another case in point is the work for racial equality within the contemporary women's movement. Since the early 1980s, the Euro-American women's movement has been transformed by increased work with women of color. While women of color have a long history of working against racism and sexism, it is only recently that white women have begun to take seriously the

35. Ibid.

political and theoretical challenges posed by women of color.[36] Writings by women of color are being published in greater numbers and are becoming central to the scholarship and activism of white women.

The coalitions, academic and political, between white women and women of color are still in the process of formation. The work of creating and sustaining such coalitions is not easy. Many of the challenges faced by women throughout the United States are present in Papusa Molina's account of the work against racism that took place among feminists at the University of Iowa from 1982 until 1991. She describes the chaos that erupted when women of color first challenged white women:

> For the white women, it was time only for guilt. There was no understanding of our rage, no clear sense of what we were talking about. The closing session was chaotic.... A lot of tears and screaming and silencing and interrupting. The group disbanded after this conference. At the time, it seemed almost impossible that white women and women of color in Iowa City could ever be in the same room together, working for the same cause.[37]

Molina describes the chaos and conflicts that emerge even when people have a conceptual grasp not only of racism but also of the interaction between various forms of oppression.

> Some women could not come back. Maybe *el miedo* [fear] came in, maybe the anger, the guilt or pure pain kept them away. The ones who returned once again began the process of questioning, of learning, of talking honestly and of exercising listening skills. ... Once again, we needed to admit that we hadn't learned how to work together.... The fact that almost all of us were lesbians and/or feminists, with an intellectual understanding of racism, classism and homophobia didn't mean a damn thing. We were stuck.... We kept meeting each Monday, we kept reading, we kept arguing. It seems that at some intuitive level we knew that our

36. Elisabeth Spelman, *Inessential Woman: Problems of Exclusion in Feminist Thought* (Boston: Beacon, 1990); Angela Davis, *Women, Culture, and Politics;* bell hooks, *Yearning.*

37. Papusa Molina, "Recognizing, Accepting and Celebrating Our Differences," in *Making Face, Making Soul*, ed. Gloria Anzaldúa (San Francisco: Spinsters, 1990), 327.

> survival...depended on our ability to go beyond coalitions and form alliances.[38]

What does it take to form genuine alliances between white women and women of color? What does it take to dismantle the cultural habits of white supremacy that destroy such alliances? Gloria Anzaldúa points to the need, once again, for specific types of practice. In order to learn from and live through the conflicts inherent in undoing the habits of white supremacy, whites do need sustenance and reassurance, but from each other, not primarily from the people who have been victimized by those cultural patterns. Anzaldúa describes the distinctive pattern of whites turning from acknowledging the depth of oppression to a focus on their feelings and concerns:

> They [women of color] were eloquent in expressing their skepticism about making alliances with whites when most white women focused exclusively on their own feelings and needed reassurances, acceptance and validation from *mujeres-de-color.*[39]

Our ability to challenge white supremacy will be enhanced as we learn to support each other through the immensely painful yet essential work of seeing, without excuses and rationalization, the damage caused by racism. We can also support each other in the critical work of examining not only the personal but also the systemic manifestations of white supremacy. bell hooks describes this process—the move from a focus on exclusively personal concerns to an understanding of political structures.

> Early on, accusations that the issue of race was raised to deflect attention away from feminism, thereby undermining the movement, were common. Many white women felt that they were being admonished so that they would examine personal expressions of racism, and failed to link that interrogation of self with an understanding of the way white supremacy works as an institutionalized structure of domination. This meant that changes in

38. Ibid.

39. Gloria Anzaldúa, "Haciendo caras, una entrada," in *Making Face, Making Soul,* xx.

> behavior within the private sphere of personal relationships did not necessarily lead to a transformation of public interactions.[40]

From her work with women in Iowa, Molina also emphasizes the need "to work at the personal level, unlearning attitudes and behaviors of oppression; and at the institutional level, we needed to actively dismantle the structures which privileged some by excluding and silencing others."[41]

At the institutional level, far-reaching changes are needed, changes that do not occur easily or without resistance. Molina restates the imperative voiced by Angela Davis: "[W]e needed to dismantle . . . white people's organizations and recreate them with diversity at their core and people of color as their leaders."[42]

Developing new structures of leadership and power that reflect our rejection of white supremacy remains conflictual, chaotic, and difficult. The attempt to live out a clear theological and moral injunction—the fundamental equality and value of all people—leads into a crucible of political conflicts, personal struggles, and painful misunderstandings. Yet as Molina reminds us, this struggle is necessary not only for growth but also for our very survival.[43]

bell hooks provides a succinct account of what is at stake in feminists' work for racial equality—trying to *create* the sisterhood that feminists once assumed was a gift.

> Let us confess! Feminist belief that solidarity between women was possible waned in the wake of tensions around "difference" with the growing understanding that the concrete forces separating us could not be overcome by romantic evocations of woman bonding. Most women were not prepared to struggle for sisterhood, to work at it arduously and patiently. Now that we know better, we have the opportunity to start anew. We no longer have to continually do the difficult work of forcing one another to acknowledge the reality of racial difference and domination. Now we must speak of

40. bell hooks, "Feminism and Racism: The Struggle Continues," *Z Magazine*, July/August 1990, 41.
41. Molina, "Recognizing," 329.
42. Ibid.
43. Ibid., 327.

how that domination can be challenged and resisted. Now we can talk.[44]

Despite the partial success of some attempts to undo the habits of white supremacy, many white feminists are still afraid of being labeled as racist, fearing the conflicts that inevitably emerge when differences are highlighted instead of being repressed. The solution, however, to the paralysis of fear and ineptitude in working through conflicts is not a conceptual one. The problem is not primarily a matter of theological symbols or doctrines. We have the concepts already that invalidate the claims of white supremacy and undergird work for racial justice. According to western theology, all humans are equal: all humans are the children of God. Feminist, womanist, and mujerista theologians have taken this claim further. We proclaim that all women and men are equal and take this belief in equality as the foundation of our theological method. Since all women and men are seen as equal, the experiences of women, our experiences of suffering, joy, pain, and transformation, should be as central in the shaping of theology as are the experiences of men. To reach this point, a great deal of recovery work is required, a recovery of the experiences of all those who have been marginalized and excluded, women of all races and classes, poor and working-class men, and men of color.

The problem now is learning how to live through and with the conflicts that will continue to emerge as marginalized groups continue to find their voice. The answer to this problem can be found only in practice—the practice of politics, of community building, of worship.

The political agenda is vast. It includes ending patterns of discrimination in employment, health care, education, and environmental safety and protection. It is not easy to maintain courage and persist in political struggles of this magnitude. It is often hard for whites who find themselves beleaguered

44. hooks, "Feminism and Racism," 43.

on all sides: working to end racial injustice but in that very struggle being challenged by people of color to recognize and change the habits, attitudes, and behaviors that come from white supremacy.

Let me give an example—five white people, all relatives at a family reunion, sitting on a porch in Tennessee on a summer evening talking, without posturing, of the pain each felt in their work against racism. A high school teacher spoke of her weariness of working for equal funding for education for black children, of working for a curriculum that did justice to the costs of racism and to the richness and complexity of the lives of people of color. Despite all her work, she was depressed, tired, and dispirited, wondering if it was worth it to keep struggling. Another woman, the director of a museum, expressed her loneliness and despair—she was an outcast in the eyes of many whites because of her work for racial equality and yet still was criticized by some blacks who wanted her to do more and who saw elements of white supremacy still present in her attitudes and behaviors. She did not think she could continue being the object of criticism on all sides. Another man, a county attorney, also expressed his despair and his fear that racism was as bad as ever.

What did these despairing, weary people need? A reminder of the need for racial equality? An indictment of the indulgence of their despair in light of the great suffering white supremacy causes for people of color? No. What was needed was neither theological affirmations nor political analyses. These people knew the theological and political reasons for work for racial justice. They were soul-sick from the cost of living that political analysis, of living out that faith. The solution to our malaise is not more analysis but participation in a community of practice in which political work against white supremacy is sustained by acts of worship that feed the soul.

What was needed that calm evening was comfort, not the comfort that elides suffering and injustice, that promises an easy resolution to complex problems, but a comfort, a sustenance, that comes from acknowledging the immensity of injustice and the cost of working against it. Such comfort is expressed well in music, in the resonance of spirituals that embody hope for justice and the costs of injustice, and in voices and instruments joining together, manifesting the beauty of human community.

Take as an example the spiritual "Balm in Gilead," which is referred to often in the writings of African Americans. Sarah Lawrence Lightfoot uses it as the title of her biography of her mother; Lewis Baldwin uses it as the title of his study of the theology and work of Dr. Martin Luther King Jr.[45]

The words of the spiritual are moving in themselves, but the full power can be experienced only in the act of people singing the spiritual together. It may be helpful to examine some of the words alone:

There is a balm in Gilead
To make the wounded whole.
There is a balm in Gilead
To heal the sin-sick soul.

Sometimes I get discouraged
And think my work's in vain.
Then comes the holy spirit
and heals me once again.

There is a balm in Gilead.[46]

This spiritual contains a forthright acknowledgment of despair and fear, the experience of working without success, without sufficient support. In this spiritual there is also a far from naive affirmation of the sustenance that does come even in the midst of despair. James Cone describes the theological and political power of spirituals and African-American spirituality as follows:

> The spirituals and the blues, gospel music and jazz, have revealed to many the depth of our spiritual and cultural will to survive amid

45. Sarah Lawrence Lightfoot, *Balm in Gilead: Journey of a Healer* (Boston: Addison and Wesley, 1989); Lewis Baldwin, *There Is a Balm in Gilead.*

46. "There Is a Balm in Gilead," North American spiritual. For a version of the text see Erik Routley, ed., *Rejoice in the Lord: A Hymn Companion to the Scriptures* (Grand Rapids: Eerdmans, 1985).

> situations of extreme oppression, thereby encouraging them not to lose hope but to keep on fighting until freedom comes.[47]

The creative healing power of African-American spirituality is clearly exemplified in the spiritual "Balm in Gilead." The power of this spiritual and the resources it embodies for work for justice are highlighted as we contrast the hymn with the scriptural passage on which it is based, Jer. 8:18-22. In this passage the writer of Jeremiah sees the ruin of the kingdom of Judah and the vanity of resistance to the Chaldean invader. The mood is one of utter despair because of the complete moral and spiritual corruption of the nation of Judah. The words are those of mourning and pain:

> My grief is beyond healing,
> my heart is sick within me....
>
> Is there no balm in Gilead?
> Is there no physician there?

The prophet goes on to decry the brokenness of the bonds of human trust and sustenance:

> Let every one beware of his neighbor,
> and put no trust in any brother....
> Every one deceives his neighbor,
> and no one speaks the truth....
> Heaping oppression upon oppression, and deceit upon deceit,
> they refuse to know me, says the Lord. (9:4-6)

From these passages of despair and longing, African Americans have crafted a spiritual of honesty, depth, and hope. To the prophet's mournful cry, the answer resounds: there is a balm in Gilead to make the wounded whole!

In this spiritual and the life-transforming affirmation of hope in spite of struggle and defeat, I find a clear example of the theological insight that is abundant in African-American spirituality. The communal performance of this spiritual, like that of so

47. Cone, *For My People,* 191.

many others, embodies a theological anthropology that allows us to withstand the conflict and pain that attends our efforts to create human networks of equality and justice. James Cone is right. The spirituals are "the logical places to turn" for our theological reflection on hope in the struggle against white supremacy. As Cone states, these songs "bestow empowerment and courage." People experience moments of solidarity when singing them. They experience connection with other people in an unambiguous declaration of the costs of injustice, the difficulty of struggle, the beauty and worth of human life that propel our struggle, and the heartfelt hope for strength in the challenges yet to come.

In conclusion, I return to Cone's pointed question: Were white theologians limited by their own racism? Yes. Given the power of white supremacy even in the assumptions of those white people working for racial justice, it was impossible to see that the tools required to dismantle the intricate machinery of racism are the tools of the oppressed. The tools of political and theological analysis can take us only so far. They can bring us to know, intellectually, the contours and costs of oppression. They cannot sustain us in the work of building a just society.

Theologians of liberation highlight the centrality of practice for the life of faith *and* as the source and criteria of theological reflection. We who are white have the theological and political resources to denounce white supremacy. We are only beginning to live out the political and spiritual practices that can rid us of supremacist assumptions. We are only beginning to live out the political and spiritual practices that can remedy the sickness in American society caused by white supremacy. What we need are practices of communal worship that embody, through music, movement, and prayer, the pain of living out the theological mandates of justice.

WALTER LOWE

8. MILITARISM, EVIL, AND THE REIGN OF GOD

Historians often speak of the twentieth century as beginning not in 1900 but in 1914. Those living before the outbreak of World War I seem to inhabit another world from that of mustard gas and trench warfare. To speak of the casualties of only one country: "[I]n these holes and ditches extending for ninety miles, continually, even in the quietest times, some 7,000 British men and officers were killed and wounded daily, just as a matter of course. 'Wastage,' the Staff called it."[1] Unimaginable. Yet that was only the beginning. "The twentieth century is probably the most war-ridden of all in Western history; at least 100 million human beings lost their lives in war—on average 3,500 a day."[2]

The term "militarism" is one feeble effort to wrap one's mind around this. It came into common usage during the arms buildup of the late nineteenth century, as people sensed the way things were headed. Many of these critics were not strict pacifists; they were not opposed to armies as such. They did not reject the *military* as such. Thus the need for another word to convey their

1. Paul Fussell, *The Great War and Modern Memory* (London: Oxford Univ. Press, 1975), 41. Works cited in the present essay are not highly technical and are offered as suggestions for further reading. For his valuable guidance, I wish especially to thank Dan Zins of the Atlanta College of Art.

2. Jan Oberg, "The New International Military Order: A Threat to Human Security," in *Problems of Contemporary Militarism*, ed. Asjorn Eide and Marek Thee (New York: St. Martin's, 1980), 47.

sense that, for whatever reason, things were slipping out of control. The amassing of arms was a process feeding on itself. The "means of security" were making the world more dangerous. That heedless, self-defeating pattern is what people meant to condemn in speaking of "militar*ism.*" Today, living with nuclear proliferation and so-called "ethnic cleansing," we use the term to glean what insight we can.

Yet those of us who view militarism from North America remain insulated from the experience. Thanks largely to the good luck of geographical isolation, we have in this century been spared the experience of invasion and devastation. Thus, probing militarism in the North American context, we confront a disturbing anomaly. We live within a "permanent war economy"; we are the largest producer of weapons of destruction in the entire world.[3] Yet the actual use of the weapons, the experience of their destructiveness, is something that happens elsewhere, "over there." For the most part, we know these weapons of destruction only as something *positive!* They strengthen our country, they fuel our economy. Despite our technological sophistication—or rather because of it—we remain blissfully naive about the pain they cause. We are distanced, disconnected. Jonathon Schell put it dramatically during the Persian Gulf War:

> We Americans, with our complete mastery of the air, wage war in three dimensions against a foe trapped, like the creatures in certain geometrical games, in two dimensions. The result is that the killing and the dying have come apart. In this war so far and for the most part, we kill and they die, as if a race of gods were making war against a race of human beings.[4]

High-tech destruction creates a sense of exaltation; we seem god-like, more than human. In theological language, this is the temptation of *pride.* Not all pride is sinful. But it is sinful when human beings seek to take the place of God; and when, thinking

3. *The Defense Monitor* 20, no. 4 (1991).
4. Jonathon Schell, "Modern Might, Ancient Arrogance," *Newsday* (New York), February 12, 1991, p. 86.

ourselves more than human, we look down on others as less. Article 16 of the Geneva Conventions (to which the United States is signatory) formalizes a minimal recognition of the humanity of combatants by requiring that parties to a conflict record as soon as possible "any particular which may assist in [the] identification" of wounded, sick, or dead persons of the other side.[5] On these grounds the United States still refuses to normalize relations with Vietnam. Now, "according to the available estimates, approximately double the number of Iraqis were killed in six weeks of combat as U.S. casualties produced by a decade of fighting in Vietnam."[6] Yet during the Gulf War "the United States refused to count, locate, identify, honor" the enemy dead.[7] One observer commented, "General Schwartzkopf's main concern is that when you get into the body-count business, you end up perverting the bomb damage assess [*sic*]."[8] Is it only Americans who are human, only American lives that count?

The reverse of pride is *sloth,* the refusal to take responsibility for one's full humanity—as if one were, oneself, somehow less than human.[9] For those most actively involved in the exercise of power, pride may be the major temptation. But for most Americans, whose knowledge of war comes via satellite and only intermittently, the besetting temptation, I wish to argue, is at least as much that of sloth. As epigraph to his novel *Howards End,* E. M. Forster penned two simple words—"Only connect." Simone Weil writes, "He who treats as equals those who are far below him in strength really makes them a gift of the qual-

5. Ramsey Clark, *The Fire This Time* (New York: Thunder's Mouth Press, 1992), 178.

6. Margot Norris, "Military Censorship and the Body Count in the Persian Gulf War," in *Cultural Critique* 19 (fall 1991): 225.

7. Clark, *Fire This Time.*

8. Loren Thompson, quoted in the *New York Times,* February 3, 1991; cited by Norris, "Military Censorship," 225.

9. Reinhold Niebuhr, *The Nature and Destiny of Man* (New York: Scribner's, 1941), 1:178–240; Judith Plaskow, *Sex, Sin and Grace* (Washington, D.C.: Univ. Press of America, 1980), 51–94; Hannah Arendt, *Eichmann in Jerusalem: A Report on the Banality of Evil* (Harmondsworth, Eng.: Penguin, 1977).

ity of human beings, of which fate had deprived them."[10] Sloth is a failure to connect—a failure to connect imaginatively and empathetically with others; a failure to acknowledge our actual connection with harsh realities; a failure to acknowledge the spiritual connection between one's own interior state and the things that are done in one's name.

Before we begin our own effort to connect, let me add a personal note. My perspective on militarism is that of a white male who, as a boy, imagined combat to be exciting. I was drawn by the promise of comradeship and action, the warrior ethos. Yet at the same time I felt a gnawing anxiety. As a student I lived in Belgium, the battlefield of Europe. Classified 4-D as a ministerial student during Vietnam, I was involved in draft resistance. Increasingly my reflections are affected by awareness of my German descent. Otto Loew, my paternal grandfather, changed the family name to Lowe at the time of World War I to make it sound more English. Thus for reasons both biographical and intellectual, I have an affinity to certain of those "other voices" who are distanced temporally as well as geographically. Along with contemporary voices from the "Two-Thirds World," I also hear those from the European past who witness to a long history of suffering and resistance.

ANALYSIS

Other Voices: The Political Alternative

Verdun, Hiroshima, Vietnam: images of the devastation wrought by war (if not the firsthand experience) have sunk deep into our collective psyche. Once it was possible to speak of "the glory of war." No longer: schooled in the absurdity of war, we all count ourselves among the disillusioned. Once-powerful words such as "courage," "heroism," and "honor" have forfeited their meaning; as often as not, they are spoken with irony. But this

10. Simone Weil, *Waiting for God* (New York: Harper and Row, 1973), 144.

means that in the very gesture of rejecting war, we are implicitly accepting mass violence as part of "the way things are," as if chaos and conflict—disorder—were the natural "order" of things.

Thus when we begin to reflect contextually by listening to those who have experienced militarism at first hand, for example those who have resisted military dictatorship in Latin America or Central Europe, we who are schooled in cynicism may be surprised. We come expecting horror stories, and such stories there are—but what these voices focus upon is the slow, step-by-step process of building communities of trust and cooperation. From South America, Leonardo Boff wrote (before he was silenced by his church) of Christian base communities in which "the new virtues find expression in class solidarity, participation in community decisions, mutual aid, criticism of abuses of power." This he characterizes as a process in which "*the field of politics* emerges as one with its own relative autonomy."[11] From Central Europe, Václav Havel propounds a "politics of hope" through "something like political clubs where people could refine their opinions, get to know each other personally, and seek to determine who among them would be the best to administer the affairs of the *polis*."[12] Americans disparage politics—those with fewer freedoms value it more.

What is this notion of the political to which these people are drawn? It is a truism to say that the military approach to a problem seeks to destroy the enemy, or prepares to do so. The political approach also has its share of conflict. But in politics does one seek to *destroy* one's opponent? Sometimes we talk this way, but I want to suggest that when we do, it is no longer politics in the proper sense of the word. For when I engage in politics, I must remember that however much we fight, my opponent of

11. Leonardo Boff, "Theological Characteristics of a Grassroots Church," in *The Challenge of Basic Christian Communities,* ed. Sergio Torres and John Eagleson (Maryknoll, N.Y.: Orbis, 1981), 142, 138; emphasis added.

12. Václav Havel, *Disturbing the Peace: A Conversation with Karel Hvizdala* (New York: Knopf, 1990), 17.

today may be my ally tomorrow. As issues shift, people forge new alliances. This fluidity makes observers nervous, but it can generate openness. Certainly it means that politicians must be to some degree respecters of persons.

The military and the political thus entail two different views of "the way things are." When a soldier confronts an enemy, he or she knows that only one person is likely to walk away. "It's either him or me." Abstractly put, it is a zero-sum game; one person's gain comes at the other's expense—until the loser dies and the winner takes all. The beauty of politics, in contrast, is that it offers an alternative to this hellish situation. It suggests the possibility of a solution from which *all* parties might benefit. By its very existence politics (in the positive, normative sense of the word that I am advocating here) promises that life, "the way things are," does not have to be an endless process of dog eat dog.

Note that the issue in this context is not one sort of politics versus another, but the political as such, politics as a way of being in relation to other people. It is this appreciation of politics as such that occurs when "the political" is set over against "the military"; or when, in the words of Boff, "the field of politics emerges as one with its own relative autonomy." This is the experience of those who have struggled to foster communities of decency under conditions of oppression. In that setting, religion and politics no longer seem as far apart as they do in our own culture. They struggle together for a future that is open and humane.[13]

Cooperation as a Natural Good

We have been considering politics as a way of relating within a particular society. Inextricably related to this is the question

13. The notion of politics espoused here draws on Hannah Arendt, *The Human Condition* (New York: Doubleday, 1958), 155–223. Cf. Paul Goodman's notion of "treason against natural societies" in his marvelous *Drawing the Line* (New York: Random House, 1946), 3–9.

of finding alternatives to armed conflict *between* societies. Now when nations are moving toward war, efforts to find a political solution are confronted with two kinds of argument. One is the argument from "*realism*": "Face it, life is survival of the fittest. Anybody tells you differently, they're trying to fool you or they're very naive." The other, the argument from *urgency:* "This is no time to sit around talking. There's a clear and present danger! Act now or it will be too late!"

Let us take the arguments in reverse order: first, the argument from urgency. Advocates of an exclusively military approach are prone to crying "Emergency!" Convinced that there is no time for talk, they may in the extreme case suspend all political discussion. Virtually every country, including the United States, has procedures by which civil liberties may be suspended, allowing a small group to rule by decree. This ever-present possibility of martial law dramatizes the tension that exists, even in the best of times, between military and political approaches. Now undoubtedly there are moments when the cry of emergency is warranted. But proponents of an exclusively military approach do tend to push this button more often than is required or justified. Repeatedly Americans were warned that the Russians were pulling ahead of them. Repeatedly they were told—on the basis of secret intelligence—that emergency measures had to be taken. Why was it that U.S. intelligence reports, which were so determinative, failed to discern that the Soviet Union was much weaker than it seemed?[14]

The fact is that those who were processing the information themselves lacked objectivity. They had developed a vested interest in a military approach (after all, this is what gave them their jobs), and this distorted their sense of the way things actually were. An atmosphere of secrecy, anxiety, and suspicion blocked their access to reality; the vaunted "realism" (the first of the two arguments against using political solutions before

14. See George F. Kennan's post–cold war reflections in the *New York Times*, October 28, 1992, sec. A, p. 15, and March 14, 1994, sec. A, p. 13.

war) of the militarist became functionally *un*realistic.[15] The military passes into militarism. For an anxious, secretive society is like an anxious, secretive individual. Blind to richness and complexity, it blunders into thickets (one thinks of Vietnam); it trips over the obvious. Studies indicate that because arrangements based on cooperation encourage feedback, they tend to last longer and be more adaptable than arrangements based on force.[16] The sociologist Philip Slater extends the point to our relationship with nature: "[T]o exercise control over the environment" is inherently self-blinding in that it limits the environment's "freedom to influence us."[17] And indeed there is some historical evidence that by becoming *disconnected*—by obstructing the feedback that is the essence of politics—military dictatorships do tend to undermine themselves. Witness the fall of the Berlin Wall.

In sum: (1) There does seem to be a certain order inherent to our social relationships. This point is worth emphasizing because we have seen in our century that, in the stark phrase of the poet Carolyn Forché, "there is nothing one man will not do to another."[18] A dictator can do many things, but then there will be consequences even a dictator cannot avoid. (2) The kind of relationship that we have called "political" constitutes a sort of natural good proper to human society, which cannot be suppressed without injury to the society. (3) Militarism might be defined as the overextension of military practices to the detriment of the political or civilian realm. Obviously, thorny issues remain regarding what constitutes an "overextension," but we

15. The "missile gap" announced by John F. Kennedy turns out to have been an example of such distortion: see Ralph E. Lapp, *The Weapons Culture* (New York: Norton, 1968), 53–54. On the limitations of *realpolitik* in the Gulf, see Christopher Hitchens, "Why We Are Stuck in the Sand," *Harper's,* January 1991, 70–78.

16. See Dietrich Fischer, *Preventing War in the Nuclear Age* (Totowa, N.J.: Rowman and Allanheld, 1984), an especially helpful book.

17. Philip Slater, *Earthwalk* (Garden City, N.Y.: Doubleday, 1974), 10; the book relates social psychology to ecology. See also Slater's *A Dream Deferred* (Boston: Beacon, 1991).

18. Carolyn Forché, "The Visitor," in *The Country between Us* (New York: Harper and Row, 1981), 15.

may have made progress in clarifying the meaning of militarism and why it might be called an evil. (4) Militarism represents a whole way of relating to persons, to society, and to the environment, a way characterized by opposition and control even to the point of annihilation.

Economics: Between Violence and Cooperation

We have been using a simple distinction between military and political approaches. Now I wish to introduce a third concept, economics; and to suggest that if the military and the political are regarded as poles of a spectrum, then the realm of economics can be located variously along that spectrum, depending on the particular situation and depending on one's worldview. There are economic arrangements that amount to a cold zero-sum calculus in which each group seeks constantly to extend its advantage over the other. Along with this may go a worldview that sees economics as being by its very nature a sort of covert warfare. But is this view of things really so infallibly accurate? Is economics invariably a form of combat? Surely there are numerous instances in which economic relations bring mutual benefit: the point is already made by the familiar proposal for economic cooperation, "Let's make a deal."

My point is analogous to that made earlier about the military and the political. In each case the danger is that the military may dominate another distinctive realm, distorting society. A distortion of economics occurs on the conceptual level when all such transactions are regarded as predatory. It occurs on the institutional level when military production dominates the economy. And in practice the matter of worldview and the matter of institution turn out to be intertwined.

As to how the distortion occurs and the price it exacts, one clear principle has been abundantly confirmed: compared to other forms of investment, money spent on military purposes is relatively unproductive. In one study of seventeen countries, "nations supporting proportionately heavier military burdens tended to have lower levels of investment and productivity growth."[19] "Every gun that is made, every warship launched, every rocket fired signifies, in the final sense, a theft from those who hunger and are not fed, those who are cold and are not clothed," to quote no less a figure than General Dwight D. Eisenhower.[20] The United States has spent massively on military production while its infrastructure—the schools, roads, and services that are the basis for future productivity—has been allowed to deteriorate. Other empires have trod this downward path. Will American history be one more demonstration that overreliance on the military tends to undermine itself?[21]

Again it is a question of worldview, "the ways things are." Militarism as a worldview has the effect of forcing things that are not inherently military (the political, the economic) into military terms. But militarism also thrives on a misnaming that works in the other direction as well—relations that *are* in fact military get disguised by reassuringly *non*military terms. A situation is called "free trade," but the weaker party is controlled and manipulated much as if under military occupation. Such institutionalized, legitimized violence is a major concern of liberation theology. A book aptly entitled *War against the Poor* documents the prevalence of "low-intensity conflict," a simmering state of virtual warfare by which powerful interests seek to control the internal affairs of various Third World countries.[22] Better described as "total war at the grassroots level," such conflict has no respect for civilians.[23] Yet we tend not to recognize it as war. "Every

19. Robert W. DeGrasse Jr., "Militarization of the U.S. Economy: Costs and Consequences," in *War in Slow Motion: The Economic and Social Impact of Militarism,* ed. Zelle W. Andrews (New York: Pilgrim, 1985), 19; the book is a guide for study groups.

20. Quoted in *A Peace Reader,* ed. Joseph J. Fahey and Richard Armstrong (New York: Paulist, 1992), 455; cf. Eisenhower's justly famous farewell address regarding the military-industrial complex, *New York Times,* January 18, 1961, p. 21.

21. See Paul Kennedy, "A Declining Empire Goes to War," in *Peace Reader,* 76–79.

22. Jack Nelson-Pallmeyer, *War against the Poor: Low-Intensity Conflict and Christian Faith* (Maryknoll, N.Y.: Orbis, 1989).

23. Sara Miles, "'The Real War': Post-Vietnam Low-Intensity Conflict," in *Unwinding the Vietnam War: From War into Peace,* ed. Reese Williams (Seattle: Real Comet Press, 1987), 317, 336.

one is greedy for unjust gain. . . . They have healed the wound of my people lightly, saying 'Peace, peace,' where there is no peace" (Jer. 6:13-14).

Religion as Part of the Problem

Familiar to visitors to Paris is the white dome of Sacré Coeur, a basilica conceived and constructed in the wake of the Franco-Prussian War. As you mount the great steps, there looms above you the silhouette of a warrior on horseback holding aloft what appears to be a cross. Coming nearer, you discover that it is not a cross but an inverted sword held high by the blade. The sword has become a cross, which with one swift gesture can become again a sword.

Since the time of Constantine, cross and sword have merged as armies were assured that "God is on our side." The Reformation brought in its wake a series of devastating wars, each side clambering to exterminate the other in the name of the God of love. Modern secularism, which Christians are quick to lament, is in part a response to the experience of militant religion. Observers of the wars of religion pronounced "a pox on both your houses," washing their hands of the matter altogether.

Granted, one needs to distinguish between the all-too-fallible church and its spiritual message, the gospel. But within the Bible itself there are elements that give one pause. Military images abound, often with positive connotation. Upon crossing the Red Sea the people of Israel proclaim, "The Lord is a man of war" (Exod. 15:3).[24] From the conquest of Canaan at one end of the Bible, one proceeds to the Book of Revelation at the other. We know how a Hal Lindsey can appropriate the imagery of apocalypse to define our enemy of the moment as the Antichrist.

Such defining is in fact crucial. To kill a group of people, you must first dehumanize them, portraying them as less than

24. See J. Carter Swaim, *War, Peace, and the Bible* (Maryknoll, N.Y.: Orbis, 1982), 1.

human.[25] That is precisely what we do when we label them "pagan," not to say "evil." Nor is it any accident that such terms abound in the language of religion. Religion thrives on powerful dichotomies: good versus evil, the blessed and the accursed. Those who view the world in such terms are often the most ready to take up arms. Peace needs moderation, politics requires compromise; whereas for the impassioned believer, there is no compromising with Satan.

Religion is a part of the problem. It may even be the heart of the problem. For militarism is most dangerous when it becomes a way of looking at all of reality, when it becomes a *worldview.* And yet isn't religion itself just such a worldview? Doesn't religion (at least in its Western forms) view all of life as a sort of battlefield between the forces of light and the forces of darkness? In Latin America, liberation theology, for all its significance, remains a minority movement. Most religious institutions do little to resist an identification of the cause of Christianity with the violent assertion, by police or paramilitary groups, of the status quo. Thus we face three difficult conclusions. (1) Much, if not all, of religion seems itself to be militaristic. (2) So far from making folk gentler, the combining of religion with militarism often encourages fanaticism. (3) Within Christian doctrine, the responsibility seems to lie with that doctrine which underwrites the demonization, namely the doctrine of evil.

RECONSTRUCTION

The Cycle of Violence

Thus the way toward theological reconstruction seems obvious. If the language of evil is a part of the problem, it would seem that theology should downplay the doctrine or drop it

25. See Sam Keen, *Faces of the Enemy: Reflections of the Hostile Imagination* (San Francisco: Harper and Row, 1986); regarding the Gulf War, see *Cultural Critique* 19 (fall 1991).

altogether. That proposal was central to nineteenth-century liberalism, which regarded wrath and judgment as primitive notions that have no place in a truly Christian doctrine of God. Is this then the direction we ought to pursue?

To respond, let us recall our earlier discussion. We described cooperation as a natural good and observed that dictatorships have some tendency to undermine themselves. Together, these theses suggest a natural ethic. Might it not be possible to distinguish between (1) *naive* self-interest, which thinks only in terms of the short run, namely, the immediate gain achieved by military conquest; and (2) *enlightened* self-interest, which recognizes that in the long run more is achieved—even for oneself—by cooperation toward the common good? If people could be educated to think in these terms, they might see that in the long run force accomplishes nothing.

A commonwealth of enlightened self-interest: this vision that galvanized nineteenth-century liberalism continues to have power and plausibility—current ecological movements being an example. For note that, contra the alleged naïveté of liberalism, it does not imagine that people will become saints: it is based on *self*-interest, after all. For my own part, I believe that something *like* the liberal vision has to be regained if Christians are to identify and address the militarist threat. But I also believe that liberalism as such is unable to surmount a fundamental problem—namely, (3) *cynical* self-interest. It is all too possible for a person to think: "Perhaps it is true that pursuing the common good is better than grasping at one's immediate self-interest. But I see something even better: for me to act *as if* I were committed to the common good; indeed for me to praise the vision of the common good, so that others will trust it—while secretly I go ahead and cheat. Imagine all those unsuspecting people laying down their arms while I am secretly stockpiling mine. What a delightful prospect!"

The cynicism of this position is thoroughly perverse. Trampling down the fragile hope of a common good, it causes the innocent to suffer, all for the sake of selfish gain. It is perverse—yet there it is, a part of "human nature." We confront here a cruelty that is more coldly calculating and more rapacious than that of the "savage" animal and yet which is "just human nature." It is in order to speak of this distortion of nature, which becomes a sort of nature in its own right, that theology resorts to such inflammatory terms as "evil" and "sin." For it is the mark of evildoers to "talk of peace to their neighbors while malice is in their hearts" (Ps. 28:3, NEB). And once sin comes upon the scene, even as possibility, chaos ensues. "Of course *I* wouldn't do such a thing. I'm a not a bad person. But those others, they might! So the intelligent thing is to prepare for the worst. In fact, the really smart thing would be a preemptive strike, get them before they get me." Thus are wars launched and lands laid waste—all in the name of peace.

A radical ill requires radical language to describe it. In the very effort to do without the language of evil, we find ourselves driven to use it. There is a tragedy here, a historic tragedy in human affairs, which I want you to feel. We really were getting close to a basis for peace, premised upon the common good. All it required was a willingness to think in terms of long-range mutual gain. And now through a tiny aperture, no more than a chink in the wall, namely the possibility of willful cynicism, violence, "the undoing of Creation," enters in.[26] It is all so foolish, so unnecessary. " 'Would that even today you knew the things that make for peace! But now they are hid from your eyes' " (Luke 19:42, RSV). War is unnecessary—yet by a deadly logic it presses upon us. For add to what we have already said the accumulated weight of history. Nobody starts afresh, each person comes bearing his or her personal prejudices, nursing his or her resentments. Add to that the reality of economic injustice. Add to that the fires of nationalism. Thus does sin multiply itself. And thus do theologians come to speak of original sin. We may piously affirm that "violence

26. William Stringfellow, *An Ethic for Christians and Other Aliens in a Strange Land* (Waco, Tex.: Word, 1973), 127.

never accomplished anything"; but which of us really believes that when some delicious, unfair advantage is lying before us, just begging to be seized?

No doubt the human penchant for violence is in some part a matter of good intentions gone astray, as liberalism would suggest; no doubt it is in some part a mark of inadequate development. But to say that it is *only* that has seemed to the classical tradition inadequate: a blindness to willful perversity on the one side, and to unspeakable suffering on the other.

The Believer's Dilemma

We have been reenacting the movement of experience and thought that led mainstream Protestant theology from liberalism to neoorthodoxy. Now I need to intensify the issue even further. Consider this recollection of actual battle:

> I was boiling with a mad rage, which had taken hold of me and all the others in an incomprehensible fashion. The overwhelming wish to kill gave wings to my feet. Rage pressed bitter tears from my eyes.... We called to each other in sobs and stammered disconnected sentences. A neutral observer might have perhaps believed that we were seized by an excess of happiness.[27]

Others describe similar experiences, a sort of exaltation that is not incompatible with fear but drives one to act in spite of fear.[28]

Now this is an experience of ecstatic self-transcendence—which is one definition of religion. Warfare can become a *religious* experience![29] In *Facing the Nuclear Heresy,* G. Clarke Chapman comes to a similar conclusion from a different angle, by focusing upon a specific form of militarism, the nuclear arms race. Chapman argues that for zealous defenders of nuclear buildup, the Bomb, with its aura of insuperable power, acquires such subjective and objective ultimacy as to constitute

27. Ernst Juenger, quoted in J. Glenn Gray, *The Warriors: Reflections on Men in Battle* (New York: Harper Torchbooks, 1959), 52.

28. See Stephen Crane's classic *The Red Badge of Courage.*

29. Cf. Paul Tillich, *Systematic Theology* (Chicago: Univ. of Chicago Press, 1967), 3:392–93.

a virtual religion.[30] Thus those who argue against the arms race may be naive in thinking that advocates of the Bomb are taking a rational position from which they might be rationally dissuaded. For Chapman it is a form of *idolatry* that Christians must denounce as heresy.

"Idolatry" and "heresy" do seem to be appropriate terms for the Dr. Strangelove phenomenon of worshiping the Bomb. "Some put their trust in chariots and some in horses, but we will call upon the Name of the Lord our God" (Ps. 20:7, NEB). But by now it is obvious that the moment we speak the words, we are enmeshed in a dilemma. For "idolator," "heretic," and "infidel" are the words that launched the Crusades and fueled the Inquisition. They invoke in the harshest terms the dichotomy of good versus evil, inviting the us-versus-them mentality by which religion has justified militaristic crusades. We must conclude, at least, that religion is high-octane stuff. Once people start using it, it is likely to explode.

Yet the fact is that people *are* using it all around us, some subtly, some at the top of their lungs. Worship of chariots, worship of bombs—many seem even anxious to sacrifice their own lives, and others', in obedience to inanimate things. It is precisely the religiousness of that impulse (its impetus toward total commitment, thus total sacrifice) that creates what I wish to call "the believer's dilemma." For if militarism is evil of such enormity, if it is indeed idolatry, how can we not denounce it as such? Yet if we start using such terms, how can we avoid perpetuating—first verbally, then physically—the cycle of violence?

The Kingdom of God

In a sense the task of "analysis," which was the announced concern of the first half of this essay, has continued well into the second half. For it is only now, with the believer's dilemma before us, that we have something like an adequate description of

30. G. Clarke Chapman, *Facing the Nuclear Heresy* (Elgin: Brethren Press, 1986), 6–8, also using Tillich.

the problem. And yet it is also true that in the course of the last two sections we have been working at theological reconstruction. This overlapping of tasks makes an important theological point. Doing contextual theology is not a two-step process of first doing an empirical analysis of a problem (which analysis would be self-sufficient in its own right) and then subsequently doing theological reconstruction (which might mean bending theology to accommodate the needs of the moment). Rather the tasks overlap; better, they are related dialectically. One must already be doing constructive theology simply in order to gain an adequate sense of "the way things are" and thus to know the reality of the problem.

We have seen something of the inadequacies of liberalism, with its insufficiently radical view of evil. In the twentieth century these inadequacies led to the neoorthodox response, for example, the work of Reinhold Niebuhr. But neoorthodoxy had problems of its own. In a sense it was too successful. For in trying to take evil with full seriousness, it exposed a reality so entrenched in human life and institutions, so fused with the ambiguities of this world, that it seemed insuperable. Neoorthodoxy's subtle awareness of the effects of original sin could seem to invite paralysis. To dramatize the way in which paralysis can happen, consider the cobra, which is (in Western culture, at least) a living symbol of evil. Remarkably, the cobra can devour a rabbit, even though the rabbit is faster. It does so because the moment they make eye contact, the rabbit is paralyzed. Trembling with fear, the victim stands frozen as the snake slowly, rhythmically, closes the distance and then, at its leisure, strikes.

My point in evoking this image is that we too become paralyzed if we stare at evil too long. We find ourselves imitating it and thus serving it, hypnotized by its power. At such moments it is absolutely crucial that there be some other reality to which we can turn our gaze. In our earlier discussion, "the political" and a possible commonwealth of enlightened self-interest served just such a purpose. In liberalism such notions were virtually identified with the reign of God. In this century, however, we have seen enough of the cobra to know that an inspiring vision is not enough. But having seen the cobra, we need to see something else, something stronger and more positive, beyond it. In this liberalism is lastingly right, that without a vision, the people perish.

Contrary to liberalism, however, what is required is not (simply) a hope or a possibility, but a reality. What is required is not something that may (or may not) be in the process of happening, but something realized and actual, something to which our gaze can turn and upon which we can rely. And it is just that, the assurance of an achieved reality, which I take to be one of the functions of the doctrine of the reign or kingdom of God. Now of course anyone who has studied the New Testament has been taught to offset the "already" with the "not yet." What that has often meant in the face of twentieth-century violence, however, is that the "already" has receded (often under the heading of "hope") to the glimmer of a possibility.

Now let us have realism, by all means; and by all means let us avoid making an idol of any present institution. But there comes a point where one must inspect certain presentations of the gospel and ask forthrightly, "Is that all there is?" For my own part I wish to affirm that, whatever else it does, Christian theology must regard the reign of God as being in a real sense *accomplished.* Certainly we have Jesus' cry from the cross, but we also have from the cross the words, "It is accomplished" (John 19:30, NEB). Those words are to be understood (as the Fourth Gospel insists) in light of the resurrection. Given *that* reality, we dare not regard the reign of God as being anything less than irrevocably established—*whatever* the appearances to the contrary and whatever may be yet to come.[31] And it is well that it were so; for nothing less will suffice, it seems to me, to reclaim us from

31. See Dietrich Bonhoeffer, *The Communion of Saints* (New York: Harper and Row, 1963), 104–5; Bruce Chilton, "God in Strength," in *The Kingdom of God,* ed. Bruce Chilton (Philadelphia: Fortress, 1984), 121–32.

that worship of the serpent that has, in our own time, taken the form of militarism.

PRAXIS

We *live out of* the reality of the reign of God, in a double sense. We *live* out of it—God's kingdom supports and nourishes us (note the maternal imagery, which balances the masculine associations of "kingdom"). We live *out of* it—the kingdom is an in-breaking event (see Jesus' parables). We cannot make of it a cozy, limited reality set apart.

We Americans, so fixated upon achieving concrete results, need to be reminded that if the reign of God is irrevocably established, then there is a sense in which we don't have to "do" anything! We do not "do"—we pray (in praise and thanksgiving, in petition and intercession). And yet at the same time prayer is a kind of doing, a form of work on behalf of the world. Or again, we do not "do" anything—we witness to what has already been done. "For Christianity *help* is not the criterion. Truth is the criterion."[32] Yet at the same time witnessing is not just words but deeds as well, and so it does become a doing (but doing of a specific kind, freed from the need to see results).

Recognizing limits, we must learn what the poor have always known, that human life is lived not just under the sign of freedom but also under the sign of *necessity*. Middle-class America makes a virtual ideology out of individual freedom. Acknowledging limits seems almost un-American; hence the deficit. But necessity cannot be wished away: that's what makes it necessity. Our response has been to displace our fair share of necessity onto the backs of other people, making them bear our burdens on top of their own. But such a thing is not done without force.

32. Alexander Schmemann, *For the Life of the World* (Crestwood, N.Y.: St. Vladimir's Seminary Press, 1988), 99—cf. Kierkegaard! On Kierkegaard as social ethicist, see *Foundations of Kierkegaard's Vision of Community*, ed. George B. Connell and C. Stephen Evans (Atlantic Highlands, N.J.: Humanities Press, 1992).

Thus does the economic realm becomes militarized. The Gulf War was fought to preserve "the American way of life." Did we mean freedom from political oppression? Or did we mean freedom from having to treat oil as a limited resource—the unreal and implicitly violent fantasy of a freedom from necessity?

Living from the reality of the gift God has given us, we can accept reality as a gift. Necessity itself can be accepted, indeed celebrated, as the form, the particular shape, by which we participate in God's redeemed creation. To take an extreme case (which must increasingly seem to be not so extreme at all), there is something positive and ecologically sound in the ascetic tradition of "prayer and work." Living out of the kingdom, one lives *into* the concrete world, which means limit and necessity as well as freedom and hope. We North Americans must stop regarding necessity as if it were inherently evil and not a part of life! And we must work to bring to light the many ways in which our necessity gets lashed to the backs of others, becoming an evil indeed.[33]

Cowardice in the face of necessity happens between societies and within a society as well. Within North America we are witnessing a "secession of the successful." Those who can afford to do so are withdrawing from a society shared with others unlike themselves, retreating behind protective walls with "people like us." The number of private security guards in this country now exceeds that of public police.[34] The reasons for this are complex, but one part of the phenomenon is a giving up on the political—a turning away from shared solutions, a virtual severing of the social contract, an announcement that "you're on your own." Anxious, uncertain, our society is increasingly receptive to devices that, in their demand for immediate results and their disdain for due process, have a disturbingly military air. Ultimately, moving in that direction represents a giving up on life, which is life together. Martin Luther King Jr. taught us that "we are all

33. See Noam Chomsky, *Deterring Democracy* (London: Verso, 1991).

34. Robert Reich, "The Secession of the Successful," *New York Times Magazine*, January 20, 1991, pp. 16–17.

caught in an inescapable network of mutuality, tied into a single garment of destiny."[35] Severing ties in the name of "survival," we press toward that final severing, which is death. "*Only connect.*" Spiritual sloth, betrayal of the common bond, the dismantling of public life—is this the meaning of militarism among the "haves" of America today?

We are thus returned to our initial reflections regarding pride, sloth, and the Persian Gulf War. What follows is difficult to write, for I, as much as anyone, want to be proud, legitimately proud, of my country. But there is mounting evidence that the United States may have been guilty of an overweening pride, an overstepping of certain boundaries of morality and humanity, in the Persian Gulf.[36] The Geneva Convention stipulates that "it is prohibited to attack, destroy, remove or render useless objects indispensable to the survival of the civilian population, such as foodstuffs, . . . crops, livestock, drinking water installations and supplies." Yet according to reports, "Four of Iraq's seven major water pumping stations were destroyed. . . . Water purification plants were incapacitated nationwide."[37] Untreated sewage poured directly into the rivers; a year later an epidemiological study found fecal coliforms in 70 percent of the water tested. Yet this is what people have been drinking, out of necessity, because for many there is no alternative. As a consequence, "the infant mortality rate in Iraq . . . has more than tripled in one year's time."[38]

The first step in connecting is to realize that there is an issue here, to connect with the experience of others enough to see that a war that causes children to drink water polluted with human waste is not a "clean" war, as some have called it. The next step

35. Martin Luther King Jr., *A Testament of Hope* (San Francisco: Harper and Row, 1986), 254.

36. None of what follows is meant to deny that Saddam Hussein's Iraq is a brutal dictatorship guilty of aggression. The question for the moment is not *whether* the war should have been launched (that is another debate) but *how* it was conducted.

37. Clark, *The Fire This Time,* 65–66; in those same pages, Clark states: "U.S. bombing hit 28 civilian hospitals and 52 community health centers."

38. Interview with Dr. Tim Cote in *Sojourners* 21, no. 1 (January 1992): 17.

would be to gather information in order to make an informed judgment.[39] It may possibly be that the reports are misleading or that U.S. military activity can be justified on specific grounds. But here we run up against a fundamental barrier or absence, an "erasure." For we have very little information upon which to make a judgment. During the war, Americans were subjected to censorship more radical than on any previous occasion in the country's history.[40] Beyond that, the media have during the war and since exercised an almost inexplicable degree of *self*-censorship.[41] The sort of questions we are raising have not been pursued; conditions inside Iraq are largely ignored.

Thus the effort to learn about Iraq teaches us about ourselves, that we live in a situation of distorted communication. It follows that the next step in connecting is to resist this situation. We cannot at present make a definitive judgment about the measures that were taken against enemy soldiers or against civilians. But we can judge that we are being denied the information that is essential in order to make that (political) judgment. And, yes, we can judge that the present radical absence of such information is not essential to military security. The Gulf War is well on the way to becoming a gulf in our collective consciousness. It is our responsibility as Christians to defend the "dangerous memory";[42] to re-member the persons whose dismemberment is forgotten; to bear in mind the pain that others bear in their bodies.[43] In a situation of distorted communication, simply trying to remain humanly aware can amount to an act of resistance.[44]

39. Here I am informally following Bernard J. F. Lonergan, *Method in Theology* (New York: Herder and Herder, 1972).

40. See *The Gulf War Reader,* ed. Micah L. Sifry and Christopher Cerf (New York: Random House, 1991), 353–91.

41. A study guide on media coverage of the Gulf War is available from the Center for Media and Values, 1962 S. Shenandoah St., Los Angeles, CA 90034. See also the special issue of *Media and Values* 56 (fall 1991).

42. Johannes Baptist Metz, *Faith in History and Society* (New York: Crossroad, 1980), 56–58, 129. On the memory of suffering, see Walter Lowe, *Theology and Difference: The Wound of Reason* (Bloomington: Indiana Univ. Press, 1992), chap. 1.

43. See Elaine Scarry, *The Body in Pain* (New York: Oxford Univ. Press, 1985), 124–28 and passim.

44. See the list of alternative news sources in *News for the '90s* (Los Angeles: Center

For Christianity the criterion is not in the first instance one of being helpful. The criterion is the truth. In the present culture it is likely that those who press for the truth will be regarded as distinctly *un*helpful. For there are signs that contemporary America has struck a Faustian bargain. Historically the country's foreign policy has swung between the poles of isolationism and interventionism. The invasion of Iraq (and of Panama before) suggests a new post–cold war strategy that fuses these two divergent tendencies, and thus creates a consensus within American culture, but which does so at great cost to others. The strategy is to intervene, but on two conditions: first, that there be massive, almost unlimited, use of high-tech weaponry; and second, that American forces go in quickly and leave quickly. The first point addresses the very high premium that isolationism places upon American lives. But it suppresses the classic just war concern for proportionality, specifically the protection of civilians on the other side. The second point addresses the concern that America not get "bogged down." But it means we do not stick around to deal with the consequences of our actions: witness what we allowed to happen to the Kurds whom we incited to rebellion in Iraq.[45]

Certainly we should not take lightly the importance of American lives. *But* "If you love those who love you, what credit is that to you? For even sinners love those who love them" (Luke 6:32). More is required of Christians than rallying to the cause of those who are like themselves. "I say to you that hear, Love your enemies" (Luke 6:27, RSV). The first step in loving those who are (or are said to be) our enemies is to connect. One concrete example: it seems to me that in the present culture Christians should go out of their way to establish relationships, friendships, with Arab persons; for Western demonization of Arabs has a long history

for Media and Values, 1990). Vigorous research can itself be a form of resistance: witness the great investigative journalists such as I. F. Stone, Noam Chomsky, and Seymour Hersh; see especially Chomsky, "The Responsibility of Intellectuals," in *The Chomsky Reader* (New York: Pantheon, 1987), 59–82.

45. This paragraph draws on Robert W. Tucker and David C. Hendrickson, *The Imperial Temptation* (New York: Council on Foreign Relations Press, 1992), 160–62, 197.

with no sign of slackening.[46] One who performs so simple an act may find that during the next cry of "Emergency!" keeping faith with a friendship (and with what friendship makes one see) is enough to get one accused of disdaining American lives; and thus enough to give one a sense of being (as Christians indeed are) a sort of alien within one's own country.[47]

"Only connect" means, in a sense, only be human; and in a sense what God asks of us is simply that we be human. Doing so in a culture given to demonization requires courage; and authentic courage is what pride and sloth, in common, lack. Thus, fittingly, we conclude our critique of militarism by appealing to a military virtue. (Boff's list of virtues, abridged earlier, includes "endurance of slander and persecution for the sake of justice, unjust imprisonment, loss of one's job. . . . ") In a darkened situation, believers must "put on the armor of light" (Rom. 13:12). The function of the doctrine of the reign of God is to en-courage, to hearten, us with the assurance that where one citizenship is contested, another is sure; we are citizens of the kingdom.[48] The reign of God is the ultimate answer (given only in praxis and struggle) to the question of how things are.

Finally, the doctrine functions to give us a norm—to show us the meaning of being human when we would not know. Militarism is but the extreme form of our all-too-human penchant for separating method from purpose, means from end.[49] We sense no contradiction between the means of war and the goal of peace. When God acts, it is otherwise. The temptations that Jesus refused were just so many proposals for separating ends (benefitting self and others) from means (some exercise of sheer power). Christ, who uniquely joins human and divine, and in so doing

46. See Edward W. Said, *Orientalism* (New York: Random House, 1978); and a special issue of *Middle East Report* 178 (September/October 1992).

47. See Stanley Hauerwas, "Whose Just War? Which Peace?" in Jean Bethke Elshtain et al., *But Was It Just? Reflections on the Morality of the Persian Gulf War* (New York: Doubleday, 1992), 83–105. Also Stringfellow, *An Ethic for Christians.*

48. See, despite its difficulties, Augustine's *The City of God.*

49. This paragraph draws on Jacques Ellul, *The Presence of the Kingdom* (New York: Seabury, 1967), 61–95, esp. 81.

shows what "human" truly is, does not separate the purposes of love from the means. As for us, aliens, refugees that we are, we cannot do the same; we haven't the capacity to follow Christ—unless we be *in* Christ. To be a citizen of the kingdom of God is precisely to be in Christ—who, as the oneness of the human and the divine, is both God's end and God's means.

LINDA A. MERCADANTE

9. SIN, ADDICTION, AND FREEDOM

THE DEMISE OF SIN, THE EMERGENCE OF ADDICTION

A friend of mine decided she had a problem with alcohol and checked herself into a treatment center. A devout Christian and Presbyterian elder, she brought along a Bible since it was an important part of her daily routine. My friend reported, without anger, that the treatment center took her Bible away. They explained that it might interfere with focusing on her addiction. She pleaded for the Bible, only convincing the staff that she also might have an unhealthy attachment to it, or a "religious addiction." They decided, however, that if she did well in treatment they would allow her to read the Bible for ten minutes before bed each night. But the Bible had to stay at the nurses' station the remainder of the time. My friend agreed to this and, in relating it, justified the staff's decision. Although she now regularly attends Alcoholics Anonymous meetings, she has quit her job and spends much time at home, particularly avoiding stores and malls because she has decided she is also a shopping addict and does not want to be tempted. She still attends church but is more careful about the extent of her involvement.

Another friend, who for years denied her heavy drinking during a difficult marriage and then as a single parent, admitted her problem. She went through treatment, stopped drinking entirely, and began to attend Alcoholics Anonymous. In the process, she became convinced that she also has a susceptibility to other addictions, such as workaholism, smoking, and codependency. Nevertheless, slowly, laboriously she put her life back together, earned two degrees, became ordained to the ministry, and is enjoying a productive and active life.

The outcomes of these two stories are quite different, but each person became convinced that she is sick, will always be in danger of relapse, and must daily practice the twelve steps of Alcoholics Anonymous, attend meetings, and maintain complete sobriety from alcohol and restrictiveness toward the ancillary addictions. Addiction, once thought to be largely confined to disadvantaged peoples, rebellious youth, and societal misfits, is increasingly seen as a sickness affecting a broad spectrum of the population. While twelve-step meetings are virtually free of cost, the various addiction treatments, related therapies, and educational programs have become a growth industry. Many affirm that the movement has saved their lives. But they would not say they have been "saved from sin." They have been made aware of their disease and see diagnosis as part of the healing process, but they are clear that they are sick, not sinning.

In 1973 psychiatrist Karl Menninger published a book entitled *Whatever Became of Sin?*[1] The book protested our culture's abandonment of personal moral responsibility. Today sin is still not a popular topic, and the addiction movement dramatically demonstrates this. To call an alcoholic or addict sinful is considered harsh, judgmental, self-righteous, lacking in compassion. In the view that sees addiction as a disease, more weight is put on the side of genetics, brain chemistry, conditioning, or psychological predilection, and less on will, morality, character, or offending God. Additionally, the types of problematic behavior included under the umbrella of addiction are proliferating: not only are excessive alcohol consumption, reliance on mood-altering prescription drugs, and the use of illegal substances included, but addiction has also become a cultural metaphor

1. Karl Menninger, *Whatever Became of Sin?* (1973; reprint, New York: Bantam, 1988).

used to describe such behaviors as overeating, overshopping, exceptional dependency upon a loved one, preoccupation with sex, greater than average religiosity, and a host of other human behaviors.

My attention to this movement began when I took a job in a seminary with a program in alcohol and drug abuse ministry. An adult convert to Protestantism, I was raised in an ethnic background (Jewish and Italian) where alcohol was used within a structured social and familial setting, was considered part of proper hospitality, and was enjoyed in moderation. I was surprised to find among some Protestants a strong reaction against or, it seemed to me, even a morbid fear of alcohol. But I taught and became friends with many people who identified themselves as recovering alcoholics or addicts. I was impressed with their stories. So I began to read the relevant literature and regularly attend twelve-step meetings, partly to check my own perceptions and practices and, even more, to experience what my students enthusiastically proclaimed as a life-saving spirituality.

I found a supportive community that took people seriously and made itself available. The principles were clear and practical, the meetings predictable, short, and without external constraint. People often found help and hope there. But there was also an ancillary program, often quite expensive and time-consuming, of therapist visits, seminars, treatments. Some participants were mandated into attending therapy, meetings, and treatment by the courts, compelled by employers, or pressured by families. I was struck by many persons' enduring identification of themselves as sick, or powerless, or needing to live a life of avoidance and restriction. When I heard claims that nearly everyone is addicted to something, I pondered the similarly universal claims of the doctrine of sin.

As I began to explore with my students the differences between sin and addiction, we agreed that for the Christian the addiction movement raises some theological questions. For although drunkenness and many other kinds of excess are censured under both metaphors, such behaviors as self-sacrifice, dependence upon or deferral to others, minimizing self-focus, and even religious zeal, conduct considered virtuous in much traditional church teaching, can be considered problematic and possibly pathological by the addiction movement. And things the church after long years of ascetic impulse is beginning to welcome as good gifts of creation—food, sex, relationships—can provoke fear and avoidance for many in the addiction movement. Some students wanted to handle all this by considering addiction just a contemporary name for idolatry. Others, however, became concerned that we were moving from morals to medicine.

DEFINING THE ADDICTION AND SIN CONCEPTS

Although our age may balk at the word "sin," there is still a recognition of evil. Many accept the reality of nonmoral evil, for example, earthquake and disease, things largely independent of human causation. There is also some recognition of tragedy or radical evil, for example, things such as ecological deterioration or famine, which have a human component but seem to go beyond or deeper than direct human culpability. There is, however, less clarity about the notion of moral evil or individual sin, that is, the idea that individuals have a measure of free choice, must take responsibility for their actions, and transgress sacral boundaries when they use their freedom wrongly. Some argue that understanding addiction as disease, that is, as nonmoral evil, effectively absolves one of responsibility for his or her actions and ultimately denies one's human freedom, which the doctrine of sin protects. Conversely, it is argued that the notion of addiction as sin places undue guilt and blame on someone who is trapped and powerless, yet someone suffering from a disease must still take responsibility for its management.

The classic disease theory of addiction has been greatly modified or rejected by researchers, but it still exercises considerable influence in the treatment movement and among the public. Because of its popularity and widespread recognition, this theory must be looked at more closely. Its acceptance is linked in the public mind with increasing rejection of or confusion about the concept of sin. Since much of the addiction movement is a lay-led phenomenon focused on pragmatics, public perceptions are very important. The movement is worth examining because it offers alternative and increasingly comprehensive explanations for the human condition. Our inherited version of the doctrine of sin also must be surveyed in order to understand what has actually been rejected. Is there an accurate portrayal of the doctrine in the movement? Is the prevailing traditional doctrine adequate to meet the challenge presented by addiction? Or must it—and can it—be reconstructed to provide a more comprehensive and helpful understanding of human behavior?

THE DISEASE THEORY OF ADDICTION: PREVALENCE, DEFINITION, CRITIQUE

The Temperance movement, which led to Prohibition (Eighteenth Amendment to the U.S. Constitution, 1920), viewed alcohol as an inherently addictive substance. Although this was not a majority view among the population, especially as immigrant groups with different alcohol practices became part of American society, the stress on self-control and self-help certainly was. The movement thus managed to galvanize a host of other reform efforts, which clustered around the Temperance cause. Through successful political action and grassroots organization (especially among small town and country folk, nativists as opposed to immigrants, and the evangelical churches), the movement eventually succeeded in having the production, transport, and sale of alcohol prohibited.[2] The movement failed, however, to bring

2. See, for example, Joseph R. Gusfield, *Symbolic Crusade: Status Politics and the American Temperance Movement* (Urbana: Univ. of Illinois Press, 1963); and Andrew Sinclair, *Era of Excess: A Social History of the Prohibition Movement* (New York: Harper Colophon, 1962).

about the promised, almost millennial goals of a crime-free, moral, and temperate society, and in many ways had the opposite effect.

What is called the "classic disease theory" emerged shortly after the failure and repeal of Prohibition (Twenty-first Amendment, 1934), although it had been a long time developing. The idea that heavy drinking could become uncontrollable and assume disease-like characteristics had been broached earlier, but moral overtones were often still present, especially when compulsive inebriety was seen as a sinful choice leading to a disease of the will. In much of the earlier thought on drunkenness, will and desire were closely linked. The new development was the ascendancy of the theory that for some people heavy drinking was not a choice, that will and desire were separate. Indeed, it was claimed that these people were especially vulnerable or "allergic" to alcohol.[3]

Experiential credibility for this theory arose from the shared stories of early members of Alcoholics Anonymous (AA), a group that began in 1935, just a year after the repeal of Prohibition. The group was heavily influenced by the evangelical Oxford Group, and there is some similarity between the Oxford tenets and practices and the twelve-step programs. Although AA's founders did not use the term "disease" to describe alcoholism, they did call it an illness, sickness, or malady.[4] This emphasis, the group support, and the focus on the spiritual condition of the alcoholic helped to produce dramatic results for people considered by others to be hopelessly degenerated. Some years later the disease aspect was supported by the work of Edwin Jellinek and the Yale Center of Alcohol Studies. When compared to the stringency of the prohibitionist view and the

3. See Harry Gene Levine, "The Discovery of Addiction: Changing Conceptions of Habitual Drunkenness in America," *Journal of Studies on Alcohol* 39, no. 1 (1978): 143–74.

4. Anonymous, *Alcoholics Anonymous: The Story of How Many Thousands of Men and Women Have Recovered from Alcoholism* (New York: Works Publishing, 1939); this is the text known as "The Big Book."

radical measure of banning alcohol completely, it seemed an improvement to assert that some people are more susceptible than others, and only they must maintain abstinence. The idea also aided the revival of the alcohol industry after repeal, allowed moderate drinkers to avoid public censure, and provided a place for heavy drinkers to find help and solace.

Although the content of the disease theory has remained somewhat vague and variable, there are certain key features. In the classic view, alcoholism is considered a clinical entity, a primary condition rather than a behavior linked to other problematic factors in the victim's life or background, and a susceptibility that is irreversible and involuntary. Loss of control is the most salient factor, whether it is seen as acquired or innate. Understanding it this way is considered a new scientific approach, far more rational and humane than allowing either the law or religion to define and deal with it. Lifetime abstinence is claimed to be the only saving path for alcoholics and drug addicts.[5] While drugs are popularly considered inevitably addictive, as alcohol used to be, alcohol addiction is now deemed person-specific. The more recently identified "process" addictions (eating disorders, codependency, sexual addiction, shopping addiction, and so on) present difficulties since many of the activities (eating, relationships, sex) are intrinsic to the human condition or a functional part of the culture (for example, spending money). The disease model is nevertheless pressed into service here, but the goal becomes analyzing and restricting behavior and changing attitudes, rather than total abstinence.

How can we explain the popularity of the disease model when it so stretches the typical meaning of "disease" and has also been either radically modified or rejected by the majority of researchers? Part of the reason may stem from a cultural rejection

5. A key work is E. M. Jellinek, *The Disease Concept of Alcoholism* (New Brunswick, N.J.: Hillhouse, 1960). See also Robin Room, "Sociological Aspects of the Disease Concept of Alcoholism," *Research Advances in Alcohol and Drug Problems* 7 (1983): 47–91.

of the concept of sin, especially when that concept is understood as harsh, judgmental, punitive, and pessimistic. To say an addict or alcoholic is sick rather than sinful is today deemed more compassionate, relieving guilt feelings, giving hope of improvement, calling for sympathy rather than condemnation.

Additionally, placing the treatment of addiction in the hands of health practitioners, rather than religion or law, accords with the contemporary inclination to look primarily to technology, science, and medicine for answers. Although values are inevitably communicated in addiction diagnosis and treatment, they are presented under the aegis of a value-neutral psychology or medicine, thereby outwardly avoiding competing religious and cultural claims in our pluralistic society. From an economic point of view, the promotion of the disease model allows addiction treatment to be covered by health insurance and puts it into the governmental, educational, free-market, and social services realms. It allows the alcohol industry to support AA methods for the vulnerable, without jeopardizing sales to the rest. It allows business to separate out its problem drinkers (and drug users) and offer (or insist upon) treatment for them, while allowing social drinking to continue for others.

Although a large proportion of our society has decided that addiction is an illness, there is no corresponding unanimity among researchers. Instead, the various fields that have an interest in addictions continue to disagree with each other, remaining fragmented and specialized, and there is no reigning paradigm to bring uniformity to the definition, diagnosis, and treatment of addictions.[6] Additionally, critiques of the disease theory, the twelve-step method, and the treatment industry abound.

For example, some researchers see the disease metaphor to be a more serious problem than actual addictions, eviscerating people's capacity to deal with perennial human problems and

6. Dennis Donovan, "Assessment of Addictive Behaviors: Implications of an Emerging Biopsychosocial Model," in *Assessment of Addictive Behaviors,* ed. Dennis M. Donovan (New York: Guilford, 1988), 3–48.

stigmatizing them for life. Doubt has been raised about the efficacy of existing treatment programs, since lifetime abstinence appears to be a rarely met goal. It has been noted that many addiction counselors are recovering addicts, staunchly committed to the model they used themselves and often closed to conflicting views. Many researchers claim the studies that popularized the disease theory are seriously flawed. Feminists insist that an admission of powerlessness is the last thing needed by women and other oppressed groups and that the diagnosis of codependency is simply another way of blaming the victim. Some critics contend that the twelve-step method is religion in disguise and that it violates separation of church and state when mandated by the courts. And there has been a discussion within sociology about the "medicalization of deviance," where treatment really becomes a means of social control.[7]

Yet the work of addiction diagnosis and treatment goes on, and people continue to seek out both self-help groups and formal treatment programs to deal with an ever-widening array of problems. What are people searching for here? Even with current neglect of the doctrine of sin, it is possible that our culture nevertheless senses the tragically distorted human condition, something all religions have noted. Is the rising metaphor of addiction really just a modernized way of looking at sin? Could it even function as a new back door to the church, since twelve-step groups are sometimes the first to introduce persons to their need for a spiritual center? Can the doctrine be re-presented using addiction language and dispelling stereotypes that helped cause it to be rejected?

Indeed, some writers move in this direction, hailing the twelve-step movement as the most vital spirituality of our time. This

7. The body of critical literature is growing. See, for example, Herbert Fingarette, *Heavy Drinking: The Myth of Alcoholism as a Disease* (Berkeley: Univ. of California Press, 1988); Stanton Peele and Archie Brodsky, *The Truth about Addiction and Recovery* (New York: Simon and Schuster, 1991); and other works by Peele; see also Peter Conrad and Joseph W. Schneider, *Deviance and Medicalization: From Badness to Sickness* (St. Louis: Mosby, 1980).

is not a surprising assessment, given AA's Oxford roots and its focus on establishing a relationship with one's Higher Power, giving over control, making restitution, and continuing in an honest life. Some see the addictive spiral as one effective way to describe how sin functions in a human life, and others have claimed that addiction—whatever its biological and psychological aspects—is at base anything one puts in the place of God.[8]

Yet we cannot ignore the fact that although twelve-step meetings have frequently met in church buildings, the intercommunication between basement and sanctuary can be very slight. Participants often use the support group in ways the church was formerly used, that is, for spiritual nurturance, mutual help, and identity. Is the addiction movement, then, in fact further weakening the hold of religious principles upon contemporary culture? Has the doctrine of sin been further repudiated by turning addiction—and a multitude of other perennial human problems—from sin that can be repented and forgiven into sickness that can only be diagnosed and managed? Are we, rather than updating the doctrine of sin, instead in a transition from a religious to a secular description of the human condition? In order to ascertain whether the sin and addiction concepts can coexist and dialogue productively, or are antithetical, it is necessary to look briefly at the prevalent traditional doctrine.

THE DOCTRINE OF SIN: ELEMENTS AND ARGUMENTS

Although the doctrine of sin was always important to Christian faith and theology, it was not systematically considered until the work of Augustine. Key for the Augustinian doctrine is the "self-imposed bondage of the will." This view was pitted against the Manichaean version, which saw sin and human finitude as synonymous and was overly pessimistic, and against the Pelagian version, which saw sin as a wrong choice that could be avoided

8. See, for example, Patrick McCormick, *Sin as Addiction* (New York: Paulist, 1989); and Gerald May, *Addiction and Grace* (San Francisco: Harper, 1988).

and was overly optimistic. Western culture has been replaying these debates ever since.

A diversity of opinion on sin has always existed within Christianity. Sin has been seen as a kind of impurity or uncleanness, bondage to hostile powers, the flesh dominating the spirit, failure to maintain divinely ordained order, loss of love, losing touch with one's innate consciousness of God, alienation from God, and lack of trust. These are not inherently contradictory explanations but facets of the dilemma in which humans find themselves. For humans have long recognized that our condition is beset by a feeling of estrangement, a loss of touch with our ground of being, an inability to realize our potential, and a lack of trust in the good that exists, or, more definitively, in God's offer of grace.[9]

In spite of this diversity, there are certain central aspects of the various Christian traditions on sin. One key is that sin is more than breaking a moral code, disrupting order, using one's freedom wrongly, or failing to live up to one's potential. There is a dominant sense of sacral violation. We were created for God; there is a purpose for our lives; and when we reject that or turn away, we offend the divine person and purposes. This rejection is not occasional, however, but endemic. Sin is a universal condition, not the problem of a few, so there is a strong sense of human solidarity and an equalizing quality to the doctrine. Also crucial, the doctrine of sin seeks to preserve an element of human responsibility and freedom, even in the face of God's sovereignty and in light of radical evil. Yet it recognizes that we sell ourselves over to a bondage, from which it is then impossible to free ourselves. Therefore, the grace of God and its manifestation in the person and work of Christ are essential.

There has always been a debate on how much we can do and how much only God can do to effect this liberation. And

9. A clear and succinct treatment of this is given in Paul S. Fiddes, *Past and Present Salvation: The Christian Idea of the Atonement* (Louisville: Westminster/John Knox, 1989). Another concise resource on sin is Robert R. Williams, "Sin and Evil," in *Christian Theology: An Introduction to Its Traditions and Tasks,* ed. Peter C. Hodgson and Robert H. King (Philadelphia: Fortress, 1982).

the extent, timetable, and depth of this liberation are also debated. But the once-for-all work of Christ is pivotal. Through the ages the church has taken different positions on when the sacrifice of Christ takes full efficacious action and how to explain the transaction. Yet there is significant agreement that the act has finality even though its full flowering is yet to be seen. This hope inspires believers, seemingly against all odds, to both participate and trust in the promise that this work is moving effectively against the evil and sins of the world. Therefore, even though an inclination toward sin remains throughout life, an antidote to the poison is available, and it will eventually heal the world.

The prevalent tradition has tended to break down sin into constituent parts, original sin and actual sin. Original sin describes the condition we are born into and the inclination we seem to inherit, and actual sin refers to our response to that condition. Although there are a number of interpretations of original sin, it does not mean, as the stereotype holds, that babies are born evil and that there is nothing good about being human, but rather that we are born into a deformed world and cannot hope to escape unscathed. Indeed, we contribute to it.

For much of the dominant tradition, the essential point has been the basic inclination called concupiscence or inordinate desire. It is not that desire is wrong, for desire also serves as motivation for good and is eminently human. But excessive, wrongly directed desire produces evil. Concupiscence, then, is either seen as sin in itself or as something that prompts one to sin. Indeed, sin can be seen as simply a desire for the good that has become perverted.

Some would explain original sin societally, that is, that we are born into a world distorted by systemic and structural evil that seems beyond human effort to correct and is added to by (yet is more than the accumulation of) human sins. Others would see the basic problem as unbelief, lack of trust, alienation from God. Original sin can also be the human predilection to turn away from God and toward self or another. As such, all humans must fight continually against a perennial drift away from God.

The doctrine of sin, therefore, does not focus solely on volition. In fact, the prevailing tradition has long acknowledged that how we act is often not much determined by our will, even when we know better (see Rom 7:16). There is a strong sense of almost biological inheritance. And both Scripture and much Christian tradition indicate that while human will and desire are crucial, evil has a power that traps us. We are born into a difficult situation and while we contribute to it, we are also the victims of it. Humans are in bondage, and only grace can free us. The focus on will is essential, however, in order to maintain the crucial element of human freedom and to explain God's goodness in the face of evil. The modern debate over this is lengthy, but a key point is that human free will is essential if we are to return God's love for us in a voluntary, rather than coerced or determined, manner.

This goal is a futuristic and holistic one, for the doctrine of sin takes the long view of human history, looking forward to the restoration or institution of God's reign, when every tear will be wiped dry, the books will be balanced, and no one will fear anymore. This eschatological focus is the linchpin to any discussion on sin in Christian theology. But even now the church lives anticipatorily in that new realm. For we look at sin over our shoulder, recognizing its true character from the vantage point of forgiveness and liberation. There are different ways to approach this. When sin is understood more as breaking God's moral law, the experience of forgiveness is heightened. When sin is understood as our entrapment, both by the power of our own wrong choices and by systemic evil, liberation is the dominant metaphor. When sin is seen as wrong use of free will, restoration and sanctification are stressed as we feel newly able to choose the good. In any case, remorse quickly gives way to gratitude. We are not meant to wallow in sin but to revel in our release. Although tradition tends to see the work of Christ having finality, on the experiential level this is not a once-for-all event but a continuing dialogue between bondage and liberation.

There are a number of contemporary problems with the doctrine, and several are relevant to the addiction debate. The prevailing tradition has seemed imbalanced and negative by focusing more on the universality of sin and less on the universal offer of grace and redemption. A backward-looking approach that focuses on the fall (Augustinian version) has tended to dominate Christian tradition, in spite of the presence of a developmental approach that focuses forward on the maturity and freedom God is producing in us (Irenaean version).[10] The modern awareness of the psychological, sociological, and historical factors conditioning all human behavior is only beginning to temper the volitional aspect of the doctrine. For in spite of the potential balance between volition and bondage in the doctrine, we have too long stressed the power and independence of the will. Indeed, much of North American theology has had a Pelagian cast.

Concomitant with a narrow use of the idea of concupiscence, we have inherited a low view of the body, an ascetic impulse that can equate sin with corporeality. Additionally, the emphasis on human sin and volition has caused much of Christian tradition to downplay the irreducibly tragic element of radical evil. And the assumption that pride is the core of sin denies or ignores the perceptions of women and marginalized groups who, being taught to devalue or negate the self, experience sin and grace differently.[11]

10. See John Hick, *Evil and the God of Love,* rev. ed. (San Francisco: Harper and Row, 1977).

11. Foundational works on the gender aspect of this point are Valerie Saiving (Goldstein), "The Human Situation: A Feminine View," *Journal of Religion* 40 (April 1960): 100–112; and Judith Plaskow, *Sex, Sin and Grace: Women's Experience and the Theologies of Reinhold Niebuhr and Paul Tillich* (Lanham, Md.: Univ. Press of America, 1980).

COMPARISON AND CRITIQUE: ADDICTION INADEQUATE AS A REPLACEMENT METAPHOR

It must be granted that there is some significant common ground between the sin and addiction concepts. Both metaphors speak clearly about the existential dilemma that humans experience, knowing the good and not being able to do it, the bondage of the will. Both claim that this problem feels inborn or inherited. And both, at least the twelve-step approach to addiction, insist that divine aid is essential in breaking the hold. This runs against the contemporary trend to expect only human solutions to problems. Both the sin and addiction concepts speak about inordinate desire, and both see it as a perversion of a desire for good. In fact, Bill Wilson, founder of AA, said many alcoholics are "seeking God in a bottle," and even the more scientific expression of addiction can explain it as a good desire gone wrong. Neither the sin/grace nor the addiction/recovery process countenances self-deception; both promote honesty, self-examination, acceptance of responsibility, confession, making amends, and service to others. Both concepts insist upon a profound reorientation, toward the transcendent (twelve-step approach) rather than self-aggrandizement, toward trust rather than unbelief, toward solidarity rather than alienation. Both concepts promote the use of support communities, in recognition that the journey is too perilous to make alone and that honesty is aided by accountability.

In a culture that finds an idea of inherited evil distasteful, the addiction-as-disease metaphor comes close to a secularized view of original sin. No matter how much the addiction movement claims a nonmoral interpretation of addiction, its view of inherent addictive-inclination has some important similarities to the traditional notion of original sin, except that it is restricted to a specific, albeit growing, population. Especially when the disease is seen as innate or inherited, the sense of having been born into a difficult situation is similar. Also, Augustine, Christianity's various theological traditions, the founders of AA, and current members of twelve-step groups have all been struggling to explain some common human experiences—how it is that we can will one thing but do another; how we can know the good but not do it; how a good desire can come to a bad end.

For all the common ground, however, the addiction/twelve-step movement is not simply the Christian message in contemporary form, as some claim, or even a satisfactory contender. But it is a contender. While it is unrealistic to expect a complete theology from a popular movement and industry with the restricted task of managing addiction, the program has gone far beyond the initial goals of its founders. For many it is being used to provide a comprehensive life plan and interpretation of reality. To critique this metaphor and movement is not to withdraw compassion and support from those who suffer with addictions and have found help there. Also, because the movement is so diverse, not all points of critique will apply to each particular program. Nevertheless, some of the more striking contrasts between the sin and addiction concepts will be briefly discussed here.

First, this is a relatively new and highly pragmatic movement, working on many fronts at once. The blending of Christian principles derived from the Oxford Group, a quasi-medical disease theory, and various psychological approaches has resulted in a confusing mixture. For instance, it is rather pessimistic, almost Manichaean, about the inherent nature of those diagnosed with a particular addictive disease. It is not their fault, but it is part of their makeup. It can be managed but not cured. They can never be "normal." Yet conversely the movement is almost Pelagian in its optimism for those who accept the diagnosis of addict. Once individuals have been taught the true nature of their disease, they are expected to develop the ability to choose and maintain sobriety, in spite of previously irresistible factors such as craving, genetics, biochemistry, and family background.

The addiction-as-disease model has serious limitations in providing a working model for human behavior. Saying this neither takes credibility away from the biomedical components of addiction nor deemphasizes the chemical changes that can result from excessive alcohol and drug use. But critics are persuasive in noting that addiction is not just a medical problem; it is also a moral problem. Additionally, as the addiction model spreads to encompass more human behavior, it pushes beyond biology and ethics and confronts metaphysical issues, for example, the nature of humankind, its relationship to the divine, the reality of evil, and the character of God. Even when a spiritual component is added to the addiction model, its indebtedness to the disease aspect forces it to face these broader issues with an inadequate, eclectic conceptual framework.

A most important distinction is in the area of freedom. In spite of all the conditioning factors we are increasingly aware of, Christian theology has not given up its stress on human freedom. The bondage of sin is real enough and intractable, but it is self-imposed at a certain point, no matter how reduced or compromised one's responsibility. And this freedom can be restored and/or enhanced—albeit only through grace—when one becomes a "new creation" in Christ. Since this new status is secured not through one's own efforts, which would make it fragile at best, but through divine initiative, one has the security of knowing that nothing can separate one from the love of God or reverse one's deliverance.

In the disease model of addiction, freedom before and after diagnosis is compromised through the apparently compassionate but ultimately debilitating reduction of responsibility. There is the intimation, especially in the twelve-step model, that the addict is not sane before beginning recovery. (Step 2 says that a Higher Power "could restore us to sanity.") Thus, censure is avoided by understanding freedom and reason as largely absent or greatly reduced until recovery begins. But relapse always threatens; it is just "one drink/drug away." In fact some claim the disease progresses inexorably even during abstinence. Therefore, lingering doubts may remain about one's ability to know and trust the self or even rightly follow one's Higher Power. Experts or the group will have to be relied upon. Indeed, a principal goal of treatment is to replace the destructive addiction with a nonchemical substitute dependency.[12] In the spiritual version of the addiction model, divine grace awakens persons to their plight and can empower healthier choices, but no once-for-all cure can be expected, not even from one's Higher Power.

Although sin—like addictive inclination—can and does linger in the life of the redeemed, there is an eschatological goal and promise of complete liberation in Christ, not just for individuals, but for all creation. There is also a foretaste and guarantee of this in present restoration, being made a "new creation" in Christ. The addiction metaphor urges "progress, not perfection" but has no teleological direction or goal, no promise of complete health. While these two positions are not totally incompatible, the addiction metaphor on its own is inadequate to replace the hope and direction received from a more comprehensive, specific, future-oriented, and present-empowering eschatology. Nor can the addiction/recovery model point to a specific or objective act of redemption that activates the promise.

Additionally, the diagnosis that someone is not sane, the victim of a disease, and always vulnerable may ultimately be as debilitating as the guilt one carries when feeling lost in sin. The message of salvation is that although at base we have sinned against God, God has the power and desire to forgive, rectify, and transform. In the addiction model, even though one is not fully responsible for the wrong done while diseased, it must be faced. Yet one can only excuse oneself for it and hope for compassion from others. A crucial difference between twelve-step spirituality and Christian theology, therefore, is not just that the former has no Christology; it also has a reduced concept of

12. For a good summary of treatment goals (and the disease concept in general), see David E. Smith, Harvey B. Milkman, and Stanley G. Sunderwirth, "Addictive Disease: Concept and Controversy," in *Addictions: Multidisciplinary Perspectives and Treatments*, ed. Harvey Milkman and Howard J. Shaffer (Lexington, Mass.: Lexington Books, 1985).

God. God is neither responsible for nor ultimately powerful over the disease, the dangerous substance or process, or the perversions that perfectly natural things can be made into by weak/sick people. Yet the twelve steps present the Higher Power as able to control the person and the process. This inconsistency and other hard questions about the relationship between God and the disease are not addressed.

A chief goal within twelve-step spirituality, besides sobriety, is "serenity." But this, similar to the type of freedom sought by ancient Stoicism, is a very internalized state. Because there is no ultimate responsibility for the disease, the true self can be seen as pure and ripe with potential, if protected. Once sobriety has been achieved, the true self can develop. But persons must recognize they have little ultimate control over anything but their own attitudes and strive to detach "with love" from everything outside that core. No doubt some of this is a useful work of personal liberation and could undergird broader action. The danger is that inclinations toward political, organized, social action—that is, toward changing the actual conditions that promote addiction—will be eviscerated. Also, for those truly victimized by society, empowerment can be short-circuited by focus on a diagnosis of personal disease and irrationality. The profound effects of the social dimensions of injustice can be glossed over, and hence injustice is perpetuated or exacerbated. While historically Christians have disagreed on the proper extent and nature of social action, there are strong themes in Bible and tradition that urge responsibility for society and culture and call for justice and relief.

RECONSTRUCTION AND PRAXIS

These and other distinctions between the sin and addiction concepts show difficulties with the addiction model. Nevertheless, as we have seen, the doctrine of sin has problems of its own. Some argue that the main difficulty has been its recent neglect by the church. But a close look at the doctrine shows that interpretive distortions and difficulties have contributed to its dismissal by many. The doctrine needs reconstruction and reinterpretation in order to address the contemporary context better. A significant change in praxis must accompany this work. The success of the addiction movement and the way it redefines human behavior only heighten these needs.

Thus, ultimately it does not matter whether the addiction movement is seen as the secularization of a religious idea, a protest against theology and culture's overemphasis on volition, or a turf battle for the definition and control of problem behavior. Redefining the doctrine of sin should not be done to "reclaim territory" but instead to satisfy the perennial obligation to present the gospel message in contextually relevant and clear terms. In some areas the reconstructive work can be done in productive dialogue with the addiction movement. And the church can also learn from the successful community-building structure that addiction groups provide for their members. A few examples will suggest some areas in which to focus attention for the necessary work of doctrinal reconstruction and practical change as the church faces the addiction issue.

In many ways sin really is like addiction, partly inherited, partly chosen, easy to get into, difficult to get out of. It is true that, just as anything can become addictive, so anything can displace God. This is a useful message for professionals in the church who are valued for, and even pressured into, certain forms of idolatry like overwork, careerism, and the "messiah complex." It is equally useful as we recognize that the church is not immune to such problems as alcohol and sexual abuse. A first reconstructive suggestion, then, is that rather than downplaying the doctrine of sin, theology and preaching would do well to explicate the components of the doctrine and to draw fruitful comparisons between the concepts of sin and addiction. A second and distinct, but closely related, reconstructive need is for the church to recognize that focusing backward on the fall, rather than forward on restoration and grace, has communicated a negative, hopeless message to many. Since contemporary theology has already shown interest in a more developmental, Irenaean attitude toward sin, we would do well to focus theological work, as well as preaching and teaching, on the goal of maturity, health, and freedom in Christ. The recovery movement, for all its attention to addiction, does hold out hope for despairing people. The church must be recalled to its task of doing no less.

While there may be some truth in the contention that the rise in emotional illness is, in fact, a result of religion's retreat from the notion of sin, that is not the whole story. The best reason to preach on sin is to highlight the power and joy of grace. Indeed, contemporary culture has a hopelessness that cries to hear of the transformative healing and liberation available. But this must not be restricted to the individual level, something both the doctrine of sin and the addiction metaphor have done. For just as the whole culture is implicated in such problems as addiction, so all aspects of culture can and must be transformed. Helping people one-by-one to get off drugs or alcohol is an inefficient solution when scores of others are prompted daily to use substances to blot out the pains of poverty, societal oppression, or a sense of meaninglessness. And it is also an unrealistic solution unless we deal with the fact that entire industries, both legal and illegal, continue to profit from these personal, ineffectual, and thus necessarily repetitive attempts at escaping problems that are broad-based and not just individual. A third reconstructive suggestion, then, is for Christian theology to focus more heavily on the systemic nature of sin and evil and to analyze the problem of addiction within this wider framework, while not losing the notion of individual complicity and responsibility. Since there are resources for a more comprehensive, systemic, and societal view of sin and evil, it would be valuable for theologies that utilize these approaches, such as liberation, feminist, and black theologies, to turn their attention to the addiction issue.

The related problem, both practical and theological, is that although the doctrine of sin at heart is a leveling concept, it has been used instead to judge, separate, and condemn. The penalty for this shows up in the addiction movement's virulent attitude toward the concept of sin. If the alcoholic or addict is loath to come up from the basement meeting and enter the sanctuary for worship, the church must do some soul-searching about its attitudes, interpretation of the gospel message, and focus of ministry. This is as much an area for practical action as theological reconstruction. However, while the church will need to repent of its blaming attitude, we are reminded by the doctrine of sin not to do so at the expense of accountability, for that essentially diminishes human freedom and dignity.

A fourth key problematic area in need of reconstructive work is Christian theology's inadequate handling of the reality of radical evil. The prevailing Christian tradition understands evil as both internal and external but has focused much attention on the internal aspects. The addiction metaphor in a sense preserves a space for external and radical evil by allowing for the ever-present and ultimately unexplainable nature of disease. Yet it ultimately rejects personal involvement in evil by giving up accountability for the disease and projecting the problem on substance, biology, process, and so on. Spurred by the North American penchant for expecting quick solutions, people flock to the addiction movement looking for remedies to distinct problems. Once there, however, they are taught they have a lifetime disease for which they are not ultimately responsible but which they will now have to manage.

Theology must face the tragic dimension of life squarely but aim for a balance between notions of responsibility and victimization. A revitalized doctrine of original sin could provide a more holistic way to explain the feeling of powerlessness while also showing the solidarity of humankind. This is ultimately more compassionate, realistic, and egalitarian than seeing only certain people as infected and vulnerable. It is also potentially empowering to insist people always have some level of choice even if they have been victimized. On the level of praxis, small groups that would focus on the daily problems of living common to us all, and work intentionally to counterbalance societal issues with individual responses, would be valuable assets in the local church. Hopefully, community-based social action would result when the societal component of seemingly individual problems became clearly evident.

A fifth reconstructive focus is the area of gender, for the traditional doctrine of sin has not taken gender seriously enough. Both the doctrine of sin and the twelve steps focus on powerlessness. But this is only productive where power-seeking or self-aggrandizement has been the prime problem. Where abnegation of self has been the prime form of alienation, leading to alienation from God and others, the exhortation to admit powerlessness is counterproductive. The doctrine of sin, with its overemphasis on pride, is culpable. A theme in the addiction movement, the problem of codependency, graphically shows that lack of self-development can be as detrimental as focusing too much on the self. When this behavior is presented as a disease, however, rather than as a more systemic, societally induced problem, the diagnosis remains stunted and counterproductive. Theology and psychology can dialogue here. There are a few resources within the various theological traditions that might serve as discussion starters,[13] but the essential task is reconstructive, with praxis growing out of it.

Finally, we still do not value creation enough, and we still fear the body. The addiction movement has exacerbated this problem it inherited from the dominant tradition. We must learn to defend our human pleasures as much as fear our excesses. Sex, food, wine, and relationships are all part of the good creation.

13. See, for example, Mary Louise Bringle's discussion of Kierkegaard in *Despair: Sickness or Sin? Hopelessness and Healing in the Christian Life* (Nashville: Abingdon, 1990); and Wanda Warren Berry, "Images of Sin and Salvation in Feminist Theology," *Anglican Theological Review* 60 (January 1978): 45.

Christians should be the chief defenders of responsibly enjoying, rather than morbidly fearing, these gifts of God. Instead many become attracted to the new legalism of the addiction movement. A concerted effort by believers and churches to appreciate our humanity and the created order is needed here. Churches can be intentional about promoting healthy ways for us to relax and play together, rather than limiting our interaction to work and formal worship.

It must be admitted that the addiction movement is filling some gaps in contemporary culture, gaps that the church has either stopped addressing or feels inadequate to meet. Thus, people have turned elsewhere. For instance, the twelve-step movement, using the idea that one must manage one's own disease, talks about such things as self-discipline, individual responsibility, and the everyday choices that build or destroy character—topics in which the church once specialized. The movement has provided a dependable, accepting environment for people who feel rejected and hopeless. Both the lay and professional aspects of the movement strive to unflinchingly face and compassionately accept persons with the most intractable and even humiliating problems. By and large, the mainstream church has either flinched, handed the problem over to science and medicine, or accepted the twelve-step model uncritically. However, while the addiction metaphor challenges the doctrine of sin—as well as church attitudes and practices around the addiction issue—it does not provide a satisfactory reformulation of the doctrine. Nor does it provide an adequate description of the problematic aspects of the human condition. Indeed, in some ways the addiction metaphor has adopted some of the more troublesome themes of the prevalent traditional doctrine, while in other ways giving up on the concept. Significant reconstructive work on sin, rather than further dismantling, is needed. For the difficulties with eliminating or reducing the idea of sin become apparent as we study the addiction movement.

That movement, however, is filling a gap in our society, providing a place of hope for the hopeless and creating a forum where the day-to-day problems of human behavior can be explored. And in its maintenance of the spiritual dimension of addiction and the need for honest living, the lay twelve-step movement is holding a middle ground between a solely moral approach to addiction and a complete medicalization of the problem. Both theology and church must take a lesson from this.

JOHN T. PAWLIKOWSKI, O.S.M.

10. CHRISTOLOGY, ANTI-SEMITISM, AND CHRISTIAN-JEWISH BONDING

INTRODUCTION

During World War II a delegation of German bishops went to see Adolf Hitler in order to protest his treatment of Jews. He caustically responded to their intervention with the oft-quoted statement that he was "only carrying out in practice what the churches had been preaching for centuries." While Hitler's remark may fall somewhat short in terms of exact historical analysis, it does point to a long-standing, undeniable, and deep connection between classical Christian theology and anti-Semitism. When all is said and done the most direct link between anti-Semitism and the church's theological tradition comes in the area of Christology.

Christian anti-Semitic attitudes have always been directly connected to interpretations of the Christ-event. Jews were seen as intimately involved with Jesus' execution, thus bringing upon their heads a permanent curse. Jews were called "blind" with respect to the new revelation in Jesus. They were said to practice a much inferior form of religion rooted in law while Christians based their faith on the experience of grace made present through Christ's coming. And Jews were described as rejecting belief in Jesus, being replaced as a result in the covenantal relationship with God by the new Christian community.

These expressions of the meaning of Christology took time to coalesce in the early church. Though some of them go back to misinterpreted or selective scriptural passages, these beliefs about the Jews essentially are postbiblical. They owe their origins to the writings of the church fathers such as Origen, Tertullian, and Eusebius, who fundamentally framed Christian identity along anti-Jewish lines.[1] In so doing they created what has been termed the *adversus Judaeos* tradition. Jesus, a Jew, had clearly become a barrier between Jews and Christians rather than a point of bonding. Nearly all Christian churches have appropriated all or part of this negative vision of the Jews as an integral part of their catechesis, preaching, worship, and theology.

ANALYSIS: ANTI-SEMITISM IN THE U.S. CONTEXT

Rosemary Ruether has demonstrated in her now classic volume *Faith and Fratricide* that anti-Judaism lay at the heart of patristic theology.[2] It became in effect the "left-hand of Christology." The great writers of the patristic era, Tertullian, Origen, Irenaeus, and Eusebius, all made it an integral part of stating the fundamental meaning of Christian identity.

In many of his writings, but especially in those directed against Marcion, Tertullian presented Jesus as the messiah who ought to have been recognized by the Jewish people, and he argued that the Jews suffered God's wrath because of their blindness. For him Jesus' severity toward Jews was completely in line with the antagonism toward Jews expressed by his Father, the Creator. As David Efroymson puts it,

> What seems significant here is not the negative picture of the Jews of Jesus' time, which was, of course, already firmly embedded in

1. See David Efroymson, "The Patristic Connection," in *Anti-Semitism and the Foundations of Christianity,* ed. Alan T. Davies (New York: Paulist, 1979), 98–117; and Robert L. Wilken, *The Myth of Christian Beginnings: History's Impact on Belief* (Garden City, N.Y.: Doubleday, 1972).

2. Rosemary Ruether, *Faith and Fratricide: The Theological Roots of Anti-Semitism* (New York: Seabury, 1974).

> the tradition. It is rather the heavy emphasis on the appropriateness of the opposition between Jesus and Jews, or between God and Jews.... Not only was there an emphatic heightening of an anti-Jewishness ascribed to Jesus; there was the additional element, apparently now crucial against Marcion, of a God who for some time had "opposed" Israel and had wanted to rid himself of the "old" covenant in the interest of something new and better.[3]

Origen's approach was marked by a particular emphasis on what he called the "spiritual sense" of the Scriptures. Reading the biblical texts in this way, he insists in *On First Principles,* is the solution to the problem of the "hard-hearted and ignorant members of the circumcision" (that is, Jews) who "refused to believe in our Savior" because they could not get beyond the *literal* sense of the text (4.2.1).

Irenaeus explained Jewish law as necessary for a time because of human sinfulness. But the coming of Jesus and the destruction of Jerusalem signaled that the time of the Jews and their law was over. According to Irenaeus, Jesus was attacking the Jewish claim to be able to know the Father without accepting the Son. He relied on the parables of the wicked husbandmen (Matt. 21:33-44) and the wedding feast (Mark 22:1-14) to "prove" that God had destined the Gentiles to replace unresponsive Jews in the kingdom.

Finally, Eusebius in his early fourth-century *Ecclesiastical History* confines the rolc of Jews to that of witnessing to divine justice. That was especially true in the first century when Jews were being punished at the hands of the Romans while the Christian church was flourishing and growing.

Over the centuries this original patristic *adversus Judaeos* tradition has continued to exercise a sometimes direct and sometimes more subtle influence on Christian theological formulation of the meaning of Jesus' ministry, death, and resurrection. It has given rise to a decided emphasis on Christ over God and Spirit in Christian thought, leading at times to what Dorothee Soelle

3. Efroymson, "Patristic Connection," 103–4.

has described as a "crypto-racist" tendency in christological expression. It has likewise resulted in a denial of any independent integrity and meaning for the Jewish Scriptures. Gabriel Fackre's remarks are very much to the point in this regard:

> The apostolic testimony to the central acts of the Christian drama, the deliverance wrought in the life, ministry, death, and resurrection of Christ, is the prism through which the light of biblical revelation is to be seen and understood. Thus the *seventy-seven percent* of the Book that is the Hebrew Bible, our Old Testament, is to be understood within its New Testament context. How the law and the prophets are appropriated in the Christian faith is determined by how their promise is illumined and fulfilled in the New Testament.[4]

The *adversus Judaeos* legacy of patristic Christianity cast a shadow over the writings of many of the prominent exegetes and theologians of the first half of the twentieth century, especially in Europe. But because these European scholars have had a global impact on Christianity, including North American theologians and Latin American liberationists, their views have special significance for this analysis. Gerhard Kittel, the original editor of the highly influential *Theological Dictionary of the New Testament*, was one important example. His view was that postbiblical Jews were largely a community in dispersion. "Authentic Judaism," he wrote, "abides by the symbol of the stranger wandering restless and homeless on the face of the earth."[5]

The prominent exegete Martin Noth, whose *History of Israel* became a standard work for students and professors alike, described Israel as a strictly "religious community" which died a slow and agonizing death in the first century A.D. For Noth, Jewish history reached its culmination in the arrival of Jesus. His words are crystal-clear on this point:

> Jesus himself, with his words and his work, no longer formed part of the history of Israel. In him the history of Israel had come, rather, to its real end. What did belong to the history of Israel

4. Gabriel Fackre, *The Christian Story* (Grand Rapids: Eerdmans, 1978), 23.
5. G. Kittel, *Die Judenfrage* (Stuttgart: Kohlhammer, 1933), 73.

> was the process of his rejection and condemnation by the Jerusalem religious community. It had not discerned in him the goal to which the history of Israel had secretly been leading; it rejected him as the promised Messiah. Only a few had joined him, and from them something new proceeded. The Jerusalem religious community imagined it had more important concerns, and kept aloof from this new movement. Hereafter the history of Israel moved quickly to its end.[6]

A third example is Rudolf Bultmann, who exercised a decisive influence over Christian biblical interpretation for decades. Unlike Kittel, who was removed from his teaching post at Tübingen in 1945 because of his pro-Nazi sympathies, Bultmann's exegesis did not carry over into politics. But, theologically speaking, his understanding of the Christ-event also left Jews and Judaism with little or no meaning after the coming of Jesus. In his *Theology of the New Testament,* he held to the view that a Jewish people cannot be said to exist with the emergence of the Christian church. For him Jewish law, ritual, and piety removed God to a distant realm while through the continued presence of Jesus in prayer and worship each individual was brought ever closer to God. Bultmann's understanding of Judaism in Jesus' day was based on totally inadequate sources in terms of understanding Second Temple Judaism and Jesus' relationship to its teachings.

The deep-seated tradition of anti-Judaic Christology has continued to find expression even in very recent attempts at theological reformulation. Liberation theologians, for example, are not free of its shadow. Gustavo Gutiérrez has written that since "the infidelities of the Jewish people made the Old Covenant invalid, the Promise was incarnated both in the proclamation of a New Covenant, which was awaited and sustained by the 'remnant,' as well as in the promises which prepared and accompanied its advent."[7] Clark Williamson, in a detailed study of Jon Sobrino's

6. Martin Noth, *The Laws in the Pentateuch and Other Studies* (Edinburgh: Oliver and Boyd, 1966), 63.

7. Gustavo Gutiérrez, *A Theology of Liberation* (Maryknoll, N.Y.: Orbis, 1973), 161.

Christology at the Crossroads in light of the basic anti-Judaic patterns for Christology set forth in the writings of Tertullian, has concluded that "each aspect of this anti-Judaic model is to be found in Sobrino's *Christology at the Crossroads*. Each theme can be documented in his text."[8]

Another major point of linkage between Christology and anti-Semitism arises from the interpretation of Jesus' approach to the law, particularly as presented by St. Paul in his epistles. Protestant Christianity has shown a marked tendency to build a great deal of its christological understanding around the belief that Jesus brought to the fore a new sense of freedom that obliterated any further need for the Jewish Torah tradition. Because Torah observance was at the heart of Second Temple Judaism, in the time of Jesus total rejection of the Jewish legal tradition amounted to rejection of the Jewish tradition as such. Christian exegetes and theologians such as Jon Sobrino have especially targeted the Pharisees and have described Jesus as strenuously opposed to supposed "Pharisaic legalism" in the name of a new freedom in the Spirit.

A new twist on this theme of Jesus' teachings as religiously superior to parallel beliefs in Judaism can be found in certain forms of contemporary feminist theology where Jesus is portrayed as advocating the liberation of women from the yoke of Jewish law. As Judith Plaskow has argued, "the consequence of this myth is that feminism is turned into another weapon in the Christian anti-Judaic arsenal."[9]

It was not until the middle of this century that serious efforts began to develop to rid church teaching of this destructive

8. Clark M. Williamson, "Christ against the Jews: A Review of Jon Sobrino's Christology," in *Christianity and Judaism: The Deepening Dialogue*, ed. Richard W. Rousseau, S.J. (Scranton, Pa.: Ridge Row Press, 1983), 148; also cf. John T. Pawlikowski, *Christ in the Light of the Christian-Jewish Dialogue* (New York: Paulist, 1982), 59–75.

9. Judith Plaskow, "Christian Feminism and Anti-Judaism," *Cross Currents* (fall 1978): 306–9; and Deborah McCauley and Annette Daum, "Jewish-Christian Feminist Dialogue: A Wholistic Vision," *Union Seminary Quarterly Review* 38, no. 2 (1983): 147–90.

adversus Judaeos tradition created by the church fathers. Vatican II's Declaration on Non-Christian Religions, subsequent Catholic documents, and various national, regional, and international Protestant documents have led the way in clearing the ground for a new catechesis and theology regarding the church's relationship with the Jewish people.

North American Christianity clearly has shared this dark legacy created by the church fathers even though the spirit of religious toleration generally operative on this continent has prevented it from being applied in the social sphere to the same extent as in other parts of the world. We have been basically spared from the violent attacks against Jewish communities that have often marked European history. Further, church legends that portray Jews killing Christian babies and using their blood for their own rituals, legends that were commonplace among Christians in such countries as Italy, have not developed in North America.

Certainly the Christian anti-Semitic legacy has concretely affected North American Jews to some degree, even if not to the same extent as in Europe and elsewhere. Jews (as well as Catholics and other religious minorities) were accorded few civic and political rights in most of the original North American colonies. At best they were granted the right to worship. Social discrimination against Jews in employment and housing was widespread until the middle of this century. And certainly we cannot overlook hate groups such as the Klan, supposedly rooted in the Christian tradition, which made Jews special targets of their attacks along with African Americans and Catholics.

One factor that considerably moderated concrete expressions of anti-Semitism in the United States was the emergence of an unprecedented interreligious coalition that was formed to counter prevailing economic injustice in the nation in the 1930s and 1940s. Though this coalition, which embraced Jews, Catholics, and Protestants, never directly generated a rethinking of historic theological understandings of each other by the participating religious groups,[10] it did instill a spirit of toleration that helped bring about a collaborative effort on a series of pioneering textbook studies in the 1950s and 1960s that significantly contributed to changes in the approach to Jews among mainline Protestants and Catholics.[11]

This experience of toleration and social cooperation was no doubt responsible for the central role the U.S. Catholic bishops played in the passage of the ground-breaking chapter on the church and the Jewish people in Vatican II's Declaration on Non-Christian Religions.[12] This declaration represented one of the most important contributions of American Catholicism to the council. It added strength to the movement begun by certain Christian leaders and theologians, some of them connected with European resistance movements during World War II, for a thorough revamping of Christianity's theological approach to the Jewish people. Their experience during Nazism—which employed the traditional anti-Semitism within the churches as an indispensable seedbed for popular support of Jewish extermination—left them convinced that post-Holocaust Christianity could not recover moral credibility without ridding itself of this vicious cancer with its theological basis.

The same was true of some of the anti-Nazi Protestant leaders in Germany, France, and Holland. They formed the nucleus of a new force within the churches that led (with some Catholic and Jewish collaboration) to the historic "Ten Points of Seeligsberg" in 1947. This initial postwar declaration on the need for

10. See John T. Pawlikowski, "A Growing Tradition of Ethical Critique," in *Economic Justice: CTU's Pastoral Commentary on the Bishops' Letter on the Economy,* ed. John Pawlikowski, O.S.M., and Donald Senior, C.P. (Washington, D.C.: Pastoral Press, 1988), 39–48.

11. See Bernhard E. Olson, *Faith and Prejudice* (New Haven: Yale Univ. Press, 1963); John T. Pawlikowski, *Catechetics and Prejudice* (New York: Paulist, 1973); Eugene J. Fisher, *Faith without Prejudice* (New York: Paulist, 1977); and Philip A. Cunningham, "A Content Analysis of the Presentation of Jews and Judaism in Current Catholic Religion Textbooks" (Ph.D. diss., Boston College, 1992). A new analysis of Protestant educational materials is being completed by Stuart Polley.

12. For the text of the declaration, see Eugene J. Fisher and Leon Klenicki, eds., *In Our Time: The Flowering of Jewish-Catholic Dialogue* (New York: Paulist, 1990), 27–28.

a new constructive theology of the Christian-Jewish relationship was followed by many statements from individual Protestant dominations and from the World Council of Churches. These documents parallel, and in some areas even move beyond, the declaration of Vatican II.[13]

The results of the professional studies on Christian education materials conducted at Yale University (Protestant) and at St. Louis University (Catholic) added further impetus to the movement for change in the American churches' stance toward Jews.[14] Both textbook studies clearly showed that generations of Christian students in North America had been presented with an understanding of the gospel in which anti-Semitism became an inevitable by-product.

The studies show that Jesus was routinely presented as the one who brought Jewish history and Jewish messianic longings to an end. Everything that the prophets had promised was in fact fulfilled in his ministry and person. As a result, there was little theological value accorded to Judaism after the Easter-event. What was of value in Judaism had been subsumed into the religion of the new covenant, which began with Jesus. Put another way, the church had *displaced* Israel as covenantal heir. Jews could continue to share in the covenantal tradition only if they converted to Christianity. Those Jews who refused to accept the gospel were destined to experience a life of misery and social exile. Even if the Christian textbooks made no specific mention of the patristic *adversus Judaeos* tradition, it is clear that this legacy continued to cast its shadow over Christian catechesis well into this century.

13. For the other documents, see World Council of Churches, *The Theology of the Churches and the Jewish People: Statements by the World Council of Churches and Its Member Churches,* with a commentary by Allan Brockway, Paul van Buren, Rolf Rendtorff, and Simon Schoon (Geneva: WCC Publications, 1988); Helga Croner, ed., *Stepping Stones to Further Jewish-Christian Relations: An Unabridged Collection of Christian Documents,* foreword by Edward A. Synan (London: Stimulus Books, 1977); and idem, ed., *More Stepping Stones to Jewish-Christian Relations: An Unabridged Collection of Christian Documents 1975–1983* (New York: Paulist, 1985).

14. See n. 11, above.

The christological tradition of the churches never advocated outright extermination of the Jewish people, although individual Christian preachers did sometimes suggest such a fate. Rather this tradition argued that Judaism was to continue until the end of days, but as an empty religion that had relinquished all status and was bereft of spiritual vitality. It was to survive as a pariah so as to highlight the superiority of the church that had accepted Jesus as Lord and Redeemer. The desperate plight of the Jewish people was also intended to serve as a warning to anyone in the Christian community who might be tempted to stray away from belief in Christ.

As Rosemary Ruether has shown,[15] the church has not been content to keep its notion of Jewish displacement confined to the theological realm. While the church as institution has opposed any notion of a "final solution" (that was something in God's hands to be accomplished perhaps as part of the final eschatological drama), it did attempt to translate this theology into forms of "social misery." As Ruether puts it, "the legislation of Christian emperors and Church councils on the status of the Jew in Christian society reflects the effort to mirror this theological theory in social practice."[16] Such efforts were to remain commonplace in Western society until the twentieth century. Even the Nazi legislation owed much to the ancient and medieval laws promulgated against Jews, although its racial basis set it apart from previous forms of anti-Semitism. In the United States a noted Catholic priest from suburban Detroit, Fr. Charles Coughlin, exploited this anti-Semitic legacy during the Depression in numerous radio sermons that reached large audiences.[17]

These two central theological trends in Christianity, viewing

15. Ruether, *Faith and Fratricide,* 186ff.

16. Ibid., 186.

17. See Ronald Modras, "Father Coughlin and Anti-Semitism: Fifty Years Later," *Journal of Church and State* 31, no. 2 (spring 1989): 231–47; and idem, "Father Coughlin and the Jews: A Broadcast Remembered," *America,* March 11, 1989, 219–22. Also see Mary Christine Athans, B.V.M., "A New Perspective on Father Charles E. Coughlin," *Church History* 26, no. 2 (June 1987): 224–35.

the church as displacing the Jewish people in the basic covenantal relationship with God and understanding the gospel as a total replacement (and rejection) of the Jewish Torah, have stood at the heart of christological statement in Christianity over the centuries. As a result, any decisive cleansing of anti-Semitism from the Christian heritage will necessarily involve some reshaping of basic christological language within the churches.

RECONSTRUCTION: A SEA CHANGE UNDER WAY

Beginning a Dramatic Reversal

The formal process of rethinking theologically the meaning of Christ, Christian identity, and the Jewish people is generally regarded as having begun with the historic meeting of Jews and Christians (Catholics, Protestants, and Greek Orthodox) at Seeligsberg, Switzerland, mentioned previously. The Christians who participated (including the future prime minister of Poland, Tadeusz Mazowiecki) produced a declaration that set Christian thinking regarding the Jewish people on a totally new course. And several prominent Christian scholars in Europe, including Karl Barth, Jean Danielou, the future Cardinal Augustin Bea, James Parkes, and Hans Urs von Balthasar, began to speak out on the question. While not agreeing completely on every point, on one critical issue their voices had a common ring—Jews must now be regarded as continuing in a covenantal relationship with God, however the church eventually might interpret the meaning of the Christ-event. The centuries-old *adversus Judaeos* tradition and its claims of Jewish covenantal displacement were now beginning to erode.

Many of the early proponents of a new theological vision of the Jewish-Christian relationship appealed to Romans 9–11 for justification of their position. Paul insists in these chapters that God remains faithful to the original chosen people. They also tended to rely on Romans for a new model for the Christian-Jewish relationship—the "mystery" approach in which Christians and Jews are both proclaimed members of the covenantal household of God despite the apparent contradiction of such an assertion in purely human terms. On the American scene, Msgr. John Oesterreicher, who would become a leading figure at Vatican II in developing the declaration on the Jewish people, introduced the works of some of these pioneering scholars to North America via the publication of a multivolume series called *The Bridge.*[18]

The process of eradicating the *adversus Judaeos* tradition from Christian theology gained new impetus at Vatican II. After a dramatic meeting between French Jewish historian Jules Isaac and Pope John XXIII it was decided that the conciliar agenda would include a statement on Christianity's relationship to Judaism. Though this was an internal Catholic document in one sense, there is little doubt that its eventual impact reached far beyond the parameters of the Catholic church. It sparked similar reexaminations by many of the mainline Protestant churches.

The actual composition of the Vatican declaration proved quite revealing, as Eugene Fisher has noted. For it showed the poverty of the Christian tradition relative to its understanding of relations with the Jewish people. Every other document issued by Vatican II abounds with references to the tradition of the church—the Fathers, papal statements, declarations by previous church councils. Not so with chapter 4 of *Nostra Aetate.* There was simply little, if any, positive tradition upon which to draw, except to return as a starting point to Romans 9–11.[19]

In other words, the church was finally picking up in the second half of the twentieth century a process that had been short-

18. John M. Oesterreicher, ed., *The Bridge: A Yearbook of Judaeo-Christian Studies,* 4 vols. (New York: Pantheon, 1955, 1956, 1958, 1961); idem, ed., *The Bridge: Brothers in Hope: Judaeo-Christian Studies,* vol. 5 of the series (New York: Herder and Herder, 1970).

19. Eugene J. Fisher, "The Evolution of a Tradition: From *Nostra Aetate* to the *Notes,*" in *Fifteen Years of Catholic-Jewish Dialogue, 1970–1985,* ed. International Catholic-Jewish Liaison Committee (Rome: Libreria Editrice Vaticana and Libreria Editrice Lateranense, 1988), 239–54.

circuited since the latter stages of St. Paul's life. Constructing a new theology of the church and the Jewish people in light of the Christ-event was clearly emerging as an epochal undertaking. Because the effort to reformulate the theology of the Christian-Jewish relationship inevitably touches upon the very nerve center of Christian identity (that is, Christology), the pace of change will likely be slow. But because of this, a renewed theological understanding of the church's linkage with the Jewish people has repercussions for the whole of Christian theology. Johannes Metz has strongly emphasized this point: "[I]t is not a matter of revision of Christian theology with regard to Judaism, but a matter of the revision of Christian theology itself."[20]

Recapturing the Jewish Jesus

The process of revising Christianity's theological approach to Judaism has been enhanced by the work of both Scripture scholars and systematicians. In New Testament studies we are now witnessing a remarkable turnabout in the basic understanding of Jesus' relationship to the Jewish community and tradition of his time. This fundamental shift in perspective has resulted from a wider grasp of Hebrew and Aramaic and a new reliance on Jewish materials from the Second Temple or so-called intertestamental period made possible through this new language facility among Christian scholars. We are experiencing a rapid end to the dominant hold of early *Religionsgeschichte* (history of religion method)—which emphasized the almost totally Hellenistic background of Pauline Christianity—as well as its later modified manifestation in Rudolf Bultmann and some of his disciples such as Ernst Käsemann and Helmut Koester. These exegetical approaches to the New Testament seriously eroded the understanding of Jesus' concrete ties to biblical and Second Temple Judaism. This in turn tended to produce an excessively "univer-

20. Johannes Metz, "Facing the Jews: Christian Theology after Auschwitz," in *The Holocaust as Interruption,* ed. Elisabeth Schüssler Fiorenza and David Tracy, *Concilium* 175, no. 5 (October 1984): 27.

salistic" interpretation of Jesus' message, an interpretation that harbored the seeds of theological anti-Judaism.

Scholars such as W. D. Davies, E. P. Sanders, Douglas Hare, Daniel Harrington, Cardinal Carlo Martini, James Charlesworth, and Robin Scroggs have been in the forefront of this "re-Judaization" of Jesus. Arthur J. Droge, in a review of Sanders's *Jesus and Judaism,* speaks of this development in blunt terms: "Like Professor Sanders, I take this to be a positive development—a sign that New Testament studies is finally emerging from its 'Bultmannian captivity.' "[21]

The Christian scholars now engaged in rethinking the church's relationship to the Jewish people certainly do not concur on all points. Major source problems and ambiguities virtually assure the continuation of these disagreements for the foreseeable future. Nonetheless, there is a growing consensus emerging among those scholars who have examined the question in some depth. This new consensus might best be expressed in the words of Cardinal Carlo Martini: "In its origins Christianity is deeply rooted in Judaism. Without a sincere feeling for the Jewish world, therefore, and a direct experience of it, one cannot understand Christianity. Jesus is fully Jewish, the apostles are Jewish, and one cannot doubt their attachment to the traditions of their forefathers."[22]

One of the most important areas of recent research, for Christology in particular, has been exploration of Jesus' ties to the Pharisaic movement. This effort has been hampered by the widespread stereotypes of Pharisaism permeating Christianity since its earliest days. An important breakthrough in counteracting these stereotypes occurred in 1985 when the Vatican document *Notes on the Correct Way to Present the Jews and Judaism*

21. Arthur J. Droge, "The Facts about Jesus: Some Thoughts on E. P. Sanders' *Jesus and Judaism,*" *Criterion* 26, no. 11 (winter 1987): 15.

22. Cardinal Carlo Maria Martini, "Christianity and Judaism: A Historical and Theological Overview," in *Jews and Christians: Exploring the Past, Present, and Future,* ed. James B. Charlesworth (New York: Crossroad, 1990), 19.

in Preaching and Catechesis affirmed that Jesus stood closer to Pharisaism than any other Jewish movement of the time.[23]

A careful examination of the limited sources now available shows that the emergence of Pharisaism signaled a profound theological reorientation among the Jewish people in their basic understanding of the God-humanity relationship. No longer was God understood merely as the parent of the patriarchs, as intimate only with a select group of priests, prophets, and kings in Israel. This God now related in a profoundly intimate way to each and every individual, whatever his or her particular societal status. Class gradations in the level of divine intimacy had been permanently abolished. All persons were now equally "children of God." This vision would lead the Pharisees to undertake a genuine, if somewhat subtle, revolution in nearly every major aspect of Israel's social life.[24]

The Pharisaic approach to Judaism focused around six basic realities: (1) "oral Torah," which allowed for continued reinterpretation of the original biblical texts; (2) highlighting the role of lay, rather than priestly, leadership in the community through the rabbinate; (3) making the synagogue—a "house of the people of God" where prayer, study, and almsgiving were conjoined—far more important in many ways than the Temple; (4) using table-fellowship meals as the ordinary locus for worship; (5) emphasizing the centrality of the resurrection; and (6) relying on parables to convey important dimensions of the Jewish faith.

When we examine carefully the ministry and teachings of Jesus as recorded in the New Testament, we are struck by the similarity to Pharisaic patterns and concerns. Jesus often uses "oral Torah" to interpret texts from the Hebrew Scriptures; his understanding of ministry seems very much in the rabbinic mode rather than a priestly one; his vision of "church" owes far more to the synagogue model than to the Temple model; he participates in

23. See Croner, ed., *More Stepping Stones*, 227–28.

24. Ellis Rivkin, *The Hidden Revolution: The Pharisees' Search for the Kingdom Within* (Nashville: Abingdon, 1978).

table-fellowship meals, including the one where he establishes the Eucharist; he preaches belief in the resurrection; and he frequently teaches in parables. This last point is especially critical for christological study because much of modern European Christology was predicated on the belief that the parables were unique to Jesus and that they were meant to stress the expulsion of the Jews from the messianic kingdom because of their failure to acknowledge Jesus as the Christ. This Christology of expulsion, based on mistaken parabolic interpretation, served to undergird traditional Christian anti-Semitism.

Despite the shared theological vision between Jesus and the Pharisees, they parted company in several critical areas. First, Jesus seemed to envision a personal bonding with the Father that went beyond anything the Pharisees could accept. Second, Jesus' uncompromising commitment to the dignity of each individual person was deemed by the Pharisees as a threat to Jewish communal survival in an era when some in the Jewish community were strongly espousing its Hellenization. Jesus also appears to have supported the outcast group called the *Am Ha Aretz* (people of the land) to a degree that troubled the Pharisees despite their own sympathy for them, though the distinction should not be overstated.[25]

Jesus likewise advocated a degree of love and respect for enemies that Israeli scholar David Flusser has described as unique. While Judaism certainly taught that enemies ought not be the object of hatred and contempt, according to Flusser it did not prescribe outright love of enemies in the direct and unqualified way that Jesus did. Flusser adds that in the New Testament this teaching is confined to Jesus himself.[26]

Several other points of contrast between Jesus and the Pharisaic movement have come to light. Clemens Thoma has con-

25. Ellis Rivkin, "Defining the Pharisees: The Tannaitic Sources," *Hebrew Union College Annual* (1970): 205–49; and Michael Cook, "Jesus and the Pharisees—The Problem as It Stands Today," *Journal of Ecumenical Studies* 15, no. 3 (summer 1978): 449.

26. David Flusser, "A New Sensitivity in Judaism and the Christian Message," *Harvard Theological Review* 61, no. 2 (April 1968): 126.

cluded that Jesus preached the actual presence of the reign of God in his activities and person in a way that emphasized that the messianic reconciliation between God and humanity had in fact already begun. For the Pharisees such reconciliation lay entirely in the future. While great care must be taken in how this difference is stated, lest we fall back into the old messianic-fulfillment Christologies that caused so much anti-Semitism in the past and that Thoma himself has rejected, there is some basis for making a distinction between Jesus and the Pharisees along these lines.[27]

Another point of contrast relates to the question of forgiving sins. Despite their willingness to modify earlier Jewish views in many areas, the Pharisees held tenaciously to the classical Jewish position that God alone was capable of remitting human sins. In the Gospels we find Jesus not only laying claim to this power for himself but also transferring it from himself to those who abide by his teachings. This was nothing short of revolutionary within the Jewish context of the time. It represented a powerful statement about the intimacy now possible between humanity and divinity because of the incarnation.

The final example of a distinguishing mark in Jesus' preaching that elicited some Pharisaic opposition has to do with his position toward the law, or Torah. The question of the law has been pivotal for the Jewish-Christian relationship, and for Christology, since the period of Christianity's origins. Yet it remains one of the most elusive.

We are now in a period of major transition on the issue. Krister Stendahl has argued that Western Christians have imposed upon Pauline writings a mind-set rooted far more in personal struggles with sin than in Paul's actual attitudes or Jesus' teachings.[28] And Gerard Sloyan has concluded that Jesus in no way abrogated the

27. Clemens Thoma, *A Christian Theology of Judaism* (New York: Paulist, 1980), 113–15.

28. Krister Stendahl, "The Apostle Paul and the Introspective Conscience of the West," *Harvard Theological Review* 56 (July 1963): 199–215.

Torah but only brought to completion some of its key dimensions.[29] Alan Segal, Peter Tomson, and Lloyd Gaston have also contributed important studies to this fundamental rethinking of Pauline attitudes toward Torah.[30]

E. P. Sanders has undertaken an extensive study of the question of Paul and the Torah and has arrived at some tentative conclusions that can be summarized as follows. Other than the demand to the man whose father has died, we find no examples in the New Testament of Jesus transgressing Torah. On the contrary, he seems to have followed its stipulations quite precisely and defended its observance against those extreme elements of Palestinian Judaism that were urging total assimilation into the Hellenistic culture. Nor would Jesus countenance a cavalier attitude on the part of others toward the law. "We find no criticism of the law," says Sanders, "which would allow us to speak of his opposing or rejecting it."[31]

What placed Jesus in tension with the Pharisaic movement on the question of Torah observance was its apparent belief that the Mosaic dispensation was "final or absolutely binding."[32] For Jesus, Torah was not final because of the embryonic presence of the final reign of God. "It was Jesus' sense of living at the turn of the ages," says Sanders, "which allowed him to think that Mosaic law was not final and absolute."[33]

The Dialogue among Theologians

Generally speaking, two constructive approaches to stating the relationship between Christians and Jews have emerged in the last half century in light of the new scholarship on Jesus' and

29. Gerard Sloyan, *Is Christ the End of the Law?* (Philadelphia: Westminster, 1978).

30. Alan F. Segal, *Paul the Convert: The Apostolate and Apostasy of Saul the Pharisee* (New Haven: Yale Univ. Press, 1990); Peter Tomson, *Paul and the Jewish Law: Halakha in the Letters of the Apostle to the Gentiles* (Assen/Maastricht, Holland: Van Gorcum; Minneapolis: Fortress, 1990); Lloyd Gaston, "Paul and Torah," in *Anti-Semitism and the Foundations of Christianity,* 48–71; and idem, *Paul and the Torah* (Vancouver: Univ. of British Columbia Press, 1987).

31. E. P. Sanders, *Jesus and Judaism* (Minneapolis: Fortress, 1985), 269.

32. Ibid.

33. Ibid., 267.

Paul's relationship to Judaism. They are usually referred to as the *single-* and the *double-*covenant approaches, though most of the theologians involved in the discussion feel neither fully captures the reality of the linkage. A few, such as Rosemary Ruether, lean more in the direction of a multicovenantal outlook, although all tend to acknowledge that in the end the Christian-Jewish relationship, whatever its special status from the Christian theological standpoint, must be linked to the wider community of believing peoples.

The single-covenant approach assigns Jews and Christians to one continuing covenantal tradition that began with God's revelation to Moses. In this perspective the Christ-event represented the decisive moment when the gentile nations entered fully into the special relationship with God that Jews already enjoyed and in which they continue. Monika Hellwig and Paul van Buren are two leading proponents of this perspective.

For Hellwig, Christianity's classical affirmation that "Jesus is Lord" is far more a prophetic promise that commits the Christian community to work toward the realization of human salvation rather than a claim about messianic fulfillment in the Christ-event. She believes Christians need to rejoin Jews in viewing the messianic event as "lengthy, complex, unfinished and mysterious," however decisive they may consider the coming of Jesus to the process.[34]

Paul van Buren's position is presented in three major volumes with a fourth now in preparation.[35] In volume 3, van Buren argues that every statement about Jesus as the Christ ultimately involves an assertion about God, who must remain primary to

34. Monika Hellwig, "Christian Theology and the Covenant of Israel," *Journal of Ecumenical Studies* 7 (1970): 37–51; idem, "From the Jesus of Story to the Christ of Dogma," in *Anti-Semitism and the Foundations of Christianity,* 118–36; and idem, "Bible Interpretation: Has Anything Changed?" in *Biblical Studies: Meeting Ground of Jews and Christians,* ed. Lawrence Boadt, Helga Croner, and Leon Klenicki (New York: Paulist, 1981), 172–79.

35. Paul M. van Buren, *Discerning the Way* (New York: Seabury, 1980); idem, *A Christian Theology of the Jewish People* (New York: Seabury, 1983); and idem, *Christ in Context* (San Francisco: Harper and Row, 1988).

Christian theology. In his view every legitimate christological statement must include an acknowledgment of the continuing covenant between God and Israel. Christology refers in the first instance to the church's critical reflection on the significance of Jesus as person. It has little or nothing to do with the Jewish concept of the coming of the messiah. So Judaism after Jesus' resurrection continues as a religion of messianic hope rather than as a hollow faith marked by spiritual blindness. As van Buren sees it, the church must begin to recognize that "Israel" comprises two interconnected, yet distinct, branches. Both are essential to its complete definition. Christianity represents the community of gentile believers drawn by the God of the Jewish people to divine worship and to make God's love known among the peoples of the world.

The double-covenant theory generally begins at the same point as its single-covenant counterpart, namely, with a strong affirmation of the continuing bond between Israel and the church. But it prefers to highlight the distinctiveness of the two traditions and communities, especially after their first-century separation, and to emphasize that in the person of Jesus a vision of God emerged that is distinctively new in some of its central features.

Several scholars have tried to develop a new theological vision within the double-covenant perspective. One is J. Coert Rylaarsdam, who has argued for two distinctive covenantal traditions rooted in the Hebrew Scriptures. The first revolved around divine union with the people of Israel in history. It was generally future-oriented. Since its basic spirit did not blend well with the sense of finality in Christ, it tended to be downplayed in the New Testament.

The second covenant focused on the figure of David. Its orientation was far more eschatological. Emphasis fell on the holiness tradition associated with Mount Zion and the divine presence revealed through the Davidic dynasty. This covenantal tradition looked to and celebrated a supratemporal order of meaning. God was depicted as king of creation and of the nation. The earlier biblical stress on Torah and history faded away. Christianity is largely the heir of this second covenantal tradition.

The key point made by Rylaarsdam is that the two covenants exist simultaneously. Recognition of this reality forces upon the church a total rethinking of its theological approach to the Jewish people, which for so long a time had been premised on the Jewish and Christian covenants as consecutive rather than parallel.[36]

In the writings of Clark Williamson we find an attempt to restate the Jewish-Christian relationship within the framework of contemporary process theology.[37] For Williamson the church's preaching about Jesus the Jew enables Christians to know the God of love and justice who was first revealed to Israel and whom Israel continues to know. Christianity is basically Judaism for the Gentiles. Yet Williamson leaves the clear impression that despite their unity in God, the church and the people Israel are two rather distinct communities.

One final example of the double-covenant outlook is found in the works of Gregory Baum. He strongly emphasizes that Judaism is not destined to disappear after the Christ-event; rather, it is destined to continue playing a central role in the process of creational salvation. He likewise argues that a reformulated Christology must include the abandonment of any claim that Jesus is the one mediator without whom salvation is impossible.

Baum retains a central significance for the Christ-event that definitely goes beyond mere gentile appropriation of the ongoing covenant with Jews, as proposed by van Buren, or understanding of Israel's God, as suggested by Williamson. What occurred in and through the Jesus of history was the revelation that God's full victory is assured, even though not totally realized at present. Hence all messianic claims must be spoken of in terms of the future.[38]

36. J. Coert Rylaarsdam, "Jewish-Christian Relationship: The Two Covenants and the Dilemmas of Christology," *Journal of Ecumenical Studies* 9 (spring 1972): 239–60.

37. Clark Williamson, *Has God Rejected His People?* (Nashville: Abingdon, 1982).

38. Gregory Baum, "The Jews, Faith and Ideology," *The Ecumenist* 10 (1971/72): 71–76; idem, "The Doctrinal Basis for Jewish-Christian Dialogue," *The Month* 224

PRAXIS: A NEW ERA IN CHRISTIAN-JEWISH RELATIONS

The more than a quarter-century of rethinking the Christian-Jewish relationship is beginning to result in a very remarkable turnabout in attitudes that have been endemic to the church's preaching, theology, and worship for centuries. In reaffirming the continuing significance of the Hebrew Scriptures in their own right, in reemphasizing the strongly Jewish framework of Jesus' own teaching and ministry, in rethinking Pauline attitudes toward Torah, and in stressing that Christianity today, however expressed, must include an affirmation of the continued central theological significance of the people Israel, contemporary Christianity is experiencing a fundamental reorientation. This basic shift in perspective on the Jewish tradition carries concrete implications for the way Christians preach, for the manner in which they use the Hebrew Scriptures, and for the way they structure liturgies and write liturgical texts.

Some examples might help specify some of the changes implied in the contemporary perspectival shift regarding Christian-Jewish relations. The first relates to use of the so-called Old Testament, which many scholars and even some ecclesiastical statements now term the Hebrew Scriptures or the First Testament.[39] In the past many Christians regarded these biblical writings as a foil for New Testament teachings or as mere preludes to the Gospels and Epistles. Now we are beginning to see a change of major proportions. Raymond Brown has said that the Jesus story can easily be distorted if one does not recite the story of Israel as well.[40] Using even stronger language, James A. Sanders has said that without the Hebrew Scriptures, "the Christian gospel is hollow, gutless, and nothing

(1967): 232–45; and idem, "Catholic Dogma after Auschwitz," in *Anti-Semitism and the Foundations of Christianity,* 137–50.

39. See Roger Brooks and John J. Collins, eds., *Hebrew Bible or Old Testament? Studying the Bible in Judaism and Christianity* (Notre Dame, Ind.: Univ. of Notre Dame Press, 1990).

40. See Raymond Brown, *Biblical Exegesis and Church Doctrine* (New York: Paulist, 1985), 135–46.

but a form of hellenistic Palestinian cynicism."[41] Following up on this theme, Fr. Brown, addressing a group of Christian ministers in Chicago, insisted that they not overfocus on the Gospels in their preaching but include other parts of the Scriptures such as Genesis and Wisdom. By extension the Hebrew Scriptures will also need to receive greater attention in retreats and adult education programs.

Second, Christians will need to be far more careful than they have been regarding their worship texts and patterns. While some of this concern goes beyond the competence of a congregational minister (particularly in more structured denominations with established liturgical texts), improvements can be made even if in a limited way. In every liturgical season there are problems with the way texts and themes are emphasized.[42] In Advent, for example, the new theological thinking about Christian-Jewish relations has profound implications for the presentation of the meaning of Advent prophecies and their pledge of hope. In Holy Week, there is the perennial challenge of ensuring that congregants do not leave the church believing Jews as a whole killed Jesus and, more importantly, that they come away understanding the continued existence of a deep covenantal bond between the two communities. In the Easter season, steps must be taken to place some of the hostile language of Acts and Peter in proper historical context.

The restored vision of continued bonding between the church and the Jewish people also forces Christians to consider Jewish viewpoints on important theological and ethical issues, not as a matter of consulting an outside tradition but as part of essential "in-house" decision making. This vision also mandates that Christians look to form coalitions with Jews in every way possible, including on ministry to the social order. This will involve creation of new models of partnership such as the program

41. See James A. Sanders, "Rejoicing in the Gifts," *Explorations* 3, no. 1 (1989): 1.
42. See John T. Pawlikowski and James A. Wilde, *When Catholics Speak about Jews* (Chicago: Liturgy Training Publications, 1987).

in ministerial training established by General Theological Seminary whereby Jewish and Christian students secure supervised ministerial placements in each other's congregations.

Finally, Christians must continue to guard against two continuing tendencies in contemporary Christian theology, both destructive for a sense of bonding with the Jewish people. The first is the frequent overemphasis of Christology to the exclusion of theologies of God and the Spirit. Christians need to right the balance here, particularly since correcting this matter can lead to a productive interchange with Jewish theology. David Tracy, for example, has praised post-Holocaust Jewish scholarship for restoring the centrality of the God-question to theological discussion.

The second tendency is to construct new theologies of liberation, be they feminist, African-American, or Latin American, in a way that downgrades the Judaism of Jesus' time. We have taken this issue up earlier, but it bears repeating. An authentic Christian theology of liberation need not be built on the backs of Jews. Quite the contrary. Understanding the Judaism of Jesus' day enhances understanding and appreciation of the liberating dimensions of Jesus' ministry.[43]

These are but a few examples of the concrete steps that need to be taken and expanded if the renewed theology of the Christian-Jewish relationship is to take root in the church's consciousness. If our efforts are successful, we will finally witness the burial of the patristic *adversus Judaeos* tradition. The process will understandably move along somewhat slowly because it touches upon the very nerve center of Christian identity. But in light of the destructive history of Christian anti-Semitism bred by this theology, moral integrity demands that the church resolutely stay the course.

43. See Pawlikowski, *Christ in the Light of the Christian-Jewish Dialogue,* 93–102.

FRANCIS SCHÜSSLER FIORENZA

11. CHRISTIAN REDEMPTION BETWEEN COLONIALISM AND PLURALISM

Colonialism is a blight on the history of Christianity, and colonial exploitation is one of the most tragic events of that history. Bartolomé de Las Casas's *A Short Account of the Destruction of the Indies* presents a frightful example of colonial brutality.[1] The Spanish conquistadores enslaved and condemned whole Mexica tribes to extinction, resulting in a "Holocaust of the Indians."[2] Their attitudes toward the religious beliefs of the Mexica in no small measure influenced their behavior.[3] They appealed to the superiority of Christian belief in contrast to Mexica practices to justify their treatment of the Mexica. Nevertheless, others, like Pope Paul III in *Sublimis Deus* (1537), appealed to Christian beliefs to defend the rights of the Mexica and to criticize colonial practices.[4]

The debate between Juan Ginés de Sepúlveda and Bartolomé de Las Casas on the treatment of the Mexica concentrated on the

1. Bartolomé de Las Casas, *A Short Account of the Destruction of the Indies*, ed. and trans. Nigel Griffin (New York: Penguin, 1992). Original title and publication: *Brevísima relación de la destrucción de las Indias Occidentales* (1542).

2. Fernando Mires, *En nombre de la cruz: Discusiones teológicas y políticas frente al holocausto de los indios, período de conquista* (San José, Costa Rica: DEI, 1986).

3. Lewis Hanke, *All Mankind Is One: A Study of the Disputation between Bartolomé de Las Casas and Juan Ginés de Sepúlveda in 1550 on the Intellectual and Religious Capacity of the American Indians* (DeKalb: Northern Illinois Univ. Press, 1974).

4. For the context of this bull, see Alberto de la Hera, "El derecho de los indios a la libertad y a la fe: La bula 'Sublimis Deus' y los problemas indianos que la motivaron," *Anuario de Historia del Derecho Españo* 26 (1953): 65–80.

issue of identity or difference of nature. Sepúlveda justified the treatment on the basis of the Mexica being different from white male Spaniards. "In prudence, talent, virtue, and humanity, they are as inferior to the Spaniards as children to adults, women to men, as the wild and cruel to the most meek, as the prodigiously intemperate to the continent and temperate, that I have almost said, as monkeys to men."[5] In Sepúlveda's eyes Mexica could not become Christians because they were different, whereas Las Casas contested this difference: "Just as there is no natural difference in the creation of humans, so there is no difference in the call to salvation of all of them."[6] In his view, the Christian belief that God's grace is universal speaks against mistreatment of the Mexica.[7] The Christian understanding of creation and salvation provides the ground for criticizing such mistreatment. Nevertheless, the Christian tradition also contains affirmations that might seem to justify it.

RELIGIOUS ROOTS OF EXPLOITATION

The colonial conquest and holocaust of the Indians challenge Christians to be self-critical and raise crucial questions: "What criteria and what possibilities of limiting power exist when two peoples meet and a superiority of arms is linked with the consciousness of superiority in possession of the sole obligatory truth? Do missions and colonialism combined form the hybrid which is responsible for the distress of the Third World?"[8] The holocaust of the Indians demands that Christians examine the degree to which their deepest religious convictions lead them to impose their beliefs, practices, and values upon others or lead

5. Quoted from Hanke, *All Mankind Is One,* 84.
6. Quoted from ibid., 96.
7. The charge has been made that Las Casas failed to criticize the kidnapping and enslavement of blacks from Africa. See Isacio Pérez Fernández, ed., *Fray Bartolomé de Las Casas, O.P., Brevísima relación de la destrucción de Africa: Preludio de la destrucción de Indias* (Salamanca: Editorial San Esteban, 1989).
8. Joseph Ratzinger, "Conscience in Time," *Communio: International Catholic Review* 5 (1972): 294.

them to resist practices of colonization and oppression. Christian theology must honestly face the problem that its biblical past and religious tradition, as well as its modern practice, entail not only resistance but also oppression.

Biblical Roots

The holocaust of the Indians calls us back to those passages in the Hebrew and Christian Scriptures that strongly link belief in God or confession of Jesus as the savior with a conviction of religious supremacy and with political domination. The books of Joshua and Judges narrate the military victory over the Canaanites. They commend the eradication of the Canaanite temples and the destruction of their idols. Joshua 24 warns the Israelites that their Lord "is a jealous God." If they should serve foreign gods, the Lord will harm and consume them (Josh. 24:19-20). Similarly the prophets condemn foreign gods as idols and their rituals as idolatry. Their prophetic diatribes are a far cry from empathic understanding or ecumenical dialogue.

The Christian Scriptures sometimes express faith in Jesus as the Christ in categories of exclusiveness and supremacy. The Acts of the Apostles has Peter proclaim: "And there is salvation in no one else, for there is no other name under heaven given among men by which we must be saved" (Acts 4:12, RSV here and below). Similarly, the Pastoral Epistles proclaim a unicity: "For there is only one God, and there is only one mediator between God and humankind, himself a human, Christ Jesus, who sacrificed himself as a ransom for them all" (1 Tim. 2:5-6). Colossians professes the uniqueness of Christ's salvation and his reign and lordship over the cosmos and over all heavenly and worldly powers.

The Gospels contain similar affirmations. One early saying, which some scholars attribute to the historical Jesus, is Luke 12:8-9: "And I tell you, every one who acknowledges me before men, the Son of man also will acknowledge before the angels of God; but he who denies me before men will be denied before the angels of God." Later traditions likewise link belief in Jesus with salvation and refusal to believe in him with condemnation. John 12:48 affirms: "He who rejects and does not receive my sayings has a judge; the word that I have spoken will be his judge on the last day."

Contemporary Practices

The conviction linking belief in Jesus with salvation and disbelief with condemnation has been at the basis of Christianity's mission to convert all nations. Throughout the history of Christianity this conviction has also been used to justify the use of force for the sake of salvation. The problem has been that physical force is justified so long as its effects are salutary. Modern Christianity's experience of religious wars and the Enlightenment's argument for toleration lead many to assume that we have abandoned appealing to the salutary use of force. They assume that the situation is radically different today and that statements of condemnation and colonialism no longer exist within the contemporary Christian world. Nevertheless, the problem remains, only in a more complex and diverse form.

The emergence of Latin American liberation theology and its translation into many languages often give the false impression that Christian religious movements are now unambiguously on the side of the oppressed and exploited. In fact, a conflict exists between two contrasting Christian missionary approaches. As Sarah Diamond has noted, "The contemporary mission field is a battleground where those who would use the gospel message to empower Third World believers confront rival missionaries eagerly bolstering dependence on world leadership and economic aid of the United States."[9]

Some North American Christian missionary movements actively seek to counter Latin American liberation theology and aggressively oppose emancipatory movements on behalf of the poor and disenfranchised. These Christian missionary efforts see

9. Sarah Diamond, *Spiritual Warfare: The Politics of the Christian Right* (Boston: South End, 1989), 205.

Central America, for example, as "one of two places in the world for which the Lord had special plans."[10] Because they consider the Latin American social reform movements to be communist-inspired and because they view communism as the great enemy of Christianity, they interpret the situation as a struggle in which Christianity itself is at stake. Consequently, organizations like International Christian Aid have siphoned off money intended for Ethiopian famine victims to Christian groups struggling against insurgency movements in Latin America.[11] They justify such practices as part of the struggle for good over evil, for Christianity over communism. In this struggle, Christian redemption is seen as an otherworldly redemption, and salvation is the salvation of the individual soul.

ANALYZING THE PROBLEM

The conquest of the Indies, traditional affirmations of exclusivity, and the political allegiances of some present-day missionary efforts point to the problem that claims of religious unicity and cultural superiority have been conducive to practices of colonial and economic exploitation. Underlying such practices are issues that Christian theology must face in reconstructing its understanding of Christian redemption. These issues are the correlation between values and the will to power, between belief and political ideologies, and between convictions of cultural superiority and oppression.

Value as Power

Friedrich Nietzsche's analysis of beliefs and morals uncovers the link between values and power.[12] Because knowledge is

10. See David Stoll, *Is Latin America Turning Protestant? The Politics of Evangelical Growth* (Berkeley: Univ. of California Press, 1990), 149.

11. See *Christianity Today,* April 13, 1973, 44–47; March 2, 1979, 50–57; and March 1, 1985, 36–39.

12. Friedrich Nietzsche, *On the Genealogy of Morals and Ecce Homo* (New York: Random House, 1967); idem, *The Will to Power,* trans. Walter Kaufmann and R. J.

interested and because valuation entails a will that the values permeate and dominate, Nietzsche links the will to truth with the will to power. The phrase the "will to power"—though its meaning is still debated—points to the intrinsic connection between religious and moral values, on the one hand, and the power of domination, on the other. This connection exists for Christian beliefs and morals just as it exists for any set of knowledge and values. Power is not a goal separate from value; rather, power inheres within knowledge, belief, and values themselves. Inherent in every creative movement, power becomes externalized as control, domination, and exploitation.

Contemporary analyses have further revealed the relation between knowledge and power. Michel Foucault has demonstrated that modern disciplinary and discursive practices involve the exercise of control and domination.[13] Jürgen Habermas has explicated a tripartite link between knowledge and interest: the natural sciences and technological control, the human sciences and understanding, and the critical social sciences in relation to emancipation.[14] Though he has nuanced this scheme, Habermas has maintained the constitutive link between knowledge and interest and has underscored the importance of ordering knowledge, interest, and power toward communication rather than domination.

The challenge of Nietzsche's analysis remains even if his antidemocratic elitism and its political reception have discredited his constructive alternative.[15] Power permeates our discursive

Hollingdale (New York: Random House, 1967). See Volker Gerhardt, *Pathos und Distanz: Studien zur Philosophie Friedrich Nietzsches* (Stuttgart: Reclam, 1988), 72–97; and Maudemarie Clark, *Nietzsche on Truth and Philosophy* (New York: Cambridge Univ. Press, 1990), 205–44.

13. Michel Foucault, *Language, Counter-Memory, Practice: Selected Essays and Interviews by Michel Foucault,* ed. Donald F. Bouchard (Ithaca, N.Y.: Cornell Univ. Press, 1977), 139–64.

14. Jürgen Habermas, *Knowledge and Interest* (Boston: Beacon, 1971), 274–300; and "Nachwort," in *Friedrich Nietzsche: Erkenntnistheoretische Schriften* (Frankfurt: Suhrkamp, 1968), 237–61. For a comparison between Habermas and Foucault on power, see Alex Honneth, *The Critique of Power* (Cambridge: MIT Press, 1991).

15. Despite Walter Kaufmann's defense, the political reception of Nietzsche remains an inescapable problem. See Michael Warren, *Nietzsche and Political Thought* (Cambridge:

practices, systems of values, and technologies of knowledge. Since Christian ideals and practices are not exempt from the permeation of power, Christians need to explicate the meaning of redemption as a belief and practice in relation to a communicative rather than dominative power.

Belief and Political Power

The relation between religious belief and social control has been analyzed within the sociology of knowledge and sociology of religion since Emile Durkheim.[16] Religious beliefs are not just private convictions; they have social and political functions. To the extent that believers affirm and value their convictions, they seek to live them out, to give them form within their personal and communal lives, and to assert their public and political significance. Their religious beliefs thereby are a component of the glue that holds societies together.

In addition, societies have often functionalized religious beliefs as ideologies to justify political systems. Alan Davies has shown several political interpretations of the Christ symbol that legitimate a nationalist, racist, or class supremacy.[17] These extend across a broad spectrum, from the Latin Christ of royalist French aristocrats to the Anglo-Saxon Christ of social Darwinian English imperialists, from the Germanic Christ of Nazi Christians to the Afrikaner Christ of South African white supremacists. Each appealed to the symbol of Christ to legitimate a position of superiority, often colonial, over other people, races, and religions.

Contemporary liberation and political theologies have made us conscious of the ideological function of belief in two ways. Their analyses have uncovered concrete cases where Christian

MIT Press, 1990); Tracy Strong, *Nietzsche and the Politics of Transformation,* expanded ed. (Berkeley: Univ. of California Press, 1988); and Bruce Detwiler, *Nietzsche and the Politics of Aristocratic Radicalism* (Chicago: Univ. of Chicago Press, 1990).

16. See Kenneth Thompson, *Beliefs and Ideology* (London: Tavistock, 1986).

17. Alan Davies, *Infected Christianity: A Study of Modern Racism* (London: SCM, 1988).

beliefs have been used to reinforce political power structures. In addition, they have emphasized solidarity with the poor and powerless and have underscored that Christian eschatology can serve as a critique of all political institutions. They have thereby sought to explicate an anti-ideological relation between Christian belief and social-political praxis. Yet the very attempt to relate religious belief concretely to society entails the danger of such belief becoming ideological and distorted. It is imperative, then, that liberation and political theologies recognize and face this danger as they go about advocating political and social change.

Cultural Superiority and Eurocentrism

Christian theology faces not only the will to power of its beliefs and values, not only the possibilities of the ideological distortion of religious belief, but also the implicit assumption of the superiority of Western and Christian culture. Evidence of modern Christianity's assumptions of cultural superiority is easily available. Even Ernst Troeltsch—who took pluralism and the diversity of world religions with great seriousness—displays typical Eurocentric assumptions when he writes: "The heathen races, on the other hand, are being morally and spiritually disintegrated by contact with European civilization; hence they demand a substitute from the higher religion and culture."[18]

The history of the contact between European civilization and the cultures of Africa, Asia, and the Americas is one of economic, cultural, and religious colonization. This history, viewed not from the perspective of European civilization but from the "underside" of history, shows not progress but exploitation and oppression.[19] It invalidates the need for a "higher culture," be-

18. Ernst Troeltsch, *Christian Thought* (London: Univ. of London Press, 1923), 1–35; quotation from p. 29. The English translation uses "race" to translate *Menschheitsgruppen* and thereby gives an unfortunate racial connotation that the German term does not have.

19. Gustavo Gutiérrez, *The Power of the Poor in History* (Maryknoll, N.Y.: Orbis, 1983).

lies progressive theories of history, and challenges evolutionary views of religion. It displays the underside of Christian missions and their salvific purpose. Many Christian missionaries were indeed heroic and generous, but their missionary activity as a work of inculturation entailed cultural as well as economic colonization. The implicit, if not explicit, intertwinement of convictions of cultural superiority with those of religious superiority has resulted in the toleration, if not support, of colonization. Even a theologian like Troeltsch who admits the equality of other world religions and their cultures downgrades native religions with the label "primitive religions."

Christian faith in Jesus as savior is now being articulated in a context that includes interreligious dialogue among the world religions; but that context also includes colonization and its exploitation and denigration of peoples, their cultures, and their religions. Any interpretation of the meaning of the Christian faith in Christ as redeemer and savior has to mitigate the will to have one's values and beliefs dominate, to prevent the ideological misuse of symbols, and to uncover hidden assumptions of cultural and religious superiority. Theological interpretations of Christian salvation should do justice to the commitments of the Christian tradition and should also prevent the ideological justifications of oppression and colonialism.

Such an approach should lead to a reexamination of the Christian belief in the unicity of Jesus as savior that has led many theologians to view his life and message as the criterion of truth that judges other religions. For example, Wolfhart Pannenberg has argued recently that "just as the message of Jesus is, in the final judgment, the criterion for the salvation of the individual person, so should the Christian judge non-Christian religions in relation to their proximity or distance to the message of Jesus."[20] Since such affirmations of Jesus as the unique criterion of universal truth have historically led Christians to

20. Wolfhart Pannenberg, "Religion und Religionen: Theologische Erwägungen zu den Prinzipien eines Dialoges mit den Weltreligionen," in *Dialog aus der Mitte christlicher*

seek power over others for the sake of bringing salvation to them, we should reflect critically, indeed self-critically, on them. In order to establish a context for such a constructive interpretation of redemption, this essay first examines some contemporary theological approaches to the issue of Christian salvation and religious pluralism with their corresponding practices and demands.

A TYPOLOGY OF CONTEMPORARY THEOLOGICAL OPTIONS

The conflict between the plurality of religions and the Christian claim to the unicity of truth and salvation emerges in all its sharpness within modernity. Though Christianity has dealt throughout its history with the problem of the religious other, it has faced religious pluralism in a very special way only in modernity. During the medieval period, Christians assumed that the majority of persons in the world had at least some knowledge of Jesus as redeemer. Indeed, Thomas Aquinas referred to the Sibylline prophecies as examples that the "redemption was revealed to many Gentiles before Christ's coming," and he thought that "God would either reveal to him [i.e., someone who had no knowledge of Jesus] through internal inspiration what had to be believed, or would send some preacher of the faith to him as he sent Peter to Cornelius" (Acts 10:20).[21] But the discovery of new worlds and the travel east to China and Japan forced Europeans to see that Christianity was in fact geographically and numerically limited to Europe. Three distinct proposals are currently made to deal with the Christian claim to unicity of salvation and the awareness of worldwide religious diversity. The proposals stress exclusivism, inclusivism, or pluralism; they call for a corresponding conversion, enlightenment, or acknowledgment.

Theologie Beiträge zur Religionstheologie, vol. 5., ed. Andreas Bsteh (Mödling: Verlag St. Gabriel, 1987), 190.

21. Thomas Aquinas, *Truth,* vol. 2 (Chicago: Henry Regnery, 1953), q. 14; quotes from ad 5 and ad 1.

Exclusive Communitarianism

When redemption is very closely linked with the Christian community, the question emerges of whether those outside that community are saved. The phrase *extra ecclesiam nulla salus est* (outside of the church, there is no salvation) has long roots. These extend back to early Judaism and the image of the boat that saved Noah from the flood. In later Jewish writings, this image became a metaphor for the salvation of the remnant of Israel, as in Wisd. of Sol. 10:4: "When the earth was flooded because of him, wisdom again saved it, steering the righteous person by a paltry piece of wood." Early Christian writings (for example, 1 Pet. 3:20) use Noah's ark as a symbol of the church.[22] Just as the ark was the means of salvation, so too is the church. Facing church disunity, Cyprian polemically used the phrase "outside of the church, there is no salvation" against groups splitting off from the church: "Whoever does not have the church as mother cannot have God as father; who breaks the peace of Christ . . . is destroying the church."[23] Later Augustine adopted the phrase but expanded the notion of church beyond that of the empirical church of his age to include Israel insofar as the church goes back to Abel.

Moreover, at that time, Christians thought that the church extended throughout the whole world. It is important that we should interpret exclusionary statements in relation to other contrasting affirmations, such as: "Christ has died for all." There is precedent for this. When Cornelius Jansenius rejected the notion that Christ died for all and when Pasquier Quesnel argued that outside the church there was no grace, their exclusive claims were condemned by the Roman Catholic church as inadequate expressions of Christian faith.[24] This tension characterizes much

22. In 1 Pet. 3:20-21 baptism corresponds to Noah's ark.

23. Cyprian, *De cathol. eccl. unit.* 6.

24. Augustine's interpretation influenced medieval theology through his student Ruspe of Fulgentius. See Joseph Ratzinger, *Das Volk Gottes* (Dusseldorf: Patmos, 1969), 341–61.

of Christian theology. On the one hand, Boniface VIII's *Unam Sanctam* (1302) declares: "We believe that there is one holy catholic church . . . outside of which there is no salvation. . . . We declare that it is necessary for salvation for every human creature to be subject to the Roman Pontiff."[25] On the other hand, the idea of baptism of desire makes the church more extensive than the visible institution and loosens the link between the visible, institutional church and salvation. As Thomas Aquinas argues, the Gentiles are saved by their implicit faith.[26] Today, the excommunication of Father Leonard Feeney, a Boston priest, for his rigoristic interpretation of *extra ecclesiam nulla salus est* has pointed to a "semiexclusive" rather than a rigorously exclusive limitation of salvation.

A similar exclusivism is echoed in Karl Barth's limiting of God's true revelation and grace to Christianity.[27] He claimed: "That there is a true religion is an event in the act of the grace of God in Jesus Christ. To be more precise, it is an event in the outpouring of the Holy Spirit. To be even more precise, it is an event in the existence of the Church and the children of God. The existence of the Church of God and the children of God means that true religion exists even in the world of human religion."[28] Similarly, Hendrik Kraemer has sharpened this neoorthodox exclusiveness of Christianity in his interpretation of world religions.[29] Such a theological approach interprets the unconditionality of the truth in a binary fashion: a belief is true or false; non-Christian beliefs are rejected as false.[30]

25. DS 870–75. The last sentence in Latin is quite stark: "Porro subesse Romano Pontifici omni humanae creaturae declaramus, dicimus, diffinimus omnino esse de necessitate salutis" (DS 875).

26. Thomas Aquinas, *Truth*, vol. 2, q. 14, a. 11, ad 5: "It was enough for them [Gentiles] to have implicit faith in the Redeemer, either as part of their belief in the faith of the law and the prophets, or as part of their belief in divine providence itself."

27. See Paul Knitter, *Towards a Protestant Theology of Religions: A Case Study of Paul Althaus and Contemporary Attitudes* (Marburg: N. G. Elwert, 1974), 20–36.

28. Karl Barth, *Church Dogmatics* (Edinburgh: T. and T. Clark, 1956), 1/2:344.

29. Hendrik Kraemer, *Religion and the Christian Faith* (London: Lutterworth, 1961).

30. Schubert Ogden formulates the issue as a binary true or false in *Is There Only One True Religion or Are There Many?* (Dallas: Southern Methodist Univ. Press, 1992).

By denying that other religions manifest a genuine revelatory presence of God, such an approach makes Christian revelation exclusive. This exclusiveness is sometimes mitigated—as, for instance, in volume 4/2 of Barth's *Church Dogmatics,* which interprets other religions as lights reflecting the true light of Christ.

The exclusivist approach stresses the necessity of belief in Christ as God's saving revelation to all of humanity and proclaims the necessity of membership in Christ's community for all. It requires *conversion* to Christ and the Christian community as the corresponding practice. Even its exceptions, for example, baptism of desire, require an implicit desire for such conversion.

Inclusive Universalism

A second approach points to the universal presence of God and God's grace throughout the world. Several contemporary proposals take this position, which also has historical roots. The early Christian apologists appealed to the notion of the *logos spermatikos* (germinal logos) to affirm the presence of Christian truth and revelation outside the confines of institutional Christianity. In the fifteenth century, Nicholas of Cusa's *De pace fidei* appealed to a broader presence of Christian truth in discussing the plurality of religions.[31] According to Nicholas, only one God exists; therefore, only one religion and only one true worship of God exist. The one God, however, is sought in various ways, is given different names, and is worshiped differently in different religions. Nicholas identified the one true religion as Christianity, but he granted that non-Christians could discover the truths of Christianity as present within their own religions.

A contemporary proposal in this vein is Karl Rahner's interpretation of the universal presence of God's grace. All religions manifest the grace and salvation of Christ, but Christianity is

31. Nicholas of Cusa, *De pace fidei: On Interreligious Harmony,* trans. and ed. James E. Biechler and H. Lawrence Bond, Texts and Studies in Religion 55 (Lewiston, N.Y.: Mellen, 1990).

the high point of the historical religious evolution. Though God's grace is present in all religions, this presence is "inadequate" or "deficient" insofar as God's most complete and more explicit presence is in Christianity—the culminating symbol of God's grace.[32] Christianity is the explicit sign that makes manifest what is hidden or anonymous elsewhere.[33]

This approach does not so much demand conversion as demand *enlightenment*. It calls for the uncovering of implicit or anonymous structures of Christian truth represented in other religions. Such an approach tends to neglect the historical particularity of each religious tradition; this particularity is seen as an exemplification of a universal human nature. The transcendental conception of human nature, as in Karl Rahner's proposal, presupposes a transcendental uniformity of human nature that underlies and comes to expression not only in all world religions but also in nonreligious worldviews.

Pluralism

A third approach takes religious pluralism seriously by advocating either a perspectival (epistemological) or a "realistic" pluralism. A perspectival pluralism underscores that the object of religion transcends all human knowledge. Every religion, therefore, represents only a distinct perspective of the one and same reality.[34] A perspectival pluralism points to the one absolutely transcendent God behind all religions that cannot be adequately grasped by any particular human word, symbol, or belief. Every

32. Georg Hegel, *Lectures on the Philosophy of Religion* (Berkeley: Univ. of California Press, 1988). Only Hegel's first set of lectures correlates the history of religions with logic. The Christian religion is not the only final religious configuration. On this see Walter Jaeschke, *Reason in Religion: The Foundations of Hegel's Philosophy of Religion* (Berkeley: Univ. of California Press, 1990), 265–311.

33. Karl Rahner, "Christianity and the Non-Christian Religions," *Theological Investigations* (New York: Seabury, 1966), 5–34; idem, "Anonymous Christianity and the Missionary Task of the Church," *Theological Investigations* (New York: Seabury, 1974), 12:161–78; and idem, "The One Christ and the Universality of Salvation," *Theological Investigations* (New York: Seabury, 1979), 16:199–224.

34. Nicholas Rescher labels the former the "complex reality view" and the latter the "perspectival reality view" ("Philosophical Disagreement: An Essay towards Orientational Pluralism in Metaphilosophy," *Review of Metaphysics* 32 [1978]: 217–51).

language, symbol, and belief as human is a finite and inadequate perspective. The inadequacy of every religious perspective requires a pluralism of religions, each representing a distinctive and limited perspective. The symbols of Christian salvation are therefore the Christian perspective of the transcendent. The Christian claim to truth is represented through a particular perspective that needs to be complemented by other perspectives of the one transcendent reality.

This perspectivalism can be criticized for being insufficiently pluralistic.[35] When a perspectival or epistemological approach acknowledges the validity of diverse religions, it does so implicitly from the Christian viewpoint of God as infinitely transcendent. It then assumes that other religions represent in their own way this Christian, Neoplatonic, transcendent conception of God. A more radical anthropological or ontological pluralism would assert that the Buddhist notion of nothingness and the Hindu notion of religion express realities that are radically different from the Christian conception. These notions are not simply ways that different cultural and religious symbol-systems express the very same transcendence that Christianity professes. The nonbeing of Buddhism does not, for instance, correspond to the negative theology of some Western mystical traditions. Pluralism, then, should not be based either on the inadequacy of every religion to symbolize in its own way the one transcendent reality or on the multifaceted nature of that one reality. Instead pluralism should affirm that reality itself is pluralistic.

Advocates of either approach maintain the truth of the other religions. Truth is relational to each perspective so that what appears as true to one perspective may appear at first glance as untrue to another perspective. Once one acknowledges the limitations of one's own perspective, one can openly acknowledge the claims advanced from another perspective. Religions, there-

35. See Gordon Kaufman, "Religious Diversity, Historical Consciousness, and Christian Theology," in *The Myth of Christian Uniqueness: Toward a Pluralistic Theology of Religions,* ed. John Hick and Paul Knitter (Maryknoll, N.Y.: Orbis, 1987).

fore, need to converse with those sharing different perspectives and advocating different visions of reality. The diversity of perspectives and complexity of reality call for this dialogue. While one is justified in claiming the truth of one's own position, one is not justified in rejecting the truth of the other's position. Instead one enters into conversation and dialogue in order to grasp other viewpoints and even a more complex religious vision.

Though pluralism might appear as a genuine alternative to exclusivism, it too has failings. First, it reduces religion to a Western view of religion and makes it an object of consumer choice. Modern Western society is characterized by its market economy. Religion becomes a commodity within this market. The choice of religion, like the choice of values and goods, becomes a matter of individual preference. The advocacy of pluralism as the solution to interreligious dialogue may mirror Western society, its values, and its structure just as much as the other approaches mirror other societies. We must be cautious not to impose Western attitudes toward religion upon other cultures under the guise of advocating pluralism.

Second, pluralism does not deal adequately with the issues of religious truth, the criteria of truth, and the relation between religious truth and social practice, especially the practice of oppression and discrimination. Two examples will help here. In recent years many Christian theologians have argued that their churches should admit women to all ministerial offices. Yet theologians who argue pro or con within a particular community often balk at advocating such arguments when they are in dialogue with other religions. They refrain from such arguments lest they impose Western and North American prejudices. What, in this situation, has happened to truth? Another example: hardly anyone questions that the cults at Jonestown or Waco symbolized distorted forms of religious life. But doesn't such an assessment imply that one uses one's own religious, moral, and cultural criteria to judge other forms of religious life as systematically distorted?

Religious beliefs as interpretations of the ultimate meaning of reality raise truth claims about reality. Those claims often determine social, political, and personal life. Religious beliefs are not simply another perspective. Pluralism and dialogue involve more than each party stating, say, the location of an object.[36] To the extent that religious beliefs make truth claims about reality and those claims affect social and political praxis, they call for dialogue that challenges as well as accepts. If a religious conviction favors colonialism, militarism, classism, or sexism, then dialogue aims at communication—a communication with an interest in transforming that religious conviction and sociopolitical practice. Dialogue aims not merely at the acknowledgment of other positions but also at a transformative practice for oneself and for others.

REDEMPTION AS COMMUNICATIVE AND TRANSFORMATIVE

A constructive interpretation of redemption should work against the limitations of the above positions, explicate the significance of the belief in redemption for human life, and take into account the problem of oppressive power. Any attempt to get a fuller grasp of the nature of redemption also has to consider three presuppositions that plague modern understandings of it. A reconstruction of the meaning of redemption is not simply a reconstruction of the tradition; it also entails taking issue with these modernist background assumptions.

Inadequate Presuppositions

The first presupposition is the reduction of soteriology to the justification of the individual; the second, the ambiguity of the historical knowledge of Jesus; and the third, the conflict within modernity between universalism and historicism. A theologi-

36. Hilary Putnam tends to view diverse moral views as distinct and diverse logical mathematic worlds (*The Many Faces of Realism* [LaSalle, Ill.: Open Court, 1987], 41–91).

cal reconstruction of the meaning of redemption stands against the background of these developments within the context of modernity.

Soteriology Reduced to Justification of the Individual

Christian theology has traditionally explicated the belief in Christ as redeemer or savior with diverse images, models, and ideas.[37] Nineteenth-century theologians sought to uncover the idea, principle, or essence underlying this diversity. One influential reduction has been the narrowing of redemption to justification, Albrecht Ritschl's influential history of redemption being a prime example. Emphasizing the justification of the individual human subject, it interpreted reconciliation and justification primarily in religious and moral categories and neglected or passed over lightly the cosmic and social soteriology of the ancient church.[38] Its major emphasis begins with Anselm's theory of satisfaction. A comparison to Ferdinand Christian Baur's more broadly conceived treatment shows the limitations of this approach.[39] Whereas Ritschl had related reconciliation to justification, Baur related reconciliation to redemption and analyzed such important classic themes as redemption from death and the devil as well as the notion of Christ's abolition of the distance between divine and human existence.

Despite such differences, both share the modernistic emphasis on "subjectivized" redemption by emphasizing the change

37. For a brief survey of Christian interpretations of redemption, see Francis Schüssler Fiorenza, "Redemption," in *The New Dictionary of Theology* (Wilmington, Del.: Glazier, 1988), 836–51.

38. Albrecht Ritschl, *The Christian Doctrine of Justification and Reconciliation* (Edinburgh: T. and T. Clark, 1900). In contrast to my argument that modern theology has reduced redemption to justification, Carl E. Braaten has claimed that contemporary theology, especially liberation theology, has insufficiently focused on justification ("The Christian Doctrine of Salvation," *Interpretation* 35 [1981]: 117–44, esp. 129ff.).

39. Ferdinand Christian Baur, *Die christliche Lehre von der Versöhnung in ihrer geschichtlichen Entwicklung von der ältesten Zeit bis auf die neueste* (Tübingen: Osianer, 1938). See Peter C. Hodgson, *The Formation of Historical Theology: A Study of Ferdinand Christian Baur* (New York: Harper and Row, 1967).

within human subjectivity.[40] Except for religious socialism, the Social Gospel movement, and the recent emergence of political and liberation theology, much of modern theology has developed the significance of redemption in existential categories of religious justification or psychological wholeness to the neglect of the social and political dimensions of redemption.

Ambiguity of Historical Rationality

A specific rationality has come to dominate much of modernity. Empirical, instrumental, scientific, and technocratic are some of the labels used to describe this rationality that counts as knowledge only a certain kind of knowledge.[41] This rationality shaped the critique of traditional metaphysics and the emergence of historical criticism. It thereby profoundly affected language about God and the interpretation of Scriptures. The application of historical criticism to the materials in the Gospels produced ambiguous results. On the one hand, historical-critical study has provided more knowledge than ever before about the New Testament writings and their environment. On the other hand, this historical-critical study has produced a fourfold crisis in the foundations of Christian theology and of Christology.

First, historical studies questioned whether faith in Christ can be grounded by research into the historical Jesus or whether some other ground is necessary. It resulted in a distinction between the *Jesus of history* (what historical knowledge tells us about Jesus) and the *Christ of faith* (what the Christian community believes about Jesus).[42] Second, historical research has led to skepticism about the historical Jesus, and some conclude that one can know little about him.[43] Third, historical stud-

40. Gunther Wenz, *Geschichte der Versöhnungslehre in der evangelische Theologie der Neuzeit* (Munich: Kaiser, 1984), 2:14–41, 321–41.

41. Max Horkheimer, *Critique of Instrumental Reason* (New York: Seabury, 1974).

42. David Strauss, *The Christ of Faith and the Jesus of History* (Philadelphia: Fortress, 1977).

43. See Rudolf Bultmann, "The Primitive Christian Kerygma and the Historical Jesus," in *The Historical Jesus and the Kerygmatic Christ*, ed. Carl E. Braaten and Roy A. Harrisville (New York: Abingdon, 1964), 15–42.

ies have discovered that early Christian beliefs about Jesus and his salvific role existed in quite diverse strains and that traditional dogma had explicated only one or two of these strains.[44] Fourth, historical-critical approaches undercut popular religious readings of the Scriptures insofar as they claim that the expert reading is the only legitimate one. They thereby create a dichotomy between the academic as the correct interpretation of Scripture and the popular as uninformed interpretations.[45] Although theology needs to heed Schleiermacher's warning against relegating Christianity to the barbarians and learning to the atheists,[46] the problem today is that the "meaning" of the Scriptures is increasingly relegated to the expert philologist and historian and is less dependent upon the centrality of the Christ cult within the present community.[47]

Conflict between Universalism and Historicism

In addition to the subjectivization of redemption and the ambiguity of modern expert rationality, a third presupposition is the conflict between universalism and historicism. Critics of modernity and of modern theology attribute a monolithic and universal understanding of rationality to them. A much more accurate assessment is that modern theology faces the dilemma between universalism and historicism, between claims of universality and those of historical particularity. On the one hand, the early Enlightenment and Deism advocated a natural religion, stripped of the particularities of positive, revealed, and institutional religion. Though Schleiermacher responded to the Enlightenment by arguing that religion exists only in individual and concrete historical configurations, he grounded religion in the religious

44. Edward Schillebeeckx, *Jesus: An Experiment in Christology* (New York: Crossroad, 1979).

45. Francis Schüssler Fiorenza, "The Crisis of Scriptural Authority: Interpretation and Reception," *Interpretation* 44 (1990): 353–68.

46. Friedrich Schleiermacher, *Two Letters: On the Glaubenslehre* (Chico, Calif.: Scholars Press, 1981).

47. See Ernst Troeltsch, *Writings on Theology and Religion,* ed. R. Morgan and Michael Pye (Atlanta: John Knox, 1977), on the significance of the historical Jesus.

dimension of human experience and saw that dimension as basic and universal. Both the Enlightenment's natural theology and Schleiermacher's "experiential" grounding of religion could be considered a "substitutional universalism" insofar as they claim that what is particular is a universal; they substitute a particular experience as and for a universal one. On the other hand, the category of individuality and its application to historical cultural periods led to a historicist understanding of reality. The nineteenth-century historical school furthered this understanding through its historical-critical emphasis on contextuality. Each cultural period represents an individual configuration of history that has no claim upon other periods or other cultures. Consequently, modernity leaves us with an unresolved conflict, namely, the unresolved problem of the relation between universality and particularity.

Christian believers stand in a paradoxical relation to the unity and the multiplicity of the modern world. At no time before in its history has Christianity become more widespread. In previous centuries Christianity was primarily a European or a Mediterranean faith, whereas today the majority of Christians are non-European and non-Western. Yet previously Christians were confident of the alleged superiority of their Western culture and the potential universality of their faith, whereas today they are increasingly conscious of their particularity. If medieval Christianity could assume that almost everyone had heard the gospel, modern theology is aware of the particularity of Christianity and the force of cultural disparity.

Therefore, any reconstruction of redemption in categories of communicative and transformative practice not only should strive to go beyond the limitations of exclusivism, inclusivism, and pluralism but should also avoid the reduction of redemption to individual subjective justification, escape the ambiguities of historical rationality, and deal with the conflict between universalism and particularism. I shall attempt such a reconstruction in three steps. First, a description of the diverse images of redemption within the Scriptures and tradition shows that redemption is not simply the subjective justification of individuals but entails a communicative and transformative practice. Second, the particularity of Christian faith is based upon the life-praxis of Jesus and its innovative reception within the constructive Christian imagination of the Christian communities that nurture and link their symbols of Christ with reconstructions of his life-praxis. This life-praxis, thereby, serves as a critical corrective and contrast to imperial, colonialist, and ideological exploitations of the Christ symbol. Finally, the universality implied in a Christian understanding of redemption should be neither particularistically exclusive nor universally inclusive but rather communicative so as to take seriously both the particularity and unity of humanity, as explicated in contemporary experience and in background assumptions about human nature.

Images of Redemption as a Transformative Praxis

The meaning of redemption is often narrowly interpreted in reference to linguistic studies and/or to the activity of Christ. A linguistic approach to interpreting redemption is much too narrow, even though the language about redemption is quite diverse and complex. Two Greek nouns (*lytrōsis* and *apolytrōsis*) are usually translated as "redemption," and the Greek verbs *lytrousthai, exagorzesthai,* and *hryesthai* are usually translated as "redeem."[48] The Greek word *katallagn*, however, is translated as "reconciliation," and the Latin Vulgate distinguished between *reconciliare* and *placare* or *expiare.* This difference eventually became lost. The noun *soteria* and the verb *sozo* (to save) are the usual terms to express salvation. The linguistic roots of the term "redemption" point to the buying or freeing of some person or thing; the meaning of the term "salvation" is much more complex.

48. See Martin Kahler, *Zur Lehre von der Versöhnung* (Gutersloh: Gutersloher Verlag, 1937), 1–38.

Another limited focus interprets redemption from the perspective of the agent of redemption. One can outline four distinct conceptions of the work of Christ.[49] The first emphasizes the redemption that God has accomplished in Jesus Christ (Paul and Mark). Another type emphasizes that God's redemptive purposes are accomplished in Jesus Christ (Luke and the Acts of the Apostles). In another, Christ as preexistent is the active agent of redemption (Colossians and Ephesians). Finally, the fourth type sees redemption as mediated by Christ. All four accounts emphasize the agent of redemption or the role of God and Christ in interpreting human redemption.

A much broader interpretive approach is to survey the diverse images of redemption and salvation.[50] Redemption from sin and guilt is one image. Other images are found in the stories about Jesus' practice of healing: the blind see, the deaf hear, the lame walk, the dead rise, and the possessed are liberated. Such images point to personal healing and making whole. Other images are political images of liberation. The Book of Revelation envisions redemption as liberation and salvation as a new world freed from Roman imperial domination and oppression. These diverse images show that redemption embraces not only sin and personal life but also political and social life, the cosmos and the world of nature.[51] The breadth of classical images of redemption shows diverse and changing conceptions.[52] It contrasts starkly to modern systematic presentations limiting redemption to justification.

A more comprehensive accounting of the meaning of redemption would have to include the following elements. First, redemp-

49. Arland J. Hultgren, *Christ and His Benefits* (Philadelphia: Fortress, 1978).

50. For creative reinterpretation of the Christ symbol, see Mark Taylor, *Remembering Esperanza: A Cultural-Political Theology for North American Praxis* (Maryknoll, N.Y.: Orbis, 1990).

51. See Elisabeth Schüssler Fiorenza, "Redemption as Liberation: Rev. 1:5–6 and 5:9–10," in *The Book of Revelation: Justice and Judgment* (Philadelphia: Fortress, 1989); and idem, *Revelation: Vision of a Just World* (Minneapolis: Fortress, 1991).

52. See Gisbert Geschake, "Der Wandel der Erlösungsvorstellungen in der Theologiegeshichte," in *Erlösung und Emanzipation,* ed. Leo Scheffczyk (Freiburg: Herder, 1973).

tion must be seen in relation to *God*. Redemption as freedom from sin and guilt signifies that human fault and misdoing do not affect only the individual human self or only a partial aspect of human life, existence, and value. Instead human misdoing affects the web of life in its very ultimacy and transcendence. Hence redemption requires a transformation not only of the human self but also of the relation of the self to the ultimacy and transcendence of life. Redemption takes place not only when we are changed but also when the very web of life is changed, as traditional theology sought to explicate when it combined subjective and objective versions of redemption. Since sin is not simply a developmental inadequacy or lack of knowledge but a distortion of reality, redemption is not simply a maturation or the obtaining of insight but rather the transformation of the structures of reality away from their systemic distortions. In classical Latin *Conservator* was the term for savior. The *Conservator* guaranteed salvation insofar as it preserved the sacred order of the world and preserved the empire in the face of war and barbarity. Since Christians did not envision salvation as preserving what had been achieved, they replaced the term *Conservator* with *Salvator.*[53] Salvation is not conservation or maturation but liberation and transformation.

Second, it is necessary to understand that redemption affects the whole human person so that persons become what they should be. Redemption is not an external change imposed upon persons but affects the core of a person's being. In the words of Karl Rahner: "Indeed the Christian faith considers redemption in the normal human situation not simply that which through God's act simply affects humans while bypassing human freedom. Instead redemption is the definitiveness of human freedom, even though redemption is indeed first of all God's act."[54] The

53. H. U. Instinksy, *Die alte Kirche und das Heil des Staates* (Munich: Kösel, 1963), 28ff. Joseph Ratzinger, "Vorfragen zu einer Theologie der Erlösung" in *Erlösung und Emanzipation,* 141–55.

54. For the relation between redemption and human freedom, see Karl Rahner, "Das christliche Verständnis der Erlösung," in *Erlösung in Christentum und Buddhismus,* ed.

freedom of redemption is not primarily a negative freedom, as it is often interpreted—that is, it is not freedom from sin, the law, death, or the devil. Instead redemption involves primarily a *positive freedom* entailing *solidarity* with God and with fellow humans.

Third, it is necessary to affirm that redemption affects *corporeality* and relates to the world of nature. Images of redemption are neither individualist nor spiritual—they do not exclude bodily existence within the world of nature. Redemption affects humans in their corporeality and worldliness. The imagery of healing from physical illness is a basic sign and symbol of redemption that extends beyond a person's individual physical existence to her or his relation to nature. Prophetic imagery refers to a heaven and a new earth.

Fourth, redemption must be seen as affecting humans in their historical, social, and political existence. The images of the reign or kingdom of God are key New Testament metaphors that speak of salvation in social and political categories. Insight into the apocalyptic origin of language regarding the kingdom of God in the New Testament has led Rudolf Bultmann to demythologize this imagery into a call for an existential decision. Such an approach cuts short the apocalyptic imagery, as does an interpretation that translates such imagery into individualistic moral categories or into transcendent ecclesial categories. Apocalyptic and eschatological language contains a diversity of images and a pluralism of interpretations.[55] Apocalyptic language is more appropriately interpreted in, but not reduced to, social and political categories.[56] The kingdom of God embraces freedom, peace, and justice not only for the individual but also for humanity and the

Andreas Bsteh (Mödling: St. Gabriel, 1982), 112–127; quotation from p. 113. See the survey in Thomas Propper, *Erlösungsglaube und Freiheitsgeschichte,* 2d ed. (Munich: Kösel, 1988).

55. For a survey, see Elisabeth Schüssler Fiorenza, "Eschatology of the NT," in *Interpreter's Dictionary of the Bible* (Nashville: Abingdon, 1978), 271–77.

56. See Johannes Baptist Metz, *Faith in History and Society: Toward a Practical Fundamental Theology* (New York: Crossroad, 1980), esp. 119–35; and idem, *The Emergent Church* (New York: Seabury, 1986), 82–94.

world. Christian redemption and salvation imply not only a positive freedom and reconciliation but also a solidarity between all humans and all of God's creation.

Particularity as Critical: Interpreting Jesus' Praxis

Appeals to Jesus are limited in many modern scholarly approaches to Christology. Some limit their appeal in part because of their skepticism in the face of the difficulty of distinguishing between what has originated in the proclamation of the Christian community and what goes back to the historical Jesus. Such skepticism contrasts with the appeals to Jesus within popular religious piety. It also contrasts with the appeals in various liberation theologies to the practice of Jesus as a resource of resistance to destructive oppression. Others limit their appeals to the historical Jesus for ideological reasons. Charles Davis argues that the historical particularity of Jesus is the basis for Christian exclusiveness.[57] A post-Christian critique might argue that the symbols based on Jesus' life, crucifixion, and death can become symbols justifying suffering and victimization. Ernst Bloch, for example, maintains that Luther's theology of the cross served this function when preached to the rebellious peasants. Some feminists view the maleness of Jesus as a significant obstacle or note that appeals to Jesus' suffering and obedience serve to urge women (more often than males) to sacrifice themselves or their aspirations.

If, however, one interprets the crucifixion and death of Jesus as a consequence of his life, preaching, and praxis, then one obtains a leverage point to place into check ideological symbolizations of Christ and to discover a resource for resistance.[58] A major problem, leading to colonial and ideological use of Christian symbols,

57. Charles Davis, *Christ and the World Religions* (London: Hodder and Stoughton, 1970), 41.

58. See my essay "Critical Social Theory and Christology," *Proceedings of the CTSA* 30 (1975): 63–110.

is precisely their dislocation from the historical concreteness of the life and praxis of Jesus. The symbolization of Christ has been diverse throughout the history of Christianity: Christ as King, Christ as Lord, Christ as Ruler, Christ as Sovereign. These symbols stand in contrast with the historical life of Jesus, even allowing for awareness of the limitations and interpretive character of all historical research. Consequently, one should attempt historical reconstructions of Jesus' life and practice not simply as a moral example but also as an individual historical communicative and critical praxis. The tension between such tentative historical reconstructions and symbolizations cut off from such historical reconstruction is healthy; even though the historical Jesus does not ground the symbol Christ, it provides a check upon the christological symbols and provides historical resources for further symbolic interpretations.

The historical particularity of Jesus can serve as a critical corrective to Christian symbols of Christ. The preaching and life-praxis of Jesus, although attainable only through revisable historical reconstructions, portray Jesus in ways that contrast with imperialistic symbolizations of Christ. Imagery and language about Christ as King, as Victor, and as Lord are triumphalistic and can become imperialistic if they are disassociated from the historical imagery of Jesus as one in solidarity with outcasts from the society and as a victim of the existing power structures. Likewise the images of Jesus' practice of a ministry of healing and inclusion countervails exclusionary practices, even though Jesus' life-praxis was limited to the extent that he most probably understood his mission solely and primarily as directed at Israel. Jesus' practice of including sinners, tax collectors, and women among his disciples points to an inclusive practice that can become even more inclusive. Because the proclamation and life-praxis of Jesus led to his crucifixion and because that crucifixion was, most probably, a consequence of this solidarity with outcasts—a solidarity concretely narrated in diverse gospel accounts—a theology of the cross cannot legitimate victimization, oppression, and colonization unless it is isolated from Jesus' life-practice.

Redemption as Communicative and Practical

The issue is to interpret the particularity and universality implied in a Christian understanding of redemption in a way that takes seriously the danger of exploitation and colonialism. To do so, Christian redemption must not be understood in developmental or in perfectionist terms, as if the Christian understanding of redemption is the high point toward which other religions tend. Nor should it be interpreted as in the thesis of anonymous Christianity, whereby Christianity is a real symbol of what is universally implicit. Nor should it be understood as a mere concrete exemplification of a universal human religiousness. Christian redemption needs to be explicated as a communicative claim and praxis of what is historically concrete. There are warrants for this from our experience in the world, from background theories about universality and particularity, and from an interpretation of the Christian tradition.

Our experience within the contemporary world provides us with rather *complex warrants* regarding the issue of universality and particularity. On the one hand, we are increasingly conscious of the particularity of diverse cultures, religious beliefs, life-habits, and political organizations. On the other hand, telecommunication and travel increasingly make the world into a global village. For example, during an earthquake in Armenia or floods in Bangladesh, one can more easily communicate between New York and a stricken village via television than between one side of the village and the other. We face a similar dilemma concerning our culture. At a time when postmodern trends in cultural criticism underscore particular narratives over against metatheories, diverse cultures realize the unity of the earth in the ecocrisis. All cultures must face the challenge of the survival of the earth.

The warrants to be drawn from the experience of this intermingling of global unity and increased particularity point toward a theological position that moves away from two approaches: one that simply points to the historicity and particularity of individual religious conviction for the sake of radical plurality and one that undermines particularity with its advocacy of a simple unity of humanity. Instead this religious formulation has to explicate at the same time both the particularity of one's own culture and religious beliefs and its relation to the global unity. Any articulation of the meaning of Christ as savior has to take into account both the unity of humankind and its radical diversity. The christological and soteriological problem then becomes the awareness of the interrelation as well as tension between the unity of humankind and particular diversity. Particularity and pluralism need to be understood in a way that they do not undercut the solidarity and co-humanity of humans. To the extent that religious beliefs are lived beliefs and affect social and political life, the diversity of religions crisscrosses with the imperatives of ecological, economic, and political life. This position, thereby, takes seriously the postmodern critique of Eurocentrism and does not understand the unity of humanity within the individualistic categories of the modern European West but rather understands it as based on solidarity with others.

Theological interpretations of redemption have often assumed specific *background theories* about human nature. They have either assumed a nonhistorical transcendental essence of human nature or an evolving human nature, or they have dissolved human nature into the particularities of specific cultures and time periods. It seems more adequate to talk about human nature with the help of a concept of historical individuality that does not fall into either the radical particularism of the historical school or the universalism in which the historically concrete is just a specific example of a universal human nature. In dealing with historical events and historical persons, one needs testimony to document the individual historical events. The genre of testimony documents singularity and yet displays a surplus of meaning that is communicative and open to new receptions and interpretations.[59]

These two observations underscore that the Christian claim to unicity should not be explicated in the categories of either individuality or universality.[60] Individuality presupposes an incommensurability between individuals and views the other as wholly other. Consequently, one's own religious beliefs appear to the other as foreign and incommensurable, just as the other's beliefs and practices are foreign and incommensurable. The necessity of dealing with truth claims and their significance for practice is minimized. Universality presupposes an underlying common human nature and practice. It undercuts diversity and plurality, which are reduced to a fundamental oneness.

Instead unicity expresses an unconditionality of the communicative claim of a historical particularity. What is historically particular remains historically particular, and yet in raising truth claims, it raises what is communicative insofar as these claims are brought before others, for their acceptance or rejection. The power of the symbol is its location in history, in a community, and in cult. The unicity of the historical stands over against the universality, though the universal enables the symbolic to develop. A dialogical and conversational model does not necessarily imply a pluralism in which there are no claims of truth and norms. It implies instead entering into a dialogue where one expects one's claims to be acknowledged as well as challenged and where one challenges others as well. Even though one affirms that no abstract universal (rational, ethical, or religious) standards exist that can assess religious differences, such an affirmation should not mean that no criteria exist or that one cannot raise issues of truth or value within an interreligious dialogue. Unconditionality and unicity are therefore not simply expressions of individuality but are expressed in the commu-

59. Francis Schüssler Fiorenza, *Foundational Theology* (New York: Crossroad, 1984).

60. See Carl E. Braaten, "The Person of Jesus Christ," in *Christian Dogmatics*, ed. Carl E. Braaten and Robert Jensen (Philadelphia: Fortress, 1984), esp. 1:557–69.

nicative act of raising claims. The affirmation of the unicity of the historically particular checks claims that reduce the particular to simply a manifestation of the universal and therefore impose the particular upon the other. The Christian affirmation of the historical conditioning of Jesus underscores the unicity of Jesus. Christian theology seeks to elaborate Jesus' significance for the other while at the same time acknowledging Jesus' particularity.[61]

Jesus is not simply an example of a universal human nature; nor is Christianity simply an example of human religiousness. Jesus is a historical individual; Christianity is a historical religion. The redemption that Christians seek to proclaim and to live is a historical and individual configuration, but one seeking to be communicative. Christian redemption and salvation are the transformative praxis of the Christian vision—a vision that is to be put into practice and communicated. The vision is therefore neither individual nor universal but communicative, for it is a particular vision and praxis that are raised with a communicative and practical claim.[62] The symbol of Christ is a symbol of the historical Jesus. The symbol incorporates and seeks to communicate the particular, which in turn is known only through symbolization. The tension between the historical Jesus and the symbolic Christ is a tension between, on the one hand, what is a historical source and critical corrective of the symbolic and, on the other hand, the symbolic as a communicative opening of the particular to new meanings and references, to new interpretations that make possible new receptions and understandings and hence a pluralistic Christology.[63]

61. The term "absoluteness" is unfortunate insofar as it stems from *absolvere,* removed from limits.

62. See my explanation in relation to transcendental and hermeneutical approaches to religion in "Theology: Transcendental or Hermeneutical?" *Horizons* 16 (1989): 329–41.

63. For an important analysis of sign, see Rebecca Chopp, *The Power to Speak* (New York: Crossroad, 1989).

CHRISTIAN CHURCHES AS COMMUNITIES OF DISCOURSE AND PRAXIS

Christian believers have a double social location: within their churches and within their contemporary culture. The Christian faith originated within the early Christian communities with their affirmation of Jesus as the center of their community life. This faith lives on and is nurtured in the life and cult of these Christian communities.[64] When Christians explicate the meaning of their faith, they explicate a faith with roots in a historical community. Their faith depends upon the historical conditions and social effects of that community just as much as it relates to the historical conditions and social effects of modern culture.

The problem of modern Christianity, Ernst Troeltsch argued, is not simply intellectual but also a matter of community. "This lack of community and cult is the real sickness of modern Christianity and contemporary religious practice generally. It is what makes it so impermanent and chaotic, so dependent upon who happens to be there, so much an amateur thing for enthusiasts, so much a matter of world-view and the intellect."[65] Along with this lack of community, modern Christianity has to contend with the historicity of the Christian tradition, the social conditions and effects of its beliefs, the diversity and validity of other religious traditions, and the interrelation between the criteria for the assessment of religious beliefs and the criteria of its culture. The meaning of the Christian faith in Jesus should be explicated with full awareness of the historical and social nature not only of Christianity but also of other religions.

Such a task faces both the pluralism and historicism of modern culture as well as the challenge of political oppression and economic exploitation. Since Christian communities have come into existence as interpretive communities, both re-creatively recep-

64. Ernst Troeltsch has noted that "the truth is that almost all forms of contemporary religiosity are variations of what was nurtured in the churches; only here are the treasures of religion alive" (*Writings,* 193).

65. Ibid., 194.

tive and communicative of the presence and life-praxis of Jesus, their task is to place their interpretive reception and interpretation of Jesus into a transformative and redemptive practice. Hence the Christian communities take up the communicative task of the realization of the redemptive praxis represented through their affirmation of Christ. This task entails an understanding of redemption that involves ultimacy, freedom, corporeality, and political and social transformation. It entails Christian communities taking as criteria of their praxis reconstructions of the praxis of Jesus; even if these are new and creative, they still provide clues to answer questions about the possibility and criteria of limiting power. As communities of interpretation and practice, churches raise with their convictions validity claims not only about the ultimate meaning of reality but also about how that meaning should transform personal, social, and political reality. Because their claims affect the ultimate meaning of reality and the intersection of this meaning with social and political reality, the churches necessarily engage other visions of reality and practice.

Modern political and liberation theologies underscore the public and political nature of Christian faith. To the extent that they interpret salvation neither in otherworldly nor in individualistic categories, they make the problem of domination acute. Their emphasis on the option for the poor, the victimized, and the oppressed offers a corrective to the problem of dominative power.[66] The intertwinement of belief and power calls for a response that is as much practical as theoretical. It calls as much for the transformation of the Christian communities and their practice as for a reinterpretation of redemption.

This relation between theory and practice has been well formulated by Gotthold Lessing's "Parable of the Three Rings."[67]

66. On interpretation of suffering, see Rebecca Chopp, *The Praxis of Suffering: An Interpretation of Liberation and Political Theologies* (Maryknoll, N.Y.: Orbis, 1986).

67. In act 3 of his drama *Nathan Wise* (1779). See Henry Allison's interpretation in *Lessing and the Enlightenment* (Ann Arbor: Univ. of Michigan Press, 1966).

Saladin asks Nathan about the truth of Christianity, Judaism, and Islam. Nathan avoids answering. But Saladin pushes him, for one must be responsible for what one believes. The parable is Nathan's response, and it disallows a simple or unambiguous answer to whether one, none, or all is true. The parable answers in terms of the practice of life—religion is true if its adherents in their life and practice show that they possess the power of God's revelation. Yet no one of the religions exhibits such an exemplary life-practice that singles it out above the others. Perhaps all do not have the true ring. The parable views the contention among the religions as theoretically unanswerable. The life-praxis of the diverse religions could in the future display the answer. The answer is left to a future praxis and to a future and greater judge than human reason and criteria.

SUSAN BROOKS THISTLETHWAITE AND
PETER CRAFTS HODGSON

12. THE CHURCH, CLASSISM, AND ECCLESIAL COMMUNITY

Working people are likely to cling to a hierarchical, authoritarian, fixed social order, which ironically has been the source of their victimization. They do so because of the precariousness of life in an age when the dream is being betrayed all around them. They cling to a privatized religion removed from their worldly struggles because in their private realm they can be themselves, the real self or "soul" can live and the wounds be forgotten. They adopt the upwardly mobile values and religious orientation of those above them because of their tenacious belief that in the end the dream will "save" them. In other words, their religious expressions have been colonized or become captive to the dynamics of domination from which they seek salvation.

—Karen Bloomquist, *The Dream Betrayed*

Why do many economically burdened Americans consistently vote to maintain economic policies that continue to disadvantage them? According to Karen Bloomquist, they do so because they identify themselves with those who have "made it," who have attained the American dream of economic security. They are unable to see their social class for what it is and to identify the forces that keep them in that class. Further, Bloomquist argues, their religious faith is "colonized," that is, invaded by these same dominant class values, and therefore their faith only further blinds them to their real economic condition.[1] In fact, in identify-

1. Karen Bloomquist, *The Dream Betrayed: Religious Challenge of the Working Class* (Minneapolis: Fortress, 1990), 48; see 47–53.

ing with the dominant class and its values, Americans look down on those less economically advantaged, and their religious faith does little to discourage them from this prejudice.

This type of prejudice against those less economically privileged is called "classism." Classism may be defined as a widespread pattern of discrimination against individuals and groups because of their social status, economic status, or way of life. Class is the division of people into societywide groupings according to social status, political and economic power, and interests or ways of life in common. Classism, therefore, is the attitude and accompanying practice of according relative value to people and groups because of their class. This relative value results in prejudice against those in other, especially "lower" (that is, less affluent and prestigious), classes. But because Americans deny that real class differences exist in America, it is almost impossible for them to see that class*ism* is a problem.

Social scientists distinguish between *social differentiation, social inequality,* and *social stratification.* The first simply is the result of distinct individual qualities and social roles; in more complex societies it issues in a division of labor or tasks, but these do not necessarily imply a hierarchical or evaluative ranking. Social inequality is the condition whereby people have unequal access to resources, services, and positions in society. Social stratification represents the hardening or institutionalization of inequality in systems of social relationships, which historically have assumed several different forms: slavery, caste, estate, and class.[2] The reasons why differentiation yields to institutionalized inequality in human societies are complex and mysterious; we cannot pursue them here. But we are assuming for the purposes of this chapter that class is not a benign form of social differentiation; rather it is a destructive way of organizing differences into a hierarchy of privileges, power, authority, and wealth.

2. Harold R. Kerbo, *Social Stratification and Inequality* (New York: McGraw-Hill, 1983), 10–24.

Before proceeding further it should be acknowledged that the present authors write from a particular perspective and social location, that of white, middle-class Protestantism. We know that we have been only partly successful in transcending our own class interests and that in what follows many features of the American experience are not adequately discussed, including Catholicism, the working classes, and minorities.

ANALYSIS

The Problem of Problemlessness

What causes American society to turn a particularly blind eye to the problem of classism? One reason is that Americans have retained, since their earliest history, a self-portrait as a society without the old class distinctions of Europe. Therefore, when we wish to define the problem of classism in relation to the doctrine of the church, our very first problem is that as Americans we have very little experience in naming the problem of classism.

Some would say that poverty in America was "discovered" only in the early 1960s. This is rather like saying Columbus "discovered America."[3] Poor folks and native peoples pursued their separate existences and knew themselves to be doing so long before they were "discovered." The discovery of poverty like the discovery of the Americas therefore says far more about the discoverers than about what they discovered.

To have *dis*covered poverty in 1960 means that poverty must have been previously covered or hidden—and this is in fact the case. The ideal of America, a classless society of free individuals as described by Alexis de Tocqueville in his *Democracy in America* (1835–40), reigned supreme through the 1950s, altered only briefly at times, as in the Great Depression. But the post–World War II affluence brought a surge in the sense that class differences

3. Barbara Ehrenreich, *The Fear of Falling: The Inner Life of the Middle Class* (New York: HarperCollins, 1990), 17.

in America were gone, if, indeed, they had ever existed. America had become "the most truly classless society in history."[4]

How then was class ever discovered when no one was looking for it? In 1962 Michael Harrington published *The Other America,* a trenchant description of the reality of poverty in America.[5] It ended up on the *New York Times* best-seller list and, read by an idealistic young president, John F. Kennedy, set the stage for the War on Poverty. Carried out after Kennedy's assassination, the so-called War on Poverty had as its stated goal the spiritual growth of the nation. Sargent Shriver, the administration's leading antipoverty official, dubbed this effort "a movement of conscience—a national act of expiation, of humbling and prostrating ourselves before our Creator."[6] For Harrington and a few other social critics, the problem of classism in the United States was real; for the vast majority of Americans, however, even the discovery of poverty led to personal introspection rather than to hard-hitting social critique.

In naming the problem of classism in the United States, therefore, we are hampered by several factors: America has been held to be a free society of discrete individuals, and American society is viewed as uniquely blessed with plenty by a beneficent Creator. In the American psyche, class differences are, therefore, almost an affront to that beneficent Creator.

To explore the church and classism in the United States we must take account of America's willed blindness to class and the peculiar sort of class prejudice that results from this blindness. Some of the church's teachings on ecclesiology can be helpful in exposing the particular American blindness to social class differences and their importance; some of the church's teachings on ecclesiology, however, contribute to the existence and maintenance of classism in the United States.

4. Ibid., 18; quoting Vance Packard, *The Status Seekers* (New York: Pocket Books, 1961), 2.

5. Michael Harrington, *The Other America* (1962; reprint, New York: Viking, 1971).

6. Sargent Shriver, foreword to George H. Dumer, ed., *Poverty in Plenty* (New York: Kennedy, 1964), 10.

The Church: From Economic Outsider to Insider

The Christian church is oriented in a fundamental way to the message and existence of a particular historical figure, Jesus of Nazareth. Strictly speaking, Jesus did not found a church in the sense of establishing an organized community; however, what he said and did was so radical and had such a powerful impact that a new and distinctive kind of religious movement began to emerge in the Jewish-Hellenistic milieu shared by Jesus and his earliest followers, and that movement then spread throughout the Mediterranean world.

Essentially what Jesus did was to proclaim the imminent coming of God's kingdom or *basileia*. In his parables he envisioned this *basileia* as essentially communal and social: it was an image of a new way of being human in the world in relation to God and neighbor that broke the logic of the old world and of ordinary human relationships under the sway of domination and control, reward and punishment. God's rule called forth a new human community, a communion of love, of liberation, of inclusion, of gratuity, of equality. The *basileia* vision implied a radical alteration in social and institutional structures, and indeed Jesus himself put this vision into practice by gathering a network of disciples that was open to all without any prior conditions or privileges and that sharply challenged traditional social divisions and stratifications. Ultimately he died because of the severe threat his message and movement posed to the established authorities.

The medieval church can be said really to begin with the peace of Constantine, because it is with this era that the close attachment between the state and the Christian church, the hallmark of medieval Christianity, began. It became legal to leave money to the church, and the church thus began a long period of acquisition of wealth that made it a rich and powerful center for the control of economic life. The church was invaded from within by cultural accommodation, an attack that proved almost irresistible. The attack from without had been much easier to recognize.

One of the important factors to take into account in describing the medieval doctrine of the church is the elaboration of hierarchy, the beginning of classism in the structures of the church itself. The lack of a hierarchy was a striking characteristic of Jesus' *basileia* vision and the earliest churches. The development of a complex hierarchy is a hallmark of both the chronological and conceptual stages of church doctrine.

Social and political metaphors—such as the City of God, the New Jerusalem, and the Perfect Society—abound. The first of these, the City of God, is especially illustrative of the way in which class structures were taken into not only the church but also the heavens that the church mirrored. There has always been some understandable confusion about the relationship of the church to the heavenly city, the City of God. For Augustine the true church or heavenly city is made up of the fixed number of saints elected before the foundation of the world and known only to God. This is the invisible church, and it is "mixed in" with the visible church, which also includes sinners, those who are not among the elect.

It is significant for a discussion of church doctrine and classism that Augustine chose a social and political image (city) for his work. Thinking of the church in sociopolitical terms made it inevitable that later theologians would assume that the church should dominate earthly society. At the same time, Augustine's invisible/visible distinction was forgotten, and the Roman Catholic Church came to be identified with the City of God on earth. The institutional church was sacralized yet remained deeply classist in structure. In contrast to the early churches, social class distinctions, gender distinctions, and racial distinctions were not challenged when brought into the earthly City of God.

Like Augustine, Aquinas's doctrine of the church as the Perfect Society is profoundly classist. The proper ordering of society into classes mirrored the divine rule in heaven. This ordering was perhaps most visible in the existence of a priestly caste, which became marked in Aquinas's time. Only males were permitted to be priests; this suited God's order since, as Aquinas cited Aristotle, women are a lower order of being, the more material principle. As heaven was hierarchical, each soul in its proper place, so should be Christendom.

In the Protestant Reformation the fundamental question was the doctrine of the church. The historical, political, economic, and cultural factors bearing on the Reformation were of great importance. States and their new mercantile classes desired to free themselves of the economic and political stranglehold of Rome and to assert their own cultural, political, economic, and even religious independence from Rome. The desire to get free of the City of God was one of the engines pulling the Reformation.

The Reformers transformed Augustine's distinction between the visible and the invisible church and used it as a powerful tool of critique of the church's visible domination of the society. According to Luther, the essential or invisible church is the "community" or "assembly" of "all those who live in true faith, hope, and love."[7] The church hierarchy, particularly the pope, can be called to account if they do not incarnate this true community in their midst.

The Protestants escaping persecution in Europe founded the "New Jerusalem" to be a "City on the Hill." The theocratic societies set up in the New World were one attempt to bring the invisible world of the elect into visibility by social organization of religious life. Those who had been persecuted for their religious beliefs in turn persecuted dissenters precisely because dissent drove a wedge between the visible church and the election of those who had been permitted by God to found a pure society in the New World. The societies founded by this vision

7. Martin Luther, *On the Papacy in Rome,* in *Luther's Works,* ed. Eric W. Gritsch (Philadelphia: Fortress, 1970), 39:65, 69–70.

were, to a remarkable degree, free of social class distinctions. This was, to a great extent, a function of the Reformation's conscious rejection of the hierarchical principle of medieval church doctrine.

The rise of various denominations in the nineteenth century is yet another example of how church doctrine is imbedded in the social and economic forces of society. In many states of the developing American society the churches had been "established," that is, financially supported, by the state. Culminating early in the nineteenth century, however, the founders' vision of the separation of church and state resulted in "disestablishment." Church bodies were no longer financially supported by state governments. When Congregationalism was finally disestablished in Massachusetts, the process was complete.

Protestant churches in the United States are voluntary associations, supported by the monies and work of their individual members. This disestablishment was the result not only of a general democratization but also of the competitive, commercial spirit of industrialization, which challenged the values of the Christian gospel and decreed them inapplicable to business. The Protestant churches were able to retain some autonomy, but at a price. The price was the loss of the independent identity of religion over against culture. Religion triumphed in America by identifying with and upholding American values. So the Protestant doctrine of the church in America became a private and secularized version of Augustine's City of God or Aquinas's Perfect Society. The church was the very mirror of social class distinctions in American society. The distinction between the visible and the invisible church, so powerful a weapon of critique in the Reformation, became a way to further American blindness to the real race, gender, and especially class distinctions in the church's life and practice. In the "invisible" church Americans are all one; in the "visible" church, however, Americans are rigidly classist. The invisibility doctrine, employed in the latter way, certainly has contributed to having classism be "the problem that has no name" in American society.[8]

RECONSTRUCTION

A Real Look at Class

In order to begin to change the relationship of ecclesiology and classism we need to begin with the factors that do separate people into quite different social and economic groups and note how these specific factors contribute to the real *existence* of classism in the United States along with its real *denial.* In front of our eyes, we have the reality of the most racially divided hour of the American week, Sunday morning worship. The realities of race in American society make reconstructing the relation of church and class even more complex. The poor are, as they always have been, mostly white in America. It is true, however, that African Americans are disproportionately poor. Class is often confused with race, as the racism of American society projects labels such as "lazy" and "shiftless" or "welfare bums" onto the disproportionately poor African-American community. As the United States has become increasingly Hispanic and Asian, these prejudices have extended to racial and ethnic minorities other than African Americans. We should not forget, however, that the terms of racial prejudice in the United States were decisively formed by the American history of slavery.

Gender analysis, too, must be added to any analysis of the

8. The authors are aware of the absence of any discussion of the American Catholic experience in this chapter—an omission that reflects not only limitations of space but more importantly limitations in our knowledge of the subject and our own social location as middle-class Protestants. The American Catholic experience is significant for a study of classism in several respects: the assimilation of waves of immigrants first from Europe and more recently from Hispanic countries and Asia, a long and close affiliation with the labor movement, and the fact that Catholic dioceses are geographical rather than denominational or voluntaristic in structure. These and other factors mean that the Catholic Church does not mirror the social class distinctions of American society in the same way that the Protestant churches do. (We are indebted to Marianne Sawicki for criticizing our chapter on this score and for suggesting the points mentioned in this note.)

problem of classism in the United States. Betty Friedan's *The Feminine Mystique* describes the malaise of educated women who wished to do meaningful work and who were, instead, shoved into "the underused, nameless, yearning, energy-to-get-rid-of state of being housewives."[9] One idea discussed even up until the 1960s was to stop wasting valuable education on women who were going to be housewives and to train them to accept their work as the basically lower-class occupation it really was and is.

Ideologies of classlessness, of freedom of choice, of white supremacy, and of patriarchy must be exposed for their part in contributing to classism. The prevailing American ideal is to be affluent, to be white, to be male. To be poor, to be black, to be female is to be other than the norm, and this is the basic definition of an "ism." Audre Lorde puts it succinctly:

> Racism, the belief in the inherent superiority of one race over all others and thereby the right to dominance. Sexism, the belief in the inherent superiority of one sex over the other and thereby the right to dominance. Ageism. Heterosexism. Elitism. Classism.[10]

Classism, then, is the belief in the inherent superiority of one class over all the others and therefore the right to dominance.

Let us clarify, however, that classism as a system of prejudice belongs in a category by itself. Ethnic, gender, and sexual differences are goods in themselves. What is wrong about racism or sexism or homophobia, therefore, is that they are denials of the essential goodness of human diversity and represent the categorization of people according to prejudiced criteria. Class, however, is not a good in itself if it is assumed, as we do, that class is not simply a manifestation of social differences but a subversion of these differences into a system of inequality and stratification. Class carries with it *necessarily* its ideological legitimation in the form of class*ism*—the belief that social stratification or class division is justified on the basis of inherent

9. Betty Friedan, *The Feminine Mystique* (New York: Norton, 1963), 206–7.
10. Audre Lorde, *Sister Outsider* (New York: Crossing Press, 1984), 115.

human inequality, or the will of God, or accommodation to the fallen condition, or productive efficiency, or some other reason. Historically, religion has played a major role in the legitimation of class.

A Real Look at the Church

Under the conditions of history, the austere radicalism of the Christian idea gave way to compromise. One of the great contributions of the theological historian and social ethicist Ernst Troeltsch was to call attention to the positive and negative aspects of this process.[11] The conflict of historical forces and interests makes compromise inevitable in human affairs, but it is possible for compromises to be good or bad, productive or destructive, and this is a distinction of obvious importance. Our attention will focus on the kinds of compromises struck between the churches and classism at several stages in ecclesiastical history.

The basic pattern, according to Troeltsch, was established very early, already in the Pauline ethic. On the one hand, the ideal of equality and the communism of love was applied purely inwardly, within the life of the religious community, free of the corrupting influence of the world. On the other hand, a thoroughly conservative attitude was adopted outwardly toward existing social institutions (property, classes, slavery, patriarchy, and so on), on the assumption that they serve the purposes of God under the conditions of sin and thus must be accommodated. The possibility of transforming the social order along the lines of the original ecclesial vision has played only a marginal role in the history of the church. The dominant social ethic has been one of philanthropy rather than of structural reform.

Thus the ancient Catholic Church accepted that external in-

11. Ernst Troeltsch, *The Social Teaching of the Christian Churches,* trans. Olive Wyon (London: George Allen and Unwin, 1931). See also Troeltsch's *Christian Thought: Its History and Application,* ed. Baron F. von Hügel (London: Univ. of London Press, 1923). The following analysis is indebted to Troeltsch at several points.

equality could and should exist alongside an interior equality. It assumed that the division of labor and classes and the unequal distribution of wealth were divine arrangements adapted to the needs of a fallen humanity. Underlying such an attitude was the theory of a *relative* natural law that applies to the fallen state—a law willed by God to maintain relative order in a condition of potential chaos. Such a law was believed to play a necessary role in the economy of salvation, although within the church it was superseded by the law of Christ. The medieval Catholic Church went a step further and introduced the complex structure of social inequality *into* the church itself, creating what Troeltsch has called a "patriarchalism of love."[12] The original communism of love was replaced by patriarchy, the dominant social pattern in the history of Western culture. The patriarchalism of natural authority, based on male domination, was softened by the Christian ethic of love, but it was, nevertheless, used to legitimate the hierarchical church and the creation of the feudal system. It was also the linchpin of an organic social theory in which individuals and groups found their proper place along a vertical scale.

These medieval tendencies were reinforced in classic Protestantism. For Lutheranism, the organic aspect disappeared while patriarchal values were heightened. The patriarchal family became central, infusing the whole Lutheran social ethic and determining the divine-human relationship. Both divine and natural law prescribed that individuals should live within their own class, according to its social standards, and not attempt to rise in the world or change existing institutions, which were ordained by God to control against sin and anarchy. The Lutheran theology of the "calling," combined with the notion of natural "orders," produced a thoroughly reactionary social ethic, which never advanced beyond the ideal of charity. Calvinism anchored its social doctrine in a theory of predestination, according to which God has ordained that many should serve and a few

12. Troeltsch, *Social Teaching,* 285–87.

should rule (the gifted and holy elect). This inequality belongs to nature and is not a result of the fall; it follows not from reason but from the sovereign divine will.[13]

If classism means the ideological legitimation of social stratification, then these medieval and early Protestant social theories are a prime instance of classism. In an attempt to strike an accommodation with the existing social order and to ensure an advantageous place for the church within it, theological doctrines were elaborated to provide both a divine sanction for present conditions and the promise of future rewards for those who obey the rules and honor present class obligations.

This basic pattern of legitimation has not been significantly modified by the modern church, Catholic or Protestant, institutional or sectarian, European or American. For the most part the post-Reformation sectarian movements remained quietistic and indifferent toward the world. Those sects that did attempt to inaugurate a new order of society in harmony with the will of God and reason found it necessary to withdraw into small, experimental communities. They did, however, spawn the vision of Christian socialism, which provided a valuable critique of the existing socioeconomic system but lacked the means to change it.

In a classic study, H. Richard Niebuhr argued that denominationalism, especially among Protestants in North America, "represents the accommodation of Christianity to the caste-system of human society." "The denominations, churches, sects, are sociological groups whose principle of differentiation is to be sought in their conformity to the order of social classes and groups." This does not mean that they are not religious movements with legitimate theological and cultic differences, but the primary factor in the emergence and preservation of denominations is sociological: they serve and reflect specific class interests. "They are emblems, therefore," says Niebuhr, "of the victory of the world over the church, of the secularization of Christianity,

13. Ibid., 620.

of the church's sanction of that divisiveness which the church's gospel condemns."[14] More recent studies have argued that during the past fifty years considerable convergence has occurred among major denominations and that they exhibit greater social and cultural similarity than they did in Niebuhr's time.[15] This may be true, but social stratification continues to exist *within* denominations and indeed has widened.[16]

Reconstructing Church and Class Together

Reconstituting the doctrine of the church in light of the existence of classism begins, as Niebuhr's work suggests, with the class differences in the existing churches. These class differences may be named and consciously rejected by contrasting them with the egalitarian and communal practice of Jesus of Nazareth and his followers.

The primitive Christian communities were shaped by the radicalism of Jesus' *basileia* vision. Some of these communities practiced a communism of love, a sharing of earthly possessions for the use of all (although goods were produced privately and the family structure was honored). In others, existing social structures such as private homes and wealth were adapted to various uses by the Christian movement. This movement called itself an *ekklesia,* the Greek word for assembly or gathering; and the early Christians thought of themselves as gathered by the Spirit of God into community for purposes of mutual service, sharing, and worship. In this community the crucified and risen Lord was experienced as alive and at work, extending his earthly

14. H. Richard Niebuhr, *The Social Sources of Denominationalism* (1929; reprint, New York: Meridian, 1957), 6, 25.

15. Robert Wuthnow, *The Restructuring of American Religion* (Princeton, N.J.: Princeton Univ. Press, 1988), 87.

16. We recognize that the pattern differs in American Catholicism because of the geographical basis of its diocesan structure, its close affiliation with the labor movement, and a long tradition of papal teaching in support of the rights of working people (see above, n. 8). But social, ethnic, and racial segregation has inevitably led to class differences among Catholic churches within the same diocese, and the coalition with the labor movement (itself severely weakened) is probably coming to an end. The fact is that to some extent Catholicism in North America has taken on the sociological characteristics of Protestantism.

mission and message. The English word "church" derives from a Greek adjective, *kuriakos,* meaning "the Lord's," "belonging to the Lord." The church or ecclesial community understood itself to be related to the *basileia* proclaimed by the Lord, but it also knew itself to be distinct from it: it was a sign, sacrament, and foretaste of the coming *basileia,* an always incomplete and imperfect earthly manifestation of the *basileia* vision.

It is not surprising that this vision and practice appealed especially to those from lower classes, the poor, who had little vested interest in maintaining existing relations of power and who sensed in Jesus a person of the people who understood and sympathized with them. But despite this appeal, Jesus' message was fundamentally religious, having to do with the redemptive presence of God in the world and the relationship of each cherished human being to God. He himself did not draw out the political and social implications of the vision. Yet the implications were fairly obvious once it became evident that the coming kingdom of God did not mean an immediate end to the world but rather offered a paradigm of its ongoing transformation in the form of a never attainable but always beckoning goal.

In order to understand more precisely what is meant by the ecclesial community, let us say that in it a new kind of corporate life is being fashioned that is free—free not only from personal sin and guilt but also from all culturally specific conditions of redemption or provincial modes of existence, whether defined by nation, ethnic group, sex, class, language, law, tradition, or piety. In this new corporate life, persons are free to be for and with the other and with the whole of humanity under God in a quite radical way, the full implications of which are still hidden. All provincial boundaries and cultural wrappings are relativized by a redemption that is universally available without conditions. The ecclesial community, unlike virtually every other human institutional arrangement, is in its very nature not privileged, restricted, alienated; it is not based on blood, sex, race, inheritance, property, or wealth, but on a distinctive kind of self-giving love, an intending for the sake of the other rather than for oneself or one's clan.[17] This at least is the *idea* of the ecclesial community—an idea directly associated with the essential meaning of Christian faith.

Yet a reconstituted doctrine of the church in light of classism is not achieved by merely asserting, once again, a myth of return to origins, that is, to the vision of Jesus, but through a contextual proposal for the church in the late twentieth-century United States. The tension created by the difference between the Protestant denominations today and the ecclesial vision and practice of Jesus and his followers cuts both ways. American society is not the Roman Empire. In fact, most political leaders are Christians and churchgoers. Therefore, a church-against-the-world doctrine, appropriate to the pagan Roman Empire, is an inappropriate model for Christianized American society. Late twentieth-century American culture demands a contextualized *basileia* vision.

New ecclesial visions have been springing up in the "Two-Thirds World."[18] These are the base Christian communities (BCCs), small groups of Christians, largely lay led, who share the responsibilities of life equally and who combine a deep spirituality with a heightened political consciousness. Spirituality and consciousness-raising are not two phenomena, separate parts of the community life, but are joined in one vision.[19] The impact of the BCCs on ecclesiology in Latin America has been enormous. At the bishops' meeting in Puebla, Mexico, in February 1979, BCCs were hailed as a priority for the church and described as "the focal point of evangelization, the motor of liberation."

17. See Peter C. Hodgson, *Revisioning the Church: Ecclesial Freedom in the New Paradigm* (Philadelphia: Fortress, 1988), 25–28, 61, 67, 69, 103–7.

18. This is a more accurate and less pejorative term than "Third World," which seems to imply that the non–Euro-Atlantic peoples are tertiary and hence less important than the so-called First World. "Two-Thirds World" is at least an attempt to state that most of the people in the world do not live in the Euro-Atlantic countries.

19. Rosemary Radford Ruether, "Basic Christian Communities: Renewal at the Roots," *Christianity and Crisis* 41, September 21, 1981, 234.

Vatican II spoke of the church as the people of God, a church incarnate from the bottom up.

Some have hailed the BCCs as the model for revisioning the church in North America. Several points need to be raised in contextualizing this analysis. BCCs challenge the ecclesiology of the Latin American church precisely because the Catholic model has a public status and an explicit identification with the ruling powers of those countries. Protestantism, the dominant model of the church in North America, has the status of private association. This model has affected North American Catholicism as well, despite unique features of the Catholic experience.

Furthermore, it must be made absolutely explicit that the BCCs are formed of the poorest of the poor who combine their deep spirituality with a concrete political praxis. In the radically stratified economic and political structure of Latin America, this combination has a profoundly subversive impact. It may be that as the United States becomes increasingly stratified in its economic life, the BCCs will be the model for the increasingly large number of poor and marginalized people our economic practice is creating. A separable question, however, is the need for an ecclesiology to challenge the private, associational character of Protestant life and worship in their alliance with the class, race, and gender structure of American society.

"Commonwealth of God" is a suggestive late twentieth-century rendering of the Greek expression *basileia tou theou,* most commonly translated "kingdom of God." This rendering enables us to see that our ecclesial life must include a vision of the redistribution of wealth, as the term "commonwealth" actually suggests. This means the church itself is put on the side of political advocacy for a radical reform of the American economic system, even as it struggles to incarnate the commonness of wealth in its own life and practice.

It is of great concern that an uncontextualized and therefore uncritical appropriation of the BCC model will fuel the worst aspects of Protestant individualism and privatization. What among the poor served as a "motor of liberation" would, in a more affluent context cut off from the view from below, most likely be reduced to a "house church," a kind of support group of discrete individuals.

Therefore, a concrete economic theory is needed to flesh out our doctrine of the church today. Herman E. Daly and John B. Cobb Jr. have proposed an economic theory that locates "person-in-community" as an alternative to the "invisible hand" of current market theory or the abstract forces of dialectic in Marxist theory.[20] In fact, Daly and Cobb note the marked similarities in the abstractionisms favored by both market and planned-economy theorists. In contrast to these abstractions, ironically so like the abstractions of the "invisible church," Daly and Cobb criticize the "fallacy of misplaced concreteness," which insufficiently recognizes the abstract character of economic theories. They propose community, they propose human being, they propose a liveable future. Perhaps we may never be able to live without class distinctions completely; but there is no question that different forms of community could yield less drastic differences in what it takes to live.

PRAXIS

As we have seen, the alliance between the Christian churches and systems of social stratification is long and deep, appearing already in the social ethic of the apostle Paul. For the most part, the churches and their theological leaders have not sought this alliance out of the conviction that the social divisions that have plagued humanity from the beginnings of civilization are a good thing. The conviction rather is that they are evil and

20. Herman E. Daly and John B. Cobb Jr., *For the Common Good: Redirecting the Economy toward Community, the Environment, and a Sustainable Future* (Boston: Beacon, 1989), esp. chaps. 8–9. Other valuable resources include National Conference of Catholic Bishops, *Economic Justice for All: Pastoral Letter on Catholic Social Teaching and the U.S. Economy* (Washington: United States Catholic Conference, 1986); and M. Douglas Meeks, *God the Economist: The Doctrine of God and Political Economy* (Minneapolis: Fortress, 1989).

that the world of which they are a part is evil and basically irredeemable. The acceptance of social classes began essentially as a *survival mechanism* on the part both of the church as an institution, which had to defend itself in relation to competing social powers, and of individual believers, who needed to be convinced that their present suffering and lot in life somehow served the larger purposes of God and would "someday" be overcome. This acceptance became institutionalized in church doctrine in extremely pernicious ways. The tragedy is that this survival strategy only reinforces and legitimates the evil from which relief is sought.

In addressing the problem of ecclesiology and classism we have attempted to identify a *precondition*, a *process*, and a *goal*. The first step, the precondition, has been simply to *recognize* and bring to consciousness the fact of the ecclesiastical legitimation of class divisions. The legitimation of social stratification by a dominant ideology is what we have called "classism," and it must be clear that the church has contributed to the legitimation process—probably more so over time than any other social institution. Some would argue, in a cynical or Marxist fashion, that this is the primary function of religion in society; otherwise it would not be tolerated. Even if (as we believe) this is not true, it is true that without recognizing the church's complicity in the stratification process, it will never be possible to change it. The church's tendency is to deny this complicity, even to pretend that social divisions do not exist, at least in democratic societies; but, as Gustavo Gutiérrez points out, this very denial perpetuates the reality of classes, and the *denial* is what he names ecclesiological classism.[21]

Once recognition has been attained, it is possible to turn to the *process*, which we shall describe as "patient transformation of the world." At this point we are influenced by the creative insights of Ernst Troeltsch and Richard Niebuhr. To Troeltsch

21. Gustavo Gutiérrez, *A Theology of Liberation*, trans. Caridad Inda and John Eagleson (Maryknoll, N.Y.: Orbis, 1973), 275–76.

it is clear not only that the Christian ideal (radical detachment from the world, radical love for the world) requires a new world order (proclaimed by Jesus as the kingdom of God) but also that the ideal cannot be realized in the world apart from compromise.[22] Refusal to compromise leads either to a fanatic attempt to force the kingdom upon the world or to a withdrawal from the world in hostility and indifference. In either case the world will remain basically unchanged, although its tragic conflicts may be deepened in the process. Against these alternatives, we must insist that *transformation* of the world is possible, often through coalitions built on compromise, while simultaneously recognizing that such transformation remains always incomplete and unfinished, always a task to be taken up afresh by each generation.

What is demanded, therefore, is *patience*—an *urgent, revolutionary* patience, that is, recognition that conditions are such as to demand radical action *and* that such action will never be adequate, recognition that the race against suffering and oppression must ever be run but is never finished. This seems to be a strange, perhaps unsustainable paradox: patience for an ongoing process of transformation, refusing either to give up on the world or to give in to it, knowing that the ideal of a true communion of free and equal persons always faces brutal facts that will suppress and destroy it, recognizing that we can shape the world situation only slightly in its successive phases, can achieve only what is practically possible in given circumstances. But this paradox is at the heart of Christian faith. Faith provides the courage and energy to carry on in the struggle of life, yielding to neither cynicism nor fanaticism, despair nor illusion.

Richard Niebuhr warns against the dangers of compromise in starker terms than Troeltsch does: while inevitable, it is also evil, and doubly so when unacknowledged. Yet he recognizes that absolute good is unattainable and that between the absolutes of

22. Troeltsch, *Social Teaching*, 999, 1005–6, 1013.

good and evil there are vast and important differences. Niebuhr warns against those theologies that appeal to transcendental criteria by which all human efforts are condemned. This, he says, "is to ignore the obligation which lies upon religion, just as a human enterprise, to substitute the better for the good or the less bad for the bad and to penetrate the stuff of existence, so far as possible, with so much of saving knowledge and so much of redeeming effort as are available." This leads Niebuhr to an ethic of creative yet realistic transformation.[23]

But what is the "better" or the "less bad" with respect to the problem of social stratification and class conflict? How can the church address this problem in creative yet realistic terms? What resources are furnished by the *basileia* vision that operates as a critical and productive paradigm throughout the church's history? This brings us to the question of the *goal* of ecclesial praxis in relation to social inequality, which we describe simply as the building of a nonstratified human community. By and large, social scientists are very skeptical and cautious at this point. They tend to operate on the basis of a conflict model of human interaction, viewing conflict as something that can never be avoided, only ameliorated or controlled or channeled. Thus we are told that "stratification systems are attempts to reduce overt conflict over the distribution of valued goods and services in a society."[24] In this sense they are a good thing since they enable societies to function with less conflict and aggression, at least for a while. Even sociologists who regard them as a bad thing, in the sense of standing in stark contradiction with democratic ideals and human flourishing, do not hold out much hope for basic structural changes.[25]

23. Niebuhr, *Social Sources of Denominationalism,* 5, 277; and idem, *Christ and Culture* (New York: Harper, 1951), esp. chap. 6.

24. Kerbo, *Social Stratification and Inequality,* 155.

25. Daniel Rossides devotes only two pages to "some suggestions for improving the American class system"—probably because he considers it unlikely that it can be much improved. The reluctant conclusion of his study is that "the United States is incapable of modifying its structure of inequality" (*Social Stratification: The American Class System in Comparative Perspective* [Englewood Cliffs, N.J.: Prentice Hall, 1990], xvii, 432–33).

From a theological point of view, this sociological pessimism is unsatisfactory, although it serves as a sober warning against naive optimism. Both optimism and pessimism are to be avoided. Post-Marxist sociology has convincingly argued that social stratification is a largely sociocultural rather than biopsychological phenomenon. In other words, it is rooted not in innate differences between human beings as individuals or as groups but in modes of social organization; therefore, it *could* be changed by changing the social structure. But making such changes proves to be extraordinarily difficult because of the self-reinforcing character of social institutions and the deep conflict of interests and inequality of power between privileged and exploited groups.

What seems to be called for, if a way is to be found between optimism and pessimism, is a change in consciousness with respect to what is acceptable in human affairs and some imaginative models of alternatives for organizing human society. In both these respects, the churches could make a contribution. We are aware of the dynamic role that shifts in consciousness can play in the course of history. In our own time there is a newly forming consensus (not yet of a majority but of a significant minority) that warfare, environmental destruction, and ethnic and sexual exploitation are simply unacceptable and highly destructive modes of human behavior. A similar consensus about the unacceptability of highly stratified social systems could also begin to emerge, and it would be possible to point out that the Christian ecclesial community affords an alternative model—the model of a beloved, liberated, reconciled, nonprovincial community in which hierarchy and patriarchy no longer have a place. There is no reason in principle why this religious model could not be adapted to secular social contexts. At the beginning of this century Josiah Royce attempted such an adaptation in an innovative philosophy of community based on relationality, loyalty, and interpretation.[26] Slightly later Troeltsch and then

26. See Josiah Royce, *The Philosophy of Loyalty* (New York: Macmillan, 1913); and

Niebuhr called for the creation of a new cultural synthesis that would replace the fragmentation, divisiveness, and individualism of modernity through an orientation to newly integrative values. Feminism, the liberation and ecological movements, and interreligious dialogue are contributing to the quest for a more holistic understanding of society in various ways. The work by Daly and Cobb, cited above, is a detailed proposal for creating small-scale, regional, socioeconomic communities as alternatives to free-market capitalism and centrally planned socialism. These visions are inspired in part by the model of the Christian ecclesial community, and their implications for social stratification have scarcely been explored.

We offer two brief concluding observations. First, the dualism that allowed the church to legitimate social classes outwardly while preserving a religious communion inwardly is no longer necessary or appropriate. Second, moving from the level of consciousness-raising and the envisioning of new models to the actual implementation of structural changes is a prolonged and difficult task that will require patience, determination, and creative leadership.

idem, *The Problem of Christianity* (1913), ed. John E. Smith, rev. ed. (Chicago: Univ. of Chicago Press, 1968).

CATHERINE KELLER

13. ESCHATOLOGY, ECOLOGY, AND A GREEN ECUMENACY

You know how to interpret the appearance of earth and sky, but why do you not know how to interpret the present time?

—Luke 12:56

What do you think of when you hear the phrase "the end of the world"? A premillennialist horror fantasy of final tribulation, complete with planes crashing as born-again pilots join the rapture of the true Christians? The final hot death of the universe? The smoke and fire of nuclear war and endless winter afterward?

My guess is that as the 1990s count down to the millennium, the rhetoric of "the end of the world" stimulates anxious ecological associations for most white, middle-class North Americans, male or female. Apocalypse is being colored green. "Increasingly, apocalyptic fears about widespread droughts and melting ice-caps have displaced the nuclear threat as the dominant feared meteorological disaster," notes Andrew Ross in his aptly titled *Strange Weather.*[1] Consider what it means that—among the religious and the irreligious alike—phrases like "the destruction of the earth" or "save the planet" have within a few years become commonplace. But if apocalypticisms have become casual, so has the casual become apocalyptic. We exchange pleasantries with a stranger and find a casual allusion to the weather—for instance,

1. Andrew Ross, *Strange Weather: Culture, Science and Technology in the Age of Limits* (New York: Verso, 1991).

when it is unseasonably warm, or cold, or when the weather weirdly bounces—rudely insinuating the end of the world. The foreboding feeling of irretrievable and unforeseeable damage reverberates in the brief silences, as we nod and shake our heads, break eye contact, change the topic.

Of course elite Western cultures tend to scorn weather talk as small talk. This condescension symptomatizes a distinctive kind of relationship to the creaturely condition. Who can afford to experience "nature" as banal, exterior, outside of immediate importance, if not those urban elites who seem to have severed the immediate bonds of dependency upon weather conditions? But have they not, therefore, also forfeited the subtle shifting consciousness of our connections to all the earth creatures who share the dependency? This abstraction from nature facilitates practices of control of the environment and the exploitation of the earth's energies to sustain artificial environments with homogenized, centralized, steady, comfortable weather. Most of us in the Northern Hemisphere are involved in this practice.

Still, even with our clipped connections to nature, we talk about the weather. It is what we all have in common. The weather is at once a metaphor for the ecological crisis and its most inescapable symptom.[2] Theologically, because this crisis is about the end of the world as we know it, it falls under the heading of "eschatology": that is, talk about end things. More precisely, I am situating it within the theological topic of "apocalyptic eschatology"—"apocalypse" meaning "disclosure" or "revelation"; "eschatology" meaning "discourse about the ultimate, or the end"; "end" coming from the Greek *eschatos* (a temporal or spatial end, edge, or horizon). Apocalypse is a type of eschatology.

This essay considers the link between ecology and eschatology. The ecological trauma apocalyptically encoded in the weather may clue us into our eschatological missions as theological prac-

2. See Bill McKibben, *The End of Nature* (New York: Random House, 1989).

titioners—our missions not to a life *after* life but to life itself. This is the ultimate message of what we may as well call the green apocalypse. Eschatology is discourse about the collective encounter at the edge of space and time, where and when the life of the creation has its chance at renewal—that is, it is about the present. One of the signs of our time seems to be that "to interpret the appearance of earth and sky" is now an essential part of—rather than contrasted to—interpreting "the present time."

ANALYSIS OF THE DOCTRINE OF ESCHATOLOGY

Eschatology remains the doctrinal lens through which Christian culture, consciously or not, imagines any end of the world. Yet since *eschaton* does not simply refer to a final, temporal end but alludes at the same time to the spatial image of an "edge," so the moving, and therefore endless, spatial horizon of the earth presents itself both as metaphor and as content of any adequate eschatology. Eschatology remains the *edgiest* Christian doctrine. The boundaries of life take on the charge of an ultimate encounter, a kind of discourse that takes place and takes time at the edge of wherever we as a people are. But the very notion of the end of the world has been distorted by the modern capacity to bring that end about, that is, to effect a manmade apocalypse. So the meaning of eschatology must also be fundamentally renegotiated. Unless it can meaningfully and effectively address the green apocalypse, Christian theology becomes a trivial pursuit at the end of the second millennium.

Let me then suggest the following simple criterion: a responsible Christian eschatology is an ecological eschatology. It motivates work—preaching, teaching, modeling, organizing, politics, prayer—to save our planet. It must inspire and challenge the caretaking, biblically referred to as stewardship, to which we, the human component of creation, are called. This is not a matter of competition but of profound cooperation with the other issues of social justice—racial, economic, sexual—to which the ecumenical churches (and this volume) address themselves. For we find ourselves at the edge of history, where the end-time consummation may mean that about one-fourth of the planet's people consume the rest of the people and life of the planet. We can well entertain the ancient metaphor of divine judgment, a *pro*spective of *retro*spective judgment upon human stewardship, simply by extrapolating statistical trends as to planetary demise.

Responsible theology recycles its own resources: therefore, rather than seeking to junk the doctrine it requires an earthbound eschatology. But is such a reconstruction of eschatology possible or even desirable? Or is it another case of liberal Christian wishful thinking? Does not Christian eschatology gather under its wings precisely that array of doctrinal symbolics that has drawn interest *away from the earth,* from natural conditions, from finitude and flesh? Sometimes eschatology has retained its biblical imagery of the resurrected body as the inhabitant of the new creation, attempting to emphasize that wholeness comes always incarnate. Early theologians such as Tertullian argued hard on behalf of the goodness of the material creation against the flesh-despising "heretics," in order to affirm the bodiliness of the resurrection. Yet this spiritual body has been conceived as free of natural limits and geographical ecologies, hence perhaps again, tragically, feeding a Christian tendency to substitute supernature for nature.

One can argue that this addiction to the unnatural is unbiblical, that Hebrew Scripture and much early Christian thought are far earthier than Hellenized later theologies. But are not the biblical roots of Western civilization themselves ecologically ambiguous, casting stewardship in terms of dominion? "Dominion" in Genesis occurs in the context of assigning human beings their caretaking tasks and their responsibility for a creation that was not their possession but the Creator's. Yet the language of Genesis meant, quite harshly, domination and subjugation. Human subjugation of other creatures thus mirrored the

Creator's controlling power over creation. Does such a doctrine of creation inevitably justify human irresponsibility precisely in the name of responsibility, as it does now in the hands of anti-environmentalist lobbyists pitting "jobs and growth" against the earth? Is it perhaps such surrender of stewardship to greed that necessitates a "new creation" by the same all-controlling Creator? Is the biblical understanding of history as moving toward the "new thing" that God will do in itself problematic? Does it prepare the way for the throwaway culture in which we live from one "new thing" to the next? With the apocalyptic emphasis upon the new heaven and earth, this new creation comes about by the supernatural intervention of the omnipotent God. In other words, when Christian hope basks in such resplendent supernatural futures, why would it worry much about mere nature? Indeed, serious concern with the natural world, like concern with bodily processes, indicates within this framework a materialism that obstructs faith. These are hard questions for Christians—but surely tough questions are preferable to tough luck.

There are many varieties of what we may call the unearthly eschatology. At their best they sin by omission: by draining energy away from our earth-home, by encouraging us to live in orientation toward a many-mansioned heavenly home. But at a certain point, the indifference toward nature implied in traditional eschatology becomes lethal. That is, its distraction from the earth complies with the destruction of the earth. It plays itself out in continual casual references to our (whose?) right to "use" (the catchphrase for this is now "wise use"), that is, use up, the rest of the creation because of "mankind's" dominion. The strange failure to develop practices of *sustainable* use within a culture in which Christian eschatologies have shaped our view of the future is then not so strange: there is no need for endlessly renewable resources if the earth is coming to an end anyway. Thus it so happens that the neofundamentalist fantasy of the rapture out of this world, just as the going gets bad, followed by a supernatural new creation, claimed such public power in the 1980s.

This was precisely the time of the most profligate development of the throwaway consumer culture.

The disregard of the creation does indeed seem to be endemic to the culture that has called itself Christian. In other words, the assumption of the imminent end of the world, however indefinitely deferred, may be the ultimate self-fulfilling prophecy.

But *why* this temptation to flee the earth, whether in a rapture that awaits the supernatural new creation or in an afterlife expectancy that for orthodoxy suggests the final resurrection of the dead at the end of history? Why has faith for most Christians through most of their history come down simply to this: the hope for an *after*life rather than for *life itself*? How did eschatology come to function as the great magnet of future reward, sucking all embodied life toward a phantasmagoric future, flattening the earth and all its delicate, voluptuous, daunting, interdependent ecologies into nothing but material means to immortal ends?

The Marxist answer, that religion has provided the opiate for the people, now looks about as fresh as Soviet army memorabilia in curiosity shops. Materialism, even the apocalyptic-prophetic materialism of the socialist vision, has overreacted against otherworldliness and thus done violence at once to what *matters*. It has totalized the worst technological utopianism of modernity. Yet at least it exposes—as an "ideology" serving the ends of capital—the sort of spirituality that distracts from the rightful needs of all human bodies and spirits. It has inspired liberation movements that challenge at its sources the suffering that Christianity has tried, however ambiguously, to address. But like Christianity, its solutions have been purely anthropocentric.

The habit of transcendence, boredom, and alienation in relation to nature seems to be a symptom of systemic suffering, of fissures within the self and its community, from which selves can find no earthly relief. But viewed from the vantage point of late U.S. modernity, we cannot but note that the symptom seems to merge with the cause: that the construction of salvation as supernatural has helped to bring about the very destruction of nature from which the earth now needs saving. When salvation means removal from the earth to a heavenly home, then our *oikos* (home) is abandoned to the assaults of those whose ultimate concern is neither heaven nor earth, but the power and wealth of their particular households. These households drain heaven and earth of what used to be called their "glory"—their energy, their beauty, their disclosiveness, and their adequacy to the needs of the whole. This makes for lousy weather.

Before we can decide to what extent Christian eschatology may share in the culpability for the present ecoapocalypse and to what extent it may redemptively address the crisis, we need to understand the crisis (Gk. *krisis,* "judgment") itself better. The following two cases illustrate types of late modern secularized "eschatologies" at work in the structures and attitudes that facilitate ecoapocalypse.

The cover of the May 1991 *Life* magazine featured the words "Our Next Home" in bold type. Beneath the photograph of a planet the caption read: "Mars: Bringing a dead world to life." NASA was pushing a project called "the terraformation of Mars," the greening of the red planet. "It's ridiculous to go all the way to Mars just to plant the flag, grab a few rocks and come home," the house biophysicist was quoted as saying. "Humanity needs a new vision, a new challenge.... Mars could provide that challenge." Far from facing the present perils to our own planet, the argument cuts in the opposite direction: precisely in the light of ecological and nuclear threat, the chief of research for NASA's life-sciences (!) branch ruminates that "it is foolish to put all our eggs in one basket. It would be wise to look for a place other than Earth where this species could make a home."

This modernist vision of the—manmade—"new heaven and earth" has metastasized as the new earth *in* the heavens. Earth, no longer a worthy challenge to the manly imagination, is disdained as a mere "basket" in which we may or may not invest all of "our eggs" (truly far from Jesus' mother-hen apocalypse of Matt. 23:37ff., which does not boldly stride toward new worlds but rather laments the self-destructiveness of this world). Why clean up our home when we can make a new one? Here we have an ultramodernist technological utopianism at work, willing to accept apocalyptic consequences for the earth while transferring traditional American progress-optimism into the heavens. It carries early modern colonialist millennialism of the new world literally beyond all horizons. Indeed it frees itself from limits precisely by its exultant idolatry—an idolatry that proclaims "the next giant step for mankind." *Life*'s writer blandly notes, with no criticism intended, that the new challenge is "to re-create Creation—to play God."

This utopianism exemplifies what we may call the eschatology of progress, an apocalypse without judgment—an apocalypse, therefore, that blithely furthers the green apocalypse. The Martian visions come and go—terraformation is merely a metaphor and a caricature of the colonizing, ultimately self-destructive progress-optimism of the West. But varieties of this irresponsible futurism thrive in the technocratic hopes of an ever unrepentant modernism. The degree to which the modern technological utopianism has begun to give up on the earth itself clearly suggests the desperate level of failure and of denial encoded in this eschatology.

More common among the range of modernist eschatologies is the well-organized and well-funded "wise-use" movement that was mounted by the corporate community to combat environmentalism. Again the terms prove unavoidably theological. But here they are pointedly *anti*utopian. This is because the right wing now identifies various progressive movements (not technologism) as the utopians to contend with. An article from *Forbes* demonstrates this nicely.[3] The author is appalled at such environmentalist rhetoric as the notion that "humanity is the destroyer of the earth." He lambasts one such ecologist as follows: "[He] doesn't want to settle for cleaner air; he wants to *roll back man's*

3. Robert H. Nelson, "Tom Hayden, Meet Adam Smith and Thomas Aquinas," *Forbes*, October 29, 1990, 94–97.

conquest of nature" (emphasis added). Indeed! The author goes on to identify "eco theology" with the "quasi-religious fervor" of the "new gospel of ecology," analyzing both Judeo-Christian and pantheist modes of environmental religion as forms of irrational fanaticism, that is, heretical divergences from the interests of late capitalism. His coup de grace comes in his revelation that dialectical materialists in search of a new cause are joining the ecological crusade. The argument seems well prepared to characterize any prophetic analysis of structural sin as "Marxist" and "utopian."

The capitalist alternative, interestingly, gets justified in Christian terms—the starkly antiapocalyptic eschatology of Aquinas "and other medieval scholastics" is vaguely alluded to as the basis for the market theory. With evident satisfaction, the author of the article concludes: "As against this fanatical religiosity, there fortunately exists in Western theology a pragmatic tradition that regards the pursuit of self-interest, the maintenance of property rights, the desire for the good life and the institutions of the marketplace as the best available accommodation to the facts of human nature. Heaven will not be realized on earth for at least some time to come." Indeed the Angelic Doctor did stand with orthodoxy against the radical apocalyptic movements of his day, like the Radical Franciscans, which rejected the right of private property. But *Forbes*'s Angelic Capitalist never existed. Unconditional faith in the "mysterious moving hand of the market," requiring the endless translation of nature and its laboring peoples into "resources" and "profit," violates classical Christian understandings both of faith and reason.

So we have here examined two varieties of secular eschatology, the first utopian-apocalyptic in its willingness to give up on the earth and expect a new one; the second realist-triumphalist in its business-as-usual attitude and its vested interest in the endless "delay of the Parousia." The first recognizes the need to "boost morale" in North America—in the light of the apocalyptic levels of destruction, no doubt—by proposing a highly unrealistic and heavenly vision of hope. The second, which represents more or less the status quo of economic thinking in North America, construes not the destruction of the ecology but those who warn of its destruction as the problem. The apocalypse it opposes is not that of the NASA scientists—that project, if it stimulated the GNP, might well be seen as appealing. Rather, it pits itself against the sort of secular apocalypticism that stems from the Hebrew prophetic tradition of the denunciation of sinful exploitation. To this it juxtaposes its free-market "realism," which accommodates "the facts of human nature," by which are meant no doubt precisely the self-interest the prophets have traditionally felt themselves called to denounce.

Note that each of these bastardized eschatologies relies on the imagery of "man's conquest of nature," either in the colonization of Mars or the Earth, to stimulate the proper attitude. The first glitters with metallic futurism; the second holds smugly to the status quo; but both aggressively ignore the real apocalypse, the one pointed to, for instance, by Bill McKibben's *End of Nature*. Each of them acquiesces in the present levels of terrestrial deterioration, seeing it as an inevitable by-product of "progress." Indeed, it is progress defined as the unimpeded, indeed accelerating, "conquest" of terrestrial and extraterrestrial nature that must yield the solutions to present problems. That, at any rate, is the basis of the modernist faith in technology, growth, and the market.[4]

There are, as we shall see, premodern, theistic antecedents for the above modern eschatologies—all unreservedly anthropocentric and androcentric. But a peculiar "thrust" toward independence from "Mother" Nature (helped by a masculinized God) and then from God "himself" (revolt of the sons from the Father) characterizes the process of secularization by which

4. For an impressive and readable critique of the growth dogma and the GNP orthodoxy, complete with a full vision of an alternative, an ecologically, communally, and, yes, theologically sound path, see Herman E. Daly and John B. Cobb Jr., *For the Common Good: Redirecting the Economy toward Community, the Environment, and a Sustainable Future* (Boston: Beacon, 1989).

modernity shapes its futures. Despite raised public awareness of the ecocrisis, corporate growth economics rages relentlessly on. The more pastors and other theological educators educate themselves as to the connections between ecology, economics, and justice, the more we may hope to shift from the model of the conquest of the earth and most of its human and nonhuman creatures to their genuinely democratic cooperation.

As feminine theology has made clear, the sexist language of conquest is no accident. The dominant strain of masculinity has required at once the subordination of nature, envisioned as female, and of females as "closer to nature." Earth, nature, and the weather—these are viewed as alternately fecund and fickle, voluptuous and capricious, dependable and treacherous females. Thus the recent and growing choir of ecofeminist theologies are among the most vital new voices in any discipline.

RECONSTRUCTION

Earlier we wondered if eschatology is itself hopelessly addicted to "the end of nature." Can there be a greening of Christian theology—verdant life up from deep roots, not just lilies on the altar? If so, a new kind of theological self-understanding, one with a method expressive of its content, must develop: we need a *theological practice of recycling*. It will issue from a kind of ecology of discourse. Discerning the toxins at work in Christianity and its cultures allows us to break down the elements of Christian hope, to cleanse them where possible of their own patriarchal poisons and late-modern-capitalist deteriorations—and to compost what will enhance life. An ecology of discourse requires the recycling of the elements of what we are—as persons grown in a culture replete with Christian influences, however disconnected these influences may be from their healthier contexts and communities of origin. Those of us somehow called or situated to recycle the Christian theological heritage must undertake this work in order to make a needed and radical contribution to our real worlds, not as a vague apology for "the tradition." The tradition will be known by its fruits.

The greening of Christian sensibility requires what Rosemary Ruether called "the conversion of the mind to the earth."[5] So eschatology itself needs reconstructing, converting—composting.

The biblical array of *eschata* present too complex a picture to homogenize. But one thing is clear: there is in the Bible no time called "the end of the world." Rather, one reads of anticipation of a day of judgment and of a subsequent renewal of the entire creation. That is, the prophetic tradition focuses the uniquely biblical passion for the "new," the future, like a burning ray upon the present. Its futurity feeds upon that rage at systemic injustice and hope for a repentance of the people that will allow the restoration of wholeness. This wholeness does not look supernatural. Rather it expresses *shalom* in intensely natural and historical terms. Hope in the Hebrew Scriptures is not for life without death but for a long, full life, lived under the shade of one's own vine and in the fullness of a community healed of the alienation from nature and culture. In a way not unlike that of Native Americans today, the prophetic vision harked back to a tribal sense of "the land," imagined as New Israel, new heaven and earth, New Jerusalem. In its incipiency, this imagery had little unearthly about it (and hence was often deemed too "materialistic" by later, especially nineteenth-century, Christian interpreters, who preferred eschatologies of the next world). Yet the Hebrew images of home, dreamed in exile, become frantic when the homecoming itself disappoints; then apocalyptic eschatology begins to emerge, bringing with it a desperate, totalizing hope, a new sort of hope for a once-for-all supernatural action of punishment and restitution.[6] But still the call for the conver-

5. Rosemary Radford Ruether, *Sexism and God-Talk* (Boston: Beacon, 1983). See also idem, "Eschatology and Feminism," in *Lift Every Voice: Constructing Christian Theologies from the Underside*, ed. Susan Brooks Thistlethwaite and Mary Potter Engel (San Francisco: Harper and Row, 1990), 111–24.

6. Paul Hanson, *The Dawn of Apocalyptic: The Historical and Sociological Roots of Jewish Apocalyptic Eschatology* (Philadelphia: Fortress, 1975).

sion of the people resounds, and still the hope does not leave the world—except to find the Power great enough to create the desired new heaven and earth. It is still a hope for the radical reformation of life on earth, a hope for a home that can be lovingly and equitably cohabited by all creatures.

What of Jesus' eschatology? Surely the *basileia tou theou* provides fresh imagery for the already ancient expectation of the New Jerusalem. His reliance on the form of the parable—replete with ecological imagery of seeds and growth—provokes a process that is neither merely individual nor merely social, neither merely realized nor futurist, a process of mutual engagement quietly unfurling to include all time and space in its commonwealth. The Pauline notion of the new creation transfers this tension into a Christocentric messianism of which, of course, Jesus himself was incapable. There is also occasional recourse to the apocalyptic anticipation of utter annihilation, which for Jesus seems to mean the final and devastating destruction of Jerusalem (the center of the Jewish world) and in Paul extends to include the cosmos.

Only in the Book of Revelation do we find a full-blown New Testament apocalyptic narrative. Here there linger few traces of the subtlety and gradualism of the parables of the divine commonwealth and few signs of the traditional prophetic trust in the possibility of repentance to "turn around" injustice self-destruction. Now fear rather than love seems to motivate fidelity, and justice is depicted not by a radically disarmed power from below but by a cosmically armed overpower. And what of nature in the Book of Revelation? Here we have the ultimate case of bad weather.

Just the first round of tribulations results in, for instance, the death of one-third of the life of the seas, the fresh waters, the arable fields, the trees (tempting to literalize as predictions of our present predicament!). Yet divine judgment intends "the destruction of the destroyers of the earth," not of the earth itself. There is a bitter clarity as to the interlinkage of the economic and political injustice of Rome/Babylon and the devastation of nature. After the cosmic violence of the final solution, the New Jerusalem appears, now dressed up as "bride of the lamb." She "comes down from heaven" as a bejeweled architecture of wish fulfillment, a place of "no more tears," where food and drink are free, and where there is "no more ocean" (the salt water of tears and oceans both evoke a primal maternal chaos and threat). The imagery remains so mythic and the structure so nonlinear as to leave this extremist eschatology open to endless reclamations—by those whose faith works for justice, peace, and the integrity of creation as well by those whose faith awaits Armageddon with the assurance of those for whom nature and its history have become expendable, soon to be replaced. But however desperate, dualistic, determinist, and farfetched the hope of John's Apocalypse appears, it does not in itself require an otherworldly or unearthly reading. Its New Jerusalem can be placed in the context of prophetic hope for a radical renewal of this creation.

After the biblical period, especially after the conversion of Constantine in the fourth century, Christian history would never settle the tension between an explosive apocalyptic utopianism, which carried within itself the prophetic social critique, and a conservative ecclesial triumphalism. Augustine split the eschatological hope for a new age of justice and cosmic harmony within history into a "City of God" transcending nature and history and a "City of Man" within them and ending soon. Christianity as the religion of the empire could too readily acquiesce in this dead-end dualism, which undermines any motivation to struggle with the institutional causes of suffering. The triumphalism of medieval Christendom emerges on this basis. The City of God could not be better realized on earth than it already is in the church; true fulfillment is only attainable individual by individual in heaven. Almost a thousand years later, a new rash of apocalyptic movements, inspired by Joachim of Fiore's prophecy of a "third status," an age of the free spirit, would briefly reopen history. Yet these insurrectionist movements and their anti-Augustinian view of history were ferociously suppressed.[7]

So it would seem that the modern belief in progress, finally in technological progress for the creation of heaven on earth or, failing that, earth in heaven, could use the old energy of apocalyptic hope for the qualitative leaps of real-world change. Capitalist triumphalism, by contrast, rests easily on the long classical orthodox tradition of conservative realism, which pits itself against any call for radical transformation of the social order. In their aggressively colonialist modalities, both move to the conquest of the world as their prerogative, increasingly freed from the inhibitions of any doctrines of God's creation and new creation. They are in tension with the biblical heritage, which cannot be unilaterally blamed for its distortions. But we might say that they exploit dangers and weaknesses already inherent in biblical texts: such as the patriarchal privilege of history over nature, of recourse to moral dualism, to control from above, to coercive power, and to hopes for a future dissociated from present processes. Though these secular eschatologies are supremely "worldly"—that is, committed to economic, political and technological self-interest—they heighten the Christian tendency to take the earth for granted. Like mom.

I have suggested as well that the ever hovering Christian (if minimally biblical) expectation that history will end soon may have shaped the horizons of modernity in peculiar ways. Late modern capitalism tortures time into something endless and undifferentiated like a line. Yet its actual practice of using the creatures of the creation as means to its own ends is bringing about the very futurelessness it denies. Its currently climaxing passion for short-term gain seems subliminally to presuppose the imminent end of the world. And through the "conquest of nature" involved in the endless stress of development and exploitation, it is bringing that end about. Christendom is surely

7. Norman Cohn, *Pursuit of the Millennium,* rev. ed. (New York: Oxford Univ. Press, 1970).

not accidentally the culture whose holy book happens to culminate in a vision of the imminent devastation of the earth, the culture that has developed the technologies and politics capable of Armageddon, nuclear or greenhouse. To the extent that the expectation for the cataclysmic end, the redemption through cosmic violence, did indeed inspire apocalyptic hope, to that extent the task of theologians at the end of the millennium is to take responsibility for defusing the self-fulfilling prophecy of worldly doom. Thus the recycling of eschatology becomes precisely a means of the *metanoia* of theology itself: of its return to the earth.

But note: a greening theology need not decry all talk of life after life and of spirit-existence as irresponsible or otherworldly. Most of the indigenous traditions we praise for their greater ecological awareness also entertain complex connections to ancestral and other denizens of the spirit-world. Christian eschatology may paradoxically learn to cope better with death by more passionately embracing life. The comforting, sustaining, and renewing powers of Spirit may reconnect us to a greater life, an interdependent, embodied, infinite life, from which death cannot separate us.

Still—reconstructing the Western relationship to the earth must mean nothing less than understanding the earth as our true home. This will be a major comedown to all conservative and most liberal theology. Home, however, does not mean "end"—indeed home allows the rootedness by which we grow *through* endings and beginnings.[8] Home takes on the edginess of eschatology only when it is itself threatened. Jürgen Moltmann has classically argued that Christian eschatology is not a matter of *end* but of *hope*.[9] We are therefore in the position of

8. Nelle Morton's *The Journey Is Home* (Boston: Beacon, 1986) combines metaphors of rooted embodiment, dynamic self-transcendence, and relationships that make up home as the companions of the journey—implicitly important eschatological figures.

9. Jürgen Moltmann, *Theology of Hope: A Contemporary Christian Eschatology* (San Francisco: Harper, 1990). It is satisfying to note how far Moltmann's social concerns have driven him into an ecological theology in recent works, notably *God in*

hoping against hope—against the false hopes of modernity that are destroying the nature out of which the future lives. Christian attention to the promised future—the future of universal fulfillment, *shalom,* resurrection—certainly can and does serve, by default or direction, the ends of the *man*made apocalypse. The question is whether Christian hope—in collaboration with other, earth-friendly traditions—can also energize the needed *home*work.

PRAXIS

All creatures—upon whom falls the rain and shines the sun, who share the weather—the endless species, threatened with premature endings, together constitute both the habitats and the inhabitants of the creation. Indeed there is no creature who is not also home to many other creatures. Inhabitant is habitat. Being at home means being a home. "The human is less a being on the earth or in the universe than a dimension of the earth and indeed of the universe itself."[10]

The Greek word *oikumene,* from which "ecology," "economy," and "ecumenism" stem, makes *oikos*, home, into "the inhabited earth." This is the earth not as a geological formation but as that portion of the creation for which we have stewardly accountability, precisely not as passing outsiders but as paramount insiders. The Greek term *oikonomos* means "house steward." The old term "ecumenacy" added the theological dimension. The *Oxford English Dictionary* defines it, oddly, as "the ecclesiastical primacy or supremacy of the world." (One would expect rather "the universal primacy or supremacy of the church.") This trope invites us to understand ultimacy as the primacy of the inhabited earth. Here pulses the central in-

Creation (San Francisco: Harper, 1990) and *Creating a Just Future* (Philadelphia: Trinity Press International, 1989).

10. Thomas Berry, *The Dream of the Earth* (San Francisco: Sierra Club Books, 1988), 195.

sight for a recycled eschatology, an ecoeschatology. It will not content itself with interfaith, interreligious, or multicultural exchange, but calls forth a *green ecumenacy,* the earthly *ekklesia* of all creatures.

Eschatology as a doctrine cannot ultimately be thought of apart from the doctrine of creation; by the same token the doctrine of creation appears as irresponsible apart from that of a new creation. Yet this response/ability—because it roots eschatology in the ongoing (albeit so far hideously neglected and thwarted) call of stewardship for the ecumenacy—is a matter of response to the groaning of the creation. This particular dimension of an eschatological ethic is clear, is revealed, to us now in a way that it could not have been during the biblical periods, when nature still laid claim to a certain ferocious inexhaustibility. In our apocalypse lies our hope. . . .

We ourselves are also in the consciousness of a prophetic minority. We ourselves are called to the work of the new creation, the renewal of creation. But this work breeds only futility if not done in and with the Spirit of the creation.

We cannot create or re-create this life. Our responsibility for the new creation is not to terraform planets or otherwise play God. It is to participate in our finite, interconnected creatureliness with "metanoic" consciousness: that is, facing up to the manmade apocalypse, resisting the North American array of postutopian cynicisms, pessimistic determinisms, reactionary Christian messianisms, and business-as-usual realisms. As earthbound Christians, we may indeed embrace a utopian realism, bound to the rhythms of earth and its indelible history, but nonetheless still "bound for the promised land"—a promising place (and time) that is the possible healing of this one.

The realistic hope for ecology today lies not in miraculous interventions, supernatural or techno-capitalist. It lies in the still-greening mass consciousness that the manmade apocalypse is unacceptable and unnecessary, that its causes are analyzable, and that we the people can make a difference. Who the "people" is makes a difference as well. Perhaps the most moving case studies in ecohope come from the far and southern reaches of the planetary ecumenacy. For instance, the grassroots Chipko movement in India, the tree-hugging women who are using Gandhian techniques to save trees from the bulldozers of development, has been renewing the face of the earth by reversing erosion and desertification, for the sake of creating a sustainable village economy.[11] Similarly, an even more pointedly woman-centered movement, led by Wangaari Mathai in Kenya, has planted millions of trees, created jobs, made fuel accessible, and promoted renewable agriculture, leading the way toward the desirable future in spite of persecution.

Americans, especially white urban ones, tend to tune out the prospect of sacrifices in lifestyle required to redress the injustices to other human and nonhuman beings, indeed just to save ourselves. Such econumbness, akin to the "psychic numbing" of nuclearism,[12] spreads readily across bodies already alienated from their own "nature." Perhaps calls to conversion and sacrifice have a chance of being heard by the not-yet-converted only if they are inscribed with the language of desire—desire not just for some abstract future but for the enhanced life of the community that already begins to form in the practice of ecojustice. That is, to liturgically sort through our garbage, to make choices based on awareness of the sinister and/or beautiful web of connections between our food, the weather, our starving and tortured fellow humans, women's bodies, and the homeless—this multidimensional work of recycling releases new ways of being together, a new sense of a common goal, of being on the edge together, of consoling and delighting each other in our edginess. We find together spiritual practices that allow us to ground, quite literally, in our bodies and our earth, the anxieties of the unknown fu-

11. Thomas Weber, *Hugging the Trees: The Story of the Chipko Movement* (Calcutta: Penguin, 1988).

12. Robert Jay Lifton, *The Broken Connection: On Death and the Continuity of Life* (New York: Basic Books, 1979).

ture. To ground the lightning terrors of apocalypse. We are here in our particular communities, in our particular times and places, with particular ecologies, histories, and spirits we must struggle to recognize. We are here to claim, to defend, and to renew our earth-home, the inhabited whole. This is, hopefully, where the practices of ministry in local congregations, national networks, and international solidarities may root its life.

We will still talk about the weather, just because we are in it together. But the damage to the earth-home now binds us all together as never before, as members of a species, indeed members of a planet. Though doused with new griefs and furies appropriate to the situation, we will find surprising possibilities for dwelling together here at the edge of history. The weather retains its unpredictabilities. The word "weather," after all, comes from the verb "to blow"—like the pneuma, the *ruach,* that blows where it will. We gain nothing but panic and cynicism by proclaiming that "nature," the world of which we are a nettlesome dimension, is dead or ending—however thin the hole in the heavens. The Spirit that brings life to life is also there, in the weird weather. Only with the holy source of all living things does hope stay alive, renewed in the power of life to renew itself, no matter what. And I suspect that life-force ebbs for us as long as we abide in abstraction from it and the weather and in spiritualities and theories that lack a vital practice and loving solidarity. The widest solidarity, the green ecumenacy, also has its roots in the tradition. A song of Hildegaard von Bingen, the twelfth-century prophet of *viriditas,* the "greening power" of the Spirit, translates itself effortlessly into the ecology of the end of the twentieth century:

> Holy Spirit, making life alive, moving in all things, root of all created being, cleansing the cosmos of every impurity, effacing guilt, anointing wounds. You are lustrous and praiseworthy life, You waken and reawaken everything that is.

JAMES H. EVANS, JR.

14. ESCHATOLOGY, WHITE SUPREMACY, AND THE BELOVED COMMUNITY

In the nineteenth century the industrial juggernaut of the Western world roared to life and with it the promise of common prosperity. However, what was utopia to some was Armageddon to others. A host of secular eschatologies circulated in the United States. Some of these gave hope to the underclasses. Marxism had its appeal to the working classes. Various agrarian reform movements spoke to those being systematically removed from the land. Socialist and communitarian groups searched for the restoration of precapitalist social values. Many of these movements were and are legitimate expressions of human longing for freedom and wholeness, and others function as cultural knockoffs of the idea of Christian hope. These secular eschatologies normally appeal to the universal hope for a brighter future (lotteries and gambling are two of the modalities through which this hope is commonly pursued) or a deep-seated desire to return to "the good old days" (an impulse aptly described by the phrase "back to the future"). In this way these secular eschatologies address the alienation and disorientation that seemed to accompany the rise of the modern industrial state.

While there has scarcely been an industrialized nation that has not been funded somewhat by a pseudoeschatological vision, the United States has been profoundly shaped by notions of the future. H. Richard Niebuhr's *The Kingdom of God in America* and

Max Weber's *The Protestant Ethic and the Spirit of Capitalism* examine this aspect of the national consciousness. Eschatological thinking has been influenced by the modern notion of progress. At the same time there is the persistent suspicion that history is dynamic but not necessarily progressive. Part of the complexity of American life is the variety of visions of the future expressed in public, political, religious, and cultural institutions. One such eschatological vision is that found in the cultural practices and institutions of those groups that are labeled as "white supremacists." White supremacy is a virulent and persistent strain in American social life. Its root system runs deep into the soil of Western culture. In the United States it has been sustained by a dubious relation to Christian doctrine and practice. The major concern in the following discussion is the relationship between Christian eschatology and the fundamental vision of white supremacy. We will examine the convergence and conflict between the ideological basis of Christianity and those groups for whom the white race is the ultimate measure of humanity. Most North American Christians would not be very comfortable with the association of the vision of the future found in white supremacy and Christian eschatology. However, such an association can help us to examine the fundamental concepts, ideas, tropes, and metaphors in traditional Christian eschatology and to assess their appropriateness for theological discourse today.

ANALYSIS

Eschatology in Modern Theology

Eschatology means literally "discourse about last things." It refers to that branch of systematic theology that has normally encompassed reflections on the immortality of the soul, the resurrection of the body, eternal judgment, and heaven and hell. It also includes discussions of purgatory, limbo, and the beatific vision. In early Judaism, eschatological discourse concerned the establishment of the kingdom of God on earth. Justice, peace, prosperity, and orderly government were viewed as possibilities within history. In later Judaism, the disappointments that followed the failure of the promise of national tranquility found expression in the apocalyptic images of the prophetic writings of the Bible. In the New Testament the explicit apocalyptic of the prophetic writings served as a backdrop for the proclamation of the coming kingdom of God, the resurrection of the body, eternal judgment, and salvation. In fact, without the gloss put on the texts by subsequent interpreters, one might say that the ministry and mission of Jesus were driven by an eschatological consciousness. This consciousness was concretized in Jesus' proclamation of God's "kingdom" or *basileia.* A central metaphor for this reality is that of the beloved community. This notion is deeply rooted both in the memory of the early church through the writings of Irenaeus and in the cultural consciousness of the United States through the writings of Jonathan Edwards.[1]

Eschatology became a central concern for the Christian community very early in its existence. The delayed Parousia and its implications for the faith had to be dealt with while preserving the promissory foundation of the gospel. Yet the early church managed to maintain its self-understanding as a beloved community in Christ. There were two major events in the subsequent history of the church that profoundly affected the church's self-concept. The first was the legitimation of the church by the emperor Constantine and Augustine's redefinition of the church from "beloved community" to the "City of God." The move from *communitas* to polis introduced radically different notions of social organization within the church. The second event was the emergence of feudal society and Thomas Aquinas's intellectual reconstruction of the medieval church along those lines. Within the emergent hierarchical structure of the church certain class distinctions became codified and identified with normative

1. I am indebted to Ms. Kimberly Parsons Chastain of Princeton Theological Seminary for this insight into the derivation of the concept of beloved community.

church order. As a result of both of these events the communal eschatological consciousness so evident in the early church went underground.

In the modern era a variety of theological positions on the meaning of eschatology emerged. The classical liberal theologies that dominated theological reflection from the beginning of the eighteenth century until the outbreak of World War I translated the eschatological thrust of the Bible into various notions of progress. Jesus' sayings regarding the coming kingdom of God were taken to mean that human and social perfection were not only possible in history but quite inevitable. Human beings as well as their social and cultural institutions were ordained for fulfillment rather than destruction. The seeds of that perfection were planted in the act of creation, and only ignorance could alter their course toward their destiny. The basic assumption was that God was at work in the world employing human talents and genius to complete God's design for the world. Behind this translation was the conviction that the eschatology of the Bible, and especially the expressive vehicle of apocalyptic imagery, were part of an outmoded cosmology foreign to the modern world. The neoorthodox theologians, who gained prominence after the outbreak of World War I, sought to reclaim part of the gospel content that was jettisoned by their liberal forebears, especially the doctrine of sin. The human slaughter that characterized modern warfare and the appearance of phenomena that had no explanation outside of the notion of radical evil convinced these theologians that human beings and their institutions were not on a collision course with perfection. Rather, human beings were infinitely capable of deceiving themselves, of hiding their true motives behind ingenious veneers, in other words, of sin. Human institutions were easily corrupted by the pursuit of power, and human history was shot through with tragedy and irony. In light of these factors, neoorthodox theologians attempted to reclaim the elements of judgment and redemption in Christian eschatology. However, neoorthodox theologians were also part of the modern world inhabited by their liberal counterparts, and it was impossible simply to present the first-century eschatology of the Bible to a world struggling with modern methods of madness and mayhem. They could not, in good conscience, claim that the course of history would be miraculously interrupted and a new reality inaugurated. Thus, they posited a theory of two historical realities, sacred history (*Heilsgeschichte*) and human history (*Weltgeschichte*). The eschatological moment, then, occurred whenever one became aware of the judgment, condemnation, and affirmation that the history of salvation rendered upon human history. Therefore, apocalyptic language became symbolic of the distance between human work in history and God's work in history.

In addition to liberal and neoorthodox strands in Christian theology, there are several others that have contributed to eschatological thinking. In process theology, the central problematic is the conflict between the claim that God is benevolent and omnipotent and the presence of radical evil. This issue is the guide to the development of the major emphases in process thought. The notion of eschatology in process theology points to the resolution of its initial problematic, that is, the end of evil, harmony within the godhead, and harmony in the human community.[2] In various forms of political theology, eschatology has had an important place, but none more central than in the theology of hope.[3] These theologians argue that eschatology, rather than serving as an addendum to systematic theology, should be its axiomatic principle. The Christian community, humanity as a whole, and the church's affirmation of Jesus Christ as the Son of God can be adequately understood only in light of the future from which God calls. In this theology, the reversals and disappointments that are part of historical reality must be set

2. See Marjorie Hewitt Suchocki, *The End of Evil: Process Eschatology in Historical Context* (Albany: State Univ. of New York Press, 1988).

3. See Jürgen Moltmann, *The Theology of Hope* (New York: Harper and Row, 1967).

in the context of a future over which God exercises complete sovereignty. In the development of liberation theology, especially in Latin America, eschatology played an important, though undervalued, role.[4] Although most observers focused on the use of Marxist social analysis by many Latin American theologians, at the heart of much of this theology was a utopian vision of the future. This vision was often couched in social language referring to "a classless society" or "a liberated existence for the poor." Yet this eschatological vision was as much spiritual as political. Contemporary feminist theologians have identified the ways that gender has influenced the development of Christian eschatology. Rosemary Radford Ruether argues that the traditional trajectory of eschatology as "an endless flight into an unrealized future" needs to be replaced by a model of *conversion*.[5] In this instance, the end of human existence is wholeness and balanced relationships between persons and between people and the nonhuman environment. In black theology in the United States the role of eschatology has been controversial, ambivalent, and contested. The highly ornate descriptions of heaven and the future in the afterlife in African-American folklore have raised questions as to whether this vision was helpful or harmful to a people struggling for health, liberation, and wholeness in *this* world.[6] The general consensus among African-American male theologians and womanist theologians is that although the eschatological consciousness of black people has been abused in the past, it has more often given sustenance to a people struggling for freedom.

The development of eschatology in Christian theology since the beginning of the eighteenth century has been defined by the requirement to reconcile the claims of biblical religion to the demands of the modern ethos. Most theological positions that emerged during this period have responded to this mandate

4. See Gustavo Gutiérrez, *A Theology of Liberation* (Maryknoll N.Y.: Orbis, 1973).

5. Rosemary Radford Ruether, *Sexism and God-Talk: Toward a Feminist Theology* (Boston: Beacon, 1983), 254.

6. See Gayraud S. Wilmore, *Last Things First* (Philadelphia: Westminster, 1982).

in somewhat different ways. Some have adjusted their understanding of the Christian faith to the demands of modernity, while others have employed biblical faith to critique the modernist spirit. However, a common feature in all of these positions is the diminution of the prominence of apocalyptic imagery in eschatological discourse.

As a result, apocalyptic imagery has been employed primarily in millennialist forms of eschatological discourse. The political origins of apocalyptic imagery are found in the biblical accounts of Jewish history. In those periods when the Jewish people felt threatened by a loss of national security, expectations that God would dramatically intervene in history on their behalf abounded. This intervention would inaugurate the kingdom of God. During these times apocalyptic ideas and literature emerged. These images of the cataclysmic confrontation between the powers of good and evil depicted more than the Jewish quest for righteousness. They also referred to the political and military hopes of an oppressed people. They lived in a world thought to be dominated by evil forces, and it would take more than human effort alone to banish them. The overthrow of the kingdom of evil would then issue forth an age of bliss and tranquility. Since the conditions that originally gave rise to apocalyptic literature were still prevalent during the time of Jesus, it is reasonable to assume that these ideas formed the backdrop of Jesus' preaching and ministry. The texts of the New Testament reflect this fact in that these ideas and images are found in the three Synoptic Gospels and in the Book of Revelation.

A key element in apocalyptic discourse is millennialism. Millennialism is the belief in a thousand-year reign of Christ in which the kingdom of God is brought to fruition. There are two major varieties of millennialist thinking. Premillennialism is the conviction that the Second Coming of Christ will precede the thousand-year reign of Christ. Postmillennialism is the conviction that the coming of Christ will follow the millennium. The former belief includes a chronology in which tribulation and strife will mark the coming of the Antichrist. This is followed by the thousand-year reign of peace and order, which is then followed by the catastrophic battle between good and evil and the final victory of Christ. Postmillennialists, on the other hand, have generally identified the reign of Christ with the age of the church, which will be followed by the conflict between good and evil and the Second Coming of Christ.

Millennialist thought took root in the United States during the period of the American Revolution and the Second Great Awakening. The establishment of a new political state and the quest for moral perfection were initially collapsed in the attempt to proclaim the dawning of a new age. However, the political pragmatism required to preserve and advance the emerging nation stood in stark contrast with the religious idealism at the heart of the quest for personal perfection. Moreover, those groups that held millennialist views most securely—Shakers, Oneida Perfectionists, Seventh-Day Adventists, and Mormons—soon found themselves marginal participants in the discourse that shaped the identity of the nation. The last major thrust of millennialist activity in the social life of the United States occurred in 1844. William Miller, a Baptist and the author of *Evidence from Scripture and History of the Second Coming of Christ, About the Year 1843,* published in 1836, calculated that Christ would return to earth between March 21, 1843, and March 21, 1844. When Christ did not appear by the appointed date, a new date of October 22, 1844, was set. When this date also came and went, Miller's disillusioned followers dispersed, and millennialist thought went underground.

The Rise of White Supremacy in the United States

It is unclear whether slavery in the United States was the cause or the result of the rise of white supremacy. However, much of the evidence seems to suggest that the systemic forces that sustained the enslavement of Africans derived their impetus from the vortex of classism and racism. George M. Frederickson observes that "the participation of lower-class whites in these disorders was induced to a great extent by the status anxieties generated by a competitive society. For those who had little chance to realize the American dream of upward mobility, it was comforting to think there was a clearly defined out-group that was even lower in the social hierarchy."[7] Within the sectional conflict that erupted into civil war were competing views of the optimum social order. In the North, the argument was that the social order should be based on achievement rather than "ascription." Therefore, the principle that stated that Africans were naturally destined to be slaves was opposed. This did not mean that the natural equality of Africans was affirmed, but rather that the basis for asserting their inequality was their supposed inferior levels of intellectual, moral, and cultural achievement. In the South, the argument was that the social order should be based on a kind of natural law that placed the master class in positions of power and responsibility. Therefore, it was possible that individual instances of genius and creativity among African slaves could be recognized and even applauded without rendering a challenge to the cosmic laws that relegated them to a "mudsill" class.

As the still-fledgling nation struggled to forge an identity, both the North and the South faced the specter of an overthrow of the basis of their social order. In the South, the resistance to the abolition of slavery rested on the conviction that an inevitable race struggle would result. In the North, the resistance to the full participation of Africans in the economic development of the region rested on the conviction that something akin to a class struggle would be inevitable. In both instances, ample cause for white supremacist attitudes could be found. However, the economic factors that shaped the fate of the South during and after the Civil War made white supremacy the centerpiece of Southern social order. Therefore, the political structure of Southern society—including the disempowerment and disenfranchisement of

7. George M. Frederickson, *White Supremacy: A Comparative Study in American and South African History* (New York: Oxford Univ. Press, 1981), 153.

African Americans—after the Civil War suggests that the economic development of the South created a complex ideological system of race and class relations that left black people at the bottom of the heap.[8]

The final three decades of the twentieth century have seen the reemergence of various white supremacist groups. Although the ideas and sentiments that sustain these racist attitudes have never been far from the surface of American social and political life, at clearly identifiable moments in history they have coalesced, challenging the stated philosophical foundations of U.S. society. In recent years several groups with otherwise different agendas have found common cause in the idea of white supremacy. Among them are survivalists, tax resisters, white nationalists, counterfeiters, Christian home educators, antiabortionists, gun enthusiasts, mercenary aficionados, and neoconservatives.[9] This broad, loosely related consortium of racists includes the more familiar coalition of groups in the Ku Klux Klan, the American Nazi Party, and the John Birch Society, as well as lesser known groups such as the Liberty Lobby; the American Front; the Covenant, the Sword, and the Arm of the Lord (CSA); and the Populist Party. The sobering economic, global, and political realities of the latter part of the century were the catalyst for the formation of "a new phase in the far-right movement, which would come to be known as the Fifth Era."[10] This new age would see the creation or, more accurately, the re-creation of the nation. It would be "an America Christian and masculine in its culture, racially white, English-speaking, and overseen by its sacred compact, the United States Constitution."[11] For the purposes of this

8. John W. Cell, *The Highest Stage of White Supremacy: The Origins of Segregation in South Africa and the American South* (New York: Cambridge Univ. Press, 1982), 101–2.

9. James A. Aho, *The Politics of Righteousness: Idaho Christian Patriotism* (Seattle: Univ. of Washington Press, 1990), 39, 59.

10. James Ridgeway, *Blood in the Face: The Ku Klux Klan, Aryan Nations, Nazi Skinheads, and the Rise of a New White Culture* (New York: Thunder's Mouth Press, 1990), 79.

11. Aho, *Politics of Righteousness,* 3.

essay several of the groups in this "silent brotherhood"[12] warrant further description.

The Ku Klux Klan had its origins in the aftermath of the Civil War.

> In Pulaski, Tennessee in 1866, half a dozen recently returned—and bored—Confederate soldiers who were looking around for a source of amusement formed an organization they called the Ku Klux Klan. Members would turn up at town gatherings dressed in outlandish outfits and publicly hazed their newest recruits. They put together a group for playing practical jokes, like draping themselves in sheets and wandering about town, spooking the public. These early Kluxers had no political consciousness at all; their only stated purpose was "to have fun, make mischief, and play pranks on the public." But soon they turned to newly freed blacks as a source of humor, recounting stories of how their nighttime high jinks frightened the freedmen. As its reputation for merry pranks grew, the Klan took on the trappings of a full-fledged civic organization.[13]

As the Klan developed, many of its internal ceremonies were modeled on church ritual. A particular target group for Klan recruiters were ministers. The Klan sought to position itself as a defender of common piety "appealing to nativist intolerance, fundamentalist frustration with the libertinism of the Roaring Twenties, and the general anti-modernist urge of the heartland."[14] Since its beginning, the Klan has waxed and waned as an influence in American life. There are five discernible periods in the evolution of this organization.

> Its First Era, during post-Civil War radical reconstruction, saw an insurgent outlaw army. It soon withered, then rose again in a Second Era in the 1920s, an above-ground political phase that attracted millions of members. The Third Era was a violent, rear-guard battle against the civil rights movement of the 1960s. The

12. For a journalistic, narrative account of recent activities of white supremacist groups in the United States, see Kevin Flynn and Gary Gerhardt, *The Silent Brotherhood: Inside America's Racist Underground* (New York: Free Press, 1989).

13. Ridgeway, *Blood in the Face,* 33.

14. Ibid., 34. Although the Klan appealed to populist values, it is interesting to note the development of an ideology of gender equality in the Klan movement in the 1920s. See Kathleen M. Blee, "Gender Ideology and the Role of Women in the 1920s Klan Movement," *Sociological Spectrum* 7 (1987): 73–97.

> Fourth Era, in the 1970s, was a public relations campaign, led most importantly by the young David Duke, who would go on to become a member of the Louisiana state legislature and, in 1990, make a run for the U.S. Senate. The Fifth Era, in the 1980s and beyond, involves both an armed underground and an aggressive above-board political movement.[15]

The Aryan Nations, the Order, and the White Aryan Resistance are interlocking groups that share a common theme of racial purity and armed resistance to the federal government. The Aryan Nations, also known as the Church of Jesus Christ Christian, was the vehicle through which several white supremacist groups forged their vision of the future of America. By drawing on the religious fervor, political frustration, and xenophobia of much of the Euro-American populace, the leaders of this organization formulated a three-pronged plan "to make National Socialism the next high Christian culture in America."[16] First, an international "Aryan Congress" would be held every year at which major white supremacists would be invited to speak. Second, a direct solicitation campaign would be initiated to enlist others who might share a general opposition to current liberal social and governmental trends. Third, special attention would be paid to the recruitment of whites among the prison population where the forces of separatism among racial groups were already strong.

The Order was a splinter group of the Aryan Nations. The first meeting of the Order was held in the summer of 1983 and included members of the Aryan Nations church who were not content with wearing swastikas and uttering the name of Adolf Hitler. Also present were members of the Ku Klux Klan who wanted action and not rhetoric. In essence, the Order was an underground terrorist group of the far right. Its members were implicated in the murder of a radio talk-show host in Denver, Colorado; the murdered man, a Jew, had regularly criticized

15. Ridgeway, *Blood in the Face,* 20.
16. Aho, *Politics of Righteousness,* 59.

white supremacist groups. The Order was also implicated in several robberies of banks and armored cars, passed counterfeit currency, and engaged in a host of other illegal activities to finance its racial revolution.

The White Aryan Resistance (WAR) represents the maturation of the Aryan supremacist movement. Its leader, rather than employing inflammatory rhetoric, states the racist premises of the movement with a kind of matter-of-factness. The focus is on discipline rather than anarchy, and its major target is young people. This does not mean that WAR is any less firm in its racist intentions than other groups. It simply means that this group has adopted modern methods of appeal and recruitment.[17]

While many white supremacist groups demonstrated a contempt for the law, one major group was founded on the principle of the conservation of law and order, the Posse Comitatus.

> The Posse Comitatus was first organized in Portland, Oregon in 1969 by Henry L. Beach, who had just retired from the dry cleaning business. During the 1930s Beach was the state liaison officer for William Dudley Pelley's Silver Shirts, the storm trooper group formed immediately after Hitler took power in Germany. The Posse believes all politics are local. Beach argued that the county sheriff is the highest legitimately elected official in the land, and that the sheriff has the right to form a posse including any able-bodied man over the age of eighteen. To the Posse the sheriff is, in reality, the executive branch of government. He directs law enforcement, including the impanelling of juries.[18]

As a constitutional fundamentalist group the Posse Comitatus believes that the federal government has exceeded the limits of the Constitution and therefore has violated the inalienable rights of its citizens. Government intervention into education, the coining of money not based on the gold or silver standard, the establishment of the Federal Reserve, the federal attempt to regulate the sale and possession of handguns, and the U.S. role in

17. For an insightful account of the rise of the White Aryan Resistance, see Leonard Zeskind's *Peddling Racist Violence for a New Generation: A Profile of Tom Metzger and the White Aryan Resistance* (Atlanta: Center for Democratic Renewal, 1987).

18. Ridgeway, *Blood in the Face,* 111.

the affairs of other nations are examples of this violation. Many Posse members believe that the nation has gone too far toward socialism and world government. Posse members claim that the Constitution establishes individual states as "separate sovereign Republics within the United States."[19] Therefore, federal income tax is a violation of the right to local government. The belief in the power of each locality to establish its own law has been one of the mainstays of white supremacy. Unwarranted incarceration, harassment, and even lynchings of black people have been justified by appeal to it. Here, the xenophobia that many white supremacist groups share has found expression in the alleged constitutional right to self-rule.[20] These groups, along with the White Patriot Party, the American Nazi Party, and the John Birch Society, among others, have carried the banner of white supremacism in the United States and abroad.

As George Kelsey pointed out, these groups are determined to provide a basis for solidarity among a race that has sensed a loss of community. This is most expeditiously accomplished by targeting certain racial groups as threats to order and civility. "By positing an enemy race, the racist ideology produces cohesion within white society. At this point, the ideology is a call to vigilance, and if need be, to attack."[21]

Although Catholics and various immigrant groups have been among the targets of white supremacist groups in the United States, African Americans and Jewish people have been singled out as primary recipients of racist venom. The attack on Jewish people is based on a complex myth in which they are accused of carrying out a massive conspiracy to control the world.

> The theoretical underpinnings for today's far right originated at the time of the French Revolution in the creation of the myth of an "international Jewish conspiracy." Evolving and expanding over the years, this myth worked its way through Europe in the

19. Ibid., 112.
20. Ibid., 109–41.
21. George D. Kelsey, *Racism and the Christian Understanding of Man* (New York: Scribner's, 1965), 42.

> early twentieth century, and was popularized in America during the 1920s, when fear and antagonism toward immigrants and naturalized aliens was at its height. Automobile tycoon Henry Ford was one of the first and most influential promulgators of the doctrine of an international Jewish conspiracy; and the idea was taken up by the burgeoning Ku Klux Klan, and added to its already busy agenda of anti-black and anti-Catholic terror.[22]

Although the myth, which began in 1797, weaves its way through a maze of casuistry and intrigue, focusing especially upon the role of secret societies in the decline of public morality that led to the French Revolution, Jewish people first became implicated in the myth in 1806, when they were accused of accumulating wealth and influence for the purpose of controlling the world. The major outlines of this myth were written down in a document called the "Protocols of the Meetings of the Learned Elders of Zion." In it, Jewish people were accused of destabilizing the social order, starting wars for their economic gain, creating huge monopolies, and inappropriately influencing national governments. In a sinister document called "The Rabbi's Speech," published throughout Europe, the anonymous author "described how once every hundred years, the reigning elders of the twelve tribes of Israel gathered around the grave of the most senior rabbi and issued reports on the progress of the grand plot to enslave the gentiles and take over the world."[23] In the modern era, the myth took root in the United States with the help of industrialist Henry Ford. Ford capitalized on the fears and insecurities of Americans during the 1920s and published a series of articles based on the "Protocols" in his newspaper, the Dearborn *Independent*.[24] The *Independent* fanned the flames of

22. Ridgeway, *Blood in the Face,* 17.
23. Ibid., 32.
24. As a young boy growing up in Detroit, I, like all African Americans in the area, was aware that the town of Dearborn, a suburb of Detroit, was all-white, was determined to stay that way, and, thus, was not a safe place for any person of color to be found after dark. It is a curious bit of irony that after years of political maneuvering to keep black people and Jews out of their town, the residents of Dearborn are now faced with the newest target of racial hate in the United States, people of Arab descent. Per capita, Dearborn has the largest Arab population of any city in the United States.

hatred by blaming international warfare on Jews, by accusing Jews of infiltrating the U.S. government at the highest levels, and by castigating them for enriching themselves at the expense of others. To these traditional elements of the conspiracy theory Ford added some new claims that spoke to the evolution of popular culture in the United States. Jewish people were accused of controlling the theater and entertainment industries, of introducing sensual and immoral "popular music" to American youth, of promoting alcoholism, of corrupting the all-American sport of baseball, and of introducing female mud wrestling to the American public.[25] In essence, the myth of the international Jewish conspiracy was employed to explain the bewildering changes in economics, culture, and global politics experienced by a people who longed for simpler days. The U.S. government was subsequently referred to by white supremacists as the "Zionist Occupation Government," and Jewish people were referred to as "demon Jews" or "Satan's offspring."

The theoretical underpinnings of white supremacist hatred of African Americans was less complex, even if the hatred itself was perhaps more severe. African Americans' skin color made them easily identifiable targets; thus there was no need for a conspiracy theory to justify their oppression. From the same Enlightenment era that gave rise to the myth of the Jewish conspiracy came the scientific and religious theories of racial inferiority, which focused on black people. The history of color symbolism in the West and its confluence with powerful religious tropes of good and evil, purity and taint, lent credence to the idea that African Americans were lower on the evolutionary scale than people of European descent. There were two major tenets in the canopy of racism against black people. First, the white race had to be protected against the taint of the black presence. Hence, complete separation was necessary. Second, the supposedly unbridled and animalistic sex drive of African Americans was the main conduit

25. Ridgeway, *Blood in the Face,* 40–41.

of their corrupting influence. In a sense, white supremacists drew on the distinctly Puritan notion of the relationship between sex, sin, and blackness to erect a scaffold upon which African Americans could be lynched both literally and figuratively. In sum, one could say that the rise of white supremacy in the United States was a particularly abhorrent manifestation of the white revolt against that sea change in American life that we now refer to as modernism.

The ideological foundation for the vast majority of white supremacist groups in the United States today is a pseudotheology called Christian Identity. This ideology is also embraced by many fundamentalist but less overtly racist religious communities such as the Church of Israel, the Gospel of Christ Kingdom Church, and the World Wide Church of God.[26] The origins of Christian Identity are difficult to locate. Some scholars trace its origins to the 1840 publication of *Our Israelitish Origin,* which was written by a Scotsman named John Wilson.[27] Others claim that it was founded by an Englishman, Edward Hine, in his 1871 book, *Identification of the British Nation with Lost Israel.* The common element in both instances was the search for the lost tribes of Israel. The conclusion of both books provided the basis for the doctrine of Christian Identity.

> The crux of the doctrine is that European Jews are not descended from ancient Hebrew stock at all but from Khazars, residents of a warlike nation of southern Russia who converted to Judaism in the eighth or ninth century. They cannot claim lineage from Abraham, Isaac, and Jacob and are not the covenant people, according to Identity's genealogists. On the contrary, today's Nordic-Anglo-Saxon-Teuton whites are the descendants of the lost tribes of the Biblical Israelites, making white Christians the true people of the covenant. To support this, Hine reinterpreted the book of Genesis with a "two seed theory." Eve was seduced by the serpent and bore a son by him, Cain, who slew his brother Abel. After that Adam, the first white man, passed on his seed to another son, Seth, who became the father of the white race, God's Chosen People. Cain's

26. Aho, *Politics of Righteousness,* 19.
27. Ibid., 52.

> descendants, Identity says, are the Jews. They literally are the seed of Satan. Other races, or "mud people" to racists, descend from others cursed by God.[28]

British Israelism, as it came to be known, was imported to Canada and the United States during the first decades of the twentieth century. It spilled over the Canadian border from Vancouver, British Columbia, into the states of Washington and Oregon. It also found its way into the eastern United States by moving from the eastern Canadian provinces into the state of Maine. An odd twist in the development of Christian Identity was the fact that some Identity believers came to regard Native Americans as the true Aryan people. "The fascination with Native Americans is also a longstanding Klan preoccupation: many Klansmen try to trace their heritage back through the blue eyes and finely chiselled features of certain American Indian tribes, to the Celts, and, finally, to the lost tribes of Israel."[29] In the context of contemporary U.S. political discourse,

> Identity theory teaches that the U.S. is God's promised land and modern Israel a hoax. British followers of Identity are starkly anti-Semitic, but it was the American Identity theologians who added the ingeniously gnostic racist twist known as the "two seed" theory. They hold that the nonwhite races are "pre-Adamic"—that is, part of the creation finished *before* God created Adam and Eve. In his wisdom, they say, God fashioned the subhuman nonwhites and sent them to live outside the Garden of Eden before the Fall. When Eve broke God's original commandment, she was implanted with two seeds. From Adam's seed sprang Abel and the white race. From the serpent Satan's seed came the lazy, wicked Cain. Angered, God cast Adam, Eve, and the serpent out of the Garden of Eden and decreed eternal racial conflict. Cain killed Abel, then ran off into the jungle to join the pre-Adamic nonwhites. ... Identity theology provides both a religious base for racism and anti-Semitism, and an ideological rationale for violence against minorities and their white allies.[30]

28. Flynn and Gerhardt, *Silent Brotherhood,* 51.
29. Ridgeway, *Blood in the Face,* 53.
30. Ibid., 54.

Identity theology, with its two-seed theory, originated perhaps by Hine and developed by his successors, became a viable alternative for disaffected fundamentalists. These fundamentalists gave to Identity theology a racist cast directed not only toward Jews but primarily toward African Americans. Identity theology gave refuge to fundamentalists who could not understand the support given to the state of Israel by many of their more well-known preachers. It is at this point—because many of the early U.S. Identity proponents were former Christian fundamentalists—that the coupling of Identity theory and Christian Dispensationalism resulted in a distinctive hybrid form.

Identity theory explains reality in basically dualistic terms. God is in conflict with the devil. The forces of light, goodness, chastity, cleanliness, and purity are locked in battle against the forces of evil, lewdness, stain, and defilement. However, unlike the traditional formal explanations of this dualism, Identity theory does not teach that this struggle goes on in every human being but that it goes on *among* different groups of people. This does not mean, however, that the tendency to assign the label of the "evil ones" to other groups of people is absent in traditional Christian theological thought. There are too many examples of the dehumanization of other human beings in the name of "the church" for that. The point here is that in Identity theory, the notion of the inner struggle of the human being is entirely absent. Thus, racist Identity followers can refer to African Americans and others as "human rodents," "pests," "germs," "viruses," and "bacteria." Certainly, questionable exegesis of the Bible is required to support the theological infrastructure of Identity theory; however, an ironic twist is that much of the support for this racist and anti-Semitic view comes from certain rabbinical texts in which the humanity of black people is called into question.[31] The apocryphal First Book of Enoch describes the origins of so-

31. Charles B. Copher, "Three Thousand Years of Biblical Interpretation with Reference to Black Peoples," in *African-American Religious Studies: An Interdisciplinary Anthology*, ed. Gayraud S. Wilmore (Durham, N.C.: Duke Univ. Press, 1989), 105–28.

cial pathology in a story in which the fallen angels of heaven succumb to their lust for earthly maidens, cohabit with them, and produce a race of black mutant devils.[32] From their twisted reading of the Bible the Identity theologians grasped an emphasis on racial hygiene and the personification of evil in "the other." This racial purity is symbolized by the ability to blush, to have "blood in the face."

Much of the compelling force of Identity theory is the result of its emphasis on an apocalyptic eschatology. In it the focus on Armageddon reemerges.

> Christian Identity followers tend to think in apocalyptic terms. Many believe that the era of the beast is fast approaching; some think the field of Armageddon is in Nebraska or Kansas. Some see in our current system of banking and commerce the very signs foretold in the Book of Revelation. To many on the fringe, this trend represents the dreaded mark of the beast, without which in Apostle John's nightmarish vision, "no one could get a job or even buy in any store" (Rev. 13:17).[33]

In this view, history will end not in the nuclear nightmare that haunts much of the postmodern consciousness but in a cultural holocaust. In order to preserve the chosen white saints of God, strict separation of the races is required. Thus, in one very elaborate scheme, the United States is divided into separate racial homelands. Navahona and Alta, California, both in the southwestern portion of the United States, are the names of the regions set aside for Native Americans and Mexican Americans, respectively. East Mongolia, in the Hawaiian Islands, and New Cuba, in the city of Miami, Florida, are the homelands of Orientals and Cuban Americans, respectively. West Israel is located in Long Island and Manhattan; Minoria, set aside for Puerto Ricans, Italians, and Greeks, takes up the remainder of New York

32. For additional insight into this topic, see Cain Felder's *Troubling Biblical Waters: Race, Class, and Family* (Maryknoll, N.Y.: Orbis, 1989).

33. Flynn and Gerhardt, *Silent Brotherhood,* 52. Also see Jonathan R. White, "The Road to Armageddon: Religion and Domestic Terrorism," *Quarterly Journal of Ideology* 13, no. 2 (1989): 11–21; and Charles B. Strozier, "Christian Fundamentalism, Nazism, and the Millennium," *The Psychohistory Review* 18, no. 2 (Winter 1990): 207–17.

City. Francia, in northern New England, is the new home of the French-Canadian community in the Unites States, and New Africa, the reserve for people of African descent, is located in the southeastern portion of the country. Some, but not all, white supremacists groups identify a "white bastion" located in the area that is now the states of Washington, Oregon, Montana, Wyoming, and Idaho.[34] This dividing of the land completes the eschatological circle of white supremacy: people with different histories (that is, who occupy different locations on the time continuum) are also people of separate lands (that is, who occupy different locations on the space continuum). Ironically, rather than a hopeful eschatology, what one finds in the ideological infrastructure of white supremacist dogma is a fatalistic resignation in which the United States—once claimed to be the promised land—is divided up among warring factions.

RECONSTRUCTION: TOWARD THE BELOVED COMMUNITY

The focus of this essay is the relationship between the idea of eschatology in mainline Christian thought and the fundamental vision of white supremacist groups in the United States. We have briefly reviewed the notion of eschatology in Christian theology and the theological roots of white supremacy. We have discussed the ways in which Christian thought in the United States is related to the vision of white supremacy. It remains to be seen, in light of that relation, how Christian notions of eschatology might be revised. The eschatological dimensions of white supremacy suggest at least three concepts that require reexamination.

The first concept is the meaning of history and hope. One of the central affirmations of the Christian faith is that there is a definite relationship between the history and hope of a people. When the people of Israel left Egypt, they remembered the promise extracted from them by Joseph, who asked that they take his

34. Ridgeway, *Blood in the Face*, 150.

bones with them (Exod. 13:18-19). The hope of Israel that lay in land that God had promised to them could never be separated from their history of enslavement, degradation, and dislocation in Egypt. The prophets constantly reminded a stiff-necked and often forgetful people that the God who guaranteed their future was the same God who brought them out of the house of bondage (Jer. 2:5-6; Ezek. 20:9-10). Jesus' ministry rested on the authority of God. This authority was mediated through, though not limited to, the history and tradition of Israel. The hope for humanity, as embodied in Jesus himself, was inseparable from what God had done in the history of Israel.

One of the dimensions of white supremacist thought that relates clearly to eschatology is that many of its adherents see themselves as a people without a history. Among many white supremacists there is a kind of *cultural amnesia* in which race is elevated to the level of supreme norm, while ethnicity is denied. It is curious that white supremacists completely ignore their own European ethnicity and elect to establish their identity by adopting the label "white" to describe themselves. Whiteness, like blackness for that matter, is a North American trope born out of the racial polarization endemic to the society. It speaks to one's political, rather than cultural, location.[35] The national myth that claims that all who come to U.S. shores are enjoined to leave their cultural particularity behind them is part of the explanation of this phenomenon. The normative cultural context of the United States is one in which all persons, except those whose lineage goes back to the Mayflower, are encouraged to dehistoricize themselves and to blend, if possible, into that normative culture. Most followers of white supremacy share with the cultural powerholders in society only skin color—race, not ethnicity. With no cultural history to draw upon, they simply invented a racial history. Besides cultural amnesia, white supremacist writings betray a kind of *political fatalism*. That is, a people

35. This is one of the major insights of Malcolm X. See *The Autobiography of Malcolm X* (New York: Random House, 1964).

without a sense of a cultural history will also be a people without political hope. In spite of the bravado and posturing of many leaders of the white supremacist movement, there is a definite fatalistic tinge to their proclamations. Within their revolutionary rhetoric is none of the optimism one would expect of persons who are absolutely certain of the rightness of their cause. Very little concrete detail is given in descriptions of the future, beyond the establishment of a "Miracle Whip Kultur" in which the white race is dominant. The lack of political substance in the vision of white supremacists is perhaps what allows them to attract a variety of followers, including those anarchists who have lost all faith in the political possibilities for community in the postmodern world. In light of these considerations, it is incumbent upon the Christian church to emphasize that without a common history, there can be no common hope. Each person must be able to find his or her place in the history of humanity told in the biblical witness, and the church is where that place should be affirmed and celebrated. Moreover, it is through the retelling of our histories and the sharing of our hopes that true community is created.

The second eschatological concept that requires revision is the relationship between creation and consummation. In a sense, this concept is analogous to that of history and hope, but on a cosmic scale. It deals with the origins and destiny of the created order. The symmetry of the biblical witness suggests a significant relationship between the emphases found in the creation accounts and those encountered in the narrative of the consummation of history. The creation accounts found in the Book of Genesis are usually cited as mythopoetic expressions of the beginning of all that is. White supremacists have fastened on that aspect of the creation narratives that deals with the origin of evil, sin, and human alienation. Much of the ideological justification for their racist views is founded on a twisted, but not uncommon, interpretation of the temptation of Adam and Eve and their eventual expulsion from the Garden of Eden. As noted above, this interpretation justifies the separation of the races that grew out of human strife.

The conflicts that are begun in the creation accounts find their resolution in the biblical accounts of the consummation of history. Thus, the Book of Revelation provides, for white supremacists, an account of rapture, tribulation, suffering, and conflict, which will issue forth in a pure, white race. In essence, if the history of the world originates with human strife, it will end with human strife. The relationship between creation and consummation in Christian theology in the North American context needs to be revised in light of the challenge of white supremacist interpretations. Certainly, violence is part of the creation narrative, and the realignment of the social order is part of the consummation narrative. The question is whether these are the central interpretive foci for creation and consummation. The creation narratives are misunderstood if they are taken to be accounts of the origins of human existence. Biblical scholars have agreed that the earliest collective memory of Israel centers on the exodus. The exodus account is actually more than the story of a mass escape from bondage. Its focus is the creation of community. It is in this context that God tells God's people, "I will take you who were no people and make you my people" (Exod. 6:7). The peoplehood of Israel is established by God's mighty acts on their behalf. Further, this community is not founded on the notion of racial purity or homogeneity.[36] This community is made up of persons whose "mother was a Hittite, and whose father was an Amorite" (Ezek. 16:45). Likewise, the Book of Revelation is not primarily concerned with the destruction of the created order but with its redemption. The final goal is overcoming sin and alienation and the establishment of the beloved community. As the writer of Revelation surveyed the horizon

36. Racial purity is not to be confused with racial or cultural integrity. The latter stresses the inherent gifts that reside in a given cultural or ethnic group, while the former is based on a negative evaluation of "the other race" and an implied vulnerability of the race seeking to maintain its purity.

of human history, he saw beyond the pain and suffering that his community was undergoing at that moment and glimpsed "a new heaven and a new earth." He saw a "New Jerusalem," a new community, and its citizens found their identity firmly inscribed in "the Book of Life."

The third concept in Christian eschatology that requires revision in light of the establishment of community is that of apocalyptic and judgment. In white supremacist rhetoric, apocalyptic language is the vehicle for the horror that results when the people of God come face-to-face with God's judgment. Although this language has often been used to instill fear in the hearts of neophyte Christians, this is not the central role of apocalyptic language in biblical discourse. The apocalyptic images found in the Book of Daniel, for example, do certainly address the impending judgment of the Babylonian Empire, but their primary purpose is to reveal the creation of community in exile. In the context of wars for territorial and ethnic conquest between Greece and Persia, the point of Daniel's vision of death and overthrow is that true community begins in the righteousness of God (Dan. 12:1-4). Likewise, the Book of Revelation speaks to the divine redemption of all that is, employing dramatic images of God's rectification of all that humanity has set askew.

The essence of this redemption is the establishment of the beloved community. The writer of Revelation first sees the beloved community as composed of the 144,000 who bear the seal of God upon their foreheads (Rev. 7:3). But that number cannot express the radical inclusivity of the community of the redeemed because the writer then sees "a great multitude which no one could number, from every nation, from all tribes and peoples and tongues" (Rev. 7:9).

The word *apokalypsis* means disclosure. The primary content of Christian apocalyptic is not disaster or condemnation but the revelation of the coming community of God. Beyond "the terrible beast" and the "lake of fire," there is the vision of a restored community in which the original harmony among persons and nature is affirmed. The writer of Revelation shares with the reader a vision that recalls the Garden of Eden. "Then he showed me the river of the water of life, bright as crystal, flowing from the throne of God and of the Lamb through the middle of the street of the city: also, on either side of the river, the tree of life with its twelve kinds of fruit, yielding its fruit each month; and the leaves of the tree were for the healing of the nations" (Rev. 22:1-2).

PRAXIS

What will it take to make the beloved community—one which truly values human diversity—a reality? The poignant story of a former white supremacist suggests that, at the very least, the civic virtues of solidarity and neighborliness are required. In 1979, Greg Withrow founded the White Student Union, later called the Aryan Youth Movement, at American River College in Sacramento, California. In 1987, Withrow fell in love and, influenced by his companion, publicly rejected his racist views. Shortly thereafter, a group of his former colleagues attacked and brutally beat him. Calling him a "traitor," they nailed his hands to a crossbeam, slashed him with a knife, and left him for dead. He regained consciousness and, with the crossbeam still on his back, hobbled down the street seeking assistance. He appealed to a white woman, who simply turned away. A white couple did likewise. But a black couple coming out of a nightclub came to his aid. They took the gag from his mouth and called the police. Reflecting on this event, Withrow observed: "I want people to see that this is what I get because this is what I created. What goes around comes around."[37] Within this story, with its remarkable allusions to the crucifixion and the parable of the good Samaritan, are the elements of the beloved community that ought

37. Ridgeway, *Blood in the Face*, 169.

to be central to the proclamation and praxis of the churches in these days of racial tension and conflict.

Historically, Christian communities have been engaged in the practices of building social structures that fit somewhere on the continuum between paradise and the apocalypse. However, the ideologies that lie behind these practices are often inimical to the formation of loving communities. It is imperative that churches recover the deep propensity for self-critique. This self-critique will plunge the churches directly into the struggles and ambiguities of their host cultures. In her book *The Politics of God: Christian Theologies and Social Justice,* Kathryn Tanner describes two types of cultures.[38] Customary cultures, as she describes them, are those in which social transformations are the results of "unreflective habits," while reflective cultures are those in which social transformations are "promoted by reflection on principles or standards of procedure, and in that way produce a self-critical culture."[39] In the United States, both types of culture are present. However, churches have rarely engaged in the sustained reflection necessary to develop a consistent self-critique. Therefore, rather than leading the movement toward justice, churches have too often limped along into the future as an unreflective response to general social change.

The beloved community, as I understand it, is a community with a highly developed and consistent culture of self-critique. The story cited above suggests that there are at least three dimensions to this self-critique. First, it makes confession possible. Withrow was able to confess his transgressions because he was loved. It was not simply romantic love but a love that shattered his allegiance to oppressive forces. Second, this self-critique made it possible to see the other in a different light. Here, the African-American couple who rescued him were able to see Withrow as another suffering human being who stood in need of assistance.

38. Kathryn Tanner, *The Politics of God: Christian Theologies and Social Justice* (Minneapolis: Fortress, 1992).

39. Ibid., 42.

Third, Withrow was able to discern, within the total context of his experience, the meaning of his own suffering in relation to that which he had inflicted upon others.

The beloved community in the United States will recognize the ambiguity that surrounds all of its practices. That is, it is always susceptible to sin. This is what Martin Luther King Jr. meant when he stated that "the American people are infected with racism—that is the peril. Paradoxically, they are also infected with democratic ideals—that is the hope."[40] This means that both the internal and external practices of the churches will be guided by a commitment to justice, realizing that imperfect justice is redeemed by love. It can certainly be argued that not every Christian community occupies that same moral ground or, therefore, possesses the same propensity toward this self-critique. However, the point is that the possibility for self-critique is in some measure present in every Christian community.

To participate in the upbuilding of the beloved community means that we must be able to share the sufferings of another, and we must be willing to answer the question Who is my neighbor? with genuine acts of compassion. Perhaps then, out of a history of pain, enmity, and hostility, we can grasp what Vincent Harding has called "one final, soaring hope."

40. Martin Luther King Jr., "Showdown for Nonviolence," in *A Testament of Hope: The Essential Writings of Martin Luther King, Jr.*, ed. James Melvin Washington (San Francisco: Harper and Row, 1986), 71.

INDEX

Key theological resources from Fortress Press—

❧

Christian Theology
An Introduction to Its Traditions and Tasks
Peter C. Hodgson and Robert H. King, Editors

The widely acclaimed and popular restatement of theology in its modern context, newly updated by the editors.
416 pages, ISBN 0-8006-2867-5

❧

Readings in Christian Theology
Peter C. Hodgson and Robert H. King, Editors

A rich selection from classical and contemporary sources on central doctrines of Christian faith.
432 pages, ISBN 0-8006-1849-1

❧

Reconstructing Christian Theology
Rebecca S. Chopp and Mark Lewis Taylor, Editors

A liberating pedagogy, which tackles and reconstructs major Christian doctrines in light of significant social or cultural challenges.
400 pages, ISBN 0-8006-2696-6